NOW MAY MEN WEEP

ISANDLWANA

NOW MAY

ISANDLWANA

A story from the Zulu War

By

Mark Hobson

INTRODUCTION AND ACKNOWLEDGEMENTS

Of all the so called "small wars" fought during Queen Victoria's reign, the Anglo-Zulu War of 1879 is maybe one of the best known. Its general appeal probably lies somewhere deep in the British mindset, maybe an unspoken yearning for the days of Empire, or possibly a secret admiration for the courage and selfless sacrifice of the Zulu people. Certainly it continues to hold a fascination amongst both young and old despite the passage of over 140 years since the events themselves took place, in a far off land of mystery and limitless beauty. Great Britain was a very different nation back then. Imperial expansionism demanded a certain amount of arrogance on the part of the ruling politicians and this was passed over to the population too. Pride in your Queen and Country and its achievments was at the forefront of these feelings of superiority, and what better way of showing your swaggering military power than to push out the boundaries of control by conquest and subjugation. If any nation objected to being ruled as British subjects, then a little force was acceptable; as long as the cost in Her Majesty's redcoats was kept to a minimum.

Different values. Different times.

Today such an attitude would be completely unacceptable. Indeed a lingering shadow of guilt about Britain's Imperial past is one of the by-products of such blustering, haughty arrogance. The reason for this is the modem-day acceptance that many of those conflicts were completely unjust, in particularly in regard to the justifications offered at the time and also the way the military went about prosecuting these wars in order to achieve their aims. This is definately so in the case of the 1879 war in Southern Africa.

Picture a proud people and their King, living in a rich and beautiful country. With their own culture, their own laws, their own customs. Leading their lives in the way they deem acceptable. But over the river that constitutes their land's boundary lives an aggressive people intent on literally stealing their country, using force of arms to achieve this. This, in admittedly a diluted outline of their predicament, is exactly the quandry that faced the Zulu people in the months leading up to hostilities. The fact that they would fight for their land, for the independence of their sovereign nation, for their very survival, is, simply, understandable. After all, the Zulu were a proud warrior people with a dynamic and proven army of their own to match the best that Great Britain could throw at them. This war therefore had all the ingredients of being anything but a gentle stroll in the park for Her Majesty's redcoats!

The story of this dramatic struggle has been told and re-told many times in the years since. Hundreds of books have been written (some by the actual participants), several movies have been made, and even a few stageplays produced, bringing to life the high drama and bloody nature of the conflict. Surprisingly only a few novels have appeared; for some reason fictional writers seemed to have steered clear of this period. Those who have tried in the past have had mixed results. Some have been good, accurate renditions, closely following real events - whilst others have been downright appalling. It seemed to me that there was an obvious gap in the market, with people with an interest in military history crying out for works of fiction about the Zulu War. Hence the reason for sitting down and writing this novel.

It goes without saying that this was indeed a labour of love for me. It comes after 25 years of study, numerous research trips to museums, several journeys to KwaZulu-Natal and many enjoyable evenings spent with dear friends discussing all manner of things ranging from the symptoms of African tick fever to the finer points of bayonet practice! For fourteen months I closed myself off from the outside world, with just the occasional weekend break, in order to complete this manuscript. For the most part I can honestly say that I thoroughly enjoyed myself, immersing myself so deeply in the events of 1879 so much that at times I did not want to return to the here and now. It was wonderfully calming to allow my mind to wander thus, to take me off to those far off places, to really feel that I was there...

I should point out that this novel is a work of fiction based on historical fact. It tries to the best of my abilities to tell the story of these momentous events, but with a certain amount of poetic license thrown in. However, I have tried to stay true to the real story in this, so the reader must bear in mind that no matter how fanciful certain parts may seem, it is basically all true. Several of the characters are fictional but the vast majority were real people taking part in real warfare. Also, I make no apology for the extreme nature of the description of the battle scenes; it is how I believe war is really fought and not some censored version. Bloody and vulgar it may be, but not gratuitous. So be warned!

In March of 1999 I and a group of friends made our first tour of the battlefields in KwaZulu-Natal. It was an experience none of us will ever forget, coming after a lifetime of obsessive interest in all things related to the Zulu War. We walked over the very ground where those momentous events occurred, rode horses through old Zululand and swam the Buffalo River at Fugitives' Drift. I can say without a shadow of a doubt that it changed my life. Those seventeen days spent with a bunch of wonderful people, wandering the African countryside, partly inspired me to write this monster. I owe my heartfelt thanks to their continuing friendship.

I'd also like to mention my great appreciation to Bill Cainan, good pal and travel companion on our trips to the battlefields. He has allowed me complete access to his large collection of books, archives and weapons in my endless search for information. Without his help this novel would not have been possible. Also a big thanks to Martin Crofts for his thoughts and ideas and enthusiasm, and Edward Cooper for his technical wizardry and IT skills.

Mark Hobson.

Dramatis Personae

BRITISH:

Sir Henry Bartle Edward Frere - The British High Commissioner for Southern Africa, sent by the Colonial Office to implement their policy of Confederation.

Lieutenant-General Frederic Augustus Thesiger, 2nd Baron Chelmsford (later, Lord Chelmsford) - The commander of British Troops in South Africa.

Brevet Colonel Richard T. Glyn - Commanding Officer of the 1st Battalion, 24th Regiment and also of No.3 Column.

Lieutenant-Colonel Henry Burmester Pulleine - 1/24th Regiment, he was left in command of the British camp at Isandlwana on January 22nd.

Brevet Colonel Anthony William Durnford, Royal Engineers- Commander of No.2 Column, which consisted mainly of African troops.

Brevet Lieutenant-Colonel John North Crealock – Chelmsford's Assistant Military Secretary.

James A. Brickhill – Civilian Interpreter for Colonel Glyn and No 3 Column

Brevet Major Francis Broadfoot Russell -Commander of the Rocket Battery, Royal Artillery that was with Durnford's Column.

Commandant Hamilton-Browne-Commander-1st Battalion, 3rd Regiment NNC.

Lieutenant Horace Smith-Dorrien- A special service officer from the 95th Regiment attached to No.3 Column for transport duties.

Lieutenant Nevill J.A.Coghill – Colonel Glyn's Orderly Officer.

Brevet Major Stuart Smith – Second in command of N Battery, 5th Brigade, Royal Artillery.

Captain Reginald Younghusband – Commanding Officer of C Company, 1/24th Regiment.

Lieutenant Teignmouth Melvill- Adjutant of the 1/24th.

Lieutenant Charles W. Cavaye- Commanding Officer of E. Company, 1/24th.

Private Owen Brooks- Private of E. Company, 1/24th.

Private Thomas P. Scott- A private of C. Company, 1/24th but attached to the rocket battery as an escort.

Gunner Edward Chisolm – Member of N Battery, 5th Brigade, Royal Artillery, under Major Smith.

Captain G.V.Wardell – Commanding Officer of H.Company, 1/24th Regiment.

Colour-Sergeant Frederic Wolfe – H.Company.

Private Charlie Noakes & Private Robert Metcalfe – Both of H.Company.

VOLUNTEERS, COLONIALS and SETTLERS:

Captain George Shepstone – Durnford's Staff Officer.

Inspector George Mansell – Officer in command of the Natal Mounted Police.

Troopers Fred & Jack Symons, and Trooper Ted Greene- All members of the Natal Carbineers, a locally recruited unit.

Lieutenant Harry Davies- Officer commanding the Edendale Troop, a unit of mainly black Christians and part of Durnford's No. 2 Column.

Sergeant-Major Simeon Kambule- Member of the Edendale Troop and a close friend of Durnford. His father Elijah was killed at Bushmans Pass in 1873.

Solomon Malaza- A trooper of the Edendale Troop.

Jabez Molife-Member of the Hlubi contingent under Durnford's command. A unit of mainly black horsemen.

Miss Frances Ellen "Fanny" Colenso- Daughter of Bishop Colenso, the Bishop of Natal, and a very close friend of Durnford.

ZULUS:

Cetshwayo kaMpande – The King of the Zulu since his coronation in 1873.

Chief Ntshingwayo kaMahole- One of the King's closest advisors and appointed overall commander of the Zulu regiments during the Isandlwana campaign.

Sigcwelecwele kaMhlehleke- Senior Induna of the young iNgobamakhosi Regiment during the Isandlwana campaign.

Mehlokazulu KaSihayo- A personal favourite of Cetshwayo and allowed to serve the King, he was also Chief Sihayo's son as well as a senior commander in the iNgobamakhosi Regiment.

Ndlela kaSashangane- A young warrior of the iNgobamakhosi.

Mnyamana kaMakhoba – friend of Ndlela and also a young warrior of the iNgobamakhosi.

Dilikhana kaBokwe & Nzobo kaBokwe- Brothers and warriors of the uKhandempemvu Regiment.

Gezindaka kaMadikane – A warrior of the uNokhenke Regiment.

Mfulandelo kaZibeme – A warrior of the uNokhenke Regiment but a rival of Gezindaka.

ISANDLWANA

CHAPTER 1

ZULULAND, SOUTHERN AFRICA. THE NCOME (blood) RIVER,
NORTH OF RORKE'S DRIFT. DISPUTED TERRITORIES.
JUNE 1878.

B revet Colonel Anthony William Durnford, Royal Engineers, guided his mount down the steep hillside with confident ease, using his one good arm with a skill brought on by necessity. His other arm, the injured left one, was tucked discreetly out of sight into the dark blue patrol jacket he wore. Once safely at the bottom, he relaxed his grip on the reins and allowed the horse to go on, following the rider ahead of him.

They'd been following the trail for over a day now, himself and the seven other men in his little command. At the head of the party, acting as guide, was the skinny figure of constable Elkington, from Pomeroy. He, together with his four native policemen, had volunteered to act as an escort for them on their patrol, partly because he knew the area so well, but also to add a little muscle. For this was potentially a dangerous situation.

They were heading for the British outpost at Rorke's Drift, twenty or so miles to the south. However, it had been necessary to make this detour across the border into Zululand, despite the risks that entailed. What with the current crisis it may have been a gamble not worth taking, but Durnford had never let danger get in the way of duty. He was confident of his own abilities. Yet, at the same time he would not make any rash decisions that would endanger the lives of his men. Once, several years before, he had made that mistake and it had cost him dearly. A price paid in blood, both for his command and himself. The result had been the loss of the use of one arm, years of pain, and sleepless nights spent tossing and turning in inner turmoil. No, he could not afford a repeat of that episode. So on this particular occasion a little caution was called for.

Elkington was a good man. He knew the terrain remarkably well, despite the fact that much of it was unmapped, but Durnford could not rid himself of the tension that had been steadily growing inside him. If they were discovered here, then the situation could turn nasty.

Durnford turned in his saddle and glanced back at the others behind him. Next in line after himself was the massive, burly figure of Sergeant-Major Simeon Kambule. He knew he could depend on him if things turned bad. They'd rode together and fought together on many occasions and he knew he would never find anyone more capable. After him was the young and eager Jabez Molife, untested in combat but from what Durnford had heard an excellent shot and a brilliant horseman. Behind the young trooper were the four policemen. Of them, he knew nothing. How they would handle themselves in the heat of battle, Durnford could not say, he just hoped it wouldn't come to that. He would be glad when they finally crossed back into Natal, back to British soil.

Durnford cantered forward until he drew alongside Elkington. He looked at the man for a moment. He seemed unconcerned.

"How soon until we reach the drift constable?" he asked, trying to keep his voice calm.

Elkington replied without looking back. "Sometime tomorrow, I should imagine. We still have a fair way to go and we need to make bivouack soon."

"Very good. I'd like to try and be close to the river before sunset if possible. That way we'll be able to get across if the need arises."

"Yes sir. I wouldn't get too concerned sir. The kaffirs around here are usually pretty friendly."

"Really? I wonder how long that will last?"

"That's a good point sir."

"Carry on constable," Durnford said, before taking up his place once again.

They continued on through the dense undergrowth and over the rocky ground, Durnford's eyes constantly alert beneath the wide brim of his hat.

*   *   *

They made camp on the banks of the Ncome River. The long drought of the last few years had resulted in the once fast flowing watercourse becoming all but dried up. Just a thin trickle of water now meandered down the centre of the channel, the vegetation along the banks having long since died back. Lying amidst the rocks that had once lain midstream was the dead carcass of an oxen, the ants and flies eagerly devouring the rotting meat.

Colonel Durnford stood on the bank, gazing off into the distance. On the horizon, a range of flat-topped mountains stretched away, while closer in was a seemingly never ending series of rolling hills, usually green and fertile but now dry and barren. Under normal conditions this was prime cattle country; once you came inland away from the tropical coastal strip-perfect conditions for cattle disease and horse sickness- you reached the cooler heights where the grass and pasture flourished in abundance and where the giant herds could thrive. It really was the perfect land for anyone wishing to settle, as had many of the Dutch Boers. Their farms lay scattered far and wide throughout the region, both across the border in Natal and further north in the Transvaal, and also to a lesser degree in Zululand.

And there lay the root of the current crisis that was brewing. The reason too for their dangerous expedition here.

Durnford removed his hat and scratched thoughtfully at his balding head.

This area of land was up for grabs. Both the Zulu and the Boers claimed it as their own. The Zulu stressed that the Buffalo and Thukela rivers were the natural boundary between their nation and the British Colony of Natal, but the Dutch farmers were insistant that they had purchased large tracts of the region back in the 1850's and that they had a right to settle there. If that is how the situation had stood then the British authorities would have been quite happy to stand back and watch the two sides squabble things out. But the previous year, in 1877, the British Colonial Office had decided to annex the Transvaal, raising the flag in Pretoria, and thus making the Dutch Boers British subjects. So then the problem became a British one.

At the same time that all this was taking place back in England the Colonial Office had decided upon a new policy-Confederation. A bringing together of all the various states and chiefdoms under the umbrela of one administration, run naturally by Britain. The reason for this was the sudden potential exploitation of the newly discovered mineral deposits further north. After years of financial investment in the region suddenly there was the chance of making a return on their costly commitments. It was too good an opportunity to pass up. The opening up of the diamond fields was too alluring and dazzling a prospect.

However, with this possible solution came the Zulu problem. If their plans were to work then the Zulu nation and their King, Cetshwayo kaMpande, would have to become a part of the Confederation scheme.

Easier said than done, Durnford thought ruefully as he scratched at the long whispy curls of his moustache. If he knew the Zulu people as good as he thought he did they would not just hand over their land willingly. And that is where he came in.

The British High Commissioner to Southern Africa, Sir Bartle Frere, recently sent out to implement the new policy, had decided to settle the border dispute once and for all. He had set up a Border Commission to investigate the two claims for ownership of the land. The inquiry was to decide fairly and squarely who was the rightful owner. He, Colonel Durnford, had been selected to be a member of the Commission.

Sir Bartle Frere, it was fair to say, had a keen dislike of the Zulu people. He had recently been manipulating public opinion to try and stir up feelings against the Zulu, quite unfairly in Durnford's view. It seemed to him that Frere was simply looking for a reason to take some kind of action against King Cetshwayo, and the upcoming report from the Border Commission should play directly into his hands. If, as was the general expectation, the Boer claim was upheld then that would be all the excuse Frere would need. As

4

British subjects then the Boer land claim would have to be accepted by Cetshwayo, and if he refused to then the use of force would be justified. Yet once again, Durnford did not think things would go quite so easily. The Zulu were a proud people. What's more they had a large Army, one that had been successfully proven in battle on many occasions.

It was a very worrying situation.

Durnford was so deep in his thoughts that he failed to hear the sound of approaching footsteps behind him. Only when the person snapped to attention, his boots crunching the dirt underfoot, did the Colonel become aware of his presence. Turning, he saw it was Sergeant-Major Simeon Kambule.

"Yes, Sergeant-Major?"

Kambule spoke in a deep baritone, in keeping with his hulking frame, his accent heavy but his grasp of English very good. "Sir, you asked me to tell you when your tent was ready."

"Of course. Have you posted the sentries?"

"Myself and Trooper Molife will take the watch, sir. I do not trust the police to stay awake." He said this without a hint of humour but Durnford could not help the small smile from flickering across his own face inspite if his inner nervousness.

"That's probably a good idea, Sergeant-Major. I'll be finalising my report for a short while so if there are any problems let me know immediately." The two men saluted then turned and went their seperate ways.

Durnford strode across the flat ground to where the tiny camp was being set up. They were in a good position, with open ground on all sides allowing a good view of any approaching trouble. The camp consisted of just two tents, his own and Elkington's, a couple of small fires where some mealies were being prepared, and the unrolled blankets that the four native policemen would be sleeping under. Around and about lay their equipment, such as their eating and drinking utensils, personal items and their firearms. The horses had been off-saddled and tied to the stump of a tree nearby where one of the policemen was feeding and watering them. Everything seemed to be in order and despite his own misgivings the men seemed to be in good spirits. Maybe he was just being over cautious, something he could not stop himself doing lately. Heading towards his tent, he lifted the flap and ducked inside.

The evenings came on rapidly in Southern Africa. Once the sun had dipped beneath the distant hills, the night quickly drew in, a blackness that was both impenetrable and daunting. To anyone unused to it it could be quite a frightening experience, lying there listening to the calls of nocturnal creatures. Colonel Durnford, having spent so much of his life here, wasn't in the least bothered. Infact, the very stillness and immensity of an African night could be soothing, a time for reflection; as long as the dreams stayed away.

He was awake now. Sitting at his small fold-up writing desk in the cramped interior of his tent, writing up the report which he would be soon handing over to the Border Commission. Above his head hung a lantern, the flickering light casting dancing shadows on the tent walls.

The report was almost complete. It included several months' worth of survey work and statements taken from those at the heart of the dispute. The conclusions he had reached were based on a totally impartial overview of the whole complicated matter, a summarization of the legality and moral rightness of the two conflicting claims. A week spent travelling down through the Disputed Territories on their way to Rorke's Drift had helped to give him an impression of the geography of the land. The result of all of that hard work sat heavily on Durnford's conscience. He knew it would be controversial, even unpalatable to certain people, but in his opinion it would essentially be the correct outcome.

Sighing heavily Durnford leaned forward over the desk and added the finishing touches to the document.

...the white man wanted the black man's land - that he got leave from the black to graze cattle in the first instance, then came over and put up a shanty, then a house. Then more Boers came, and so on, until, as the Zulus told us, the Boers were like a toad that comes hopping and hopping until it hops right into the middle of the house.

Durnford paused momentarily, asking himself for one last time if he was doing the right thing. Finally, when his mind was settled, he signed the report in a flourish.

Standing, he stretched his aching limbs which were stiffening after the day's long ride. He decided a short stroll outside would help before he settled down for the night. Passing through the tents opening he wandered across to the dying embers of one of the campfires, and waited for his eyes to adjust to the blackness.

Craning his face up towards the sky, he scanned the multitude of stars that stretched from horizon to horizon. He never ceased to be amazed by their beauty, no matter how many times he looked upon them.

A sudden flicker of white light drew away his attention. Durnford glanced out towards the distant horizon. Then it came again. Lightening, dancing a merry dance beyond the distant range of the Drakensberg Mountains, and briefly illuminating their outlines.

He shivered as memories of another night came back to him, a night of death and pain and heartache spent in those very mountains.

Durnford tried to push these thoughts away. In their wake lingered a peculiar sensation of ill-omen. A dark foreboding that gripped him in its icy claws.

CHAPTER 2

The grey-haired gentleman sitting at the ornate desk by the french windows, garbed in all his official dress, did not look up when the knock on the door came. He was re-reading the document spread out before him for the third time, a frown of irritation creasing his forehead. When, a few moments later came further polite knocks, he reluctantly responded, but still without lifting his gaze.

"Yes?" he grumbled in an insolent voice.

The huge double doors which stretched almost from floor to ceiling were pushed gently open and in walked a young coloured man, perhaps aged about twenty, dressed in loose fitting cream trousers and a pristine white shirt. He paused just inside the large, sunlit room, and addressed the man seated before him in a soft, lilting voice.

"The Lieutenant-General is here to see you, Your Excellancy."

"Good. Show him in."

Sir Henry Bartle Edward Frere, The High Commissioner to Southern Africa, continued to run his eyes over the papers on the desk. He heard the approach of steady footsteps down the hall

8

outside and only when they came through the doorway and into his office did he finally drag his gaze away and look up. Frere came to his feet to greet his visitor.

Standing before him, tall and gaunt and looking as severe as he always did, resplendent in uniform and with his dark beard neatly trimmed, stood the overall commander of British Forces of the region. Frederic Augustus Thesiger, 2nd Baron Chelmsford, forever immpecable in both manners and gentlemanly conduct, bowed his head in his typical Old Establishment way. Beneath his left arm he carried his hat. His right came forward in greeting.

Frere reached over the desk and shook the proffered hand. "Welcome, Frederick," he said with a half-smile replacing his troubled expression.

Lieutenant-General Thesiger nodded and replied with a simple "Your Excellancy."

Frere looked beyond his friends shoulder towards the coloured youth who was hovering just inside the doorway. "Refreshments I think. What would you like Frederick?"

"A glass of water would be nice."

"The same for me, if you would," Frere instructed. Once the doors were closed again he indicated the seat opposite. "Please...sit." He lowered himself into his own chair once again.

Pulling open one of the desks drawers he lifted out a gilt-edged cigar box, flipped open the lid, and offered one to Thesiger. The Lieutenant-General politely turned down the offer and instead picked at a piece of fluff on his trouser leg. Frere returned the box without bothering with a smoke either.

"You're looking well Frederick, despite your journey. I must congratulate you on the successful outcome of your recent campaign on the Frontier. Tell me, how did things go?"

Thesiger looked straight at The High Commissioner. "They went as well as can be expected considering the problems. The Xhosa showed their usual reluctance to fight us, deciding instead on guerrilla tactics, which was most annoying for the men. But they gained good experience from it. I don't think the kaffirs will give us much of a problem again. I just wish the final result had been a little more decisive."

"Well that's the natives for you," Frere responded. "They're good at hiding amongst the Bush and little else. But at least it is one more problem out of the way."

The doors opened once again and the two men broke off from their conversation while their drinks were served. Taking a sip of his drink, Thesiger peered curiously over the rim of his glass at the young man as he once again left the room, closely studying his features. When he was gone, he lowered his hand and glanced at Frere, one bushy eyebrow raised. "A Zulu?" he asked politely.

"Yes," Frere replied, "but a Christian Convert. One of Colenso's flock. I brought him down with me from Pietermaritzberg. He does his job adequately. Actually, that nicely brings me to the reason for calling you here."

Thesiger replaced his glass onto the silver tray that had been left on the corner of the desk. He meticulously wiped a few water droplets from the precisely curled lips of his beard.

"You mean, the Zulu problem?"

"Yes. The Zulu problem." Frere turned in his seat and looked out through the french windows behind him, looking towards but not really seeing the blue expanse of Table Bay and the Atlantic Ocean beyond. When he continued, his tone had taken on a certain edge. "You are aware Frederic of the Border Commission that I had set up a while back? Looking into the question of ownership of the Disputed Territories?"

"Of course Your Excellancy. I await their findings with intense interest."

"Well you need wait no longer. Their report is on my desk." He continued to stare out through the windows. He tried to appear calm but inside he was seething with anger, but it would not do to reveal his inner frustrations. "It does not make good reading."

Lieutenant-General Thesiger carefully lay his hat beside the drinks tray and reached over for the documents lying on the desk. Sitting back, he crossed his legs and started to read. For ten minutes he patiently went through the entire report, turning page after page, with neither of them saying anything. Frere occassionally reached for a sip of his water but he studiously avoided making eye contact with his companion, preferring instead to wait until he had finished. When finally Thesiger replaced the document the High

Commissioner turned back and leant his elbows on the edge of the desk, hands clasped before him.

"A surprise, what?"

"Yes. It certainly affects our plans for Confederation."

"Temporarily, hopefully only temporarily. It is a setback though, there's no denying it. However, I have always being a believer in perserverance. No problem is insurmountable. Of course at the moment only a very few people know about the outcome of the investigations. It may be wise to keep it that way."

"The Colonial Office will need to be told."

"Quite right." Frere looked steadily at Thesiger, and the Lieutenant-General did not fail to spot the slight twinkle in the man's eyes. "There are occassions when the length of time it takes to communicate with London can be a damn nuisance. On the other hand, at times it can work to our advantage. If you understand what I am saying."

The Lieutenant-General understood perfectly what was being suggested here. He may not have been a beauracrat but he still knew how the political machine worked.

"While we wait for a response from the Home government we must bide our time," said Frere. "An opportunity will present itself in due course. In the meantime we still have the worry of the security of our border with Zululand. You and I know what a threat the Zulu Army pose to the good people of Natal and the Transvaal. You only need to read the newspapers to see how worried the citizens are. Cetshwayo only needs to give the word and his regiments could be across the river in moments, between 40,000 and 60,000 bloodthirsty, celibate warriors bent on a rampage of death and mutilation. The death of a white man means nothing to a despot who has murdered thousands of his own people. The situation is completely intolerable!"

Sir Bartle Frere rose from the desk and started to pace the room. Thesiger watched him, awaiting for what he could guess would come next.

"I think it is pretty clear, at least it is to me, that one day soon Cetshwayo must be made to, ah, 'Kiss the Rod'. Do you agree Frederic?"

"On every point Your Excellency."

"Good." Frere paused in his walking about and spun on his heels, the soles of his shoes squeaking on the polished floor. He pulled his regalia straight and then put his hands behind his back. "I'm sending you to Natal. I want you to begin an appraisal of the military situation. Of Zulu strengths and weaknesses and how best we can exploit those weaknesses if military action becomes a necessity. Also you must make arrangements for the security of the border. Your plans must be flexible and be able to either take on a defensive posture or an offensive capability. You will be in overall command of any future operations there. Do you understand what I'm asking for?"

Thesiger looked out through the French windows. A frown flitted across his face and he turned to look closely at Frere. "I gather we are talking about a possible war with Cetshwayo?"

"Yes. If that is what it takes to solve the Zulu problem."

"And what military assets will be available to me? I think currently we have just five battalions of Infantry in the country and they are allready under a heavy workload due to various commitments. The Zulus, Your Excellancy, are of a different breed to the Swazis and Xhosa and as you know are well renowned as gutsy and determined. They may actually stand up and fight. It would certainly help if we requested for reinforcements."

Sir Bartle Frere was nodding along to what Thesiger was saying.

"Also, we have a distinct lack of cavalry. They would give us greater flexibility and mobility if we are to pin the Zulu impis down and force a fight. I think at least a couple of regiments."

Frere lifted a hand to stay any further requests, a look of concern shadowing his features."I'm not sure whether the War Office will agree to that Frederic. What with trouble brewing in Afghanistan they may not be able to spare them."

Thesiger shrugged, his mind already working around the problem. Frere strolled back around the desk and resumed his position in his seat. He drank more water and then returned the empty glass to the tray. "What about the local units that were raised a while ago, couldn't we use them?" he suggested.

"Most of them are poorly trained and armed. They're mostly used as border guards and such like. I suppose we could beef them up by taking men who can ride out of the Infantry Battalions and using them as NCO's to instill some disipline. Yes, it might be adequate, given time. There is one area that we fall short in which is a big worry though."

"What's that?"

"Manual labour. The roads leading up to the Zululand border are in a very poor state and would need constant maintenance. Also, there are numerous rivers that would have to be negotiated. Just getting over the border will prove a challenge. I doubt if the engineers and sappers we already have will be able to cope with all that work. There is one possible solution to the problem..."

Frere waited for the answer, not at all sure whether he would like it when he heard it. Thesiger took a deep breath and went on. "If we could raise several contingents of native levies, they could help with the workload as well as be a valuable addition to our scouting parties." "Do you think that's wise? Could they be trusted?"

"Yes, I don't see why not, as long as we draw them from chiefdoms that are traditional enemies of the Zulu. Infact I think they would relish the opportunity to exact a revenge upon them. It would mean cutting back on our requests for large reinforcements."

"I take your point. Do you think it could be done?"

The Lieutenant-General thought carefully for a moment before responding. "I think I know just the man for the job."

"Really? Who is that?"

"Durnford."

"Durnford!" Frere cried aghast. He recoiled back in his chair as though the name had somehow stun him. "Are you sure Frederick? I mean, the man has got a history!"

"Yes, I realize that. But the Colonel does know this country and its people better than anyone. Despite his...inadequacies...in my opinion he is still the most qualified for the task. Also, the blacks seem to like him, for some reason."

Sir Bartle Frere huffed and puffed over the idea for several moments, clearly troubled by the prospect. Yet he knew that what his friend had said was basically true, despite his own misgivings. Finally he acquiescented and gave a reluctant nod of approval.

Both men were silent for a short while. Each understood the significance of what was being discussed here. They were setting in motion a chain of events that once underway could quickly gain a momentum all of its own, to such an extent that it may prove impossible to stop. Yet neither man doubted for one minute that they were doing the correct thing. Being in positions of high authority, Frere as the British political representitive and the Lieutenant-General in his capacity as overall commander of the military, meant that such important decisions ultimately rested with them-once they gained approval from London. That being the case it also meant that they would have to take responsibility for any setbacks or mistakes. But the two of them possessed good judgement. Their confidence was high.

Thesiger eventually broke the silence. "It will not be an easy campaign, if it does come to war. The geography of the land will create untold transport problems. Hopefully this drought, if it lasts for a few more months, will come to our aid in at least making the rivers fordable. Yet I am certain of success. Rest assured, Your Excellancy, the matter is in good hands."

Frere's grin was broad. "I'm sure. I'm absolutely sure Frederic. Now, will you be staying for lunch?"

"I'd better not. There's much to do and I have to get on."

"Of course." Frere pushed himself to his feet once again. He took up the report from the Border Commission, holding it at arms length as though it might somehow contaminate him. "I will try and surpress these findings for as long as possible. This probably isn't the correct moment to tell Cetshwayo that his claim was successful. I'm sure we can find a better time and place, hopefully in a manner that will be to our advantage." He stepped around the desk and glided across the room.

Thesiger stood and followed him into the corner. Sitting on the floor was a large cast-iron safe. Taking a heavy key from his pocket Frere bent and unlocked the door, then drew it open. He placed the document inside on the top shelf. Then closed the door with a resounding thud. Once the safe was securly locked Frere and Thesiger stood looking at one another.

The High Commissioner and Lieutenant-General shook hands.

CHAPTER 3

ZULULAND/NATAL BORDER. THE BATSHE RIVER VALLEY.
3 MILES EAST OF RORKE'S DRIFT.
28th JULY 1878.

Tall and imposing but very popular amongst the group of young warriors that were with him, Mehlokazulu kaSihayo of the Ngobese led them down the side of the steep hillside. Some, like him, were on horseback, but the majority, perhaps two hundred, preferred to walk. All were well armed. They carried their large, raw-hide shields, their knobkerries and *iklwa* stabbing spears, with ease. A few owned obsolete Brown Bess muskets or elephant guns and they showed them off with pride, carrying them high. Each and every one of them were buzzing with excitement. They were looking forward to the fight ahead.

When they were close to the valley floor Mehlokazulu called them to a halt. He slipped down from his horse and moved over to a cluster of rocks nearby. Taking a position on the biggest boulder he squatted on his haunches and motioned the others across. His companions gathered around him, similarly crouching down or sitting in the grass. Gradually the sound of their chatter dropped away.

Taking hold of a small bone container that was hung around his neck on a leather thong, he poured the crushed tobacco into the palm of his hand, picked up a pinch and proceeded to sniff the powder up his nostrils. Following his lead, his companions did likewise with their own supplies.

For ten minutes they took snuff, a group of Zulu warriors preparing for the coming confrontation.

That morning Mehlokazulu had made a terrible discovery. His father, Chief Sihayo kaXongo Ngobese, a firm favourite of the mighty King Cetshwayo, was at the royal *amakhanda* at Ondini, and so he had instructed his son to oversea things at their homestead. During his absence Mehlokazulu had heard talk concerning two of his father's wives, gossip he thought until he had found the proof for himself. The two women had, it appeared, taken lovers. Both were with child. He had refused to believe such ugly talk at first, and had actually struck the person who had told him, beating him hard about the head. Afterwards Mehlokazulu had retired to his hut, sitting in a sulk and wondering what to do

Eventually he had decided to go and confront the two wives about it. Storming across the large homestead he had approached the hut of the principal wife first, at the top of the *umuzi* enclosure opposite the main gate, the place where his father would normally spend most of his time when here. As he'd come close to the dome-shaped thatched but he had hesitated for some reason, covering the last few strides slowly and quietly. With great stealth Mehlokazulu had crept close, going to the side rather than to the low entrance at the front. Bending low he had strained to hear any sounds from within.

On the rock at the valley bottom Mehlokazulu felt himself shake with anger and indignation. He remembered full well the sound of a male voice talking in hushed tones, in a secretive manner, from inside the hut. Shaken, he had fled, racing away to the bush outside where he had hidden himself.

It was true. His father's principal wife had taken up with another man.

Mehlokazulu had been torn as to what to do. Should he confront the illicit lovers and reveal to them that he knew of their secret? Or should he await the return of his father? After much consideration he had decided to seek advice from his uncle and brothers, for he was unable to hold the news to himself alone.

They, like him, were shaken by the scandelous news. But overriding the shock was a profound feeling of anger and acute embarrassment. Things would be so much better if they could rid themselves of the problem. So, after a short discussion, it had been decided that they should deal with the problem themselves, before Chief Sihayo returned from Ondini.

Together the four of them, Mehlokazulu, his two brothers Bhekuzulu and the young Mkhumbikazulu, and their uncle Zuluhlenga, attacked the woman's hut that same night. Storming inside they had discovered not only the principal wife and her lover but also his father's second wife along with her man too. In their fury the four warriors had begun beating and lashing out at the occupants. In the dark and confusion the four miscreants had somehow escaped, much to Mehlokazulu's seething anger, but not before the principal wife had been cut badly on the arm. They had given chase but the noise of the fight had brought everybody else in the *umuzi* outside and in the general uproar the two women and their lovers had slipped away into the night. For the time being Mehlokazulu and his brothers and uncle had given up.

Throughout the long hours of darkness the four of them had talked about the situation. The women had definately left, were no doubt hiding somewhere and probably too petrified to return and face the wrath of their clan. They would never be allowed to return. Normally that would be punishment enough, to be cast out as traitors and be forced to spend the rest of their days as fugitives, but to Mehlokazulu it seemed as though they had escaped lightly. Not only was he angered at their treacherous and disloyal behaviour but he was also acutely embarrassed that they had been seeing their lovers right under his very nose, and at a time when he had been trusted with the important task of overseeing the daily life of the homestead during fathers absence. What's more, they had escaped from out of his very grasp. He felt personally insulted, and for someone like Mehlokazulu, an ambitious and vigorous young warrior who held rank in the iNgobamakhosi regiment, it was almost too much to take. He would have his revenge, as soon as he'd discovered their whereabouts.

Early the following morning, before the sun had appeared from behind the distant hills and the land was still dark, Mehlokazulu had returned to the but where his fathers wife lived and ramsacked the place, smashing the earthenware pots and tearing the sleeping mats, breaking everything that he could find as his fury was released. His father's wives would suffer for this. They were evil, probably they had even bewitched his father so complete was their betrayal and if that was so then only the punishment of death would satisfy Mehlokazulu.

Leaving the *umuzi* through the gateway at the lower part of the homestead he had clambered to the top of the steep hillsides that overlooked the river and waited for sunrise. Gradually the distant peaks had come into view as the new day dawned and for a long time Mehlokazulu had looked out over the vista, running his eyes over the hills and crags hoping to catch some sight of the two men amd two women. Nothing. He'd seen nothing. They could have gone anywhere. If they had travelled through the night then they could be beyond the horizon by now. Glumly, he had wandered back down towards the kraal, wondering what to do next.

Just then he had heard a voice calling out his name. Looking up from the ground, he saw running towards him from the kraal a familiar figure. Familiar because of the headring he wore which made him an *ikehla,* a man who had been granted permission to marry. The *isicoco* stood out high on the head to indicate their status, but this particular one was even more prominent because of the shaven hair around it. Instantly he recognized who the man was, his uncle Zuluhlenga. Waving a stick to attract Mehlokazulu's attention, the older man had come trotting over.

He had exciting things to say. While Mehlokazulu had been gone stories had come that the two wives of Chief Sihayo had been seen during the night. A young herdboy, setting out early with his cattle to the pastures close to the bottom end of the valley, had seen two men and two women skulking through the undergrowth. At first he had thought nothing of it, but then he had noticed that one of the women had an injured arm. His curiosity gaining the better of him, the boy had quietly followed the group, not very easy when he had a small herd of goats with him. He had watched them for quite a distance, over many hills and small valleys, but eventually he had been unable to go any further when they had crossed the big river.

Mehlokazulu had all but grabbed at his uncle's arm upon hearing this. "Which river did they cross?" he had asked in alarm.

"The river that goes by Shiyane, and by kwaJim, the one you must cross to get to the land of the white man," his uncle had replied.

"They have gone to the place of *abelungu,* the pallid sea-creatures? Weugh!" Mehlokazulu had thrown his arms up into the air in outrage. "They not only betray my father but they seek to hide in the land over the river. For this they will be punished severely."

"You must be careful Mehlokazulu kaSihayo. That women speaks with our dead ancestors and she will surely bewitch you when she see's you."

"I am not scared of her. My fathers name is Sihayo kaXongo Ngobese and he must be shown respect by his Great Wife. That is how it will be!" With that, Mehlokazulu had stormed off to seek as much help as he could. He would not be able to do this alone.

*   *   *

It was time for them to go.

After their rest, and taking their snuff, they were ready for the confrontation.

Mehlokazulu was sure this was the right thing to do. His father, after the shock of hearing about his wives unfaithfulness, would surely be thankful. Possibly even the mighty King Cetshwayo, whom Mehlokazulu sometimes served during the *umKhosi* festival as a favoured member of *zembekwela,* one of the King's class of personal servants, would be so impressed he might even bestow on him further privileges.

Putting away his snuff container and picking up his large shield and assegai, Mehlokazulu rose to his full height. Those around him, his brothers and uncle, and his friends, and those who had joined their vengeful mission, stopped what they were doing and looked up. Once he had his audience, Mehlokazulu began, speaking in a loud voice that demanded silence.

"Tell me, should women who are possessed by such wickedness, by such thoughts of betraying their Chief, thus live? Are we to ignore this betrayal and let them lie with their men, while my father buries his face in the ashes of his shame? While they run, do we sit on the ground like leopards with no claws?"

The others in the gathering acknowledged his words with a series of sharp clicks from their throats. A few of them buzzed like angry bees.

"Or we may cross the great river that divides our land from the land of our white enemies, who let them shelter in their kraals, and bring down our wrath on them!" Mehlokazulu paused for dramatic effect, relishing the way his people sat listening spellbound to his every utterance. "What shall we do?"

Bhekuzulu, the middle brother, called out in answer. "They have brought great shame on father! We cannot sit crushed like broken stalks! We must go and finish what was started!"

Mehlokazulu snarled in agreement to his brothers words. "What shall we do?" he asked them again.

"We must eat them up!" came the wild response from all, in a single roar that ripped the morning air apart.

They crossed the river a little below where the silty drift was, out of sight of the home of where the white farmer had once lived, which they called kwaJim, 'Jim's place', close to the foot of the hill that so resembled an eyebrow that they had thus called it *Shiyane* hill.

With Mehlokazulu at the head, they made for the place where they knew one of the fugitives was hiding.

According to the boy Mswagele had given her shelter.

They knew about Mswagele. He had once lived in their *umuzi,* many harvests ago, but now he was a servant of the white people. Their magic had seduced him and he had gone over the river, building a small kraal close by the water. If it was true and he had offered his father's cheating wife a hiding hole then perhaps he should be punished too.

Mehlokazulu was aware of the risks they were taking by crossing over into the white peoples land. He had heard stories about how powerful they were, how they controled the fire demons and could make their guns, some as thick as a man's body, speak with great fury. But, although he was a little in awe of such sorcery, he wasn't afraid of it. They had their assegais, and in the hands of an accomplished man, they could move as fast as a snake. They were a match for anyone.

As they moved away from the river the stillness of the morning became apparant. Even their passage through the tall grass hardly made a noise, so expert were they at moving with stealth. Their appearance would come as a complete surprise. He noticed that one or two of the younger men, no more than youths really, were getting a little excited and Mehlokazulu had to warn them to keep quiet. He wanted nothing to go wrong.

After a short while the homestead of Mswagele came into view. It lay a little away from *Shiyane* hill and Mehlokazulu realized that they would probably be in view of kwaJim's once they arrived, but it didn't matter. The whites could not interfere. This was a Zulu matter and he would not be stopped from doing things in the Zulu custom. It was the only rule he knew, it was the law as set down by Shaka.

Mehlokazulu trotted on ahead and at his signal the men on foot started to run to keep up.

As they neared the cluster of beehive huts that made up the small homestead, he noticed a few figures running about in panic. Then a sound came to him, a cry of fear as the approaching group were spotted. "Namp' amaZulu!" went the alarmed shout - the Zulus are here!

They had lost the element of total surprise that he had wanted, but Mehlokazulu thought it made no difference now. It was too late for his father's wife to escape and there would be no hiding place for her anymore. As one body, the Zulu warriors dashed forward, their fleet-footedness taking them over the rough ground in a blur.

By the time they reached the first hut a small group of men had gathered to meet them. Mehlokazulu saw that they carried an assortment of assegais and knobkerries and he at first thought that Mswagele's followers were going to fight them. He prepared himself for the clash that was surely to come, but just before the two groups met another figure suddenly appeared from amidst the huts - Mswagele himself, waving a stick about his head. To Mehlokazulu's amazement the older man suddenly set about his own people, thrashing at them and shouting angrily. Unsure, Mehlokazulu called for his own people to wait.

They looked on as the amusing spectacle of Mswagele punishing those around him continued for several moments. With squeals and yelps from those he hit he tried to knock some sense into them. Mehlokazulu understood what was the matter; Mswagele must have seen the size of the raiding party descending on his home and immediately realized that to stand and fight would be hopeless. There could only be one outcome and he probably didn't relish seeing his home being burnt to the ground around his own ears, and so he was trying to prevent his followers from fighting. A wise elder, he was, thought Mehlokazulu.

By the time he had finished beating them it was a contest as to who they were more frightened of; their kraal head or the small Zulu impi watching them and laughing.

When everything was settled the old man turned and asked the Zulus what it was they wanted.

Mehlokazulu answered. "My fathers cheating wife, who came to seek shelter here. Bring her out and we will leave you unharmed and your house still standing."

Mswagele tried to look confused but Mehlokazulu saw it for the ploy it was. "What are you to do with her, young kwaSihayo?" he asked.

"She will be punished. My families shame demands that so. I tell you Mswagele, that she is blighted with *umThakathi*. The parasite of evil witchcraft inhabits her body, she was smelled out by our witchdoctors! Do you really wish her to remain here?"

These words had the effect that Mehlokazulu had been hoping for. A ripple of palpable fear passed through the small cluster standing before them, and soon a low murmur of alarm could be heard amoungst them. Mswagele himself looked scared. Without hesitation, he turned and barked out an order to his people. Two large men slipped away and disappeared into one of the huts.

A moment later they reappeared, dragging a screaming woman between them.

Chief Sihayo's Great wife had a formidable personality, someone who would normally instil fear into most individuals. She also had a temper. She wasn't one who would normally give way to panic, so it came as quite a shock to see her quivering with fear as she was marched out of the kraal and thrown to the ground. Immediately three or four Zulus rushed forward before she had a chance to rise. They hurriedly tied a leather collar around her neck, then, using two attached lengths of rope, they dragged her to her feet once again. Mehlokazulu's people became uncontrolable with excitement. A sea of assegais were thrust to the sky and in unison two hundred feet were slammed down hard onto the earth, sending up a cloud of dust from the parched ground. Several of them, getting carried away, charged forward a few feet and leaped into the air in mock combat; this was called to *giya* as each individual tried to outdo one another with their boasts about how they would prove themselves in combat when their time came.

All of this was starting to have quite an effect on Mswagele and his people. A look of terror was starting to appear on their faces, so to calm things Mswagele stepped forward and spoke loudly to Mehlokazulu. "If your people are to wash their spears, then do so over the river. Not here. Take her with you! Do not come to my home and create terror. Go Mehlokazulu kaSihayo!"

Mehlokazulu, his heart beating fast in his chest, told the old man he had nothing to worry about. Their quarrel was with Chief Sihayo's wives and nobody else. Even their lovers weren't to be harmed, for surely they had been bewitched? Satisfied that he was doing the right thing, he turned his horse and led his men away from the kraal, much to the relief of Mswagele.

They went back over the river, pulling their captive along with them.

Once they reached the far bank she seemed to realize what fate lay in store for her. She started to beg for forgiveness and threw herself prostrate on the ground infront of them. But Mehlokazulu felt no pity for her. Cheating on a husband together with accusations of witchcraft could mean only one punishment. It was not for him to decide.

At Mehlokazulu's command they took the woman up to the top of a small knoll. Here the men holding the ropes forced her to stand, although her quivering legs made this difficult. Then Zuluhlenga, his uncle, stepped forward. Brandishing a knobkerry he unhesitatingly smashed her in the face hard, not to kill or render her unconcious, but to break her teeth. He hit her again, then again, repeating the process until all the teeth had been knocked out and her mouth was a grotesque mask of red.

When this was done the now barely concious woman stood before them, only remaining on her feet because of the men holding her upright by the ropes attached to the neck collar.

Getting down from his horse Mehlokazulu passed through the chanting and leaping crowd and pushed his way to the front. Taking his uncle's bloody knobkerry he stepped behind the sagging, terrified woman. He raised the weapon. Then smashed it down on the back of her skull, killing his father's cheating Great Wife with a single blow.

Mehlokazulu stood there amidst the screaming and roaring crowd. He did not feel remorse, only pride. It soared in his chest. Then he cried out loud above the surrounding tumult.

"Ngadla!" - I have eaten!

CHAPTER 4

DURBAN, BRITISH COLONY OF NATAL. DURBAN REDOUBT.
6th AUGUST 1878.

In February of 1488 two storm damaged ships, sailing 1,400 miles further down the African Coast than anyone had been before, rounded the Cape of Good Hope. Their weary, and somewhat mutinous crew, commanded by Bartholomew Diaz, managed to haul their stricken vessels to Mossel Bay where they dropped anchor for much needed repairs and also to make land to replenish their supplies of water. As they reached shore in their surfboats they noticed, off in the near-distance, a group of Hottentots (descended from primitive Bushmen), watching them. Before Diaz or his crew could make contact they fled, disappearing over the sandunes into the bush.

They weren't long in returning, but this time they were greater in number. After once again observing these strange white-skinned people, they eventually found the courage to attack the landing party to try and drive them back into the sea, whence they had come. In the ensueing melee Diaz fired a crossbow at one of the natives, killing him instantly, and so fearful were the Hottentots of this demonstration of the white man's power that they took off once again.

The landing party, anxious to be away from this strange and wild land, hurriedly replenished their water casks and likewise

25

departed. So incensed were the crew with their captain at risking their lives that within days they all but threatened to take command of the two ships, using force if necessary, unless they immediately returned home. Diaz, having little option, complied. It was to be a decade before the next white explorers came back to this part of the African continent.

On Christmas Day in the year 1497, Vasco da Gama the Potuguese explorer who had recently reached India, was sailing north along the same coastline, admiring the green and fertile hills that stretched away into the distance. So taken was he with its beauty and unexplored hinterland that he decided to give it a name there and then; he called it *Terra Natalis.*

During the next century and a half the Portuguese established their trade routes via the Cape of Good Hope. Along the way they established a series of bases on the East African coast, further north of the region briefly visited by Diaz and da Gama. It was considered too big a risk to create a stopping off point there as the rugged coastline had already claimed several vessels and the native Hottentots were of an unknown quantity. Infact the Portuguese now had a name for the various clans that lived in the area; taken from the Arab word for infidel - Kaffir.

By 1652 the Dutch, being better mariners and of a hardier nature, had taken over the trade routes from Portugal. But they lacked ports of their own, so on 6th April and under orders from the United Chartered East India Company they made landfall at the Cape and established a settlement at Table Bay, later to become Capetown.

Table Bay was looked upon as no more than a stopping off point for the ships rounding the Cape, a place for the crews to rest and replenish their stocks. The people living there were not in the least interested in what lay to the north, all of their attention was on the blue expanse that was their only lifeline with home. The native tribe, the semi-nomadic 'Choi people, were easily appeased by the liberal bribes of goods such as brandy and tobbaco. However, within a few years a number of settlers grew to love the land and decided to try their hand at farming, their produce being much welcomed by the townsfolk as well as the crews of the various ships that set anchor there. Gradually the frontier was pushed out. Soon the farmers, mostly Dutch but with a sprinkling of Germans amongst them, started to cut their ties with Table Bay and a fierce independant streak started to flourish in them. Each farm - they named themselves Boers after the Dutch word 'farmer'- became a self-sufficient community with no need for outside help. The size of each holding was staggering to the Boers; the average farm was about 6,000 acres and with a variety of hardy grasses that flourished throughout the year it was prime cattle country. Also, there was a significant absence of the tsetse fly. All in all, these early frontier settlers had never had it better.

The further north and east they spread the more they came into contact with the native Hottentots. The Boers fiercly drove them away so determined were they to claim the land for themselves. In 1713 an outbreak of smallpox amoungst the natives helped the Dutch and thereafter they met little resistance. For the next half century and more they had a virtual monopoly of all the land in this part of Southern Africa.

By 1793 all of this had changed. The Dutch found themselves competing for the lucrative rights to the trade routes with Britain and a series of bloody wars between the two nations followed. It was a contest that significantly weakened the Dutch maritime powerhold over the area to such an extent that Britain eventually was able to take Capetown. It was briefly snatched back in 1802, only for the British to push them out, this time permanently, four years later.

Further to the north in Natal, the stretch of land that Vasco da Gama had cast his envious eyes over while sailing in the *San Gabriel,* great events were about to unfold. In 1816 a small native clan of just a few thousand, led by a dynamic and ruthless leader by the name of Shaka kaSenzangakhona, emerged as the dominant tribe. These were the Zulu, descended from the Nguni people, and in a bitter struggle that lasted until 1820, Shaka virtually wiped out any who opposed his clan. This bloody series of brutal wars, a time of cataclysmic turmoil became known as *mfecane* 'the crushing'.

Gradually news of King Shaka's exploits reached the British at the Cape. Intrigued by this mysterious person and his mighty Zulu nation - for they had conquered vast tracts of land and amalgamated with many beaten tribes during the years of *mfecane* - a few hardy individuals set out to establish contact with them. Upon arriving in Natal these first white adventurers were so over-awed by Shaka's power, and he in turn intrigued by them and the strange gifts they brought with them, that the Zulu King granted them a tiny portion of his territory. An area just to the south of the Thukela river it was named Port Natal.

Back at the Cape the Dutch Boers had grown tired of British rule. Promised compensation for the land that had been taken from them by the Crown, they became dissilusioned by the pittance they finally, and after much wrangling from the British authorities, recieved. By 1834 they had had enough. A small expedition was sent out to look for suitable farming land further to the north and when the Kommissie trekke returned with favourable things to say about Natal many farmers decided they had no option but to pack up their belongings and go. The Great Trek was underway.

It didn't happen overnight. Infact things only reached their height by 1837 and the vast majority actually chose to head to the vast and seemingly endless expanse of the Interior. But a trickle of Boers did start to reach Natal. In the meantime Port Natal had been renamed Durban, after the then Governor of The Cape Colony, D'urban. The Zulus weren't happy. Shaka was now dead and the new King, Dingane, felt that the number of whites beginning to settle on his land was getting out of hand and so he decided to settle the issue. He lured a party of Boer leaders to his royal residence on the pretext to discuss a treaty about purchasing some land but then had them murdered. Then he sent out his army to attack the Boer camps which had grown up in the foothills of the Drakensberg mountains where hundreds of men, women and children were slain in a terrible night of bloodletting. Next it was the turn of the fledgling community of Durban. Falling on the British the Zulu impis destroyed the small community and drove the settlers into the bush.

The Dutch demanded revenge. Within a few months they were back with a large force of well armed men and this time they were ready for what Dingane had to throw at them. On the banks of the Blood (Ncome) River they did battle with an enormous Zulu army and utterly defeated it. In the aftermath of their humiliation Dingane's brother Mpande sided with the Boers and eventually drove the Zulu King out of their land where he was eventually put to death. Prince Mpande became King Mpande and as a reward to the Boers for helping him gain the Zulu throne Mpande granted them Natal, comprising that land bounded by the Buffalo, Blood and Thukela rivers.

In far off Capetown the British grew alarmed. Forever suspicious of independent white states on their doorstep, especially of those who might form alliances with rival European nations, they realized that they had to take Natal back and return the Boers to the Imperial fold. In 1842 British forces moved north to occupy Durban. Infantry, supported by a man-o-war firing from the bay, attacked the Boer fort that had been built on the hillside overlooking the town and after fierce fighting they retook Durban and secured Natal for the Empire.

British troops raised the union flag over the Durban Redoubt. They were here to stay.

*   *   *

Durban Redoubt occupied a commanding position overlooking the town. Set back slightly from the outskirts, the fort was placed on a strategic hill, allowing for good views of the bay area to the south, the Indian Ocean to the east, and the rolling slopes disappearing into the bush westward. Any ships landing here had to first navigate the treacherous sandbar that all but blocked the entrance to the sheltered bay and then to come around the Point, before lowering anchor. The forts position had been set in 1842 and despite various changes to its defences over the years it more or less occupied the same tract of land.

Standing atop one of the forts earth ramparts was Colonel Durnford. Raising his pair of binoculars to his face he scanned the port area below, looking at the various ships and boats that sat at anchor. One in particular drew his attention. It was the most recent arrival, having come around the Point about one hour ago. HMS Active, rocking in the gentle swell with her masts lowered.

Durnford knew that she carried important passengers. None other than Lieutenant-General Thesiger and his staff themselves. He'd been informed of their visit about a week ago but hadn't been given the reason why; however, he could hazard a pretty good guess. The reaction to the delivery of the Border Commissions report had been a curious one. Instead of being a major setback to Frere's Conferderation plans the High Commissioner had all but ignored the findings and was proceeding with his own private agenda as though nothing had happened. Indeed his attitude had taken on an even more belligerent manner, his words becoming more war-mongering by the day. And now he had dispatched the General to Natal, presumably to oversee things in person and no doubt to report directly to Frere and keep him informed as to how things were proceeding. The whole affair was starting to leave an unpleasant taste in Durnford's mouth.

He turned the binoculars onto the town itself. Amoungst the jumble of wooden buildings set out in a grid pattern, the coming and going of the townsfolk, and the general bustle of a busy community at work, he searched for the General and his entourage. They would be coming straight to the fort along the main roadway from the Point, Thesiger preferring to ride on horseback rather than take the short train-ride. After several days at sea that was understandable.

After several minutes of looking Durnford finally spotted the group heading up towards the back of town.

He immediately recognized the General. Wearing the dark blue undress uniform that he always wore while on military business and with swagger stick in hand, he rode at the front with his various staff members and escort grouped around him like so many sycophants. Thesiger had a way about him that always drew the eye, thought Durnford. Maybe it was his body language, the way he rode so straight-backed and pointing things out with the stick, or perhaps his style of talk with his staff forever ready to agree with over-exaggerated nods of the head. Whatever, Durnford had no problem picking him out amidst the dense group coming in his direction.

They seemed to be in no rush. It was almost as though they were on a pleasant Sunday afternoon ride along Rotten Row. There was no sense of urgency about them whatsoever, even though they were infact a day late in getting to Durban. Durnford, while not particularly paranoid, could not shake off the notion that the Generals dawdling was a personal slight aimed at himself. But no, Lieutenant-General Thesiger may have his faults but he was most definately a gentleman and he always treated people, whatever their class, with the utmost courtesy. He was faultlessly polite. Very popular amoungst the men apparantly. Then what was it that Durnford found disquieting about the man? He did sometimes come across as arrogant, but then that was just his upbringing. The man had supreme confidence in his own abilities, a trait that could be misinterpreted as a refusal to delegate or to take on other people's opinions. Yet once again, was that a fault or was it an advantage for a high ranking officer to have? Durnford once again asked himself. Perhaps it was necessary to stamp ones authority on a situation, partly to dissuade disobedience but also in an effort to appear to be in total control of events. After all, The General did have a good track record, even if in Durnfords's opinion he had not yet had to deal with a fully worthy opponent. Chasing the Xhosa through the bush was one thing. Taking on the Zulus would surely be a different state of affairs entirely! If it came to war, and Durnford's soldier instincts suggested it could, was Thesiger the right man for the job?

It was a dilemma that had preoccupied Durnford's mind these last few days. Whereas he himself had many years of experience concerning african warfare to call upon, admittedly not all of it good, the Lieutenant-General was comparitively new to the country with just one campaign of any note to date. In his opinion High Commissioner Frere was taking too much of a risk. And as for the Generals staff... He trained his binoculars on the figure riding alongside Thesiger, talking in an animated fashion to him.

Brevet Lieutenant-Colonel J. N. Crealock, Assistant Military Secretary to the 2nd Baron Chelmsford. A small and fussy little man in Durnford's eye, forever flapping around his superior like some kind of idiotic toady. His presence was usually a waste of time. And he was also the most sarcastic and irritating individual Durnford thought he had ever had the displeasure to meet. A foolish person made more so by his facetious ways. He liked nothing more than to put people down with a withering stare and flippant words, his West Country burr coming from his tiny mouth a most annoying experience to those who it was levelled at. A fancy beard that he brushed morning, noon, and night into a long and straight mane completed the picture. Durnford disliked the man with a passion.

As he watched through his glasses Durnford saw the Lieutenant-General make some remark to his Military Secretary. Crealock, with a glance towards the fort that they were approaching, leaned across and said something back, his mouth close to Thesigers ear.

Up on the earth ramparts Durnford wondered what they were talking about.

Lieutenant-General Thesiger asked his Military Secretary, who was riding his horse half a pace behind his own, "who is that person up there on the parapet?"

"Why General, I do believe it's the good Colonel Durnford, our illustrious welcoming committee and genial host for the day."

Thesiger nodded, paying to ignore the manner in which the answer was delivered. He was aware of the history of animosity between the two men but was content to allow them their petty squabbles, as long as it did not affect their conduct. Rivalry between officers wasn't necessarily a bad thing. It stopped them becoming complacent. It also made for an amusing sideshow to the monotony of certain duties that, as commander-in-chief, it was necessary for him to perform.

As they headed up the hill towards the fortifications perched on the top, Thesiger found himself wondering about 'the good Colonel' that Crealock so disliked. Durnford was an enigma to Thesiger. Thought of so highly by his men, especially the black Christians who had stayed loyal to the Colonel over the years, but disliked by the colonial population. That was understandable, after what had happened at the debacle at the Bushmans River Pass six years previously. The settlers and farmers still held Durnford responsible for the death of their sons and brothers and fathers on that rainy and windswept mountain. Yes, he had made some bad mistakes, mostly as a result of bad intelligence and an ill-timed attack. His natural hot-headedness and questionable boldness had led the column of mounted men into an ambush that had resulted in a panicked withdrawal and a number of dead being left behind. But Durnford had somehow got the majority of his men down from the mountain despite the predicament they were in. He had shown a great deal of personal bravery in doing so, not without injury to himself, an injury that he still carried with him to this day as a constant reminder of that dreadful experience. Afterwards he had become, and still was, a hated figure amoungst the white population. Thesiger had asked himself many times over whether their dislike of Durnford was justified.

It was a question the Lieutenant-General had been unable to provide an adequate answer to.

Certainly there was no doubting his courage. He was always willing to put his own life at stake alongside his men, preferring to be in the thick of the action rather than well to the rear where it was safe. But was that the right thing to do? Was it really the job of a Brevet Colonel to be leading his men into battle in person? Couldn't a high ranking officer with years of experience have more of an influence over events by choreographing the movements of his men from a place of safety and quiet and calm? He could be very rash when the pressure was on, of that Thesiger had no doubts. Plus, did the man's sympathies with coloureds - as proved by his recommendations in the Boundary Report - have an adverse effect in his decision making? Could he be relied upon if he found himself in a tight spot? There were, in Thesiger's eye, just too many unanswered questions.

Yes, Durnford had a history.

He also had a wealth of knowledge concerning the rigours and problematic nature of warfare in Southern Africa. He did indeed know this land intricately and its various peoples as though he had lived amongst them all his life. That kind of knowhow may have come at a price for the Colonel and had not been gained overnight, but it could prove indispensible in the coming weeks and months. In short, Lieutenant-General Thesiger could not do without Durnford. His faults, and they were many, were far outweighed by the advantages to be gained from any contribution he could offer. As for his influence over the blacks...well that could hopefully be put to good use too.

Turning to Crealock, who was working his jaw vigorously as though chewing on further disparaging words about Durnford, Thesiger said, "come along, we have things to discuss with Durnford. First, however, I suggest we eat. The mind always works better on a full stomach, don't you think?"

"A fine observation sir. Very, so very true," agreed Crealock.

DURBAN REDOUBT. MID - AFTERNOON.

Lunch was over, and the three of them were strolling along the verandah of the main barracks building. The Lieutenant-Generals small military escort had taken up a position by the main entrance to the fort, waiting at a discreet distance but close enough if suddenly called upon. Not that it was expected. Still, they lent a regal air to the proceedings dressed as they were in their splendid dark uniforms with polished metal fittings gleaming in the winter sun. These were men of the Imperial Mounted Infantry, chosen as the General's personal escort, and they took great pride in their appearance.

Occassionally, the voices of the three high-ranking officers reached them, but they paid no attention to what was being discussed. They were not privy to the delicate matters at hand.

Thesiger, walking a little infront of his companions, reached the end of the verandah and turned to ask Colonel Durnford a direct question. "Can it be done Colonel? If Lieutenant-Governor Bulwer does give the go-ahead, would it be feasible to form a body of native levies, sufficient in size, to carry out the task?"

Durnford looked down at his feet for a few moments before responding to Thesiger. "Well that would depend on what their role is to be General. Are we talking about a labour force to supplement my own engineers, or would they be required to engage an enemy in combat? Plus, if a negotiated settlement becomes impossible and 'other measures' are called for, how large a campaign would we be talking about?"

Thesiger gave a somewhat sly smile before he answered. "The High Commissioner has all but given me a free hand in how I achieve his aims. Because of the nature of the Zulu and their fighting qualities I intend this to be a much bigger campaign than the recent one on the frontier. I have no doubts as to what the final outcome of any war will be but I do not intend to take any unnecessary risks. My only concern is that Cetshwayo's impis will try to avoid engagement."

"Pardon me for interrupting, General, but I've never known a Zulu warrior to shy away from confrontation."

"Yes, that may be so," Crealock uttered quietly, stepping up to Thesigers side and looking straight at Durnford. "But the nature of their enemies to date since the rise of the Zulu nation must be called into question. This time they will be facing the cream of Her Majesty's infantry, armed with the most modern of weapons. They will be no match for the Martini-Henry. In the face of massed volley fire delivered by highly disciplined and cool soldiers they will crumble away. Just look at what happened to them at Blood River."

"Good point Crealock. If a few Boer farmers could hold them at bay then we need not worry unduly," Thesiger remarked.

"Oh, I am not questioning the professionalism of our men, General. It's just that if we were to launch an invasion of Zululand then not only will they be defending their land but they will also be fighting to protect their King and their wives and families. They will not give in easily. At Bushman's Pass the-"

"Bushman's Pass...yes," mused Crealock as though talking to himself. He twiddled with his beard as if preoccupied with something. "Of course, success or failure often depends on leadership quality."

Durnford felt his face flush with anger and he had to all but restrain himself from loosing his cool. That would not do, at least not in front of the General.

Beside him, Thesiger stepped between the two and headed back along the verandah, hardly able to hide the amused smirk on his face. Durnford and Crealock exchanged a brief look before following along in his trail.

"Do not concern yourself with the small detail of this campaign Durnford. I will take care of that. Your expertise lies in another department. That is where I need your help. Principally in the fortification of any forts and building of ponts, as well as keeping the tracks passable to our transports. Your intimate relations with the blacks in this country also comes in handy, hence my request concerning these native levies. As to your question about their purpose," Thesiger looked around at Colonel Durnford, " I will require them to be able to fight alongside our men, alas as a reserve force only to be used if our boys become over burdened with duties, you understand?"

Durnford merely nodded.

"I plan to cross into Zululand with five columns, each from widely spaced points along the border. This should enable us to pin down the main Zulu army at some stage and force them to fight. It will also make it extremely difficult for them to slip past us and launch their own invasion of Natal. Your native force would furnish all five columns so it would have to be of significant size.

"Five columns you say?" said Durnford. "In that case I suggest we form five regiments, each of about a thousand men. Finding sufficient recruits shouldn't be too difficult. We ought to also have white officers and NCO's. With some training and armed with Sniders they should be quite a competent body."

Thesiger's forehead creased into a frown as he listened. "I'm not too sure whether the administration will be too happy about having five thousand blacks armed with firearms roaming the countryside. We may have to compromise somewhat. I think if only one in ten has a gun, that will suffice."

Durnford wasn't happy with that. To him the Generals plan of invading with five columns would stretch their infantry battalions very thinly. Surely they would need all the help they could get. Yet there was little he could do.

"Very well," he said, trying to hide his frustration. "I think one exception would be necessary. I'm going to try and raise a mounted unit, of about five hundred men. The people I have in mind are brilliant horsemen and excellent shots, they've rode with me many times, and I can vouch for their professionalism. Arming them with the best firearms would give us a very potent force of cavalry, an area I understand we are a little weak in."

"Yes, that's true," agreed Thesiger. "Fine, yes an excellant idea Colonel."

They continued walking along the wooden verandah, enjoying the shade it provided. Reaching the end Thesiger rested his hands on the rail and looked out across Durban to the Indian Ocean beyond. It was a beautiful view in what was a beautiful country, a land that soon would probably turn red with spilt blood. Sometimes the business of war brought him great shame.

"Just to clarify one point General," Durnford asked, "what is the Home Governments position on the matter?"

Thesiger continued to stare off into the distance. His sallow features and hooked nose reminded Durnford of a bird of prey. "Our views differ somewhat, Colonel. We have been given the task of implementing Confederation by the Colonial Office. They seem to want us to resolve the Zulu problem using peaceful means, but London is a long way away, and our view of the situation here is in contrast to theirs. I'm afraid that it is wishful thinking if they think we can subdue Cetshwayo without force of arms."

"So a quick and successful campaign is called for," put in Crealock. "An example of Imperial might will go a long way to discouraging any future ideas of rebellion, from the blacks as well as the Boer states. A little flexing of our military muscle will do wonders."

"I'm aware of the difficulties we face," Thesiger told them as he turned back to face his companions. "We face terrible problems with our transport, for instance. Finding sufficient wagons and teams of oxen to keep the five columns moving is proving to be a daunting task, and moving over the countryside will be a very slow and laborious business. All of our lines of communication will need to be given round the clock protection, so you will need to construct forts at regular intervals along our axis of advance. I've put in a request for further units of Engineers so that should ease the burden somewhat. Also, I've asked for some special service officers to be sent out to help with transport duties."

"And extra Infantry? Are we likely to receive any?" asked Durnford.

"The High Commissioner has promised to do all he can. What we have at the moment should be adequate to form a decent defence of the border. We have the 2nd Battalion of 'The Buffs', the 1st Battalion 13th Regiment, the single battalion 80th and 90th Regiments and both the 1st and 2nd of the 24th Regiment. They've all had good experience of fighting conditions in the field in South Africa, so we can depend on them with a good deal of confidence. But we definately need further reinforcements if we are to carry out offensive operations in a hostile country."

Crealock, ever the polite Military Secretary, put in gently, "morale is very high amongst the men. Especially in the twenty-fourth, who had a good time of it on the Frontier recently. We have a very capable force at our disposal."

"That's correct," agreed Lieutenant-General Thesiger. "They are the backbone of our Infantry. I intend to put them in the Centre Column, which will strike out from Rorke's Drift for the heart of the Zulu Kingdom. The area is close to the Disputed Territories and also Chief Sihayo's district so they will not have it easy, but I'm confident they will be more than capable of dealing with any situation they find themselves in."

Mention of the name Sihayo made Durnford look up. Wasn't it his son's who had been involved in the recent border incident? Was it just coincidence that one of Thesigers columns was going to be passing through the same area? Durnford couldn't but help a feeling of unease start to spread through him like some fever working its way through his veins. He didn't care for the way the General was preparing for what looked increasingly like a war with the Zulus, a war that in his opinion would be very different, and harder fought, than the one seen recently on the Cape Frontier.

"We have been presented with the perfect opportunity to quell Cetshwayo's military ambitions," Thesiger remarked, breaking through his ruminations. "I say it is our duty to grasp that opportunity."

Duty. Yes, it was duty above everything else, thought Durnford. He would follow his orders despite his misgivings because he was a professional soldier. But where was duty leading them?

To war. It was leading them to war.

CHAPTER 5

KINGWILLIAMS TOWN, EASTERN CAPE. BARRACKS OF 1/24th,
MILITARY RESERVE.
LATE AUGUST 1878.

Kingwilliams Town was typical of most garrison towns. The military personel and the civilian population lived cheek by jowl, each reluctantly putting up with the others presence with a mixture of necessity and dependency. The townsfolk recognized the fact that they needed the security the Infantry Regiments gave them from the often hostile Bantu across the Great Fish River. The officers and men of the various military units that were barracked here enjoyed the proximity of townlife and all the distractions from their day to day routine that this offered. Occassionally tensions between the two did fracture the mostly amiable relationship, but generally the mood was good, even friendly. As long as the soldiers mostly remained stationed in the military reserve at the northern end of town and kept their bawdry nature to a minimum, while the townsfolk did not interfere with the way the army ran their show.

A small stream, the Fleet Ditch, seperated the military reserve from the rifle range and the Mule Train where the army mounts were stabled. Between the two was the old town, the heart of colonial Kingwilliams Town centered on Prince Alfred Square. Because of

39

the close proximity of the reserve many of the residents had gradually moved a little to the south where they had started to build the new town. This area was more upmarket. It contained a Town Hall, some botanical gardens and The Pensioners Village, and the residents renamed Fort Murray Road - the main route out from the reserve - Alexandra Road. It soothed their sensibilities somewhat. A railway line ran from here to East London 40 miles to the east, passing a British/ German village and the new cemetery - the one close to the rifle range being full - that was positioned on the outskirts of town. All in all Kingwilliams Town was a hotch-potch of army buildings and locations mixed in and amoungst the civilian areas, a sprawling settlement stretching for several miles from north to south.

Kingwilliams Town was the capital of British Kaffraria, a garrison town and peacetime headquarters of four regiments. The first battalion, twenty-fourth regiment had only recently returned fom the Frontier War against the Xhosa's, arriving back at barracks over the last few weeks, bringing with them a number of sick and wounded. The fighting that they'd seen had raised the mens spirits and a feeling of confidence filled the ranks. All veterans of African warfare, they felt at ease in their enviroment. Jovial and high-spirited at their success they looked forward to the next campaign, wherever that might be.

One of those who had been wounded during the Xhosa fighting was Private Robert Metcalfe of H-Company, 1/24th. His injury, recieved when their post at Mpetu had been temporarily surrounded, was only slight. He had lost his footing while skirmishing with the enemy and had sprained his right ankle badly with the result that upon returning to Kingwilliams Town he had been excused duties and confined to barracks until fit for duty.

Normally Private Metcalfe would be more than satisfied with the prospect of spending time resting and avoiding the monotony of the day to day duty of army life. Anything was preferable to that.

But today was a Sunday. And on Sunday's, after the service given by the regimental Chaplain, there was always the boxing competition to look forward to. And today was H-Company versus E-Company. Confined to the barracks building as he was he would miss all the fun.

So Private Metcalfe was in a funk.

The barracks building that housed H-Company was a long, stone-built affair. Stretching along the centre was a narrow wooden table that served as a place for the men to sit, either to write letters or read those that arrived occasionally on the infrequent mail steamers, or maybe to drink the gill of rum they were allowed each day. The surface was usually cluttered with odds and ends; tin mugs and saucers, half-eaten loaves, lanterns that were lit at night, maybe the occassional bible or two.

Down each side of the room were row after row of tiny and uncomfortable beds, their mattresess and pillows stained and smelly. Above, on the wall behind, each man had two shelves on which to place or hang his personal possessions or kit. It wasn't much, but to the men it was their own personal space which they guarded with their lives, or so it sometimes seemed.

Private Metcalfe's bunk was at the far end, furthest from the door and tucked into the corner. He did not mind. It meant he was close to one of the windows, which afforded him a partial view of the parade ground outside. Many a time he would sit in his place at the table and stare outside, not really seeing the activity out there but instead trying to picture in his minds eye images of his family and home, wondering what they were doing right at that moment. He never became particularly homesick for he enjoyed army life tremendously, but sometimes, oh sometimes it would be nice to be able to see them, hold them, talk to them. England seemed such a long way away. In another world completely.

He was sitting there at this moment, as he had done a lot over the last few days. Writing yet another letter home. There was little else to do with his time.

Dear Mother,

just a few lines to let you know how things are going here. The injury to my leg, which I mentioned in my last letter, is doing fine. In another week I hope to be back to normal. It was nice to have the rest at first but sitting by myself all day can be so monotonous and 1 will be glad when I can join me mates once again.

Now that the fighting is over there is little to occupy the men and life can be very tedious. It may sound strange but we will all be glad when we are on the move again.

We have heard a rumour that things in Natal are hotting up. Cetewayo and his people, the savage Zulus, are said to be game for a fight. Lately some of his men have been acting and talking in a very bloodthirsty way, and so the general feeling is that they need to be taught a lesson. Our new General seems to delight in the prospect.

I hope we won't go, mind you mother, I am no coward, it is not the fighting that I care about but it is such a distance to march!

Would you please tell Mrs Noakes that her Charlie is in good health. As he is not able to write very well he has asked me to pass this on. I know how she worries so, therefore me and Charlie have made a pact that if one of us should fall in battle - God forbid that it does not happen - that as long as there is life in the other we shall remain by his side, but if he is dead, then he may save himself. Now, I do not want this to worry you. I'm sure this state of affairs will never come about. But we are soldiers and these thoughts do come to us occassionally.

On a lighter note, how is my baby brother doing? I'm sorry about forgetting his birthday, so tell him when I come home I promise to try and make up for it.

Well that is all for now. Please keep writing. I miss you both dearly. Your loving son,

Robert.

A noise from outside drew his attention. It was the sound of men cheering, coming from the dirt parade ground slightly down the slope. Pushing himself up from the table Private Metcalfe hobbled over to the window and pushed it open, then leant his elbows on the windowsill.

He could see the crowd gathering down there, just beyond the flagpole. The boxing contest would be about to get underway.

A somewhat guilty smile flickered across his lips. Mrs Noakes, back in far-off England, was unaware that her boy was one of the fighters today. It was a serious business, this inter-battalion boxing bout, and her Charlie was one of the best. His mother really had no comprehension just how much her son had grown up since joining the army. But let her remain safely cocooned from the realities of army life. Let her have her romantic notions and daydreams. There was no need for her to be alarmed unnecessarily.

Private Robert Metcalfe wondered how his best friend Charlie was doing.

Private Charlie Noakes, best friend of Robert, stood at the centre of a crowd that must have been several hundred strong.

He looked around at the sea of bearded and grizzled faces, saw the gleam of anticipation in their eyes, noted the expressions of expectation that dared him to let them down. He knew that most of them had money riding on the contest and so they let him know what would happen if he lost. A wall of noise filled his head, some urging him to fight hard and making unsavoury threats if he delivered anything less than victory. Words flew back and forth, swearing and cheering or chanting his name. Many reached out and patted him hard on the back. He recognized them all and he felt a burden of responsibility weigh him down. He even saw amoungst them a sprinkling of officers; his own C.O. Captain Wardell was there, standing towards the back and on tip-toes, as well as Colour-Sergeant Wolfe, broad beams on their faces. And wasn't that Lieutenant-Colonel Pulleine himself, self conciously scratching his nose but just as excited as the rest?

The tumult seemed to reach a crescendo as the start of the contest neared. Everywhere there was roaring. Yelling voices with mouths open wide revealing blackened teeth, spittle flying this way and that.

He turned to look across at his opponent, who was waiting for him, all eager and keen to get things going. Private Owen Brooks of E-Company was taller than average, about six feet thereabouts, with a body to match. Dressed like he was in just his navy-blue trousers with scarlet seam down each leg and heavy dust-encrusted boots, no tunic or undershirt and with his braces hanging loose at his hips. Thickly bearded and with a nose flattened by numerous blows from many a previous fight, he looked every inch one of the 'old sweats', with nigh on twelve years' service to show for it. Private Noakes tried to remain confident. It would be a hard bout but he knew he was good. His reputation for being a very capable fighter had grown considerably over the last few months, with some justification he thought. There was no doubting that he had a talent when it came to these bare knuckle fights.

The fight began quite suddenly, as they so often did. There was no preamble, no handshakes between opponents. They just came together in the centre of the gathered crowd and commenced to beat seven bells out of one another.

Skill wasn't called for here, nor was finese. This was a pure slugging match.

The two of them came in hard with punches to the face and body. Noakes felt himself being hit hard around the head as he weaved and dodged around but he was also landing some heavy blows on his opponent and knew they were hurting him from the grunts and cusses he could hear above the din of accompanying cheering. Fairly soon the two of them were bleeding from numerous cuts around the face, a result of such brutal, bare knuckle boxing contests.

After a couple of minutes they both broke away to regain their breath, circling each other like stalking leopards.

Amidst the shouting and applauding, Noakes could pick out a few individual voices, calls of "damn good show" or "they don't half go at one another!" and "keep it up son, you've got the bugger worried".

One of those watching was Lieutenant-Colonel Henry Burmester Pulleine, second-incommand of the first battalion, a dapper and energetic individual and well liked by the men. He was standing alongside a fine looking officer, young and athletic in physique and going by the name of Teignmouth Melvill, with the rank of Lieutenant, and acting adjutant to the 1/24th. With his scarlet undress frock and officers forage cap at a jaunty angle, he seemed boyish in manner with an infectious grin as he watched the contest.

Turning to the younger man Pulleine passed comment on the fight, his voice a little reedy and lacking in authority in contrast to his rank. But he could not hide his enthusiasm as he said, close to his companion's ear, "it's all very exciting, is it not Melvill? I've never had the pleasure of seeing a boxing contest before."

"It certainly is sir," Lieutenant Melvill responded cheerfully. "I get the impression the boys take it very seriously." He drew his commanding officers attention to the men closeby who were eagerly waving their money in the air.

Pulleine laughed, finding the whole thing a jolly caper. "Yes, well the men deserve a little fun."

The two boxers exchanged another flurry of punches, then stood off again. Private Noakes bided his time and waited until he saw an opening, then thrust hard with a left jab, following through with a swinging punch with his right, then a left uppercut. To his surprise he saw Owen Brookes rock back on his heels, momentarily stunned, and so Noakes pummelled him quickly with blow after blow.

The men of H-Company cheered him on, led by Colour-Sergeant Wolfe, a big-boned and gruff man with a dark, drooping moustache. Cupping his hands around his mouth he leaned forward and shouted encouragement above the din, for, unknown to the boys, he too had surreptitiously had a gamble on the outcome. "Hit the blighter!" he called, "lay into him, boy, don't let up!" He suddenly noticed Captain Wardell eyeing him in a surprised manner, taken aback -in an amused way- by his conduct. Ever the proffessional once again, Wolfe straightened himself and set his expression in granite.

Owen Brookes, despite his stature and experience, was starting to waver under the repeated blows he was coming under. His surprise at being outboxed was starting to be shared by his pals in E-Company, much to their nettle. Their shouts of encouragement were now turning to calls of derision as they vented their spleen at him. Bloodied and bowed and humiliated he felt his legs begin to go and there was nothing he could do to prevent the inevitable.

Sensing the moment, Private Charlie Noakes hit him hard in the kidneys. His opponent grunted loudly and then crumpled to the ground, all fight in him spent.

A roar went up from the crowd and he was suddenly swamped by people keen to congratulate him. Hands slapped him on the back amidst shouts of "Bravo! Bravo!" and all around helmets were waved aloft as they celebrated his marvelous victory.

Someone came up to him. "Wonderful fight boy! You did the company proud! Here, take this, you deserve it." With that he shoved a bottle of 'squareface', their nickname for gin, into his hand, then eagerly shook his other palm.

Private Charlie Noakes basked in the glory of the moment. He was, for the time being, the toast of the battalion. Right then, life seemed wonderful to him.

Flushed with victory he came barging through the doors so triumphantly that he caused his friend, Private Metcalfe, to sit bolt upright from where he'd been laying on the bed. Behind him came his many supporters, still cheering him or talking excitedly amoungst themselves about their good fortune and the money they had won. Dashing forward, Charlie Noakes came down the room towards where his friend was sitting with a look of astonishment on his face.

"I did it Bob!" he called like a giddy child, "I only beat Owen Brookes! You should have been there."

Robert Metcalfe came to his feet, a great beam on his lips. "Really? You're not kidding me, you scoundrel?"

Shaking his head, Charlie could hardly speak. He just laughed with joy and soon his friend was laughing along with him too. After a moment Charlie managed to say, with difficulty,"And look what I won!" He held the bottle of gin up for the other to see.

Robert snatched the bottle from his grasp and held it up to his eyes, shaking his head in disbelief. "You lucky... This calls for a celebration I think."

He hobbled over to the table and quickly found a knife to dig out the cork from the neck of the bottle. While he filled two cups, Charlie splashed his face with some water from the bowl they kept on the windowsill, washing the blood from the numerous tiny cuts around his chin and nose. A few of the others joined them and eagerly held out their cups which Robert dutifully filled. Then, all together they drank a toast, and Charlie - almost bursting with joy - told his friend all about the fight, blow by blow, in typical bombastic detail.

When he was done Robert broke away for a moment. Going across to his bed he rummaged around beneath the corner of his mattress and brought out a thin silver box. He came back over and flipped it open, revealing the contents to Charlie.

"Where did you get those from?" he asked in amazement as he looked at the cigars inside.

"I'd rather not say," Robert responded, and gave him a knowing wink. He held the box out. "Go on, you deserve one."

"But I've never smoked before."

"Well it's about time you learnt sonny!" someone called, and everyone laughed.

Grinning broadly the young soldier took one and shoved it into his mouth and someone produced a match. He inhaled deeply, too deeply, and choked and spluttered on the smoke until tears came to his eyes. When he had recovered sufficiently Robert told him to try again, taking it easy this time. He did so. And this time he savoured the experience.

"It's good, yes?"

"Glorious," he answered, feeling every inch the man he was. "Bloody glorious!"

CHAPTER 6

ZULULAND.

THE ONDINI *IKHANDA,* KING CETSHWAYO'S ROYAL RESIDENCE.
MAHLABATHINI PLAIN.

SEPTEMBER 1878

Situated north of the White Mfolozi was the heart of the Zulu Kingdom. Here stretched the Mahlabathini Plain, a broad expanse of undulating grassland crossed with occassional small streams or dongas and surrounded by a rim of hills and mountains. The plain was dotted with up to thirteen *amakhanda,* the military barracks for the Zulu regiments, the *amabutho,* which formed the main Zulu army. Only during a general muster of the King's warriors or during the annual *umkhosi* harvest festival would these mighty kraals be full, or when a review of the royal herds took place; at other times single regiments would be summoned by him to perform specific duties and they would spend their time away from home housed in specified *ikhanda.*

Each Zulu King would have a favourite *ikhanda.* These were known as the *komkhulu,* the 'great place', where he would spend most of his time and they would thus take on the role of the royal residence. King Shaka's was kwaBulawayo 'Take Out The Old Man', once situated further to the south but moved onto the plain following

48

his death. For Dingane it was eMgungundlovu in the Mkhumbane valley. He was eventually ousted by his brother Prince Mpande, who set up a royal residence by the name of kwaNodwengu 'The Place of the kresistable One' which was amongst those on Mahlabthini Plain. Finally, following his coronation in 1873, the present King, Cetshwayo kaMpande, had a new homestead built close to his father's. He named it oNdini-or at times it was referred to as Ulundi- from the common root *uNdi,* meaning 'the heights'.

Mahlabathini was as spectacularly beautiful as the rest of the kingdom. Anybody with cause to travel across its broad expanse would have to walk with care for the ground was littered with stones and thorn bush, mimosa trees or the bizarre euphorbia trees. Numerous streams such as the Mbilane would need to be negotiated, and a variety of game still prowled the countryside despite the periodical great hunts ordered by the King or the parties of white hunters that by the 1860's had vastly reduced the more profitable elephant or buffalo herds. On the hills surrounding this great natural ampitheatre were the remnants of ancient forests, the crests of ridges and bluffs crowded with stinkwood and milkwood trees, sneezewood and ironweed.

Cresting a low rise somewhere towards the centre of the plain one would get their first view of Ondini, and an awe-inspiring sight it would be.

Like the ordinary clan *umuzi* the 'great place' consisted of a circle of huts built within a surrounding palisade of tree branches and thorn, but on a grand scale. Whereas a family homestead might consist of half a dozen huts, Ondini held as many as 1500 and covered perhaps ninety acres of land. Arranged in rows four deep these beehive shaped dwellings encircled a large open area that would serve as cattle pen to the King's herd or a place of assembly where his regiments might gather to recieve their orders in times of war. Approaching the *ikhanda* one would be struck by its sheer scale. After two hours of hard walking across the plain one would feel as though they were still no closer than when they had first cast their amazed gaze upon it from atop the rise. Eventually more details would be revealed: the gateway on its lower edge; individual figures walking amidst the huts: smoke rising from uncountable potsherds where meals were being prepared for the thousands who lived here, four, five, six or more to a hut.

Towards the top of the homestead was a seperate fenced-off area, the King's private quarters that were referred to as the *isigodlo.* Access to this part of the homestead was strictly controlled and only his chief councillors or favoured individuals were allowed here, and only at the King's say so. For it was here that the King resided with the *isigodlo* girls, given to him as gifts

from the many chieftains and men of great rank that were spread throughout the kingdom, a honour that was thought of as a great priviledge to those fortunate enough to be chosen to live with their King. In the welter of fenced passageways that made up the *isigodlo* these girls performed the everyday duties of life in the King's court, the many chores that he and his family demanded. However, a select few would reside within an even more secretive area, the 'black *isigodlo,'* a portion of his private quarters where no man but the king himself was allowed and where instant death was brought upon anyone who transgressed this rule. Here the king would indulge himself in the pleasures of *ukusoma* with the chosen girls, a form of external sexual intercourse that was permitted before marriage. Guards placed outside would ensure the king was never disturbed whilst thus occupied.

Whenever the King wished to observe the comings and goings of people in his royal *ikhanda,* his 'great place', when he chose to watch the daily life of his many subjects who shared his residence with him, he would stand atop a small mound and peer over the fence of the *isigodlo.* From here he would look out upon them. And if he was seen so doing, then it would cause individuals to drop prostrate before their King, and cry the royal salute, *"Bayede!"*

A salute for King Cetshwayo KaMpande.

'The Slandered One'- Cetshwayo KaMpande, was born in 1832 at one of his father's many *amakhanda.* emLambongwenya, near to the primoral Dlinza forest in southern Zululand. His accession to the throne had been, like all aspects of Zulu royal life, complicated. As a young boy, Cetshwayo had grown confident that it would be his right to suceed his father, being as he was the eldest son of Mpande's 'great wife'. However, Mpande had 29 sons in total, all of whom made strong claims to be regarded as heir to the throne.

Cetshwayo was the most popular of them. Enrolled into the uThulwana regiment as a cadet his reputation as a warrior had soon grown, and when military success followed in one of his father's military campaigns his prestige and dynamic nature soon made him the obvious choice to follow in Mpande's footsteps. But Cetshwayo's popularity concerned the then Zulu King, who was acutely aware of the bloody history of Zulu royal succession. He himself had lent a violent hand in the overthrow of his own brother, and before that King Shaka had been murdered by none other than that said brother, Dingane. Alarmed at the possibility of a similar fate for himself Mpande had his son sent over towards the coast, where he hoped distance would keep Cetshwayo's ambitions in check. He also made it clear that he had not ruled out the possibility of making another of his sons, Prince Mbuyazi, heir apparant. Mpande is said to have commented, "two bulls cannot live in the same cattle kraal".

Cetshwayo's fury at his fathers snub was so great that it became increasingly obvious that some form of bloody clash between the two rival brothers was imminent. Despite his father's attempts to snuff out any support for Cetshwayo, the young prince still maintained a massive following within the Zulu army. He was a sympathetic person who, inspite of his royal status, showed great concern for the welfare of the ordinary Zulu man, woman and child. He also expressed a desire to try to reclaim pride in the nations past glories and to restore the power and prestige of the old order, so weakened by both Dingane and Mpande. His ideas grew in popularity. Soon, he could call on the support of as many as 15,000-20,000 warriors, a formidable force when compared to Mbuyazi's paltry 7,000 fighting men and 13,000 women and children who would only be a hindrance in any battle.

The clash came in early December 1856 on the northern banks of the Thukela River. It was as one sided as predicted. Mbuyazi and his followers were utterly routed, trapped against the fast flowing waters at their backs. As Cetshwayo's warriors thundered into them the killing became indiscriminate with the men mixed in with the women and children and cattle, a nightmare that they had no possibility of escaping from. It became the costliest single battle in Zulu history leaving 12,000 dead littering the sandbanks or washed out to sea. One small tributary stream was so clogged with bodies that from that day foreward it would be called by the name Thambo - or simply 'bones'.

Despite the terrible cost in lives the battle secured Cetshwayo as heir to his father's throne.

No one dared oppose him now. Even Mpande had no choice but to accept the outcome and acknowledge that Cetshwayo would indeed be the next King of the Zulus.

Mpande need not have feared his eldest son's birthright and the manner of his own death. He died peacefully as an old man after thirty years of rule. For several months his body was kept in his hut and allowed to dry out, and when the empty husk was finally buried in his principal homestead, kwaNodwengu, at least one of his loyal retainers was buried along with him. In the following year, 1873, Cetshwayo was crowned King in a grand ceremony witnessed by a party of white representatives from the British administration from over the Thukela.

To mark the occassion they presented Cetshwayo with a cheap crown and photographed the coronation for posperity. The crown lay at this moment under a pile of rubbish inside the King's hut while the photograph hung on the wall, alien objects, amusing curios.

Cetshwayo was a large man in both appearance and bearing, traits that gave him an air of regal authority. His broad chest and thick arms, large midriff and powerful thighs were testimont to his legendary appetite but in contrast to this fearsome appearance he had a pleasant and open face with tiny but intelligent eyes.

From his private residence in the *isigodlo,* served by his retainers and *umdlunkulu* girls and surrounded by the thousands who shared with him the 'great place' at Ondini, set in the magnificence of the Mahlabathini Plain between the Black and White Mfolozi rivers, Cetshwayo KaMpande, King of the Zulu, ruled his mighty kingdom.

The iNgobamakhosi regiment was a young *ibutho,* made up as it was of men mostly in their mid-twenties and therefore in their prime. Being the first regiment set up by the King not long after his coronation, they were a proud and eager body of warriors whom had great favour bestowed upon them by Cetshwayo. Their name meant 'The humblers of kings', and a more apt name there was not.

One of their number was Mehlokazulu KaSihayo. A junior Induna of the iNgobamakhosi, he had recently being summoned to Ondini with his *ibutho* for their king had called upon their services. Living five or six to a but Mehlokazulu and his friends had been spending the time cultivating the fields, planting and reaping and sowing, or sometimes they had been sent out to collect thorn bush to carry out repairs to the King's 'great place' or some of the other military *amakhanda* scattered across the plain. It was mundane work but none of them resented these labours for it filled the young men with a hearty sense of well-being to know that their work was much appreciated by their King, who showed them such kindness for their efforts. After all, he owned their lives, just as he owned the lives of all his subjects, and it was his will to call upon them to do these necessary tasks.

Mehlokazulu had another reason for been here. He was one of the few chosen to serve in the *zembekwela,* a select few of the King's favourites who were his personal attendants and who were sometimes, but only with the King's permission, allowed into the *isigodlo.* It was a position of great importance and some of his friends were a little jealous of the duties his role demanded. Some of the older *izikhulu,* that is the great men of the nation, the hereditary chiefs, were downright disgusted of the priveledges he enjoyed and tensions sometimes ran high. What rankled them even more was that despite his young age, they-although much older and more powerful-had to show him, a mere youth, their utmost respect. Mehlokazulu felt great honour, and amusement, at this.

Before travelling to Ondini, Mehlokazulu had needed to undergo the necessary cleansing ceromonies after the killing of his father's 'great wife'. In their culture it was thought that when a person killed another person they were tainted with evil spirits, a contamination that made them *izinxweleha;* they were unable to rejoin normal society until this pollution inside them was expelled, and if they went into the King's presence thus stained then they would bring evil influence on him.

Anybody needing to go through the cleansing rituals would be seperated off from any others for several days. It was a procedure that was revolting but essential and Mehlokazulu remembered it well. Each day he had been required to go down to a nearby stream holding aloft the still bloodstained and gore splattered knobkerry that he had used to administer the fatal blow.

After stripping naked and bathing in the water, Mehlokazulu had carried out a procedure called *ncinda'*, the sucking of medicine from the fingertips. The medicine in question was revolting, consisting as it did the excrement and stomach contents of some small animal and boiled in a potsherd. When ready he had placed his fingers into the substance and sucked at them, the abominable compound making him nauseous and faint. Then, while chanting the words "Come out, evil spirits; come out, mtakati; fall, mtakati," he had squirted the mixture out through his mouth while jumping over the sherd this way and that, spitting all about. For several days this had gone on until any remnant of contamination was gone. Only then could he rejoin his comrades and travel overland to serve his King.

One final procedure had needed to be performed before he'd been able to enter the 'great place' of his King. One of the senior *inyanga*, a herbalist sometimes appointed to carry out such cleansing rituals, had sprinkled him with further protective medicines. The doctoring now complete, Mehlokazulu had been handed a sprig of wild asparagus which he was to wear in his hair as a symbol of his status as a hero-iqa we-someone who had killed an enemy of the King.

For the iNgobamakhosi regiment to be temporarily housed at Ondini was a great honour for Mehlokazulu and his companions. It was, however, a situation not without its problems. One of the other regiments present, indeed they were here on a permanent basis and were therefore referred to as a 'white assembly', was the uThulwana. The men in its ranks were older than their opposite numbers and often in the past they had complained bitterly that the young 'boys' of the iNgobamakhosi paid them little respect, often taunting them that they were unable to keep their much younger wives happy. The fact that many of these girls had once been promised to the warriors of the iNgobamakhosi but had been taken as wives by the older men caused a great deal of hatred amoungst Mehlokazulu and his companions. Last year things had come to a head, in the form of a bloody clash between the two regiments right here at Ondini and in the kings presense. Cetshwayo's senior councillors had insisted that the young iNgobamakhosi be barracked elsewhere after the incident and inspite of the *ibutho's* commander, Sigcwelecwele KaMhlehleke, bitterly complaining, the king had really been left with no option if further violence was to be avoided.

Now that the iNgobamakhosi were back, even only temporarily and at the King's request, tensions were high.

Mehlokazulu and his friends were at that moment in the hut they shared together. Sometimes a young *udibi* boy, a cadet who helped them with their everyday chores, would sleep with them but only if there was room, and Mehlokazulu preferred just himself and his companions. Sitting on his sleeping mat up against the side of the hut he was making a plume out of long, black sakabuli feathers which when done he would insert into one of his leopard skin headbands to be worn on some future ceromonial occassion. Some warriors liked to cover themselves with fancy costumes at all times, but Mehlokazulu preferred to wear the minimum of costumes for it allowed more freedom. A simple loin-covering, an animal headband with flaps over the ears and thin strips of fur around the wrists was usually all he wore. Today he also had a snuff spoon pierced through the earlobe and the bone snuff container was hung around the neck.

Their work for the King was done and so Mehlokazulu found the time to add the finishing touches to his regalia. His friends were performing similar tasks, talking quietly amoungst themselves. Ndlela KaSashangane was adding more cow tails to the necklace he often wore, brushing them out straight so they covered his chest, while Ndlela's close friend Mnyamana KaMakhoba was splitting the ends of several ostrich feathers to later be fastened into his hair which was built up in a popular three-horned, stubby fashion. The remainder were likewise occupied, each working diligently.

This was how life was spent by Cetshwayo's warriors. For them, their time at Ondini was pleasing, their work rewarding.

"Let the men of the regiment muster! Is the order heard?"

"It is heard!"

They came pouring out of their huts at Sigcwelecwele's command, hurrying into the large central enclosure. A few who lagged behind were thrashed by their pot-bellied commander, hit around the shoulders with his knobkerry, not hard enough to cause serious harm but sufficient to make them move that bit faster.

Mehlokazulu likewise hurried his section along, haranging them for not being the first to answer the call. He pushed his way to the front, curious to know what the summons was about. When he saw the pile of freshly butchered meat lying in the dust close to the kings fence a ripple of excitement passed through him, a feeling shared by the hundreds of men around him. A wave of chatter passed through the ranks. This could mean only one thing. The King, evidently pleased at their work, was to reward them by providing food for them from his own herd.

Mehlokazulu felt humbled at his king's genorosity.

Usually it was left for them to find provisions for themselves, not allways easy when the crop yield was low at the time of drought that currently plagued the land. This night, however, they would eat well.

A hush descended when the King appeared, crouching low to pass beneath the arched gateway that led to his *isigodlo* then rising to his full height again and moving forward towards the gathered crowd. As if on a hidden command the whole mass of warriors dropped to a squatting position. Their eyes remained fixed on their King.

Slowly he walked over to the mound of glistening meat, a broad beam on his face.

Immediately about a dozen senior men from the regiment dashed foward, Mehlokazulu and Sigcwelecwele amoungst them, and flung themselves on the ground before him. They awaited his command. It came in the form of a single word. Remaining crouched low each man reached out and grabbed a large slice of the proffered food and then retreated, holding their prize aloft and singing the King's praises.

Rejoining his section, of which he was the commander, Mehlokazulu watched with the others as the King returned to his private quarters, the little ceremony at an end.

Their repast could now begin.

*   *   *

The food was not ready until late into the night. Since sunset the meat had been stewing in a large, earthen pot, the top of which was sealed with cement. This was partly to enhance the flavour by not allowing the steam to escape but also to prevent any discreet sampling of the feast from taking place when knowbody was looking. The aroma from the dozens of other cooking pots bubbling away in their quarter of the kraal sent a mouth-watering aroma wafting along on the nighttime breeze as the succulent juices in the meat hissed and popped.

When theirs was finally ready Mehlokazulu emptied the contents of the pot onto a square mat and brought the meat over. A circle of eager faces were soon crouched around him as he placed it on the ground.

Carving off one piece at a time he handed them out to every third man, who in turn split it into three portions with his teeth and handed a third to each man to his left and right. Soon the sound of chewing and gulping filled the air, and Mehlokazulu started on his own piece, which naturally was bigger than those he had handed out.

The men were hungry and the food was quickly devoured, not a slither of meat being left in their teeth or a droplet of juice on their fingers. When they were done they sat and chatted, some drinking beer, a feeling of contentment in their now full stomachs.

Mehlokazulu noticed the figure coming towards him from out of the shadows. He saw it was Sigcwelecwele. The *ibutho* commander squatted down beside him and looked closely at him. Mehlokazulu felt uncomfortable under the older mans scrutiny, and glanced out of the corner of his eye at the bearded face.

After a few more moments Sigcwelecwele spoke, his tone hushed and confidential.

"The King is pleased with our work. He shows great genorosity in providing food for us, even when he is heavy with troubling problems."

"It pleases me that he is satisfied," responded Mehlokazulu. A worried frown crossed his features. "May I ask what worries him so?"

"He fears the white men are soon going to take his kingdom from him. He talks of war, and how the whites will try and take our crops and our homes. It is troubling him greatly."

"The King need not be frightened. They are not as strong as they think. If the whites do start a fire then they will perish like so many ants. We will go and stab them if the King demands it!"

"Ah! be quiet Mehlokazulu, or you will start a war all by yourself." Sigcwelecwele poked at the ground with his knobkerry. "The King, he ponders your fighting spirit and is worried about your fiery nature. He knows about the fight that you had in the white mens land."

"Is he angered?" Mehlokazulu asked in alarm.

"No. He understands your reasons for killing Sihayo's 'great wife'. Do not forget, the King was once young and rash too. But he is alarmed that the white indunas may be angered. Things do not look like they will be as forgiving."

Mehlokazulu thought about this for several moments. He hoped he had not created a disaster for his King. When he glanced back up at his commander he was surprised to see the faintest trace of a smile on the older mans face.

"You are fortunate that the King is so fond of you Mehlokazulu, or things would be bad for you." He slowly pushed himself to his tired legs, leaning on his stick for support. "Soon, the regiment is to depart, the boys are to return to their homes now our work is done. But you, he wishes for you to stay. You are to remain here and work in the 'black' *isigodlo.*"

Mehlokazulu felt himself glow with pride upon hearing this, tempered though it was with the worrying news his commander had just shared with him. The prospect of war did not scare him; he was a Zulu warrior and was confident that no foe, whatever the colour of his skin and no matter what evil magic his weapons may contain, would be any match for them. He had killed once, to protect his family name and also to rid his King of an enemy, and if he was ordered to do the same again then he would do so without question.

He would, if called on, enter the heat of battle unflinchingly.

CHAPTER 7

DURBAN.

MID-DAY / 23rd SEPTEMBER, 1878

S ir Bartle Frere looked across towards Thesiger and asked him, "so tell me Frederic, how go your plans?"

The High Commissioner, Lieutenant-General Thesiger, and Lieutenant-Colonel Crealock, were seated at a large dining table set out beneath a white canvas awning erected on the lawn infront of the main barracks building at the Durban Redoubt. They were currently in-between courses of a splendid lunch that Thesiger had organized for Frere who had just arrived that morning in Durban. Up to this point their conversation had avoided all talk of the upcoming military operations, instead conducting idle chit-chat as they enjoyed the pleasant winter sunshine. Now the pleasantries were over and it was down to business.

Thesiger gave a perceptible sigh before answering. "They are progressing adequately. Our transport needs are the main concern. For an endeavour this large the sheer number of oxen wagons is staggering. Everything that our battalions need, our ammunition, tentage, food supplies, even fodder for our horses, will need to be taken forward as the columns advance, and each battalion alone would need a minimum of seventeen wagons. Then you have the

Royal Artillery, the Engineers, the local volunteers, all of whom need their own transport. What makes matters even worse is that our own wagons are totally inadequate for the conditions and I've found it necessary to either hire or purchase local ox-drawn wagons from civilian contractors that have a wider wheel base."

"Some of them have been charging exorbetent prices," Crealock added. "Our young officers are somewhat naive when it comes to financial matters and these civilians - some of whom are Boer farmers I might add - have tried to make the most of our problem."

"Crealock is correct. The problems are not insurmountable, but they do worry me."

"Do you not think that your plan of five columns is maybe a little ambitious in that case," Frere asked mildly.

Thesiger thought about the question briefly. Then he gave his rather diplomatic answer. "Our plans have always been open to a certain amount of flexibility. Depending on the conditions and circumstances.

"Of course," Frere said, aware that he had ruffled the General's feathers a little. "I do not presume to tell you how to carry out this invasion. My time in India taught me that the best approach to achieve a given aim is to give free reign to the individual tasked to the job. That person should carry on as he see's fit with as little interference from me as possible. I still stand by that rule. It has never failed me in the past. The man on the spot does have the best judgement of the situation after all." He smiled warmly across the table at his companions.

Thesiger accepted the apology graciously. Then he moved on. "I was wondering, Sir Henry, about our conversation about requesting further reinforcements? Have you had any response from the Home Government?"

"Well, as I implied at the time, London seems preoccupied with other matters. Yes, I did put in a request for more troops but I think it highly unlikely that they will be able to spare us the numbers you asked for. Hicks Beach seems to prefer a peaceful resolution to this crisis, and that we should re-double our efforts to avoid an armed clash if at all possible."

Thesiger exchanged a brief glance with his military secretary, who for once seem unable to offer him succour. Pursing his lips, he tried to point out the impractibility of such an approach. "We are dealing with a murderous despot who commands a vast army just over the river from

Natal. The recent border incident has shown vividly just what his people are like. Do the Home Government not see what a precarious situation we find ourselves in? It is my firm belief that our present state of peace - if it can be called such - depends on the sufference of the Zulu King, a peace that if he feels so inclined he could shatter with no provocation whatsoever. The current state of affairs, where our people live in daily fear of his vast army falling on them whilst they sleep in their beds, cannot be allowed to continue."

"Yes, it is intolerable. Natal's citizens have an inherent right to expect protection from their aggressive neighbours." Frere glanced away and looked up at the union flag that fluttered in the breeze above the outpost. "What's more, we are talking about a murder here. No one, British citizen or otherwise, should be permitted to invade territory belonging to the Queen to plunder or perpetuate acts of violence against someone seeking sanctuary under our protection. If we were to stand back and do nothing that would be an outrage almost as unforgivable as the actual slaying itself."

"So our plans go ahead, with or without approval?" Thesiger queried.

"Yes."

"Of course, with one quick and decisive victory to show for our independent actions, there will be all-round support from London. That is why a short campaign is called for. And that can only be achieved with more military assets."

"Your point is made Frederic," Frere assured him with a warm smile.

Thesiger gave a polite nod.

"I will put in a further request for more men to be shipped out with all haste."

Frere reached out for his wine glass and took a sip. Returning it to the pristine tablecloth he clasped his hands together and leaned forward over the table. "Five columns then. Do tell me more.

"Of course." Thesiger took a moment to gather his thoughts, then proceeded to explain his plans, giving a condensed version of how the campaign would proceed. "The first column, the Right Flank, will be commanded by Colonel Pearson of the Buffs. They will be based at the Lower Drift near the mouth of the Thukela where the engineers are currently looking into the feasibility of building a substantial earthwork fort on the Natal bank. From here they will advance to the abandoned mission station at Eshowe where they will pause and gather their supplies before resuming their advance on Ulundi, but this second movement will depend on the progress of the other columns. No 3, that is the Centre, column will be under Colonel Glyn, and will cross at Rorke's Drift. The track there is one of the oldest routes into Zululand and leads more or less all the way to the Zulu capital. They wll be the strongest of our columns as I expect that route - the most direct into the heart of the country - to be the most contested. Up-country will be No 4 column, Left Flank, led by Colonel Wood and based at Utrecht. From here they will move forward to Bemba's Kop on the Ncome River and thense on with the proviso of supporting Glyn and co-ordinating his movements with his advance. No 2 column, commanded by Colonel Durnford and made up largely of his native levies, will move forward from the Kranskop escarpement on the middle drift, another major entry point into Zululand, in support of either Pearson or Glyn and depending on the circumstances. Our final column, No 5, is to be based up in the Transvaal and will be under the command of the good Colonel Rowlands. Their main role will be to act as a defensive force to discourage any Zulu raids into the Transvaal as well as to keep a wary eye on the troublesome Boers.

This, as you can tell, is a massive venture that we are undertaking. We always knew that eventually, despite the politicians attempts to find a diplomatic solution, we would have to deal with the Zulus with force. That is why our invasion must be on a scale that the Zulu King will find impossible to confront. We must overwhelm him and his people from the very moment our forces cross over into his kingdom."

Crealock, who had been sitting quietly, his eyes flicking from face to face, decided to add his own opinion to add weight to his commander's outline. "The General is of the opinion that if we can break the back of the Zulu army at the earliest opportunity, in a set-piece engagement, then all resistance thereafter will crumble. Apart from a few mopping up operations the bulk of the fighting will be over within a matter of weeks."

"If fortune follows the brave," Thesiger said as he toyed with his napkin, "then the whole bloody business should be finished before the Colonial Office is even aware that the invasion has begun."

"Yes, that is our dilemma," observed the High Commissioner. He stroked his small, white moustache, his mind turning the various problems over. "The Colonial Office have granted me a degree of automony in regards to Confederation, a position that I interpret as having a free hand. Even so they continue to urge caution. If I keep in putting in requests for more reinforcements they are obviously going to question their role. And the less forewarning they have of imminent military operations the better. Timing is everything."

"It's a tricky business we find ourselves in," agreed Thesiger.

"And of course we still face problems here. We must try to massage public opinion and make them see that removing the Zulu threat will have benefits for all. The Boers for one thing will be glad to see the back of Cetshwayo. But others, I'm sorry to say, are proving harder to convince."

"You refer to Sir Bulwer I presume?" Thesiger asked. Beside him he felt Crealock bristle at the mention of the Governor of Natal's name.

"Yes."

"He still objects to the raising of native levies?"

"He objects to the whole idea of having a war Frederic. His mind-set is on the far distant future rather than the present and holds the view that a conflict now will sour the race-relations in this country for years to come. Not just of white against black but if we do pitch Natal's native population against the Zulus then also black against black. He feels that a general insurrection could then spread throughout the whole region with all the speed of a bushfire."

"Does he not see how putting down the Zulus will discourage such a possibility? Is he really that narrow-minded?" Thesiger asked bitterly.

Frere spread his palms and then brought them back together. Gripping them he gently shook his hands to emphasise his words. "I'm sure that with the right sort of approach his views can be changed. These things call for delicate diplomacy. Of course, in the meantime Colonel Durnford must continue with his efforts to organise his native troops with all haste. I feel the tempo of events is starting to quicken, and it may not be long before they are needed."

"Well, all the indications I am recieving suggest that he is making excellent progress. His knowledge of the various tribes and their cultures is making the Colonel a godsend for us. Admittedly, Colonial society still shuns him after the misfortune at Bushman's Pass, but he is nonetheless an excellent officer of Engineers, and seems to be coming into his own. He has quite thrown himself into the tasks I have set him."

"Good...good..." the High Commissioner mused. "It seems your recommendation for him is proving spot on."

"Of course, I feel we should hold back on our final judgement until we have seen how they perform under battle conditions," Colonel Crealock offered, a little too quickly. His comment-or rather the hidden insinuation within the words-did not go unnoticed by the other two gentlemen seated at the table. However, neither of them felt the need to reprimand him. The acrimonious nature of the two Colonels' relationship was well known, and, if the truth be said, starting to become rather tiresome for the High Commissioner and the Lieutenant-General. Their silence was enough to stay any further biting remarks from Crealock and his features took on a distinctly sullen look.

Instead, Frere said, "I intend to move up to Pietermaritzburg within the next few days where I hope to catch up with Durnford. I would like the two of you to accompany me."

It was a polite request but said in a way that to decline was most definately not an option. Both Thesiger and his military secretary inclined their heads.

The three men's attention was then diverted by the arrival of the second course: Roast Terrine of lamb with mint sauce and seasonal vegetables, and a glass each of Sauvignon. It was served by a Punjabi waiter splendidly dressed in white.

"Oh, how wonderful!" Frere exclaimed in delight, all worries and concerns over the momentus events that loomed on the horizon temporarily pushed to the back of his mind. This glorious meal being set before them captured their full attention. Other matters could come later.

Above them, the Union Flag fluttered in the breeze. In this tiny corner of Empire.

PIETERMARITZBURG.

FORT NAPIER.

MID-AFTERNOON / 23rd SEPTEMBER, 1878.

The lone figure riding along the main dirt road out of Pietermaritzburg was easily recognizable to the four sentries guarding the main entrance to the fort, that sat perched atop a low hill just outside of town. The colour of his horse, white with speckled grey markings, told them who it was approaching. They called out to their Captain, who was inside the small bell-tent just off the roadway, and when he joined his men the small group readied themselves to snap to attention when the new arrival came past.

But then the horseman stopped momentarily and turned his mount sideways, the rider glancing back the way he had come.

The men on sentry duty waited patiently.

Sitting astride Chieftain and holding the reins in one hand, Colonel Durnford looked out over Natal's provincial capital, Pietermaritzburg.

The busy streets, congested with a variety of mule and cattle drawn wagons ranging from small spider carts to larger ox driven transport creaking under the weight of goods, and pedestrians walking too and fro along the wooden walkways that lined the streets, a community going about its business, the white Colonial buildings such as Government House in its wooded grounds and the large Court Buildings at the end of Longmarket Street had gradually given away as he had rode through just a short while ago. On the outskirts of town were the thatched roofed mud huts of the native quarters, and beyond these the fields where black labourers worked the land. A circle of hills surrounded the town, a hazy purple in the afternoon sunshine, dotted with the occassional farm building.

This was Pietermaritzburg of 1878.

It was a pretty town with a charming Victorian quality to it but despite its picturesque buildings and pleasant setting nestled

65

amidst the hills, the aroma of mimosa trees which were coming into bloom mingling with the sweet scent of jessamines and gardenias and fuchsia trees covered with a profusion of orchids that hung down from the branches making the air seem like an English conservatory, Durnford always felt happier once he was leaving. Whenever he had cause to visit the town he could not fail to detect an air of hostility from the townsfolk. An enmity that was directed at himself. The legacy of Bushman's Pass, that was the reason. Even now, after five years, the good people of Natal still blamed him for the debacle that had cost them the lives of their sons and fathers, brothers or husbands. It was his foolhardy nature that had killed them, his hotheadedness, his rash and badly orchestrated scheme to launch the attack. His ambition that from the outset had been a blue-print for disaster. The accusations were as varied as they were ignorant, but they all came down to basically the same conclusion; that he was a liability when in command of men. These taunts and vehement comments - at times of such a blasphemous quality that they even made Durnford, a hardened and seasoned soldier, balk at their vulgarity - had eventually become too much. Now he spent as little time as possible in Pietermaritzburg and the other frontier towns. He preferred the familiarity of camp-life. As well as the distraction of soldiering.

Today was an exception. Seated on his mount atop the hill he looked down on the town, a sinking feeling tugging at his heart which had grown steadily worse as he had rode along the dirt road back to camp.

The reason for his dejection was simple. He had just spent the afternoon in the company of someone who meant a great deal to him, and who after only a half hour he was allready yearning to see again.

That person was Frances Colenso, daughter of Bishop Colenso, The Bishop of Natal. Durnford had known the Colenso's for a number of years. He had been drawn to the Bishop because of a genuine sympathy for the Bantu peoples and their plight in this fast changing land. Colenso's views, like Durnford's, were unfashionable amoungst the settler society and coupled with their very proper English social standards the family had soon come into conflict with the white populace. It was maybe this shared 'notoriety' that led to the close friendship the Bishop's family and

Colonel Durnford had for there was little denying how comfortable he felt when in their company. Whenever the opportunity allowed he found himself visiting their home in Bishopstowe, not for spiritual guidance but because he genuinly liked them. And over the course of these many visits he had found himself growing increasingly closer to one of the Bishop's daughters. Frances, or 'Fanny' as she preferred.

A weak and frail young thing who bore the marks of the consumption that plagued her, Durnford nevertheless was mesmerized by her beauty, and grew to care for her a great deal. He hadn't known it at the time but Frances also developed strong feelings for him from the outset, and soon they found themselves spending more and more time in each others company. It did not take long for opinionated gossip to begin. He, a married man with a wife back in England, and she, the daughter of such a public person as the Bishop of Natal, should have known better than to form a relationship of the sort they - narrow-minded and full of tittle-tattle - wrongly imagined.

The truth was that Durnford would never behave in any other way than the perfect gentleman. He was an officer of Her Majesties Army and therefore his manners were impecable. Her bearing was equally befitting her background, and fiercely protective of her fathers unorthodox sentiments, she would never behave in a way that would bring embarrassment to her family.

Yet despite this very correct air they adopted, scandal still followed them wherever they were seen together.

Today he had arranged to meet her during a brief break in his heavy workload. She had travelled the six miles to Pietermaritzburg, a sure sign that she shared his enthusiasm to be together. Maybe she was aware, like he himself was, that they would have precious few opportunities to spend time with each other over the coming weeks and months. Hense the exquisiteness of their time together and why Durnford, sitting astride Chieftain on top of that rise, cherished those few hours as he cast his mind back...

...He could hardly take his eyes off her as they strolled along the riverbank towards the bridge. She wore a cream coloured dress of finest linen with lace edgings and a wide-brimmed straw hat, tied around with a cream ribbon. Resting against her right shoulder and protecting her from the hot sun she held a fine lace parasol while on her hands were matching gloves. Her face, soft and pale, was framed by two loose strands of hair the colour of honey. Durnford longed to touch it, to feel its softness run through his fingers. He longed to hold her face in his palms and savour the silky skin.

Suddenly aware that she was watching him, he quickly cast his eyes away. Fanny smiled and moved closer. They were alone in this quiet part of town, where open parkland stretched all the way down to the waters edge, and she took advantage of the privacy by passing her hand through his arm and gently resting it on his sleeve. Looking down at her once more, Durnford smiled back. They walked on.

"I do so like this time of year," Fanny told him. "If you close your eyes you could almost imagine we were back in England. The aromas and birdsong, they remind me of home."

They strolled on a little further. Alongside them the stream, only a thin trickle now, gently wound its way passed.

"Do you miss home?" she suddenly asked him.

Durnford paused before answering. "I think about it quite often," he said," but I don't especially long to be there. The damp and coldness is not good for my arm. When I did return a few years ago all I could think about was the day I would come back here."

Fanny smiled up at him and rested her cheek against his arm.

"I feel more at home here. I was enchanted with the place the moment I first arrived. The country and its people are so glorious, especially the Bantu. They are fine men, very naked and all that sort of thing, but thoroughly good fellows."

"Yes."

Ahead of them a small mule cart with a single black rider passed over the bridge that spanned the stream. A few moments later they moved beneath the steel and brick structure, the shadows cool and alive with buzzing insects. They emerged again into the bright sunlight.

Fanny screwed up her face and made no attempt to hide the contempt in her voice when she said, "I just wish more people shared your view William, instead of their beligerent superiority over the coloureds. We could all live peacefully side by side if only they made more effort. I hate all this talk of war and conquest."

Colonel Durnford felt a little awkward at this. He was in a difficult position, caught as he was between a rock and a hard place; the rock being his belief that all peoples were equal whatever their race but the hard place being his patriotic and christian view that they, the British, were here not to violently subdue but to enlighten and civilise. The dilemma was that to achieve those aims a more robust form of persuasion than mere religious teachings and the spreading of the word of God was often needed. He admired Bishop Colenso immensely for his patience, but being a soldier for all these years had taught Durnford to look at both sides of the arguement; appeasement or direct military action with a definate and clarified objective? It was a conflict that had been taking place inside his conscience more and more over the weeks and was still unresolved.

"They are difficult times, that is true," he offered weakly and wondered how he could steer the conversation away from this topic.

Fanny must have sensed his predicament for she said hurriedly, "I'm sorry William, it is most unfair of me to talk of such things. I know you have your duty. It is that what worries me most and sometimes my concern manifests itself in a rather fervent manner."

"You do not need to apologize. You are correctly very passionate in your beliefs," Durnford responded. "But tell me, what worries you so?"

"You worry me, William," Fanny whispered and her cheeks became flushed.

A twinge of guilt crossed Durnford's face, for he felt bad at having caused her distress. He slowed his pace a little and asked, "Tell me why."

"Because if, as I fear, there is to be a war and you do your duty, then I cannot bare the thought that you might be harmed...or worse." A shiver seemed to pass through her at the mere mention of her fears. "It is something I dread everytime you go away."

Durnford saw as clear as day that these words came from her heart and it caused a small lump to form in his throat. He tried to think of something encouraging to say to allay her fears but could not. They walked on in silence for several moments following the path up the gentle slope away from the stream. Ahead of them Fanny's carriage waited, the driver dozing in his seat, while nearby Chieftain waited with his usual patience. They came to a halt, neither of them wanting to depart, but wishing they had more time together.

Durnford glanced across and saw that Fanny's eyes were downcast. She was normally so strong willed and often brazen in character. Her illness had implanted a degree of impatience in her as perhaps she was - and it pained him to consider the possibility - aware of the brevity of the time left to her. This day, she appeared so young and vulnerable, like a little girl.

"There is still a chance that a war can be averted," he whispered feebly, knowing his words would not fool her.

"Do you believe that?" Fanny asked, still unable to meet his gaze.

Durnford thought about lying to her, to give her a small hope that would sustain her through the difficult days ahead. It would be so easy to do that. So easy, but so wrong. And besides, Fanny wasn't as naive as all that.

"No. No, I don't," he finally admitted.

Fanny turned to face him, her features pinched with concern. Under the shade of the parasol her eyes darted to and fro as she looked his face over, his eyes, his whiskered jaw, his high forehead. She took in as much detail as possible lest she never be given the chance again. Then she reached into the cuff of her dress and withdrew something, passed it over.

It was a small piece of folded muslin. Dumford looked down into his palm where she had placed it.

"I want you to keep it, to remind you of me."

"I don't need anything to remember you by, dear Fanny. What is it?"

Fanny reached out and carefully unfolded the muslin for him. Inside was a lock of hair. Golden hair, belonging to her. Durnford stared down and found himself unable to speak for his mouth was suddenly too dry. Then she folded it once more and closed his fingers around it.

"Keep it in your pocket, close to your heart," she whispered. That way I will be with you allways wherever you go."

"Fanny...I..."

But she placed a finger upon his lips stilling any further words. The moment was exquisite for them both, a few seconds that stretched for infinity. A precious moment that would see them through the terrible trials that lay ahead...

...Colonel Durnford gently patted Chieftain's neck tenderly and then turned him and made for the entrance to Fort Napier. As he passed the men on guard duty he returned their crisp salutes and nodded at the Captain. He headed straight for the barracks.

CHAPTER 8

NATAL.

HELPMEKAAR, NEAR THE BORDER WITH ZULULAND. OLD TRADERS
TRACK.

EARLY OCTOBER, 1878.

Slumped forward in his saddle and with his eyelids heavy
with fatigue, James Brickhill followed the old traders track
as it wound its way through the broken countryside. He
had set out from home early that morning, leaving his brother
behind at the store they shared, taking the one horse and a single
mule packed with his few possessions. The day had grown hotter as
the sun had reached its midway point and soon the valley bottoms
through which he passed were dusty and stiffling, with little breeze
to bring any relief. He had soon found himself dozing. He was
content to allow his equally weary horse to find its own way for they
had been along this route many times before, and as he drifted in
and out of sleep the beast plodded steadily on.

Occasionally he would be jerked awake as the track crossed a
dried up river bed, or dongas as they were known, or when the
horse tried to navigate a particularly steep slope. Brickhill would
take the opportunity to glance around to gain his bearings, or to drink
some water from his canteen, or to remove his wire-framed
spectacles and wipe his face with a sweat stained rag.

As they journeyed he used these rare moments of wakefulness to think his situation through. It helped to pass on the dullness of the ride, for the countryside meant little to him after all these years of living here, even though the panoramas were dramatic and spectacular.

Two days ago he had decided to go and seek employment with the British. Hearing of the growing liklihood of war between them and the Zulus he had found the prospect of joining them too exciting to ignore. Work at Knox's store was dull in comparison, monotonous and tediously wearying for the soul-not to mention financially unrewarding. He found it neither fulfilling nor stimulating; nothing about it satisfied the adventurous streak inside him. However, the possibility of warfare and all the glory it offered... the idea inflamed his passion to such a degree that once the idea was planted in his head there had really been no changing his mind.

His older brother completely disagreed. When he had informed him of his plans to leave, strong words had been exchanged between them both as he had tried to persuade James not to go, using all kinds of arguments to keep him there, including emotional blackmail; he was, after all, his big brother, and it was therefore his job to keep him from coming to any harm. What would people think if he allowed him to ride off to war to get himself killed? They would never forgive him. He would never forgive himself!

It had made no difference. His mind was made up.

Besides, the fighting would not last long, if what the British said was true.

He would soon be back, with money in his pocket and a hundred tales to tell!

His brother, seeing there was no way he was going to be able to get him to change his decision, had reluctantly helped him to pack his things. He wasn't happy about the situation but what could he do? If James was determined to go and seek his glory on some bloody battlefield then the least he could do was to try and ensure he returned in one piece. First off, he insisted he take his horse for James' old nag would surely kill him even if the Zulu didn't. Also, he must allways carry a bible on his person, especially if he did find himself in the thick of any action. Lastly, he should use his instincts and not blindly follow the example set by others; if a situation looked bad then there was no disgrace in riding away - after all, he was a civilian and not a soldier tied to his regiment!

Listening to this brotherly advice, James Brickhill had been filled with a sense of destiny. This was a big step he was taking, a life-changing decision he was making. It was very possible that he would never see his brother again nor return to their home; even if no harm came to him, he knew that once he had tasted the excitement of military adventure he would find it very difficult to return to this humdrum existance. There would probably be no going back once he had embarked on this venture.

The night before leaving had been a long and sleepless one. He had lain awake listening to the rustling of insects in the thatched roof above his head. During those long, and strangely lonely, hours he had thought hard, asking himself if this was the right thing to be doing. Was he being too rash? Was he being disloyal by leaving his brother like this, just on a whim? He asked himself these, and other questions, over and over, his mind wracked with indecision.

By the time the sky was starting to lighten with the first streaks of dawn James Brickhill had come to a decision. He was going.

It had probably never really being in doubt. In truth, those hours of tossing and turning were nothing more than his guilty conscience pricking him. He didn't want to let his brother down by going off like that but was that a reason to stay? If he didn't go he was damn sure he would regret it, and he might never get as good an opportunity as this ever again and he certainly did not want to spend the rest of his life living this dreary life. So yes, he was going. He was certain.

Within fifteen minutes James Brickhill rode away from home, while his brother still slept.

It hadn't even been fully daylight. He had not looked back at the small ramshackle building as he had departed, and soon it would have been lost amidst the rolling countryside anyway even if he'd wanted to. He had rode resolutely on to wherever his destiny lay.

The best place to find employment would be in Pietermaritzburg but he had heard that there was a small military presence in the nearby settlement of Helpmekaar about a dozen miles away so he had decided to go there first and see what the situation was. From there, if necessary he could travel down the border road and calling off at Greytown pass on to 'maritzburg and even on to Durban if he could find nothing on the way.

Helpmekaar was set atop the Biggarsberg heights, a lofty plateau with panoramic views right out across the Mzinyathi valley all the way into Zululand beyond. When the Voortrekkers had pushed north into Natal to seek their 'promised land' they had come upon the high, table-topped ridge. Uniting together they had made a cutting through the hillside and then established a tiny settlement there which they had named Helpmekaar - "help one another" - to mark the occassion. It had been a tiny place then, and in the intervening years had hardly grown any bigger. All it consisted of was two wattle and daub buildings with a small chapel a couple of miles away, but it must have held some interest to the British. Why else would they be there, in such a godforsaken place? Maybe he would find out when he arrived.

Brickhill pushed on.

Soon he came upon a colossal outcropping of rock the size of a barn. By some freak of nature the stone monolith had been split in two right down the middle, the pair of halves leaning apart. Growing out from this fissure was a stunted tree.

Here, the old traders track he had been following likewise seperated. The way to the right led down towards the distant Mzinyathi River while the left hand trail branched up the side of a steep slope, the beginings of the Biggarsberg plateau. Brickhill urged his horse to the left. His mule, which was tethered to his saddle, dutifully followed on.

Within several minutes the track became very difficult to negotiate, due to the steepness of the slope and the large boulders and loose rock that impeded their way or made the ground hazardous. Brickhill had to dismount a number of times to lead his horse and mule by the reins, pushing his way through dense thorn trees and spikey aloe plants. One compensation for the arduous trek was a cool breeze that picked up the higher they went, an indication of the size of the plateau they were climbing.

At long last they reached the top.

Brickhill paused for a moment to regain his breath and to sip some water. Standing close to the edge of the escarpement he looked out towards the hazy peaks in the distance. There lay Zululand. A place that held excitement and danger, adventure and risk. He felt a flutter of giddyness go through him as he considered what possibilities lay in store for him out there.

After several minutes he turned and led his horse away from the edge, trundling through the waist high grass. He followed the trail for a short distance but it soon petered out as the plateau opened up and as he came around a small hillock the tiny hamlet of Helpmekaar came into view.

The two buildings were close to a dirt road, this being the way to Msinga and Greytown. But Brickhill's attention drifted away towards a group of men clustered together beside a small stream where they were watering their horses. He headed in their direction, drawn by their dark corduroy uniforms and white helmets. As he neared them he thought he recognized what unit they belonged to for they were a familiar sight around the farms and towns of the border region. These were men of the Natal Mounted Police, he saw, a mounted unit of semi-professional irregulars who were better trained and turned out than the average colonial unit. They were also well armed with Swinburne-Henry carbines which they carried with a special kind of swagger.

There were about twenty or so in the group. Some were standing around while others were clustered near a small fire where they were preparing a meal. The smell of fresh coffee drifted over and it drew Brickhill across.

On seeing him approach the men stopped what they were doing and those sitting came to their feet. One of them, a handsome looking sort with dark eyebrows and a heavy black moustache, folded his arms and sucked on a meerschaum as he studied this stranger who approached.

Brickhill stopped several paces away and raised his hat in friendly greeting. "Hello there." The man opposite nodded back.

"I was passing through so I thought I'd stop off," he continued. "I don't believe we've met?"

The tall man stepped forward, moving with ease for someone so big. When he spoke it was with a firm and authorititive voice. "I'm Inspector Mansel and these are my men. Who might you be sir?"

"Brickhill's the name. James Brickhill, of Knox's store."

Mansel shoved the pipe back into his mouth and reached out to shake his hand. "It's nice to make your aquaintance Mr Brickhill," he mumbled around the wooden stem as they shook, then he asked, "would you care for some coffee?"

Brickhill beamed happily. "I'd be delighted!"

"Then park yourself on a rock. It's a long climb coming the way you came and you must be tired. Trooper," he told one of the men, "fetch the man some coffee."

Brickhill moved into their midst, saying hello to them as he did. A few answered in a likewise fashion but most did not. He gratefully lowered himself onto a boulder, sighing with exaggerated relief. Around him a see of faces watched him curiously. After a few seconds they resumed their own seats.

A tin mug of coffee was handed to him and he sipped at the tasty beverage.

Inspector Mansel, one of his riding boots resting on a log that lay in the grass, started to talk quite casually, apparantly keen to chat away. He seemed a descent type, thought Brickhill. Immensly strong and powerful but friendly enough.

"So tell me Mr Brickhill, what brings you up here? By the look of your pack animal you must be journeying quite far."

"I'm on my way to Pietermaritzburg. To offer my services to the British for this war they're planning," he said proudly.

To his consternation this caused a few guffaws amoungst the others. All except Mansel, who just smoked his pipe quietly. Brickhill did not let their response put him off.

"I heard you were up here. I was curious to know why."

"Oh, we're out here to see if this place would make a good position to set up a supply depot. The British want to come through here if they do decide to move against the Zulus."

Brickhill listened with interest. "And will it?" he asked.

"It's a good location. Cool, and with plenty of water. And it has a splendid view over the surrounding countryside. I don't see why it shouldn't meet their requirements."

"So it's a big venture their planning then?"

"It would need to be. The Zulus will be no pushover."

Mansel looked steadily at him as though summing up his worth. The others, as surly a bunch as he had ever seen, scowled and glowered as they studied him in a more contemptful way. After a minute or so the Inspector continued to speak. "So. You wish to fight in this war do you?"

"Most definately," Brickhill replied enthusiastically.

Tapping the bowl of his pipe on the heel of his riding boot, Mansel slowly shook his head and grimaced.

"Is there a problem with that? I did hear they wanted as many volunteers as possible, especially those with local knowledge."

"You know the Zulu well do you?" Mansel asked and this brought more quiet laughter from his men.

"I've lived in these parts most of my life," he said, feeling a little piqued at the mens attitude. "And I speak the language fluently. I can ride, and I can shoot."

"Ah," Mansel's eyebrows lifted, "but have you ever fought in a campaign, Mr Brickhill? Have you ever killed a man?"

Brickhill looked down at his feet and sipped his coffee. When he raised his head again he told him that he hadn't done either.

"It's a messy business, taking another persons life, be he white or black. It's not easy to shoot a man at point blank range or to run him through with a sword. It stays with you for ever. Are you sure you are ready for that?"

"I'm ready. I've thought about this long and hard Inspector," he lied. "I'll do whatever is asked of me. It's not something I'm entering lightly."

They stared at one another long and hard and Brickhill held his ground with steely determination. Mansel must have seen the resoluteness in his eyes for eventually the faintest trace of a smile appeared on his lips. He said, in a simple way, "It's your decision," then he stood upright and stretched his back. Scratching at his chin he then asked Brickhill, "you speak Zulu you say? That might come in helpful. I hear they're looking for interpreters down in Pietermaritzburg."

Brickhills eyes lit up at hearing this.

"After we've finished up here we're heading down there ourselves. You're welcome to accompany us if you like, unless you prefer to travel alone."

"No, no. That would be much appreciated. How long will you be before you're done?"

Mansel glanced around at his men, who were lounging about. "That depends on how much I have to kick these malingerers into shape," he snarled, and the troopers got the message for they grudgingly came to their feet and brushed the dirt and grass from their uniforms. Turning back to Brickhill, who was trying to keep the grin from his face - and failing - he said, "about two or three hours should see it. There's not much more for us to do, it's only a rudimentary survey their asking for. That will give you time to rest yourself and feed your horses."

The men were starting to move away, kicking dirt onto the fire and collecting their odds and ends. One by one they saddled up. Mansel went with them. Once he was seated on his horse he told Brickhill that they would pick him up on the way once they had completed their tasks. Then he rode away.

Brickhill watched the little troop go.

Then he thought to himself, quite merrily, how well the first day of his new life had gone. He hoped this was the beginning of what would turn out to be a marvelous adventure.

CHAPTER 9

THE INDIAN OCEAN / OFF THE EAST COAST. ONBOARD ONE OF
THE TROOPSHIPS ENROUTE FROM EAST LONDON TO DURBAN.
17th NOVEMBER 1878.

Carrying the men of the 1st Battalion, 24th (2nd
Warwickshire) Regiment, the troopship cut through the
heavy swell and turbulent seas as she journeyed up the
east coast of Southern Africa. They followed the same route set by
Vasco de Gama, who on Christmas Day of 1497 had given Natal its
name. Whereas he had been pushing out the boundaries of
exploration and navigating in unknown waters by 1878 this was
now a tried and tested course. It was still potentially dangerous.
Many a good ship and her crew had met a tragic end on this stretch
of coast, smashed into the rocks or swamped by mountainous
waves, and countless wrecks lay submerged in their watery graves.

Relatively speaking, today was a calm day, although the men
gathered on the pitching and tilting deck would not describe it as
such. But then, they were unused to being at sea. They much
preferred to march the great distances across land, as they had
done in the recent war with the Xhosa's, rather than take to the sea.
This was an unwelcome hardship that they had to endure. It was
much quicker than travelling overland the several hundred miles
from Kingwilliamstown to Natal but despite this and if given the

choice the vast majority would have chosen to trust in their own two feet to get them to their final destination. But they were not the ones who made such decisions. They just obeyed their orders, like the highly disciplined soldiers that they were.

What made matters worse was the intolerably cramped conditions on board. Not only was there the companies of the 1/24th but also the other various attached units, together with their amunition supplies, their baggage, food and water for the voyage, the officers horses and various pets down below, medical equipment, the farriers equipment, the field bakery ovens and furnaces, tents for the headquarters staff, tents for the regular infantry, tents for the commissariat, stores of fodder, entrenching tools...the list was endless, and it all needed to be stored away someplace and tied down and protected from the elements. The ship was a noisy, sweaty, smelly, hell made worse by the constant motion as she drove forward through the waves, bucking this way and that, creaking and groaning.

The atmosphere below decks was stiffling in the mid-day heat and so most of the passengers preferred to be up top where they could at least gain some relief from the stiff seabreeze and fresher air. However, space here was at a premium, with several hundred bodies sprawled or standing in a crush. Tempers often flared and dustups were not uncommon. A few passed the time by playing cards, others tried to write letters, while a few sang songs to the accompaniment of the battalion band playing such tunes as *Nancy Lee* or *'I'm Leaving Thee in Sorrow, Annie'*. Many just sat around smoking their pipes and talking amoungst themselves, or took the opportunity to catnap before the real rigours of the upcoming campaign began in earnest. One or two, unable to cope with the constantly rolling ship, stood by the rail, their faces an unusual shade of green.

One of these was Lieutenant Melvill, looking nothing like his usual well presented self. Today his hair was awry and the top button of his tunic was undone and he had none of his customory bounce.

He hated these seajourneys. God how he wished it was over.

His stomach, cramped up and enduring more misery than it could cope with, cried out for them to make landfall.

Leaning out over the rail he stared down at the choppy waves sluicing along the side of the hull. This made him feel even queasier, and so he closed his eyes and tried to ignore the gurgling sounds emanating from his tortured insides. Therefore he did not notice the young man who came across the deck towards him, a spring in his step and a cheerful smile on his face. Walking briskly up to Melvill he slapped him merrily on the back.

"A wonderful voyage we're having old chum, don't you agree?" he asked loudly.

Lieutenant Melvill turned and stared balefully at him. He said nothing for the moment, just turned back and looked off towards the horizon.

Trying to keep a smile from appearing on his face the other officer continued, "I see you're enjoying the view. That's a good idea. Do you mind if I join you?"

At last, and with a weary sigh, Melvill managed to say, "why can't you just leave me alone?"

Pretending to be taken aback the young blonde haired man said, in an aghast tone, "well that's not a very friendly thing to say. Cheer up. We only have two more days to go until we arrive."

"Thankyou for reminding me, I'm forever gratefull." He turned once again to peer at his companion more closely and then slowly shook his head. "You know, that beard doesn't suit you at all, Coghill."

A hurtfull look came across Lieutenant Coghill's face and he stroked the newly grown beard that he sported with dented pride. A fellow officer of the 1/24th, Lieutenant Nevill Coghill had thought it made him look dashing, but after what his friend had just said he was no longer sure. It was all the fashion these days, to see who could grow the most fanciful moustache or beard. Shrugging the matter off for the time being he started to chat away.

"So I see you're not feeling any better?"

"I feel worse, if that were possible."

"Well not to worry. Once we reach port and start on our way you'll soon forget all about this. Infact, you know what? I think you'll probably laugh about it."

"You think so do you?"

"Of course. We will have more exciting things to occupy our minds with. It's a thrill, going off to fight the Zulus, don't you agree? I'm relishing the prospect. You know, the word is that we should get to see some proper action this time. The boys are very keen."

"Well I hope you're correct. This damn journey had better be worth it," Melvill grumbled in response.

Coghill looked at him sympathetically, seeing from his friend's appearance just how much he was suffering. "Look. Why don't you join me and the boys for a game of cards. Captain Wardell is there and so is Charlie Cavaye of E Company. It might make you feel better. Anything's better than standing here feeling sorry for yourself." He placed a comforting arm around Melvill's shoulders. "What do you say old chum?"

"Oh, I don't think so. I wouldn't make good company. Just look at me."

"Nonsense," Coghill replied. He took a hold of his friend by the lapels of his tunic and gently turned him around. He fastened the top button and then brushed his shoulders, then told him, "You can come to my cabin and freshen up and you'll be smart enough to have an audience before the Queen herself."

Still protesting that he did not really feel like playing cards, Melvill nevertheless allowed himself to be steered away from the rail and through the doorway that led to the officers quarters. He supposed it wasn't good for the men to see him in such a funk.

In the meantime, the troopship pressed on, carrying its cargo of human freight off to war.

Elsewhere on board the cramped ship and just a little way down the deck from where the two officers had been standing, Privates Robert Metcalfe and Charlie Noakes sat talking quietly. In the corner closeby lay Colour-Sergeant Wolfe. To the accompaniment of his snoring they discussed the coming war, or rather their expectation of one.

"The way I see it," Charlie Noakes said in between mouthfulls of food," is that this Cetshwayo has been allowed to get away with things for too long. He's just asking for a beating and it falls to us to give him what he deserves."

Private Metcalfe watched his friend carefully. He had placed his folded blanket on the deck before him and he was using it as a table to eat from, spooning preserved potatoes and rice from his messtin and occassionally gulping at a tin cup of dark coffee. He ate as though he was ravenous, but then he always seemed to be, using every spare moment to fill his stomach with any available food he could lay his hands on.

He smiled to himself, and went back to his own task.

He was dyeing his white cork helmet a shade of brown using some infernal mixture of animal dung and syrupy coffee which one of the lads had prepared for him. Experience had told them that the dazzling white headgear was far too conspicuous in the bright and dazzling African sun and so before any campaign began most men took the precaution of first removing the brass regimental plate from the front and then changing the colour of their helmets to something more subtle. He worked away deligently, enjoying the sunshine and the company.

"I don't think it will take too long to put him straight," Private Noakes was saying. "We will just have to march into his country and when he takes one look at us he'll be begging for mercy. I think we'll have a jolly good time. What do you say, Robert?"

"You may be right. But don't forget that the Zulus have a reputation for being very keen when it comes to a fight. They might not be the pushover you think."

His friend looked up at this and said, "but surely they won't be a match for us? They're just a bunch of savages aren't they? Come now, Robert, you're not saying that they will really want to fight us are you?"

"That could be the case. You have to remember that every Zulu boy is trained to fight from when they are old enough to pick up a spear. It's in their blood. Warfare is their way of life."

"So," Charlie said in a rather sceptical voice, "they will really be willing to fancy their chances against us? Their spears against our Martini-Henry's? Come now! How dare they think that? Ah!" He laughed out loud and shook his head at his friend's suggestion.

"We'll see."

"If you don't mind me saying so, I think the sun has gone to your head. Perhaps you should put that helmet back on otherwise you might start thinking the Zulus will give us a thrashing."

Robert smiled back, enjoying the banter.

"Besides, they won't even have time to get close enough to use their spears. A few volleys from these beauties," he said, patting his rifle which lay beside him," will keep them at bay. They're man-stoppers they are. Then we have our bayonets. A bit of deft play with the old lunger will send them running with their tails between their legs."

"Alright, you've made your point." Robert turned his helmet around in his hands to see whether he had missed any. Happy with his work he set it down on the deck to dry in the sun. "But tell me this. What will you do, my friend, if they do keep on coming? If, despite the volley fire we put down and the artillery firing away and our mounted men cutting them up, what if they do charge home? What if they come right up to us, face to face, and it's your bayonet against their assegai. How would you feel then? If they kept on coming, relentlessly, right through our storm of bullets! All I'm saying is that we should be prepared for that. We should, if necessary, be ready to stand shoulder to shoulder and take it in our guts."

"Steady now," Charlie implored, a little unnerved by what his friend was saying, "you're starting to put the jitters in me."

"I'm just pointing out that the Zulus are of a different breed of men than the average native. We cannot assume they will behave like the Xhosa's, forever trying to avoid a fight. These chaps, well they will come at us at some point, I'm fairly certain."

Charlie did not say anything back for the moment. He sat and ate his meal, quietly dwelling on his friends comments. Finally he did speak, and it was in a rather sombre mood now, in comparison to his plucky manner of just moments ago.

"I heard some of the officers talking earlier," he said under his breath. "They were talking about how the Zulus like to...rip people up...when they kill them. Not happy to just stab a man the once but time after time they keep on sticking you with their spears. Do you think it's true or were they just spinning a yarn?" He looked straight at Robert and he suddenly seemed the young man that he was once again, a little scared about what awaited them. "If it is, I don't want that to happen to me. It's...it's not...well it's just not cricket, is it?"

"Hopefully you'll never need to find out."

"If I live and die then I hope you are right." He pushed his food away no longer interested in it. He turned and gazed off into the distance, looking towards the horizon where the sea met the sky.

Beside them, Colour-Sergeant Wolfe stirred. With a groan he rolled over and then pushed himself up into a sitting position.

Wiping a hand across his heavy moustache he peered bleary-eyed at the two Privates.

Then, and to their surprise for they hadn't known he had been listening to their conversation, he gave them some advice. "Just use your wits boy. God gave you a brain so use it and you should be affright. Otherwise we'll be sending you home to your 'ma one piece at a time, and she wouldn't like that now would she? As long as you hold steady and stick with your mates then you'll do fine, 'cause they're the ones that count, your pals. You look after them and they'll return the compliment. Ain't that right Metcalfe?"

Without waiting for a reply he stood and walked off, to see to his duties.

Robert Metcalfe and Charlie Noakes took stock of his words.

GOVERNMENT HOUSE, PIETERMARITZBURG.

22nd NOVEMBER 1878.

Set in its wooded grounds just off the intersection of Longmarket and West streets, its grandeur in keeping with the Victorian feel of the provincial capital, Government House was the ideal setting for the High Commissioner's official residence and administrative offices. Since arriving in Pietermaritzburg several weeks earlier, Sir Bartle Frere had set to work orchestrating his ambitious plans for the ruthless suppression of the Zulu Kingdom. From here he had set in motion all the political machinery necessary to achieve those aims. They had now achieved a momentum of their own, he'd thought smugly to himself on several occassions, and there would be no going back now. There would only be one outcome; war with King Cetshwayo.

There were just one or two minor obstacles remaining.

So he had called this meeting with the Lieutenant-General to conclude matters.

Things had been going well, and they were making good progress, when there came a knock on the door. Breaking off from what he had been saying Sir Bartle Frere watched as the door opened and in came one of his assistants. The man quietly strode across the polished floor and handed something to Thesiger who was sitting patiently by the desk.

Frere saw that it was a telegram.

His assistant left and the High Commissioner waited while Thesiger opened and read it.

He noticed the colour suddenly drain from his face. Sitting bolt upright in alarm Frere leaned forward over the desk. "Is everything alright Frederic? You look dreadful." he asked.

The Lieutenant-General was unable to respond at first. He sat there for a moment, stiff with shock. Then he re-read the telegram, making certain that his mind wasn't playing some cruel trick on him. Finally he slumped in his chair and closed his eyes and the hand in which he grasped the piece of paper shook.

After about a minute he opened his eyes. Frere was looking at him with an expression of deep concern etched into his features.

Before he could speak Thesiger had to clear his throat.

"Your Excellancy, I've just recieved some bad news from home. Last month my father, The First Baron Lord Chelmsford, passed away."

"Ah." Frere pursed his lips. "I'm so sorry to hear that Frederic. You have my deepest sympathies." He waited and watched as Thesiger sat with his head bowed and a pained expression

on his gaunt face. The High Commissioner pushed himself up from his chair and walked over to the corner where there was a jug of fresh water on a slender side table. Pouring some into a glass he came back over and handed it to the Lieutenant-General, who dumbly took it and sipped some.

"Do you wish to adjourn the meeting Frederic? You will have arrangements to make for your journey home."

Sighing heavily, Thesiger shook his head. "The timing is unfortunate, but I won't be travelling back to England. As much as it pains me to be away from my family at such a time, I feel it is essential that I remain here. My place is in South Africa, especially at such a crucial time."

"Are you sure?" Frere asked in surprise. "I will understand perfectly if you went. We can allways try and postpone things until such a time you can return."

Thesiger tried to smile his thanks but it came out looking more like a grimace. "That's very kind of you," he whispered after taking another sip of water, "but we both know that to delay things would be inappropriate right now. Our plans are too far advanced to even wait a couple of months. No. We have put an enormous amount of effort into this and I should stay and see things through." He ran a hand over his face and tugged gently at his grey beard.

"That is very commendable of you Frederic. I have to say your energetic approach to this whole business has been top-class. I do not think I could have managed it without you." The Lieutenant-General accepted the praise with a slight incline of his head.

Then something occurred to the High Commissioner. "You do realize that with your father's unfortunate death that the title of Lord Chelmsford now passes on to you, Frederic?" The lieutenant-General admitted that this had not occurred to him.

"So I suppose from here on in, I should always refer to you as such," Frere went on with a gracious smile. Then, in a rather formal manner and using his official voice which he saved for such occassions, he asked, "Shall we continue, Lord Chelmsford?"

Temporarily putting aside his personal grief, the new Lord Chelmsford took a deep breath and tried to get his mind back onto the more immediate problem of sorting out the finer details of their military plans. There would be ample time to dwell on his loss at some later stage.

"I have been considering your suggestion of reducing the number of offensive columns from the origional five to something more manageable. Our transport infrastructure is proving to be a source of major concern. Therefore, I think we could go ahead with our plans, but using just three columns instead. The other two, Colonel Rowland's column in the far north and Colonel Durnford's at the middle drift will remain this side of the border to act as buffers against any Zulu incursions into Natal or the Transvaal. However, they will remain ready to move forward in support if called upon to do so. Three columns should be sufficient to do the job."

"Well that's good," the High Commissioner remarked. A slight smile appeared on his face. "I've also just recieved word that Governor Bulwer has finally given approval for the formation of the Natal Native Contingent."

Chelmsford could hardly contain his pleasure at hearing this news, coming as it did after the bad tidings he had just had.

"Wonderful...may I ask how you managed to sway him in our favour?"

The High Commissioner fiddled with a piece of paper, trying - but not very hard - to hide how pleased he felt with himself. "Oh, I just pointed out how vulnerable the citizens of Natal are under the constant threat of a Zulu invasion, and how a great many lives might be lost in such an eventuality. I think he suddenly realized that he had no wish to have such a calamity on his conscience...as I gently pointed out to him." Frere glanced up and met Chelmsford's gaze.

"Very wise of you," Chelmsford replied.

He reached into his documents satchel which rested against the foot of the table and pulled out a map. He unfolded it and spread it out on Frere's desk. It was a map of Zululand, the best that was available to them, even though there were vast tracts that were a blank with the word *Unexplored* penciled in. There were a number of lines on the map drawn in various coloured inks.

"These," explained Chelmsford, "are the intended routes that our columns will take. And here are the various supply depots that are currently being set up close to the border, the forward staging areas if you like from which they will move out from. Obviously now that we have these additional units at our disposal I shall need to make several ammendments."

Frere looked at the map with keen interest, his eyes lighting up as he visualised how events would unfold over the next few months. "Has Durnford finalised his plans in regard to the NNC," he asked.

"Yes. He has settled on forming three regiments. The 1st Regiment will be three battalions strong while the 2nd and 3rd will each have two battalions. A total of just over seven thousand men. He allready has sufficient volunteers to fill the ranks and has in place a training programme set up and ready, with officers and N.C.O's and drill instructors. Everything is in place to form them with short notice. So now I can give him the go-ahead. As his plans are allready well advanced it means the NNC is, to all intents and purposes, ready for operations as from now."

"Excellent!" beamed Frere. Running his eyes over the map once more and satisfied that everything was progressing well, he stood up from the desk and wandered over to look out of one of the windows. He glanced up towards Fort Napier, perched on top of one of the hills that formed a protective ring around

Pietermaritzburg. From here he could just make out one of the gun emplacements on the embankment. Continuing to look through the window he said, over his shoulder, "we have just one remaining obstacle before we can begin, Frederic."

Lord Chelmsford's attention was drawn away from studying the map at the High Commissioner's words. He looked across at him. He waited.

"As a condition to giving his approval for the forming of the NNC the Governor wishes for us to make one last push for a peaceful settlement to this dispute."

"I see," Chelmsford responded. He thought about this for a moment, then said, "but Cetshwayo's response has been somewhat negative so far. He is refusing to bow to our demands. Take his last communication as an example, which does nothing to deal with the problem in my mind. What was it he said? 'He hereby swears, in the presence of Hamu, Mnyamana, Ntshingwayo and all other chiefs, that he has no intention or wish to quarrel with the English'. Hardly the kind of response we are wanting."

"Nevertheless, we must be seen to be making all efforts to avoid the very serious nature of an armed clash with the Zulu Kingdom. We must explore all other avenues first, and only then, when we have run out of alternative options, can we legitimately turn to military means."

Frere turned away from the window and looked over at Lord Chelmsford.

"The Lieutenant-Governor has called for a meeting to take place, between our own representatives and a Zulu delegation, at the Lower Drift on the 11th of December. The intention is to try and resolve the crisis in as amicable a way as possible. Our previous good relations with the Zulus prior to this current crisis will be highlighted in the hope of reaching an agreement."

A scowl had shadowed Frere's face as he spoke. He disapproved of this whole approach but his hands were tied.

"I'm afraid we will have to deliver the findings of the Border Commissions Report to the Zulus. We cannot put it off any longer."

"Is this the correct time to do that, Your Excellency?"

"As I've said, we have little option. However, if we can attach certain 'conditions' to the border award, we may be able to manipulate the occasion to our advantage."

Lord Chelmsford straightened himself in his chair and spread his hands out on the table before him. In measured tones he asked the High Commissioner exactly what he had in mind.

Sitting down once again Sir Henry Bartle Edward Frere began to explain.

ALONG THE BORDER ROAD.
TWO DAYS MARCH FROM PIETERMARITZBURG.
26th NOVEMBER 1878.

Dog-tired, with the blazing sun beating down on them and dust in their eyes, H Company marched relentlessly on. Without thinking, each man followed the person infront, their heavy boots crunching down on the dirt road, over and over. For mile after mile, and hill after hill.

With the rest of the First Battalion/24th they were marching upcountry from Durban, moving towards the border with Zululand. They had been on the march for the last few days, covering up to twenty miles a day and sleeping out under the African night sky. It was hard and punishing, but the men did not complain, for they were used to such things. This was what soldiering was all about; marching for several hundred miles, fighting a short and sharp war, and then marching all the way back again. They had done it before and, God willing, they would probably do it again.

So on they went.

Each man carried a full accoutrement of equipment, that is the basic belt, braces and frog to which were attached the ammunition pouches to the front, a haversack for rations either on the hip or slung over the shoulder with a water bottle, while strapped to the rear was a blanket or greatcoat. At the bottom was the valise. Thus fully worn, this 'marching order' together with a Martini-Henry rifle weighed about 57 pounds, a heavy load that when on long marches tended to dig into the small of the back and pulled the men down. At the left hand hip was "the lunger", the 22inch socket bayonet, which jangled and sometimes chaffed the thigh.

Encumbered and weighed down, marching over the hilly country, the mens strength soon became sapped.

But the men bore their burdens well. Some chatted away or took the opportunity to admire the stunning vistas around them. Others whistled a popular tune. A few told lewd jokes. Several men had thrust spears down their rifle barrels, trophies from some previous campaign, which they carried with pride.

All in all, and despite the hardships of campaigning and living in the open, the mood was good. They looked forward to the coming fight.

Amongst the men of H Company, Private's Metcalfe and Noakes walked side by side, several ranks back from Colour-Sergeant Wolfe who led his men on from the front with purposeful strides and the occassional snarl when anybody lagged behind. They were talking generally, with Robert telling his friend about his family and life back home, with Charlie listening or asking the occassional question with keen interest. As they walked they noticed a slight commotion up ahead. The two men craned their necks to see what the problem was but from here they couldn't tell. But as they neared the scene of the disturbance a ripple of laughter passed back down through the ranks like a breeze skimming over a field of corn. At last, they saw what was causing this hilarity.

At the side of the road one of the men from one of the companies up front had dropped out of the column. The reason being that the webbing holding his equipment had snapped, thus spilling all of his things all over the place. When they saw who the unfortunate person was it caused them both to burst out laughing, their mirth probably even greater in volume than their companions'

It was Private Owen Brooks, chief bully of E Company and the first battalion in general.

They watched him scramble about in the dust for his things, his CSM berating him at the top of his voice, his red face and spitting lips just inches from the poor mans ear. And when, in his attempts to collect the spilled equipment, he accidently kicked his mess-tin down the slope at the side of the road and was forced to go racing after it, this caused even more hilarity from those passing above.

That is, until they spotted Colour-Sergeant Wolfe coming down the line at the double, all clenched white teeth and bristling moustache and eyes stuck out like organ-stops, almost apoplectic with rage. "Who told you to laugh?!" he screeched in their faces. "Did I give you permission to laugh? Did I? You're a disgrace to the regiment, that's what you are! Now move your backsides up that hill or I'll pull you there by your bleeding ears until they come right off your 'eads! Move it! You're the most pathetic bunch I ever laid me eyes on!"

Still sniggering amoungst themselves and nudging their neighbours in the ribs they nevertheless did as they were told, footslogging up yet another steep hill. Behind them, the unfortunate Private Brooks continued to try and sort out his bundle.

On cresting the rise a spectacular view opened out before them.

As far as the eye could see there stretched, right to the very horizon, a neverending rolling landscape of hills and crests and mountains in varying hues of green and brown and yellow. There must have being several hundred, or possibly a thousand, different elevations contained within this panorama. And above there was a marvelous dome of unbroken blue that quite possibly went all the way to the distant sea. It was a breathtaking sight which stopped all conversation as each man took in the beauty of it.

They marched on and followed the dirt road down the far side of the rise they had just ascended. From this elevated position they could see it stretch away into the distance, a brown ribbon that weaved and curled its way through the landscape for mile after mile.

They doggedly went on. The column of men kicking up clouds of choking dust.

A little further on they came across a small collection of native huts gathered near the roadside. As they passed the whole family came out to stare, from the old, white haired grandma down to a tiny infant standing there completely naked. Running about and barking at the soldiers passing by was a dirty mongrel, which nipped and yelped at their feet. A few of the lads kicked it away until some kind soul threw it a morsel of food which took its attention away.

As he passed them Charlie waved cheerily but they just stared back with blank expressions on their faces. Turning to Robert he asked, "Why do they look so sad? We're here to help them, to protect them from the Zulus."

Robert just shrugged his shoulders. "The sight of us lot is probably scaring them witless." "In what way?"

Robert glanced across at his friend. Sometimes his naivity puzzled him. "Well how would you feel if several thousand soldiers came marching past your house, dressed in strange clothes and speaking a foreign tongue, and armed with all manner of weapons? I know I'd be asking myself what their real purpose is. At the end of the day, they'll be wondering if, after we've given Cetshwayo a good licking, they'll be next."

"I see what you mean," Charlie said after thinking about it for a moment. He lifted the nib of his helmet and wiped the sweat from his forehead with a rag. They trudged on for several more paces with Charlie glancing back at the cluster of huts. "So what you mean is, they're not sure who to be afeared of the most. Us or the Zulus?"

"Exactly. They probably think that once this war is over we won't be in any hurry to leave. They'll have swapped one enemy for another."

"You know," Charlie replied thoughtfully, "if that is the case, then they have every right to look scared."

"You'd be best if you didn't think about it too much," Robert advised him. "Best if we just follow our orders. That is what we're paid for, ain't it? If they say jump, we jump and if they say run around in circles..."

"Then we run around in circles."

Elsewhere in the ranks of H Company, as well as the other companies that made up the 1/24th, several dozen similar conversations were taking place. All were concerning the likelihood that they would soon be seeing some action, a prospect that both excited and scared them in equal measures.

The further north they marched, the closer they came to seeing how they would stand up to the ordeal of the bloody violence of war.

*   *   *

The First Battalion marched into Pietermaritzburg two days later.

Coming in through the outskirts, and winding their way through the wide streets and avenues, past the crowds of onlookers who waved and cheered their arrival, with children running and skipping alongside and members of the well-to-do families looking from their balconies, they turned onto Church Street, marching with a bounce in their step despite their long and arduous slog. A few waved back at the townsfolk, with wide grins on their bearded faces. Even the surly CSM's enjoyed the reception they recieved, although they would be damned if they allowed their men to see it.

One of those who was watching from outside the Colonial Buildings on Church Street was James Brickhill. He watched them march by from amidst the cheering crowds, standing on tip-toes to get a glimpse of them.

For twenty minutes, rank after rank went by.

When there was still no end in sight to the column of British redcoats, Brickhill turned away and pushed his way to the back of the crowd. Once he was clear of the crush he pulled his hat down by the nib and set off along the street.

Since arriving in Pietermaritzburg a number of weeks ago with Inspector Mansel and his men, James Brickhill had been frustrated in his attempts to find work. The British column that was rumoured to be preparing to cross into Zululand from Rorke's Drift hadn't at that stage been present in the city, the few units in the vicinity being stationed at Fort Napier closeby. He'd failed to find employment there, the few posts having quickly been snapped up by others. After spending a week moving from government building to government building in a fruitless search he had started to become very despondent.

His mood hadn't improved when the Natal Mounted Police troop had left the city. They clearly had plenty to keep them busy, patrolling the countryside or escorting various convoys. He had felt very envious at their departure, wishing he could go with them. Instead he had been left to drift around by himself.

At one time so miserable had he become that he had even contemplated going home. But that would mean admitting he had been wrong to set out on what his brother thought of as a ridiculous flight of fancy in the first place, and he could not stand the notion of feeling like a failure. Nor did he much relish seeing the smug smirk on his brother's face. So he had resisted the temptation, not wanting the humiliation.

Then he had thought about moving on to Durban. Surely there would be more going on there, what with all the troops disembarking and the build up of military units growing with every day? Yes. That's what he would do, he had decided the day before yesterday. There was little point in staying here.

However, this very morning and just as he had started to organize his departure from his lodgings, news had come in of the imminent arrival of a British Infantry Regiment, passing through Pietermaritzburg on their way north towards Helpmekaar. He had realized the worth of waiting for maybe a couple more days, and instead of setting off for Durban he had come down to watch the soldiers march in.

Now walking down the street and squeezing through the crowds of onlookers, Brickhill turned down a narrow roadway to where he had hitched his horse and mule. Walking away from the throng of people he quickly made his way there.

He was glad to see they were still tied up where he had left them, just outside the doorway to Bullock's Chemist. The young coloured boy who he had asked to watch over them was still there, sitting on the edge of the wooden walkboards. On seeing his approach the youngster leapt to his feet and smiled happily.

Speaking in Zulu, the boy's native tongue even though he was of the Thembu clan, Brickhill thanked him for staying. Then he asked why he was in the city alone and the boy told him that he had been running an errand for his mother who happened to be a servant of Mr Macleroy the bank manager. When he, Brickhill, had asked him to watch over his horse and mule then he had thought it only right to help.

Brickhill smiled. He understood what the boy was hinting at. Reaching into a pouch on his waistbelt he took out a coin and flipped it in the air. The youngster caught it deftly, said thankyou, and skipped away. Watching him go for a moment he turned and prepared to saddle up.

Just then a voice called out from further down the street.

"Excuse me there," it said, and Brickhill looked around.

Two men were watching him from their horses. Both wore the uniform of high-ranking officers of the British Army. One of them, a short and somewhat portly looking middle-aged man, with thinning hair more than compensated with a fine, bristling moustache that curled down below his chin, lifted off his hat and smiled cheerfully. His companion was thinner and taller but very smart, with black hair slicked down across his forehead and a slightly hooked nose.

"I'm sorry if I sound nosey," the shorter one said in impeccable english, "but I couldn't help but noticing that you are fluent in Zulu."

Brickhill stepped away from his mount. "That's correct. Yes I am."

The two British officers exchanged a glance.

"Sorry. We should introduce ourselves. I'm Colonel Glyn and this is Colonel Pulleine. I'm the commander of the battalion that has just arrived."

Brickhill's attention was suddenly aroused. He introduced himself and then shook hands with the two officers.

"As you can probably gather we are moving up towards the border. However, I do lack good interpreters to take with me. You wouldn't by any chance be interested, would you?"

"Colonel, please tell me more," Brickhill said with an enthusiastic smile.

"Well, it would be dangerous work, travelling with my staff at the head of the column. I would need you with me throughout. But because of the risk I can vouch that you will be well paid, plus all your needs would be catered for. What do you say?"

Brickhill did not need to think twice. He could not believe his good fortune. Not only would he be joining with the invasion force but being attached to the colonel's staff would put him at the heart of any action. He could not want for more.

"Colonel, I would be honoured to accompany you," he proclaimed loudly.

The two men grunted appreciatively and Glyn turned to his companion. "It seems we have struck gold Henry. How fortunate we were to come across this young gentleman."

"Yes," agreed Pulleine. Then he said, "It's very kind of you Mr Brickhill. Can you be ready to move out of town within the next couple of days?"

"I can be ready much sooner than that if you wish."

"Ha, ha, that won't be necessary," Pulleine replied. "The men need a rest before we push on. However, if you have the time, we could do with your services immediately."

Brickhill nodded eagerly and quickly mounted his horse. Then, riding side by side with the two officers, he went with them to the end of the small street and turned onto Church Street and joined with the column of redcoats marching through the city. How quickly his luck had turned around, he thought.

The 1st Battalion, 24th (2nd Warwickshire) Regiment, plus one new recruit, were drawing ever closer to war.

CHAPTER 10

NATAL / ZULULAND BORDER.

FORT PEARSON, AT THE LOWER DRIFT OF THE THUKELA RIVER.

11th DECEMBER 1878.

The three year drought that had ravaged the area had finally broken.

As the year drew to a close, bringing with it the scorching heat of summer and the wet season, then the rains had returned. With a vengeance. Once dried-up river beds had become transformed overnight into raging torrents as the parched land refused to absorb the torrential downpours, and the water had simply run off the slopes into the valley bottoms. So the majestic rivers that ran from the Drakensberg mountains to the sea bubbled back to life.

Very quickly the land became fertile. Crops that had suffered so badly were revitalised.

Yet that very same rain made the rivers impassable to any traffic travelling over the countryside. The roads and tracks, always notoriously difficult, became a nightmare quagmire of mud. And so Lord Chelmsford's Army, moving up towards the border in preparation for his anticipated invasion of Zululand, became bogged down. The build-up did continue, although with immense difficulty and arduous labour. His grand scheme, planned in meticulous detail and dependant on precise timing, suffered its first serious reverse. Not at the hands of their enemy.

By nature.

*　　　*　　　*

From a geographical point of view the Lower Thukela Drift had become the most favoured route in and out of Zululand over the years. Having spent its fury up in the mountain passes, by the time the Thukela River reached the Indian Ocean it was usually a calm, broad expanse of slow moving water. What's more, at the drift just three or four miles inland from the river mouth, the water was very shallow. So during the dry season or times of prolonged drought it was therefore possible to cross on foot. It was also conveniently close to the port at Durban just down the coast. And so as a result the white gun traders and hunting parties used it as the main crossing point between Natal and the Zulu Kingdom.

Over time this occassional traffic cut a fairly well defined traders track that meandered north from the small community of Stanger down to the rivers edge. To take advantage of this passing trade someone had built a ramshackle wayside inn at the side of the track named Smith's Hotel, a convenient resting place for those just embarking on or returning from a trip across the river. From the verandah the guests could take potshots at crocodiles basking on the far bank, if they felt suitably bored.

On the opposite side of the track and just across from Smith's Hotel a large knoll overlooked the river. From the top one had a commanding view of the countryside for miles around, with the broad sweep of the Thukela three hundred feet below and the long sandbank that marked the river mouth in the near distance. Here an advance party of 170 men led by a Lieutenant Main of the Royal Engineers had constructed a well-built earthwork fort atop this knoll and christened it Fort Pearson after the commanding officer of the coastal column. Once complete the fort had been garrisoned by a naval brigade, about 230 strong, sailors and marines of HMS Active which had recently arrived in Durban. They brought with them two 12-pounder Armstrong guns, two 24-pounder rocket tubes and a Gatling gun. Also in the vicinity was a unit of twenty members of the Stanger Mounted Rifles to augment this force.

Below the bluff was a small ledge that ran along the riverbank. As one approached the waters edge one would see to their right a large wild fig tree, and below its spreading branches someone had erected a canvas awning. Gathered here in the shade - for the day was hot and unforgiving despite the recent downpours - was a large group of people locked in conference, the white representitives either standing or seated at a small table, the blacks resting on their haunches as was their custom.

Their meeting was of vital importance. The outcome of these discussions would be of immense significance for both parties. They would, put simply, decide whether or not a war would be fought.

Mr James Lloyd, the photographer from Durban who had been setting up his three-legged contraption on the grass, bent down underneath the black shroud of his camera and peered through its tiny aperture at the Zulu delegates seated by the wheels of a wagon. He saw the elderly men scowling back, not sure what to make of the fearsome looking device pointing at them. One of them - Mr Lloyd thought it was the chief *induna* - nervously nudged his neighbour as though warning him to be on guard. Savages! he thought, then released the shutter.

A murmur of unease came from the Zulu delegates gathered on the ground. Their leader, and representative of King Cetshwayo, Vumandaba kaNtati, pulled his blanket tight around his hunched shoulders and stared balefully at the white men seated at the table opposite him. He had felt uncomfortable since first arriving a short while ago. When he and his two companions, their eleven subordinates and forty or so attendants, had walked slowly down the far riverbank at the appointed hour they had found a number of white men waiting for them there. Because of the heavy rains the river was swollen and so it had been necessary to come over by boat. This had created a few tense moments as they had allowed the white men to row them across, and then when stepping out onto the bank and going over to where the meeting would be held they had seen for the first time the heavily armed guard standing by.

They had not been told about this. What were the white men thinking? That they would be so foolish to attack them while in the process of trying to negotiate a bloodless settlement? The fools! They had come to try and prevent a war, not to start one right here.

Settling into their positions the Zulu delegates had looked across at their British counterparts.

The four men seated at the table had each been handpicked by the High Commissioner himself. Each one prided himself on his professionalism and expertise regarding such occassions as well as their strong sense of duty. They were: Charles Brownlee, Commissioner for Native Affairs Cape Colony; John W. Shepstone, Secretary for Native Affairs in the Cape Colony; Brevet Colonel Forestier Walker, officer of the Scots Guards and Frere's Assistant Military Secretary; and Henry Francis Fynn, magistrate of Msinga district.

Behind them and attentive to their every need were their assistants and various attendants, as well as numerous observers to the proceedings.

Finally, their military escort, made up of about twenty marines and twenty bluejackets, each man heavily armed and supplied with additional ammunition.

The atmosphere between the two groups was therefore understandably tense, with both parties watchful and untrusting. Careful glances were exchanged and whispered conversations held as each side tried, to varying degrees of success, to sum one another up.

Finally, at eleven o'clock, J.W.Shepstone pushed himself to his feet. Picking up a leaf of papers from the table he cleared his throat and began to read out loud. Off to one side, a small and scruffy-looking man going by the name of H. Bernard Fynney, a border agent who was fluent in Zulu, translated what he said sentence by sentence for the benefit of the Zulu delegation.

Shepstone read out the Border Commission award, for so long hidden in a safe in Cape Town, kept back by the High Commissioner Sir Henry Bartle Frere for five long months. Until now. The Zulu *iziduna* listened carefully. As was their normal practice they would remember the announcement word by word, a skill which they were remarkably adept at no matter how long and convuluted such messages might prove to be. Afterwards they would repeat these memorized passages to their king with unnerring accuracy.

As Shepstone spoke the expressions on the faces of the Zulus did not change. They squatted on the grass and listened intently, showing remarkable restraint. For the news was good, at least for them. It gradually dawned on them that the Border Commissions decision was coming down in their favour.

Firstly a general outline of the Boer and Zulu claim to the disputed territory was made, and then Shepstone, reading directly from a copy of the report he held in his hands, announced the following decisions. No concession of land had ever been made by the Zulu nation to the Boers. The Boer insistances that they had legally purchased large tracts of terrain could not be proven to the satisfaction of the members of the Commission, firstly because the area of land in question was far too vague to be reliably pin-pointed, also because some of the documents that purported to contain zulu signatures were very obviously forged with names and dates altered, and mostly because despite the Boer claims to have governed the territory in a fair and diplomatic way no official civil bodies of office had ever been established by them, bringing the legality of their jurisdiction into question. In short the Boer demands for land rights would not be upheld. The only concession they would have was the payment of compensation by the Zulus to any white farmers already living in Zulu territory who would now have to leave, unless allowed to stay by the rightful owner, King Cetshwayo.

Vumandaba, the chief *induna,* looked at his companions when Shepstone had finished reading. A brief flurry on conversation errupted between the Zulu delegates accompanied by hands waving and gesticulating in the air. Then the elderly man turned and gave his thanks to the four men seated at the table, which Fynney translated.

The Zulu elders and their attendants rose to leave.

Shepstone held up a hand and asked them to wait.

Vumandaba looked around warily.

Then, with his words being translated, Shepstone announced that he would like to present the Zulus with a prize bullock as an indication of their goodwill. In return he asked if they would stay and continue discussing the matter further, after a break for lunch.

With reluctance, but understanding that the gesture of offering them the bullock gave him little option, Vumandaba agreed to the suggestion.

Having now set up his camera on the verandah of Smith's Hotel, Mr Lloyd photographed the proceedings taking place beneath the branches of the large tree. With the people gathered there and the river behind them and Zululand stretching away beyond he thought it would make a reasonably good photograph. Nothing very special, but reasonable.

Turning to a group of people standing beside him and watching with interest, Mr Lloyd asked if any of them knew what was likely to happen once the discussions continued. They all shrugged their shoulders. Nothing very special, they thought.

They couldn't have known it, but the small cluster of onlookers were very wrong.

Vumandaba knew something bad was about to happen from the moment the meeting resumed. He could tell by the expressions on the white mens faces. Gone were the cordial looks of before, the respectful nods. In their place were heavy scowls and grave frowns. They had obviously returned with serious things to say.

Shepstone's next speech was delivered in a much more belligerent way. With a deep voice that was tinged with threat, he delivered a bombshell set of demands that the British administration expected the Zulu King to comply with. These were necessary for the future well being of all citizens, both white and black, living in the border region. The Zulu people were a threat to peace. They could not be allowed to remain so while the British stood by and did nothing to protect their citizens.

To the growing horror of the Zulu delegation Shepstone set out the following demands:

1. Chief Sihayo's brother and sons were to be surrendered to the British Administration to be tried by Natal Courts for the recent border incursion.

2. A fine of 500 head of cattle was to be paid for Mehlokazulu's outrages.
3. A further fine of 100 cattle was to be paid for other outrages that had recently taken place along the border.
4. A renegade Swazi called Mbelini, who had repeatedly raided parts of the disputed territory, was to be handed over along with his associates-these would be named at a later date.

The Zulu delegation, sitting with stunned looks on their faces, were bluntly informed that their king had just twenty days to comply with these first demands.

More were to follow.

1. Promises made at Cetshwayo's coronation were to be adhered to: principally that no Zulu was to be executed without being granted a trial as well as the opportunity to make an appeal.
2. Every Zulu was to be free to marry without awaiting permission from their King.
3. All Missionaries were to be allowed to return to their abandoned mission stations in Zululand and free to teach, and any Zulu converts wishing to attend could do so with no intervention or intimidation from the Zulu leadership.
4. A British Resident was to be stationed in Zululand to enforce these provisions.
5. The Zulu Army to be disbanded and the current military system abolished.
6. Any future disputes involving a European should be heard in the presence of both the King and the British Resident, and no sentence of expulsion from Zululand was to be carried out without the approval of the British Resident.

Thirty days were given for these demands to be met.

Having finished delivering his speech Shepstone sat down in his seat and the four British envoys sat watching their Zulu counterparts in silence.

For a few moments a complete hush descended as the news slowly sank in. Then Vumandaba, astonished at the chain of events, cried out in dismay and lifted his arms into the air before letting them drop back down to the ground. His companions joined in, crying out in anger and confusion. One or two of the armed men standing nearby visibly tensed at this sudden commotion and only a stern look from Colonel Walker prevented them from taking further, more direct action, to control the situation.

The four British representatives conferred for a few seconds.

Then Vumandaba suddenly spoke out aloud, addressing them directly. Fynney translated his words.

Shepstone slowly shook his head. No. There would be no further talking. They did not have the powers to discuss the terms of the demands or to negotiate them. They had been granted thirty days to comply which was deemed more than sufficient. He then informed them that they would be given a copy of the conditions to take with them, just to make sure their king fully understood the seriousness of the situation. A strange move since the British knew very well that knowbody in the Zulu court could read a word of English.

Finally Shepstone told them in no uncertain terms that a failure to meet the demands within the allotted time would thus result in a formal declaration of war.

Silent once again the Zulu delegation accepted this catastrophic news with dignity and in a calm and corteous manner. It was out of their hands now. Rising they bid the British farewell.

CHAPTER 11

HELPMEKAAR. FORWARD STAGING AREA OF CENTRE COLUMN.
MID DECEMBER 1878 -EARLY JANUARY 1879.

Throughout the month of December the small hamlet on the Biggarsberg heights saw the arrival of men and equipment as the Centre Column started to gather in preparation for its part in the impending invasion. The first to arrive were four companies of the 1/24th, arriving tired and bedraggled in pouring rain, and with weary and aching limbs they pitched their tents on the open piece of ground beside the dirt road, away from the edge of the escarpment to escape the worst of the wind-driven spears of rain that lanced down out of leaden skies. When they were done they ate a sorrowful meal of preserved meat and bread. Then, certain unlucky individuals were picked for sentry duty to watch over the camp throughout the night, these piquets being posted on the edge of the plateau overlooking the Mzinyathi valley. The rest of the camp turned in. Lights were extinguished. The exhausted men slept.

Over the next few days the rest of the column came in. The various Volunteer units arrived, mostly colonials and settlers who had offered their services to make up for Lord Chelmsford's lack of mounted men, small bodies of men of varying degrees of discipline and effectiveness. They provided their own uniforms and horses but had been given government-issue firearms and equipment and they gave themselves such fancy names as The Natal Carbineers, 60 strong, and The Buffalo Border Guard who had come down from Fort Pine, and The Newcastle Mounted Rifles under a Captain Bradstreet. They camped next in line beside the Infantry.

Next to reach the new campsite and adding to the noisy and cramped conditions were the 3rd Regiment, NNC, two battalions of the newly-formed native levie force that would complement the centre column and provide much needed manual labour and scouts. They came along the dirt road in high spirits, apparently looking forward to the upcoming fight against their hated foe, the Zulus. Singing and capering and hopping about they made for a pleasant distraction to the white troops who came out to watch despite the awful weather. A few of the Volunteer's commented how splendid they were, what a fine body of men they presented, while others muttered under their breath how ridiculous and badly disciplined they were.

Other units arrived over the following days. The Imperial Mounted Infantry. The 5th (Field) Company, RE. The Army Service Corps. The Army Hospital Corps with their cumbersome ambulance wagons.

Still on the road from Pietermaritzburg was the 2/24th which was expected to reach Helpmekaar sometime in early December. Even further away but making steady progress were the six guns of N Battery, 5th Brigade, Royal Artillery, under Brevet Lieutenant-Colonel Harness and his second-in-command Major Smith. They had being forced to march overland all the way from the Cape Frontier to Natal and would therefore probably be amoungst the last to arrive. Chelmsford and his headquarters were still in Pietermaritzburg overseeing the last minute details and using every available moment left before their ultimatum to the Zulus expired to bring his forces up to strength; he would arrive at the forward supply depot shortly.

Along the border road and fast turning it into a rutted quagmire struggled convoy after convoy of ox-wagons, bringing up the supplies of food and ammunition. The change in the weather had come at the worst possible time and on occassions the transport system, allready strained to breaking point, simply ground to a halt. Only the superhuman efforts of the transport officers kept the buildup on schedule. Elsewhere in the country the same picture was being repeated over and over at the Lower Drift, at Kranskop, at Utrecht, and in the Transvaal. The five British columns were gathering, the men marching forward towards the border, poised to launch the invasion if the go-ahead was given.

In the meantime, time was running out for the Zulu people.

Of course, this was precisely what Lord Chelmsford and Sir Bartle Frere were hoping for. Not only that Cetshwayo would be unable to meet the British demands within the allotted time but also that it would prove impossible to carry them out in any case.

For one thing, the Zulu king alone was not in a position to make any important state decisions by himself.

The Zulu Kingdom was made up of various clans that over the years had either been conquered by them or who had allied themselves to the Zulu nation. The hereditary chiefs of these clans made up the *izikhulu*, they were the 'Great Ones' who sat on the *ibandla,* the King's Inner Council. So powerful were they that the King could ill afford to ignore their advice, and on occassions they even overruled him when they met to discuss matters of national importance.

So when the Zulu delegates had returned from their meeting with the British at The Lower Drift and passed on the set of demands to the Inner Council, the British knew very well that they would in no way be willing to bow to these terms.

Chelmsford and Frere had manipulated the situation with consummate skill. The demands that they had issued on that fateful day were purposefully harsh, biting deep at the heart of the infrastructure of the Zulu nation. Cetshwayo and his *ibandla* may have been willing to pay the fines and even to hand over Sihayo's sons if it helped to appease the British but to abandon the military system and disband the zulu army, the *amabutho,* would take away the King's power as well as strangle the social, political and economic lifeblood of the nation as a whole. For the *amabutho* was more than just an army. They performed many other services for their king. They tended the king's massive royal herds, they brought in the harvest each year, they built or repaired the numerous *amakhanda* that were the most visible sign of his power. They had important functions to serve at the great national gatherings or they took part in the frequent royal hunts. They could be called upon to do the king's bidding whenever he so desired it. So the *amabutho* system was a very effective method for the king not only to centralize power and give them a feeling of national pride at the work they did but it was also a means of the young men of the nation to show the extent of their loyalty to their monarch.

Therefore, when the British demanded that this way of life be dismantled they knew what Cetshwayo's response would be.

So their military preparations continued.

As the weeks progressed Cetshwayo sent message after message to the British, appealing for them to reconsider. Were they really willing to destroy Zululand for the sake of two foolish children? he asked. But when his pleads for them not to lay waste his country fell on deaf ears he then asked them to give him more time. He would collect the cattle to pay the fines but as the rivers were all in flood he would need more than the twenty days to send them from Ondini to Natal.

But Frere was having none of it. He described the Zulu king's attempts at delaying matters as "pitiful evasion." No exceptions would be made. Cetshwayo knew what he had to do.

The clock was ticking.

Christmas came and went. The first deadline passed.

Early in the New Year the High Commissioner took the next important step towards war. He issued a notification to announce his intentions to the citizens of Natal, wording it very carefully lest he upset anybody's sensibilities. He sent a copy by dispatch rider to Lord Chelmsford who had left Pietermaritzburg that very morning for the border. Galloping down the dirt roads and with the communication sewn into the lining of his tunic the rider hurried after the General, hoping to catch up with him before sunset.

*   *   *

Accompanied by his small staff and military escort Lord Chelmsford trotted at a gentle pace down through the deep thorn valleys close to Msinga, on the road to Helpmekaar.

"The problem is," Chelmsford was saying, thinking aloud, "is that it has proven nigh on impossible to obtain any reliable information regarding the condition of the roads over the border. Even those who should know, the traders and farmers and so on, have failed to supply us with the right sort of knowledge. They have only ever looked at these routes simply from a trader's point of view and not a military one. Moving a few small carts laden with their goods is one thing, but moving an entire army forward against armed opposition is another prospect entirely. That is why, gentleman, we are to a certain extent stepping into the unknown."

He pointed off towards the east, indicating the hills in the distance. "Much of the terrain out there - Zululand - has not even being explored by white people. Hense the inadequacy of some of our maps. That worries me."

Colonel Crealock, who was by his General's side as always, replied, "Our native scouts would be able to give us good, local information, my Lord. Many of them come from the border region."

"True. However, most of the advance reconnoitreing will be done by our mounted units, especially the local volunteers. I'm sure they will prove invaluable. We must push them far out in front of our columns and scout the terrain thoroughly. My instincts tell me that if we are to meet the main Zulu Army on the field of battle it will be sooner rather than later, probably quite soon after we cross the border. We must be well informed of the enemy's movements to prevent any nasty surprises falling upon us."

As they trotted their horses along the well worn track the small party of men took in their surroundings. The rain had temporarily ceased making for another blisteringly hot afternoon, the reason for their economical pace. Several miles ahead of them they could see the large mass of the Biggarsberg heights, the most dominant feature for miles around. Chelmsford estimated that in another two hours they should reach Helpmekaar; just in time for dinner he thought pleasantly.

A short while later he called a halt. The men dismounted and each one found a rock or a spot on the ground to rest. The last stretch of their journey would be up the steep slopes of the plateau and their horses needed a break. As a precaution Chelmsford ordered the men not to remove their saddles.

They spread out and a quiet hush descended. Only the buzz of insects could be heard. Chelmsford's Naval ADC, Lieutenant Milne, took the opportunity to observe the countryside through his powerful telescope, and a few of the other officers joined him. After a half hour they prepared to set off again.

It was as they were doing so that somebody called out that a rider was approaching from the south. All eyes turned in that direction and, sure enough, galloping towards them along the dirt road came a lone figure, waving at them to gain their attention.

After a few minutes the rider reined in his horse and breathlessly climbed down. He hurried over to Chelmsford who noticed his tunic and riding breeches were caked with dust and sweat. He had apparantly come far. Saluting his General he reached into his tunic and pulled out a small leather dispatch wallet, which he handed over.

Chelmsford opened it and read the following dispatch while his staff looked on:

NOTIFICATION BY HIS EXCELLANCY THE HIGH COMMISSIONER.

In July last an armed body of Zulus, retainers of the Chief Sihayo, led by his sons and brother, entered Natal and took away by force a refugee woman, who was claiming protection from the resident magistrate of Msinga. This woman was dragged across the border, and, it is believed, murdered. This act of outrage was promptly brought to Cetewayo's notice by his Excellency the Lieutenant-Governor of Natal, but no explanation or redress could be obtained from Cetewayo. Twenty days were allowed to the Zulu King to surrender the sons and brother of the Chief Sihayo for trial, and as this term expired on 31st December, 1878, the High Commissioner entertains no hope that it is the intention of the Zulu King to afford the redress which her Majesty's Government has a right to demand.

Therefore I hereby make known, for the information of Cetewayo and all the Zulu people, that I have placed the further prosecution of this and all other demands for redress and reparation in the hands of his Excellancy the Lieutenant-General Lord Chelmsford, commanding her Majesty's Forces in South Africa, with the request that he will take such steps as he may find necessary to protect the British territory from further aggression, and to compel the Zulu King to comply with all the demands made on him for satisfaction due to the British Government, or for the greater security of the British territory, or for the better and more peaceable government of the Zulu people. Lieutenant-General Lord Chelmsford will carefully notify to all Zulu chiefs and people who may come within his reach that the commands of the British Government are made on Cetewayo, as much in the interests of the Zulu people as of the British nation, and that till the 11th January the Lieut.-General will be willing to recieve and to transmit to me any intimation of the unqualified acceptance by Cetewayo of all the terms offered to him. If such intimation of unqualified and complete acceptance be recieved by the Lieut.-General before the 11th January no .further hostile movement will be made, unless rendered necessary by the action of the Zulu forces, and up to the above date Lord Chelmsford will be ready to consider any steps which the Zulu King may propose for the purpose of giving real and permanent effect to the demands of the British Government. But unless all these terms be fully complied with by the above date, the Lieut.-General will no longer be bound by the terms of the 11th December, but will take such measures as the forces under his command will permit for compelling the submission of the Zulu King; always bearing in mind that the British Government has no quarrel with the Zulu nation, and that the future good government and well-being of the Zulus is as much an object of the steps now taken as the safety and protection of the British territories of Natal and the Transvaal. And I do hereby warn all residents and inhabitants of her Majesty's possessions and colonies in South Africa, of whatever race, to be guided by this, my notification, and I do strongly charge and command all her Majesty's officers, ministers, and subjects, and all others whom it may concern, to govern themselves and to act accordingly, and to take due notice of and to pay due regard to the tenor thereof.

H.B.E. Frere,
High Commissioner.
Pietermaritzburg, Natal, Jan. 4, 1879.

When he had finished reading Chelmsford handed the dispatch over to his military secretary. While Crealock hurriedly ran his eyes over it the General informed the rider that he should join them on their journey to Helpmekaar, where he could rest for the night before returning to Pietermaritzburg in the morning.

By the time Chelmsford had pulled himself into his saddle Crealock was done.

"Good news, is it not my Lord?" Chelmsford heard his military secretary say.

He turned his horse to face his small command, and from the expressions on their expectant faces he saw that they were waiting - or to be more precise, wanting - him to say something profound. So he did, speaking in a crisp and strong voice.

"The communication I have just recieved, direct from the High Commissioner himself, gives me final authorization to commence hostilities. We are to prosecute the forthcoming war to its full conclusion, that is to force full compliance of his Excellancy's demands from the Zulu King."

He waited a moment while the news sank in, seeing people exchange glances of satisfaction at this welcome news.

"We face a difficult campaign gentlemen. Once we cross the border I expect you to set a fine example to the men how the British Army conducts itself against an enemy who will, I'm sure, meet us with great vigour on the battlefield. We must be robust in our actions and be willing to suffer the hardships of a hard-fought war. Half measures do not answer with natives. The only way to make them believe in our superiority is to thoroughly crush them. Then, and only then, will they understand that further resistance will be pointless. I shall strive to make that clear to our enemy at the earliest possible opportunity."

CHAPTER 12

THE BRITISH CAMP AT RORKE'S DRIFT.
LATE-AFTERNOON, 10th JANUARY 1879.

Several miles south of where it joins with the Ncome (blood) River, the Mzinyathi crosses a shelf of bare bedrock before making a splendid sweep around a perculiar shaped hill called Shiyane. This drift made it possible to cross the river on foot at times of low water. White traders, once they became aware of the huge number of potential customers just over the river in Zululand-selling their goods, which included antiquated muskets which the zulus so craved, in return for hunting rights-soon made it one of the more favoured crossing points from Natal to the Zulu Kingdom.

One of the first to arrive and exploit this situation was a veteran of the seventh Cape Frontier War, the War of the Axe, of 1846. James Rorke decided, round about 1849, to settle in the northern extremities of Natal, an area teeming with game of all kinds and still with a relatively small white population. He chose an area of land measuring a thousand acres or so on the banks of the Mzinyathi close to the drift because of its easy access into Zululand and one of the first things he did was to name the crossing after himself, a small display of self-extravagance for this quiet natured man. Thus Rorke's Drift it became.

On the western slopes of Shiyane hill, a site which offered a wide and open view both into Natal and Zululand, Rorke built himself two large buildings. Both were thatched. One of them served as his house which he devided into a number of small and cramped rooms for him and his wife to live in. Some of them he for some reason left windowless and with no connecting doors, they only opened out onto a long verandha that ran along the buildings length. The second building was used as his store to hold his goods. Out to the front Rorke established a garden where he grew various vegetables and fruit.

It was a pleasant location if somewhat isolated. A hunting trail came down the Biggarsberg from Helpmekaar twelve miles away and crossed his farm on its way to the river a quarter of a mile further on. As the years progressed and Rorke and his wife lived their quiet existence a steady trickle of hunters and traders passed along this trail. Even a few Zulus from over the border came in to purchase his goods, exchanging rare animal skins for his much sought after items, and, because they had difficulty in pronouncing his name they usually referred to him as Jimu while his farm they called *KwaJim's*. He got on well with them and a mutual trust slowly developed between them.

But times were hard. And events would soon overtake them.

As the British influence in the area increased so did the tensions between the Crown and the Zulu nation. The implied threat that the Zulu people represented and to which Rorke totally disagreed with was used to bring about the inevitable confrontation and as his farm fell within the disputed territory that was at the heart of the dispute they both decided, in 1875, to sell their property. It was quickly purchased by the Norwegian missionary Society who at the time were keen to establish a foothold in Zululand and convert the local native population and having a station on the border would go a long way towards achieving that aim. A deal was agreed.

Just three months later James Rorke died after a short illness. He was buried at his favourite spot below Shiyane.

It wasn't until 1878 that the new owner moved in.

He was the Reverand Otto Witt, who moved in with his wife and young children. They quickly converted the store into a makeshift church but left the house relatively unchanged. He also renamed Shiyane hill. He decided it would now be named Oskarberg, after the Swedish king. As 1878 progressed so the military confrontation between the British and the Zulu king Cetshwayo come closer. Hardly had they moved into their new home when the first bodies of Imperial Redcoats started to arrive and Lord Chelmsford comandeered the site to be a forward supply depot of his Centre Column. The church building became, yet again, a storehouse. The gardens were soon trampled underfoot by the passage of hundreds of men and animals and wheeled transport. Bakeries and ovens and tents sprung up all about as the column marched down from Helpmekaar towards the border. Fences were torn down to be used for firewood. The narrow track became a wide welter of mud and slime. The appearance of the place changed beyond all recognition. Once a farm, then briefly a mission station, Rorke's Drift was now a British army camp.

Witt could do little about it. He sent his wife and children to live in a house several miles away for he did not think it dignified for them to be surrounded by so many men and for them to live in such noisy and smelly conditions. He himself stayed. To keep an eye on his property.

Standing on the front verandah of his new house the Reverand looked out at the hustle and bustle of the various military units passing to and fro. Below the mission the gun crews of 'N' Battery were going through yet more drills, their commander, Lieutenant Colonel Harness, and his second in command, Brevet Major Stuart Smith, pushing them relentlessly to a high level of efficiency. In the process the wheels of the six gun pieces were cutting up the ground, leaving deep ruts in the rain-soddened land. Witt tutted to himself and stood there with arms folded and shaking his head. Why here? he asked himself. Why here?

Everywhere he looked it was the same. A company of Redcoats marched passed through the rain. A cluster of horsemen galloped up from the river. Yet another convoy of heavily-laden wagons were just rumbling in. What a sight! What an awful desecration!

He was still casting a disgruntled eye over the proceedings when he became aware of somebody walking up towards him. The person stopped alongside him on the wooden verandah but Witt did not turn, for he knew who it was before looking. Instead he continued to watch the line of wagons that were just turning off the muddy track to take up position on the flat ground below the shoulder of the hill.

After a few moments the new arrival said, rather apologetically, "why, Mr Witt, I'm awfully sorry about all of this upheaval we're causing. I'm most embarrassed."

Witt turned and looked at him only briefly, then turned his severe eyes back towards the line of wagons and their bellowing oxen. As he watched they started to foul on his ruined garden.

The man beside him, a British Officer named Gonville Bromhead, followed his gaze and he chewed awkwardly at his lower lip. "I'm sure the British Government will offer you full recompense for any damage caused to your property," he said. "And it is only a temporary thing. This war will not last long they say. In a few weeks from now your home will look as it did before we descended upon you."

Witt raised his eyebrows in apparant disbelief, which he finally voiced in broken English, his accent so strong that Bromhead-already a little hard of hearing-had difficulty in understanding what he said.

"Let us only hope you are right, my friend."

Lieutenant Bromhead frowned underneath the brim of his helmet. He did not know what else to say. He stood and watched the rain, which was starting to come down heavier now.

"Your company is to stay here, I believe?" Wirt asked him.

"That's correct sir. On garrison duty. The boys aren't too happy at the prospect for they think they'll miss all the fun when the column crosses."

"But an important job, is it not?"

Bromhead paused before answering, and when he did he sounded a little peevish. "So they tell me, sir, so they tell me."

Reverand Witt glanced at his companion, who he had taken a liking to over the past few days since he and his men had arrived at the drift. The hard look on his face finally relaxed.

"You also do not sound pleased. You wish to go over the river and fight, instead of stay?"

"Of course. Forgive me, Reverand, but I am a soldier and fighting is my business. It is all I have known for most of my adult life.

Garrison duty may be important but it is hardly glamorous work and my lads feel niffed that we are being left behind."

"Niffed?" Witt asked confused.

"Beg pardon sir?" Bromhead asked and leaned his ear closer.

"Never you mind, my son." He patted Bromhead on his shoulder. "And don't you worry about all of this. I will be staying here to watch them take apart my house brick by brick."

"I'm sure it won't come to that. It will be nice to have you here though. The next few weeks are sure to be tediously dull for us unlucky ones."

They both laughed gently.

Meanwhile the preparations went on around them.

"Tell me again what you have heard Mr Fynney. Crealock here says you have some vital information for us. Please, in your own time."

Chelmsford, together with his staff and the border agent, Mr H. Fynney, were walking along the slippery river bank away from the new army camp that was still forming up on the lower slopes of Shiyane/Oskarberg hill. Just below them, the brown waters of the Mzinyathi raced by. The river was in spate because of the heavy rains and passage on foot was no longer advisable, certainly not for the British Infantry, and so work was under way to construct a pontoon which, together with an improvised barrel raft, would be used to ferry the men across once the invasion commenced. The work should be done by sunset. If so, then it fitted in perfectly with Chelmsford's plans to begin the crossing in the morning. However, the news that Fynney had just passed on to his military secretary was a little disturbing, even though it had been expected for some time.

Chelmsford thought the little man was somewhat shifty. He also thought he could do with a thorough wash and a change of clothes. Nevertheless, inspite of his shortcomings, the man was very good at his job. He had recently compiled a list of all the chief Zulu Indunas together with a detailed analysis of all the various Zulu regiments, including their individual regalia and the location of their kraals, which Chelmsford had printed up in a pamphlet and distributed amongst his invasion force. This would help them immensly in the coming war. The information was top-class, and Chelmsford had told him so personally. Now he had more news to tell. Just how he came across this information was a mystery to Chelmsford and he did not ask too many prying questions. All that mattered to him was that Fynney was proving to be an invaluable asset.

He waited patiently for him to respond.

"Well you see General, it's like this." As they walked he shoved his small clay pipe into his mouth and sucked on the smoke in between each sentence. "My sources inside Zululand, and, mind you, they're very reliable as you well know, have brought something to my attention... News which I happen to think is very important... In view of what is about to happen..."

Behind them Chelmsford noticed his military secretary silently fuming. He caught his eye and the General gave a little shake of his head to warn Crealock off from speaking forth his exasperation.

"It is only over the last few days that they have noticed, mind... About two or three days to be precise... It took them a while to get the news to me... After all, they are taking a risk in talking with white people right now, as I'm sure you can understand."

"Yes," Chelmsford acknowledged. "It is surprising what dangers people living under a despot are willing to take."

"Yes... A despot our Mr Cetshwayo most certainly is..."

"Their courage will not be forgotten when all of this is over Mr Fynney, you can have my word on that. We only want what is best for the Zulu people." Chelmsford drew them to a halt close to some trees, where they sheltered from the rain. He looked directly at the little man and asked him politely, "what news did they give you, my friend?"

"It's about the young men General."

"I presume you mean the Zulu warriors?"

"That's right."

"What of them?"

"Well they've disappeared sir."

"Disappeared?"

"Completely... All of the young men along the border have gone, vanished... We've seen lots of them recently, groups of warriors watching us watching them, keeping an eye on what we are up to... Then, a few days ago, they just got up and went, pulled back from the river and left... The lot of 'em... They've hopped it sir..."

"I see." Chelmsford turned his gaze on the hills across the river. So green and verdant now after the rains. And so empty of Zulu warriors, according to Mr Fynney. It could only mean one thing.

"Crealock, you understand what this implies?" he asked.

The Colonel moved closer to his General.

"Cetshwayo must have called a general muster," Chelmsford explained, although he was pretty sure his secretary had worked it out for himself. "They've being watching us get ready and now they've finally realized that they have no option but to fight. They are drawing back from the border and will probably form their impis somewhere near their capital. Oh, I'm sure they have left a few men behind, to watch us and maybe to try and slow down our advance, but it is apparant to me that they mean to meet us in force some distance inside their country."

"That's just what I was thinking," put in Fynney, just for the record.

The rest of Chelmsford's staff officers stood in a cluster and thought hard about the implications of precisely what this latest development actually meant. What it did mean, and they were all quick to come to this same conclusion, was that a big showdown with the main Zulu army was now inevitable. The only question was where and when? This intelligence just handed to them suggested that somewhere within the Zulu hinterland Cetshwayo's regiments were gathering and preparing. Their job would be to find them and destroy them. Hopefully on ground of their own choosing.

The younger officers could not help feeling a certain amount of nervousness. Some of them had never seen action before. That they soon would was a sobering thought.

Lord Chelmsford stepped out from under the sheltering branches of the trees and moved up towards the edge of the river. Once more he looked into the distance.

"Mr Fynney, that range of hills in the distance there. What are they called?"

The small man reluctantly joined him in the pouring rain and followed the General's pointing finger. "That is the Nqutu Range sir."

"But that hill there. The one that is seperate from the rest, on the right skyline. Isolated all by itself?"

"That one is called Isandlwana."

"Ah. A strange name for a strange hill. It seems to crouch like some sleeping beast, does it not?"

Fynney said nothing and just shrugged his shoulders.

"Unusual," Chelmsford commented, "It draws the eye."

Behind him Colonel Crealock gave a polite cough to gain the Generals attention. Chelmsford glanced at his secretary, who asked him, "Do we still go ahead as scheduled my Lord? Or does this latest intelligence change things?"

Chelmsford smiled and seemed most animated for once. "On the contrary! If the Zulus wish to offer themselves up for destruction then it will save us the bother of hunting them down. We cross tomorrow and will set up a temporary camp on the opposite bank, that is in Zululand. The crossing may be opposed so we should be on our guard. Then, after we have scouted ahead, we will begin to move forward along the route towards the Zulu capital." He pointed in a generally eastern direction. "If my reckoning is correct our path should take us fairly close to that hill there. The one called Isandlwana."

Chelmsford moved away from the river and surveyed the large British camp spreading out on the flat ground. Men and equipment were arriving from Helpmekaar all the time but the majority were already in place. Tonight he would order the evening tatoo to be sounded early for he planned on a very early start the next day. Apart from last minute preparations everything was ready. His invasion force was poised. Tomorrow would see them at war with the Zulus.

CHAPTER 13

ZULULAND. THE ONDINI *IKHANDA,* KING CETSHWAYO'S ROYAL
RESIDENCE. MAHLABATHINI PLAIN.
EARLY-EVENING, 10th JANUARY 1879.

With the army fully mustered and gathered in the central enclosure, and thousands more on the hills surrounding, it seemed that the men that made up the many regiments stretched from there to the sea.

The *amabutho* had come in over the last few days after the order to gather was sent out, either by runner or by being shouted from hilltop to hilltop, the men stretching out the syllables of important words so that on still days the calls carried great distances and echoed from hill to valley to mountain. In very short time the regiments had gathered at their local *ikhanda* and then set off on their journeys to their King's kraal. Those living close were expected to arrive by the following sunset, and over the next day or so they would be joined by those who had furthest to travel. From all over the country groups of men came, travelling light for they did not wear their full ceromonial regalia on this occassion as it was not the usual *umKhosi* festival that they gathered for. This was a general muster for war. Over mountain ranges and rivers they came, all converging on the same point. Ondini.

Once the whole army was gathered together they moved into the central enclosure and took up position depending on the seniority of their regiments. The older, often married regiments, were at the top near the *isigodlo,* while the younger men were down near the gates. Others had to contend with watching the proceedings from outside the fence so many men were there.

With such a crush of people and with the excitement of the occasion often overwhelming them, vicious stick fights occasionally broke out. These were quickly broke up by the regimental *izindunas* and the offenders carried out in disgrace, their heads often split open by the heavy knobkerries used liberally on them.

The army was given beer to drink and food to eat and then they waited for their King to appear before them.

The excitement built as the day drew on. Towards the end of the afternoon the skies cleared and they watched the sun set behind the western horizon.

Finally the King stepped out of his hut and came through the gate of the *isigodlo.* He moved into the central enclosure, dancing and shouting out "Ima! Ima! Ima!- Stand!" In his right hand he carried the sacred spear called inhlendla with its crescent-shaped blade and which he thrust repeatedly at the sky so that it glinted in the setting sun.

The multitude before him craned their necks to get a glimpse of him. The mass of people seemed to swell forward like a wave crashing at his feet. And he danced about, and he held aloft his spear, and he cried "Ima!."

His army of warriors picked up this chant and in so doing they were letting it be known that his reign would continue. Then, to add to their encouragement, they started to sing the mournful song of *ingoma,* a praise to his ancestral spirits. Finally they roared the royal salute, some 30,000 voices roaring in unison, over and over. "Bayethe!" The sound swelled and lifted out of the *ikhanda* into the orange sky. They stamped their feet onto the hardpacked earth kicking up clouds of swirling dust. To anyone present it was the greatest spectacle of their lives.

They felt simply invincible.

After a long time the King stopped dancing and the men stopped chanting and a suffocating hush descended.

Then this portly man turned and addressed them, his voice carrying far in the sudden stillness.

"Is this the whole impi then?" the King called.

"Bayethe!" came the single-throated response.

"My children, our enemies wish to lay waste our crops. Our good labours will have been in vain. I see a terrible storm coming and it is the white man. These white dogs are waiting on the far side of the river that seperates our two lands, but they mean to cross and come over. They come closer, like the sea on the rising tide steadily gaining ground."

An audible gasp came from the crowd as they listened.

"They mean to destroy us. They say I am a bad King, but do you complain?" "Bayethe! Ima!"

"Some of our children have done wrong they say. I am ordered to give them over to the whites. But they are only boys and it was a wild freak of theirs. Tell me, am I to hand them over?"

"Weugh!" they cried in alarm at this suggestion, and a buzz of uncertainty spread amongst them like some infectious disease.

"What will they demand next? The whites used to be our friends but now they wish to fight a war. I fear that if we do not fight then we shall not long remain in our good houses."

The King prowled around infront of the gate leading to the *isigodlo* and his intelligent eyes watched them for their reaction. In the faces of those nearest him, the older men fortunate to be at the front, he saw a pride blazing inside them. Their eyes were eager and wide as they remembered their past glories. Some of them he knew had fought under the great Shaka. The younger ones were also keen for battle, he could tell by the way they panted with excitement. Soon they would be seeing nothing but red, the red blood of their enemy, the whites.

"Lift up your guns!" he cried. "Show me them."

Across the vast assembly a few arms were raised holding a variety of old firearms. The majority of the warriors did not possess a gun however.

"So there are no guns?" the King mocked. "Each man with a beast from his place must bring it up next day and buy guns!"

Cetshwayo once more lifted up the sacred spear and the reflection of the setting sun on its surface seemed, just for a second, to glint in the eyes of every warrior present. They were filled with a fire that made even the King shiver with emotion. Then he turned and walked back through the low gate of the *isigodlo,* hearing the roar behind.

"BAYETHE!"

CHAPTER 14

THE BRITISH CAMP AT RORKE'S DRIFT.
BEFORE DAWN, SATURDAY 11th JANUARY 1879.
DAY OF THE INVASION.

The pre-dawn stillness was broken by the haunting sound of trumpets carrying through the camp area.

It was dead on 2 o'clock and the men were being roused early from their sleep. They struggled to get themselves dressed in the darkness. Muffled curses could be heard from inside the hundreds of tents as they stumbled about, searching for their equipment, their minds slow to respond to the summons. Their protests were in vain. Orders were orders and they each knew that today there was good reason for this early start.

At the urging of their NCO's the men started to appear from their tents, some still fastening their belts or adjusting their webbing, or rubbing hands over tired faces. When they came out into the cold air it was enough to chase away any lingering dregs of sleep. A steady drizzle was falling and the men reluctantly fell-in, shivering as they dressed their ranks and awaited further orders.

The night before Lord Chelmsford had decided on the order that the column would cross. He was keen to have a strong force on the far shore as soon as possible, incase the Zulus did put in an early appearance, therefore to achieve this he ruled that the men would cross at three seperate points simultaneously. The first regular Infantry to move would be the 1/24th, who would cross by pont and under cover of their sister battalion, the 2/24th, who were to line a ridge on this side and watch them safely across. At the same time the 1st Battalion of the 3rd Regiment, Natal Native Contingent, under their Irish commander Hamilton-Browne, were to wade over in the chest high water a little downstream while the 2nd Battalion/3rd would do the same but a mile or so upstream from where the pants were. The various mounted units would accompany the NNC, and when on the far shore they were to push the perimeter of this bridgehead outwards in order to secure the surrounding area and to act as the eyes and ears of the column whilst the remaining men, then the wagons, were ferried over. The six guns of the Royal Artillery would take up position on the lower slopes of Shiyane hill, their muzzles trained on the far side of the river, the men poised for any eventuality.

With all of this worked out in advance it was just a matter of issueing the necessary commands to set things in motion. It still, however, took time. Limbering up the guns and moving them over the rough ground to their assigned position was a time consuming process, as was getting the British Infantry down to the rivers edge. All of their camp equipment had first to be packed onto the wagons and the animals fed. The NNC found it difficult to follow orders for very few of them spoke English and very few of their officers spoke Zulu. Other means of making them understand were soon discovered; the threat and often the use of violence. Their NCO's, a brutal and unruly bunch at the best and made up of ex soldiers and runaway sailors and east London boatmen and other such undesirables, were more than willing to use their fists to move their men along. Their language was equally unsympathetic. Under such duress their black charges soon learnt what was required of them.

By the time the column had moved down to the waters edge and were in their various positions the rain had stopped. It had been replaced, as was often the case at such an hour and at this time of the year, by a thick, low-lying mist that seemed to seep out of the damp earth. It lay over the land in every direction and cut visibility down to a few dozen yards.

This caused Lord Chelmsford additional concern. He was already worried that the crossing would be opposed by their enemy and this mist would aide the Zulus if they did decide to fight. His men would be unable to spot them until they were virtually right on top of them, by which stage it might be too late. Yet he could not call a halt now.

Accompanied by his staff he rode up and down on the Natal shore and nervously peered into the thick mist. Finally he decided he could wait no longer. The order to begin the crossing was given.

Down below the men of H-Company, 1/24th, were beginning to get restless. They were standing close to the wooden pont that would very shortly be ferrying them across to enemy territory. Infact they would be the first to go over and the waiting was making them nervous. This, they all agreed, was the worst time. Those final few minutes of hanging around before they moved out. They just wanted to be on their way, to be doing something, for if they were busy then they had little time for considering the possible dire consequances of their actions, the terrible fates that might be awaiting them, hidden somewhere in the mist. Anything was preferable to this horrible waiting. Their faces were etched with lines of tension and despite the fact that the day was still cold their throats became dry from their growing anxiety. Even Colour-Sergeant Wolfe was strangely quiet for once.

At long last the order was passed down.

The men shuffled forward onto the wooden decking of the pont.

Creaking and groaning under their weight and rocking slightly in the fast flowing water, the boat moved forward as men on shore worked the hawsers. Heaving on the ropes they watched as the pont disappeared into the mist.

One of those on board was Private Robert Metcalfe. Bunched around him were his mates. Normally a cheerful lot today they were very subdued as each man peered ahead and tried to pick out the far shore. Robert felt his stomach suddenly tie up into a tight knot and he gripped the butt of his Martini-Henry that little bit tighter as they floated further out over the river. Quickly he stole a glance over to the man at his side.

Private Charlie Noakes did not look back. Infact, he did not look anywhere, for he had his eyes tightly shut. A slight sheen of persperation covered his ashen face. He had a sudden overwhelming desire to go to the latrine and he fidgeted from foot to foot to try and ease this embarrassing discomfort. Then he started to whisper a prayer to himself, something he hadn't done for a long, long time, and he wondered why the idea should suddenly have come to him now. It did not make him feel any better.

Robert was about to ask him if he was alright but a sudden thump on the underside of the pont informed everyone on board that they had reached the opposite side. The banking stretched gently away into the misty greyness, dotted here and there with aloe plants and thorn bushes. Beyond that they could see nothing.

With Colour-Sergeant Wolfe ordering them forward at the double the men of H-Company jogged up the Zulu bank and were soon lost from sight.

Back over on the Natal side of the river, Lord Chelmsford and his staff, together with the rest of the column, waited anxiously. The minutes that followed were spent in fretful silence as they awaited a response from the company just sent over. Many of them, from General on down, were half expecting to hear a crash of volley fire to announce the commencement of battle. Each man present stared into the thick fog that obscured all view of what was happening over there. They each knew of the stories of Zulu prowess, of how they could creep up on an opponent with relative ease and dispatch them with hardly a sound. Some had dismissed these tales out of hand as nothing but ridiculous hokum. However, right now, it seemed that this was a very real possibility, especially in this weather. A frightful thought occurred to many men standing there; were those men who had just gone over being slaughtered this very minute, their poor bodies disembowled as they stood doing nothing to help.

A disheartening uncertainty seemed to smother them all.

Then there came a cry. A single voice calling out.

"This side is clear! Send the others across! I say again, the way is clear for the column to come over!"This was met by a buzz of relief that was shared by every single man and a nervous laughter passed through the ranks.

"Well, you heard the man, Colonel Glyn," Chelmsford said to the column commander. "Shall we start the men across?"

The first hurdle had been passed. British troops were inside Zululand.

While the Infantry was in the process of crossing on the ponts a little further upstream the 2/3rd NNC, together with elements of the mounted volunteers, were preparing to wade across. A point in the river where the water was only chest deep and the bottom rocky and firm had been discovered and it was decided that they could cross here on foot. A body of cavalry led by Major Russell went first, splashing their way over and clambering up the slippery bank on the far side. Next it was the turn of the Natal Kaffirs, distinguishable by the red rag they wore tied around their heads. At first they were reluctant to go. In the early morning light and the damp fog the water looked very uninviting to their near-naked bodies and they stood on the shore shivering and with their teeth chattering. Finally they dragged themselves down to the waters edge and took the plunge.

Fearful that there might be crocodiles lurking in the area the first Company moved out across the river in two single files with each man holding hands with the person to his front and rear to form a double chain right across to the opposite side. This left a pathway through the centre for the remainder of the battalion to pass through. Immediately upon entering the cold water they had started to hum a sort of war-chant, and each Company that then moved through this passage joined in, creating a peculiar buzzing sound that to their white NCO's sounded like a huge swarm of gigantic bees. The noise carried over the water. It was a strange spectacle that amused their officers but it seemed to work for in a very short time the whole battalion was safely on the Zulu bank.

The same could not be said for their companions downriver.

The 1/3rd had been ordered to ford the river on a wide and sweeping bend where the flow of the water was much faster. In order to gain the far bank the men pushed into the water enmasse and swept forward so that the weight of those behind carried the men at the front across. Mostly, it worked. A few unfortunate individuals on the outer edges lost their footing however and went under. Despite the attempts of their friends to hold onto them a few were lost, their drowning bodies together with their screams carried rapidly downriver. Nobody ever learnt for certain exactly how many men were swept to their deaths in this way for a full count had never been made in the first place. It was probably only a handful, their officers insisted. The matter was therefore soon forgotten.

The dangers of crossing the Mzinyathi at this pointwas not just confined to those wading over on foot. Members of the Mounted Infantry were also using this stretch to reach the Zulu bank and one of them suddenly found himself in difficulties as he reached the halfway point. Here the river was up to the troopers saddle bags and very fast flowing. His mount had lost its footing and before he had chance to react both man and beast were being swept downriver in a torrent of white spray.

On shore a cry of alarm went up.

With hardly a second thought for his own safety a Captain Hayes urged his own horse, a splendid white charger, into the raging torrent. Miraculously he somehow managed to grasp a hold of the drowning trooper and dragged him to safety by the white webbing of his drenched uniform. To the sound of cheers from his companions Captain Hayes got the man back onto dry soil, who then thanked him profusely and much to his embarrassment.

The trooper's horse was not so lucky. Its battered and broken body was found eight miles downstream several days later.

By this time the sun had risen and the mist quickly began to dissipate. In the space of a few minutes full visibility returned and the crossing could now be more effectively covered by the six guns of the Royal Artillery. This came as a relief in more ways than one for several of the mounted units had wandered off into the mist upon reaching enemy territory and they were mightily glad when they were able to find their way back to the main body of the column that was starting to gather on this side of the river. As ordered they now started to establish a long line of videttes on the ridge overlooking the crossing, their eyes scanning the hills in the near distance.

By about six-thirty the bulk of the 1/24th and 2/24th were safely over, as were the NNC and mounted volunteers. They joined the men on the high ground and formed a rough skirmishing line that stretched for almost three miles. With no sign of any resistance from their Zulu opponents the men at last began to relax at their posts. The sun climbed higher in the sky and the morning grew rapidly warmer, drying their clothes. They settled down as the long process of bringing over the transports got underway.

While all of this was going on Lord Chelmsford had been overseeing operations from the Natal bank with a growing feeling of satisfaction. With no opposition from the Zulus everything so far was on schedule. A short time later he announced that he would now cross the river. His staff gathered about him and they were ferried over on the barrel raft.

Once on Zulu soil a strong cavalry escort made up of about a hundred Mounted Infantry and some Natal Mounted Police were quickly formed up in column and Chelmsford took his place at the front. They were to ride north to meet up with the commander of No 4 column, Left Flank, Colonel Wood who had been sent instructions to likewise ride south. They would, if all went well, link up about a dozen miles upriver where information and fresh instructions would be exchanged. Chelmsford intended their two columns to synchronize their movements but also for Wood to hopefully draw off any Zulu forces he could to hopefully give the Centre Column a clear run to the Zulu capital. Therefore this impromptu meeting in somewhat strange circumstances had been called for.

When all were ready Chelmsford and his cavalry pushed through the British perimeter up on the ridge and set out to the north at a steady trot. He left Colonel Glyn in charge of the crossing, informing him as he rode away that they should be back by the middle of the afternoon.

The morning wore on and soon became scorching hot.

Moving the transport wagons was tiring and laborious work. Only one wagon and its draught oxen could be fitted onto the pont and barrel raft at any one time, and it was a slow process of loading them and then working the hawsers back and forth. Also, the banks on either side were steep and muddy and difficult for the animals to negotiate so a company of the Native Pioneer Corps set to work making a deep cutting on each side of the river to ease the situation. Still, it was monotonous labour for the transport officers and conductors.

For the men up on the ridge there was nothing much to do except wait the day out. There was very little shade to be found and the hot sun started to have a detremental effect on their alertness.

Conversation soon died away. It was too hot to sleep. The air was filled with the sound of buzzing insects.

Towards the right hand end of the line were the Natal Carbineers. Just sixty strong they were a close knit group made up of men drawn from settler society formed into an armed body to act as a local defence force in times of crisis. They had agreed to join Chelmsfords invasion force because of a promise that each man would be given land to farm on once hostilities were over, and also because they had no love for the Zulus. They enjoyed their outdoor life and the companionship it offered and amoungst their ranks were more than a few family connections.

For example there were the two Symons brothers, Jack and Fred. Inseperable as children and still so now, they sat together on the grassy ridge. With them was their friend Ted Greene.

They had each constructed a kind of shelter to escape the blazing sunshine. This comprised of four assegais stuck into the ground and a large cowhide shield taken from some of the Natal kaffirs resting on top under which they lay. The shade these three shelters provided was extremely welcome to them, but they were still uncomfortably hot. They each wished for something to do for this heat would be more tolerable if they were at least being kept busy. As it was the morning seemed neverending.

Sometime towards mid-day they were given a brief respite from this tedious inactivity. As they lay there watching the ponts leisurely moving from river bank to river bank and the steady buildup of supplies and transports on this side gradually increase the gentle sound of lowing cattle drifted to them on the soft breeze. Everyone who heard it turned towards the noise.

In the near distance stood the solitary figure of an elderly Zulu watching them with great curiosity. Closeby was a small herd of cattle.

Quickly the men came to their feet and reached for their firearms, their eyes carrying out a quick search of the surrounding countryside. They soon established that there was knowbody else, such as armed Zulu warriors, in the vicinity. So an order went out. The herdsman together with his cattle was to be brought in. The task of doing this fell to the Natal Carbineers.

Mounting up as fast as they could they set off at a gallop, digging their spurs into their horses flanks and whooping and cheering as they charged over the rocky ground. Trooper Fred Symons found himself near the front and the excitement of the moment gripped him. As he rode he felt a wild thrill pass through him and he stole a quick glance at those around him, seeing that they shared this sensational feeling. What a wonderful spree this was!

In the space of a couple of minutes they had covered the ground between the river and the lone herdsman. He made no attempt to flee but instead he just stood there with a slightly bemused look on his face. In very short time the lead carbineers had comandeered his cattle and were questioning him. No resistance was offered and the whole affair was over in no time at all, with the old man and his beasts being brought back over to the British position with very little trouble. They had made their first catch of the day. It had been an invigorating, if short-lived, diversion for the men.

Across the Mzinyathi River, on the lower slopes of Shiyane where they had set up their guns, the men of N Battery, 5th Brigade, Royal Artillery, watched the horsemen come back in with their captured cattle and the single prisoner. They laughed and shook their heads and joked about how brave they had been in taking on the cream of the legendary Zulu Army. What courage they had shown, what reckless disregard for their own safety! They went back to their duties with a spring in their step, polishing the barrels of the seven pounder guns and keeping their vigil of the crossing going on below.

Opposite them a new campsite was being set up. The first on Zulu soil it stretched along the river bank, row after row of round white tents, growing larger with each wagon that was brought over. Supplies of food and ammunition and all the other paraphernalia that was necessary to keep the invasion on course was being stacked to one side and covered over with tarpaulins incase the unpredictable weather broke again. Horse lines were strung between wooden posts and a special area reserved for the cattle and transport was set up downriver so that the camps water supply wouldn't be contaminated by the draught oxen. The ambulance carts crossed next, then the veterinary surgeon with his half dozen pack animals weighed down with his baggage.

Midday came and went. The Imperial soldiers ate bully beef and biscuits washed down with a pannikin of muddy coffee, while the native levies were given a handful of mealee's and water. A few patrols were sent out to scout the immediate vicinity but they came back to report that no contact had been made with the enemy. All they had come across were a few deserted homesteads that had apparantly been abandoned with some haste. Of the Zulu Army there was no sign. It seemed that they had indeed pulled back from the border area.

Lord Chelmsford also had no run-in with them. While the rest of the Centre Column was still being ferried over and beginning to establish itself on Zulu soil he and his cavalry escort had riden north along the eastern side of the Mzinyathi. Shortly after nine o'clock and about ten miles into their journey a cloud of dust had been spotted on the horizon and coming in their direction. They had grown a little tense as it approached wondering whether it was being kicked up by friendly forces or by a large Zulu impi deploying for attack. Ten minutes later they had their answer. A column of horsemen, trotting steadily towards them.

It turned out to be Major Buller and the Frontier Light Horse. Greetings were exchanged and the two groups dismounted. Buller then explained that this was the advance force and that Colonel Wood should be arriving shortly for the rendezvous with Lord Chelmsford, but in the meantime he would bring the General up to date on what the Left Flank Column had been doing.

The news was good. Colonel Wood had brought his column across the Ncome (Blood) River the day before and had established his first campsite at Bemba's Kop close to the Lyn Spruit stream. He had also spent a great deal of time rounding up Zulu cattle and they had so far captured almost 2000 up to the present time. Yet, like the Centre Column, they too had met with no armed resistance so far. All was quiet and not a shot had been fired in anger.

As they were chatting Colonel Wood himself had finally arrived. He apologized for the delay but he explained to Chelmsford that they had broke off from their march to give chase to a couple of zulu herdsmen. He'd brought their prisoners, along with more captured cattle and a few goats, with them. Chelmsford had brightened considerably at hearing this and he announced that he would immediately question the two in person. They were brought forward and with the help of the interpreter, James Brickhill, he started to ask them about what they knew of the whereabouts of the Zulu Army.

It turned out they knew very little. They were only boys and had not even known that a war was underway. Frustrated, Chelmsford spelled out to them in no uncertain terms that he had crossed into Zululand in force and would be seeking the total surrender of their King and the destruction of his impis. He then let them go. He hoped they would take this news all the way to Ulundi, thus leaving Cetshwayo in no doubt what fate awaited him and his people.

Returning to the matter at hand he and Colonel Wood began their meeting, where he gave his friend his new instructions.

They then took a leisurely lunch before going their seperate ways.

Chelmsford was back at Rorke's Drift by the middle of the afternoon.

On his return he had spent some time alone in his headquarters tent considering what options lay open to them over the coming days.

It was becoming increasingly apparant that their planned advance would now be much slower than originally forecast. The recent heavy rains had had a detremental effect on the condition of the track and parties of Engineers would have to be sent forward to make some repairs to it before the heavy supply wagons would be able to move forward. A series of intermediary campsites would also be set up along the way with convoys moving their supplies too and fro as the column inched forward. Therefore it would be several days before they could advance from the river.

In the meantime there was other pressing matters for them to think about, most notably a wish to have their presence felt now that they were in Zululand. So he sent for the column commander, Colonel Glyn.

When he arrived Chelmsford beckoned him forward and they both leant over a map which he had spread out on his desk. He started to explain the situation to him.

"You see Richard, if we follow the track eastwards after a few miles it drops into this valley here and crosses this stream, the Batshe. Apparantly the ground around here is of a very boggy nature with numerous springs popping up here and there. We will need to lay down a new surface before we can attempt to get our wagons across." Chelmsford paused and kept his finger on the map at the point the track crossed the stream. "That is when our first major problem arises." He slid his finger up the stream and tapped at the map.

Colonel Glyn leaned his face closer to the map and squinted at it. He nodded, and then said quietly, "Yes, I see what you mean." His dark moustache twitched.

"Somewhere here, further up the valley, is KwaSokhexe. Chief Sihayo's homestead. Obviously we cannot send the pioneers forward into hostile country without first dealing with the threat his people pose, nor can we just bypass them altogether and leave them in place to either threaten our flank or to harass our supply lines. What's more, our intelligence suggests that they mean to try and oppose our advance, although we haven't seen anything of them as of yet."

"Plus we have the little matter of the involvement of his sons in the border incident last year and the fine imposed on him which has still to be collected."

"Precisely."

Colonel Glyn straightened himself. "You wish me to take some form of action against him?" he politely enquired.

"I do indeed. I think it is time we demonstrated our intentions to the Zulus. It's not my plan to sit here on the border and wait for them to come to us, we must take this war to them. First thing in the morning I want you to take a sizeable portion of our force forward to the Batshe valley and attack KwaSokhexe. You can expect to meet some determined resistance so it should give the men a fairly robust test, and we can see how they acquit themselves."

"I'm sure it is nothing they can't handle. The men are keyed up for a fight."

"Quite."

"And what of Sihayo's sons, my Lord? Are we to apprehend them?"

Chelmsford half smiled as he rolled up the map. "Only if they lay down their arms without a fight, which I think is hardly likely. They are fugitives after all and wanted for murder. It might be the case that they are not even there but have answered the Kings muster at Ulundi. But the rules of engagement are no different

136

than usual: prisoners are to be taken if possible and no women and children are to be harmed. That last point must be made clear to our native contingent. Apart from that, you are to use whatever force you think the situation warrants."

"Very good my Lord."

"Don't look too worried, Richard. I will be there to watch the attack should you need any guidance."

"What about Sihayo's kraal itself?"

Chelmsford slid the map into its leather case and fastened its straps, then placed it inside a wooden trunk. He carefully closed the lid. Then he turned to Glyn and said darkly, "burn it to the ground."

*   *   *

With the onset of dusk the operation to bring the column across into Zululand was coming to an end. It had mostly gone as planned. Only a few boxes of supplies - along with several members of the NNC - had been lost, and both were easily replaceable. A single company of the 2/24th were to remain on garrison duty at Rorke's Drift, while the artillery would cross first thing in the morning. The new campsite that nestled along the rivers eastern bank was complete. A screen of picquets were posted and darkness quickly came on. The men settled down and turned in early. Soon, everything was quiet.

The long wait was nearly over.

In the morning Lord Chelmsford's Centre Column would be going into action

CHAPTER 15

ONE MILE ALONG THE TRACK INTO ZULULAND. EAST OF THE
BRITISH CAMP AT RORKE'S DRIFT.
BEFORE DAWN, SUNDAY 12th JANUARY 1879.

For the second day running the men of the Centre Column were
on the move early. The first pale beginnings of dawn were yet to
streak the eastern horizon as the camp came to life and the various
units formed themselves in column. The supply wagons were to be
left behind for this was not to be a general advance forward, and as
they would be back in camp by early afternoon they only took a
days rations with them. So it did not take the men long to get
themselves ready. Within a half hour they were on the move.

The Volunteers and Mounted Infantry led them into the
darkness with Lord Chelmsford and Colonel Glyn at their head.
Behind these were both battalions of the NNC, the 1/3rd
commanded by Hamilton (Maori) Browne, the 2/3rd by
A.W.Cooper, but with the whole force of natives under a somewhat
peppery natured Scot called Wilsone Black. Next came four
companies of the 1/24th. The Second Battalion was to follow them
on sometime later.

A multitude of shimmering stars shone brightly from the clear
sky, in stark contrast to the misty start to the previous day, but as
the column progressed and left the campsite behind they gradually
started to dim as the dark african night finally came to an end. On

leaving the riverbank the dirt track they followed crested a slight rise before dropping into the Batshe valley beyond, and by the time the lead units were disappearing over the brow of the hill the distant horizon was starting to brighten. The ground beyond was marshy and as they neared the stream that lay at the bottom they soon found themselves splashing through muddy water.

Soon it was light enough to see the valley they were making for. On the western side was a long, low, stony ridge that ran for several miles towards the Nqutu range, but across the stream the eastern side was dominated by a series of large crags and precipitous cliff faces, the lower slopes of which were boulder strewn and covered in a tangle of dense bush and thorn trees. This was known as Ngedla hill. Somewhere at its northern end, where the valley twisted back around on itself, was Chief Sihayo's homestead- KwaSokhexe.

At the head of the Column Lord Chelmsford lifted a pair of binoculars to his face and studied the rugged hillside a mile or so in the distance. He then handed them to Glyn, whose horse stood alongside his own. As of yet they could see nothing of the enemy. All seemed quiet. It made the two men nervous; either they had caught the Zulus napping or they were lying in wait for them. After a moment or two they continued forward, the long, snaking column behind following on.

A little further along the track and the sound of lowing cattle reached their ears, and once again they called a halt. This time they finally spotted some tiny figures in the distance, herders quickly shepherding their cattle up the valley bottom away from the approaching army. A quick discussion ensued between the two men, Chelmsford doing most of the talking, and they soon came to the conclusion that they had been spotted by the enemy who were hurrying to safety. It mattered not. They hadn't planned on a surprise attack anyway. This was to be a show of force, to give the Zulus a clear idea of their overwhelming superiority, and what better way than to go marching up to the gates of their kraal with a powerful body of armed men?

It was decided that before crossing the Batshe a plan of attack needed to be worked out. So with the sun starting to climb higher in the sky and the dawn chill soon gone Lord Chelmsford and his staff and Colonel Glyn and his staff all dismounted and held a brief meeting beside the track.

They would go in with a two pronged assault. The mounted men, which comprised of the Natal Mounted Police, the Mounted Infantry and the smaller Natal Carbineers, all led by Lieutenant-Colonel Russell who was marvelously attired in the uniform of the 12th Lancers, would sweep into the low ground at the southern end of the valley and ascend the hill from that direction. Once on the summit they would sweep any of the enemy who were up there before them, squashing any resistance and capturing as much cattle as possible. While this was going on the main attack would be taking place below them in the valley floor. This assault, against the numerous caves that pockmarked the cliff faces and where the bulk of any resistance was expected to be, would be the task of Hamilton-Browne's battalion of native troops and the 1/24th companies being commanded by Captain Degacher on their left. Later, the 2/24th and 2/3rd NNC and who were two or three hours behind, would move up the valley to destroy Sihayo's homestead itself and finish off any zulus there. The whole fight would be short, lasting maybe an hour, two at the most. Then the whole force would march back to camp with a good days work under their belt.

The necessary orders were passed down the line.

*　　　*　　　*

While the British were making their plans the Zulu men who had stayed behind to defend their home readied themselves for the expected attack. Most of them were middle-aged or older for the majority of the younger warriors had gone to Ondini to answer the King's muster. They were, nevertheless, keen for a fight. They had been watching the redcoats for the past few days, growing more and more alarmed as the number of white soldiers and their native slaves had steadily grown. When they had finally crossed over the river to their territory just the day before then they had known that a battle was unavoidable. It still came as a shock to see the column marching on their own homes however, and in such numbers.

A lot of blood would be spilt today. They would fight tooth and nail for every cave and boulder and crevasse. Their white enemies would see how the Zulu man fought.

When the young herdboys had come running in with their cattle shouting the alarm the men came running out of their huts with weapons in hand. Many of them owned firearms, a mixture of old flintlocks and muskets and elephant guns which they had acquired from white traders over the years, although their age and condition meant they lacked accuracy. The quality of the gunpowder was also poor. Yet this was the best they had. The rest were armed with traditional assegais and shield.

Running with sure-footed ease they sprinted over the rough ground. Leaping from boulder to boulder and making good use of any cover they soon found themselves good hiding places amongst the many caves and rocky fissures that scared the hillside. Still more climbed to the top and moved south, out of sight to anyone looking up from below.

Then, being careful not to show themselves, they peered around the rocks or through the vegetation and sought to get a glimpse of the white soldiers.

They waited patiently as their enemy came closer.

Commandant Hamilton-Browne, on horseback at the front of his battalion, could sense his men getting more and more nervous the further they descended into the valley. Whereas they had been quite chirpy on the march up, dancing and singing their war-chants, they had now fallen quiet as the imminence of battle grew ever closer. Having said that, their lack of fibre wasn't a complete surprise to their officers and NCO's. These Natal kaffirs, as they referred to them, were full of bluff and showmanship but their fighting spirit was somewhat wobbly at the best of times and when faced with an enemy of the likes of the Zulus they tended to show a marked reluctance to take the fight to them. The trouble was they needed to be led from the front and this was when the quality of their leaders was often drawn into question. Drawn from the dregs of colonial society the Contingent's officers weren't the most disciplined of men either and for the pittance that they earned they felt disinclined to put their own necks on the block. So there was little option: the onus to take the attack forward fell to Commandant Browne himself.

Ahead of the NNC the mounted men peeled off to the right. He watched them splash through the shallows of the Batshe and go cantering towards the southern end of the hill. Here there was a gentle slope that would allow them to ascend to the top relatively easy but this would still take them a little time during which the infantry would launch their attack from the valley floor. Hamilton-Browne waved his men forward into the gap the horsemen had left.

He saw that Lord Chelmsford and Colonel Glyn were waiting for him beside the stream where they had been holding their discussion. The Irishman trotted up to them and gave a crisp salute, which the two men returned.

"Are you ready for the off Commandant?" Chelmsford asked jovially.

"Yes. I've told the men that I expect nothing but the best from them. Poor niggers are a trifle nervous but I'm sure they'll settle when they have the first shower of spears tossed at them." Hamilton-Browne laughed out loud and the General, out of politeness, smiled back.

"Yes, well." He turned in his saddle and pointed off towards the rugged cliff faces over his shoulder with his swagger stick. "You see those krantzes there? They're full of Zulus and cattle. I want you to go down and deal with them and take what lifestock you can. On no account are you to fire on them before you are fired at first. Also, I shall hold you responsible that no women or children are killed. The British Army does not slay civilians. Do I make myself clear?"

"Well it's clear to me sir, but as you know most of my command are not British. My boys have a different way of fighting."

"Not when they are under Her Majesty's authority. It is down to you and your officers to get the message across to them. Any breach of this ruling will be dealt with very severely. Deal with the problem Hamilton-Browne. Me and Colonel Glyn shall be watching your attack go in from our vantage point. I want this to be a clean and quick operation, no messing about. You have your orders."

Commandant Browne nodded and trotted away, a deep frown etched on his face.

However he kept his thoughts to himself as he returned to his battalion and set about deploying them for the attack. He decided that his two best companies, each made up of disaffected Zulus who had come over to Natal some time back due to some dispute with their own people, would bare the brunt of the assault. One of them he would keep in the centre around which the initial push forward would be concentrated and which he would lead in person. The other he would send out to the right flank where they could hopefully occupy the high ground, once they had flushed out the enemy, from where they could lend some covering fire for the rest of the battalion. Not that the men were the best of shots. Infact he was more concerned about receiving casualties from his own guns than from enemy fire, so much so that he would prefer to take the attack in close and trust to the steel! He would have to keep a tight control of them.

When the men were ready and strung out on a long line he paused for a moment to consider their objective just over the stream.

He immediately recognized an area that could prove to be the toughest nut to crack. Just opposite him was a deep crevasse that cut deep into the cliff-face. Its entry was wide but strewn with enormous boulders and overgrown with dense vegetation, but as it disappeared into the valley side the walls closed in like a V-shape, the tip of which was hidden in deep shadow. It was a good position to hold. A dozen sharpshooters placed there would be able to hold back a whole column for as long as their ammunition lasted. He thought it a pretty good bet to think that the Zulus would see how vital it would be for them to hold on to this spot at all costs. The place could be a deathtrap.

Despite his misgivings he knew he could not delay any longer. The General was watching him closely.

Hamilton-Browne climbed down from his horse and handed the reins to one of his men. Then he pushed his way through the battalion's ranks to the front and gave the signal to advance.

It wasn't easy keeping the formation together as they splashed through the stream and up the gentle slope beyond. The line started to waver in a number of places and his officers and NCO's found it necessary to bully the men into continueing on.

After a short way the ground suddenly worsened. Large boulders blocked their way and loose rocks underfoot made the going difficult, and the hill became steeper the nearer they came to the valley wall.

Up to this point they had seen or heard nothing of the Zulus. This now changed. From out of the nooks and cranies there came the sound of a war chant being sung, one strong voice leading the others, all to the accompanyment of assegais and knobkerries being rattled against shields. The NNC, already uneasy, hesitated for a moment before nervously shuffling forward.

Just then this singing stopped. Then a single voice called out, speaking in heavily accented English.

"WHY DO YOU COME HERE? WHY DO YOU WANT TO FIGHT US? WHO ORDERS THIS?"

The words echoed around the gorge, bouncing from valley wall to valley wall. It brought the British to a complete halt.

Lord Chelmsford and his staff sat on their horses in dumbstruck silence. They had not expected this and it left them slightly bemused. Major Wilsone Black was the first to respond and when he did he spoke for all of them. Arching his eyebrows in surprise he said, and with complete sincerity, "Why I do believe these savages are talking to us. Jolly good of them to make the effort and learn the language."

Those around him burst out laughing and even Chelmsford couldn't stop a grin from appearing on his face.

They each continued to look over towards the enemy positions, waiting to see what happened next.

Commandant Hamilton-Browne turned when he heard someone approaching and saw that it was Captain Duncombe, the only Zulu-speaking white man in the battalion. He reached his side out of breath for he had rushed over from his position. Despite this he looked excited and keyed up, a covering of sweat on his red cheeks.

Hamilton-Browne looked at him closely, then at the cliffs, then back to Duncombe. He shrugged his shoulders and said, "Well I suppose you ought to answer."

The young officer nodded eagerly and cupped his hands around his mouth.

"BY THE ORDERS OF THE GREAT WHITE QUEEN!" he shouted back in English.

They waited a few moments with their eyes scanning the cliffs. Then, just as Hamilton-Browne was about to order his battalion forward again, there came a single rifle-shot.

About twenty feet away one of the NNC men went down, screaming and clutching his thigh. Blood fountained into his face as he rolled about on the grass in agony.

There was the briefest of pauses, then all hell broke loose as the Zulus let fly with everything they had, firing as quickly as they could reload their antiquated guns.

The 1/3rd found themselves heading into the heart of an intense and deadly firestorm.

CHAPTER 16

THE BATSHE RIVER VALLEY.
SUNDAY 12th JANUARY 1879.

The firing came at a terrific rate, ricocheting off the boulders amoungst which the men tried to find cover behind and slicing the tops off the long stalks of grass. It was badly aimed but the amount that was being laid down made the chance of being hit very high nonetheless. All along the line the NNC men went to ground, leaving just their white officers standing exposed. Hamilton-Browne saw this and lost his temper altogether. Ignoring the rounds whizzing around his head he stomped up to the nearest man who was lying prostrate in the grass and picked him up off the ground by his bandolier.

"You cowardly scum!" he screeched in the man's face. "Get on your feet and move forward!"

But the man was simply too petrified to even respond and his body went rigid with fear. Hamilton-Browne dropped him and turned to take out his fury on the officers instead. "Get these niggers moving, you damn fools! I want the whole battalion on its feet and moving forward! Now!"

They did as they were instructed, moving amongst the men and hitting out with either their fists or their rifle butts, threatening them with all manner of blasphemous language. Reluctantly they came to their feet but still crouched low and glancing back over their shoulders to where they preferred to be: about a couple of miles in the opposite direction! Eventually the battalion was ready. Hamilton-Browne, out in the front, pulled out his revolver. He quickly checked that it was loaded and then called out at the top of his voice,

"CHARGE!"

He dashed forward into the galling fire, making straight for the entrance to the V-shaped crevasse. Somewhere to his right he heard someone scream and was dimly aware of one of his officers dropping to the ground, his arm split open from elbow to wrist. He did not stop but kept on running and he soon found himself clambering over the large boulders that blocked the opening to the crevasse, his revolver at the ready and searching for a target. He slipped down behind a rock which was big enough to provide him with shelter, and then turned to see how the rest of his command was doing.

He was confronted with a shocking sight.

Apart from the young Lieutenant who had taken a hit in the arm and was dragging himself back to the rear, not a single man of the battalion had gone forward with the charge. They had all squatted down on the ground once again, but this time they had been joined by their officers and NCO's. Their attack had quickly descended into a complete shambles and all under the eye of the General.

Commandant Hamilton-Browne, fuming and screeching in rage, was for the time being all by himself.

Back over the Batshe Colonel Glyn saw the assault begin to stall. He felt an acute sense of being under observation as all eyes turned to him for an explanation. After all, he was commander of the Centre Column and his Lordship had personally given him control of the attack. Any failure at company or battalion level would ultimately be seen as a failure of the overall commander. He had to do something to retrieve the situation quickly. Making a snap decision, he turned to Major Wilsone Black, who was sitting in his saddle and staring straight ahead with a blank expression on his face.

"Major, it appears the Native Contingent has run into difficulties. Perhaps you could go forward with a detachment of the 24th to give them support."

"At once," Black growled, and then he cantered away towards the Imperial infantry who were getting ready to begin their flanking attack off on the left.

Things were getting pretty dicey, Hamilton-Browne thought to himself as he hunched down in the shelter of his rock. This was a hot little corner. At the moment there wasn't much he could do about the situation except wait and hope that someone noticed his predicament. After about five minutes and when there was still no help coming he seriously considered making a dash back to his own lines where at least he could try and organise a second charge. He was just about to do that very thing when he at last spotted movement coming from the direction of the stream. Redcoats! About four companies of them starting to deploy into the valley a little to the north, and heading his way a small detachment led by none other than Major Black!

Hamilton-Browne watched them come up behind his own battalion and then pause as they fixed bayonets.

The effect on his own men was marvelous. Fearful of the enemy fire ahead of them but even more scared of this line of infantry marching towards them with their bayonets glittering in the sun, they had no option but to advance into the mouth of the gorge. They came to their feet enmasse and resumed the assault.

Major Black led them on. He had drawn out his sword and was swishing it dramatically above his head, yelling and urging the men forward in ringing tones. In his other hand he held aloft his hat which he waved from side to side like he was greeting a dear friend. Just then a bullet cracked through the air closeby and clipped it out of his grasp. It spun through the air before landing on the ground. Undaunted and with an insane grin on his lips he bent and scooped it back up, beat it against his thigh to get the dust off, and then shoved it back upon his head. He turned to the men around him, who stared back like he was mad.

"Stay with me boys!" he yelled at them. "Let's give them some back! Pour it into them! POUR IT IN!"

They seemed to understand him for every man with a gun let it off in an instant, firing a wild volley and not taking a blind bit of notice as to which direction they were pointing the business end. It was a hellish moment for Hamilton-Browne, who flung himself face down as the bullets zipped and whirred over his head.

In the next instant Major Black was alongside him. "What a surprise to see you here," he joked.

Hamilton-Browne just glowered back. Nevertheless, he was glad to see him, and he quickly came to his feet and started to appraise him of the situation.

While they were speaking the deadly firefight went on. With the Imperial infantry now in support, the British were able to return accurate fire which not only kept the heads of any Zulu marksmen down but also started to pick them off one by one. It was a slow process though. The enemy had chosen their positions well and it soon became apparant to everybody that the only way to dislodge them and take the gorge would be to close with the Zulus and prise them out at the point of the bayonet.

The order to be ready for another charge was passed around. It would be a messy business and they expected to take casualties but the enemy had to be cleared and the task to do this had fallen to them. When all were ready everybody leapt to their feet when the word was given and poured into the entranceway of the crevasse.

Suddenly about twenty Zulus came from amongst a pile of rocks on the left, heading straight for them. A second group of over thirty dropped down from above where they had been hiding amoungst a clump of dead trees part way up the cliff-face. A fierce melee of hand-to-hand fighting erupted, with the NNC and Imperial infantry on one side, Sihayo's warriors on the other. Amongst the Zulu was the Chiefs youngest son Mkhumbikazulu, who was eager to get at the British and defend his father's honour. He rushed up to the first man he saw who happened to be a member of the NNC and wearing a red rag tied around his head. Their shields clashed together but Mkhumbikazulu was more agile of the two and with startling dexterity he slipped the bottom of his shield around the edge of his opponent's and flipped it up, pulling the man off balance and exposing the whole left side of his body. He thrust with his stabbing spear and it made a horrid ripping sound as it sliced neatly in between two ribs, then withdrew it again. The NNC man yelled in agony and began to topple over as his blood jettisoned out of the gaping wound, and Mkhumbikazulu stabbed again, this time through one of his buttocks and out through his groin. He slipped the blade of the assegais clear once the man was down. For a few seconds he stood and gloried in his handiwork watching his opponent squirming in the bloody grass at his feet. Then he finished him off, quickly disembowling him to release his spirit so that it wouldn't swell in his stomach and contaminate Mkhumbikazulu with *mnyama.*

He turned from the corpse and charged back into the fray looking for another opponent. This time he wanted a white man.

Everywhere he looked there were struggling figures, wrestling with one another and slashing with assegais or bayonet. Firearms were being shot at point blank range and the whole scene was soon obscured by gunsmoke and dust. Through the furore he spotted his next man. Mkhumbikazulu pushed his way through the crush of people to get at him.

Hamilton-Browne spotted him at the last second. He'd already taken down two of the enemy to his front, using his revolver, one through the gut and the other with two shots in the back. Spinning about he just had time to see a third Zulu rushing at him from out of the dust, a bloody assegais allready thrusting towards him. Without thinking, the Irishman fired before he'd had a chance to aim properly.

He was lucky.

The bullet struck the Zulu in the head and took away most of his face as well as a large portion of his brain. Hamilton-Browne watched as the body seemed to crumple to the ground in slow-motion, pumping gore into the tall grass.

Closeby he saw two more NNC rankers fall. Neither of them came to their feet again. Beyond them, Major Black ran his sword through a tall Zulu who tried to pull himself back off the blade. They both fell to the earth amid a flurry of arms and legs.

He could do nothing to help for he had his hands full in trying to keep some kind of control over his men. It was impossible to tell how things were going at the moment, everything was too mixed up. All he could do was yell encouragement to them.

"Keep at it lads! Let them have it!"

They fought off the initial flurry and somehow managed to push the Zulus back yet not without loss. At least two or three men were dead and maybe a dozen wounded, and no doubt some of them had fallen to gunshot wounds or assegai stabs inflicted by their own side in the pandemonium. The heavy fire fell away and for the time being settled into a slower exchange, the Zulus still up amoungst the caves and rocky fissures but pushed further back into the depths of the V-shaped crevasse. The British now occupied the entranceway, trading shots with their opponents from around the boulders they hid behind.

Hamilton-Browne crouched low and reloaded his revolver. His face was caked with dust and sweat, a result of the fierce fighting which had infact only lasted a matter of a few minutes. He struggled to get his breath back.

Just then he heard a cry from behind and he spun to see a white officer falling to the ground. He immediately recognized him. "Good God Harford!" he cried in alarm. "You're hit, man!" He dashed over and came down on his knees beside the prone body, and cried out for a stretcher bearer.

There was no need. To his amazement Lieutenant Harford lifted his head from the grass and beamed merrily at him. "I most certainly am not hit sir." Then he held out a hand to show Hamilton-Browne something that he held. It was a large black beetle, ugly looking to the commandant but obviously not so to Harford, judging by his excited state. "I have caught such a beauty, see. It's the first one I've seen of its kind since I arrived. Isn't it wonderful?" And with that he gently blew out the creature's wings as if to emphasis his point.

Reaching inside his tunic he pulled out a small tin box and he delicately placed his new discovery inside it, all the while reeling off a series of latin names which meant absolutely nothing to Hamilton-Browne whatsoever. And throughout the whole episode bullets continued to strike the rocks around them, pinging this way and that.

The commandant of the 1/3rd crouched down beside him, partly to avoid being hit but also to make himself heard. With exceptional patience for one who possessed such a fiery temper he said mildly, "Henry Harford, don't you think you ought to return to your company? Your men are in need of a little leadership right now?"

Lieutenant Harford suddenly appeared to cringe with embarrassment. "Yes...yes," he blabbed and came to his feet looking around.

"They're over there," Hamilton-Browne told him patiently, still speaking softly. "Pinned down."

"Yes, I see them now. Thankyou."

Then he was gone, his prized possession still clasped in his left hand.

Over on the left the detachment of the 24th that had come up with Major Black to 'encourage' the NNC forward had swept up the hillside under a heavy fire from the cliffs above. They had so far being lucky, having taken no casualties yet. Their charge had come to a sudden halt however, for several Zulus hidden in a large cave on the opposite side of the crevasse had poured volley after volley at them bringing them up short. The whole detachment had gone to ground and scrambled in the dirt for a hiding place.

Privates Metcalfe and Noakes had become seperated in the rush up the slope and now they were lying low and out of earshot from each other. They could see one another and at least could tell that they were both uninjured, but they both knew, as did all the other men in the group, that they were in trouble. They could neither go forward nor back but were trapped where they were, a stalemate and at the mercy of their Zulu opponents.

Lieutenant Harford, now back with the right flank of the NNC, saw that the Imperial infantry were in trouble. He could also clearly see the source of that trouble for the cave where the Zulus were firing from was just above his own position. Several dead Zulus had fallen out of the entrance and were suspended in a grotesque fashion below, tangled up in creepers and vegetation, but about half a dozen or so still blazed away. Puffs of thick smoke belched out from within its shadowy depths.

He hurridly pocketed the small tin box and then took out his revolver. He quickly glanced around and called over one of his N.C.O's. The man rushed over and fell in next to him, keeping down low behind the jumble of rocks. Harford explained about the cave and that he wanted to clear it of enemy warriors, also that he wanted the N.C.O to accompany him for they couldn't rely on their natives. After a slight pause the N.C.O nodded his agreement.

"Let's go then," Lieutenant Harford said and in an instant he was up and running for the cave, revolver pointed out in front.

The ground here was very steep and it was necessary to pull himself up over the rocks with his free hand. About twenty feet from the entrance to the cave he clambered over an extremely large boulder and slipped down the other side. On the other side he got the shock of his life. A Zulu was waiting for him, sitting in a squatting position and glowering at him with venem in his eyes. Harford recoiled and in a flash brought his gun around to fire at point blank range. But in the split second before he squeezed the trigger he saw all was not right.

The Zulu hadn't moved a muscle. When Harford had unexpectedly dropped in the warrior had simply sat motionless, not flinching or showing any alarm. And this made Harford pause.

He looked again.

Then saw what it was.

The man was dead. A tiny round hole in the centre of his forehead was the only outward sign from where Harford stood poised. He carefully moved sideways, all the time keeping the barrel of his gun trained on the Zulu, just in case he was wrong. He soon saw he wasn't: the whole of the back of the man's head was missing, blown away and splattered on the rocks behind, but he had somehow remained in a squatting position and therefore giving every indication that he was still alive. Breathing a heavy sigh of relief, Harford spun away to continue his run up to the cliff.

He froze solid.

Standing in front of him was another Zulu, this one very much alive, and holding a flintlock rifle with the muzzle aimed just inches from his face. Harford could do nothing as the trigger was pulled, except close his eyes and prey it was instant.

Nothing happened. He snapped his eyes back open as he realized that the cap on the gun had snapped, and now the Zulu was flinging it to one side and running away in panic.

Harford could not believe his luck. In the space of a few seconds he had literally stared death in the face twice and on each occassion had come through the other side unscathed. His sheer joy quickly turned into an indignant anger and he gave chase, his revolver up. As he ran after the Zulu Harford fired six quick shots at his fleeing back. This time it was the turn of the Zulu to be lucky for of the six rounds only one found its mark, hitting him on the hand and taking away three of his fingers. He yelped but did not pause, skipping up the steep hillside and then disappearing into the cave.

A little below Harford paused, unable to believe how bad his aim had been. He took a moment to reload the gun yet was so annoyed with himself that he lost his cool alltogether and threw the useless thing away, then cried out for the N.C.O to give him his weapon.

The N.C.O wasn't there. He'd remained behind, having convinced himself that Lieutenant Harford had lost all his senses due to sunstroke or some other such malady, and he'd had no wish to join him on some suicide charge. He'd seen the Zulu aiming the gun at his face and convinced that he was a gonner turned to shout down the slope, "Captain Harford is dead! The lunatic is dead!"

"I must disagree! For the second time, I am not dead!" Harford called back. "What's more I am a Lieutenant!"

With that he continued his reckless charge up the hillside, but now without a weapon save raw courage.

He reached the mouth of the cave but he could no longer see any signs of the Zulu marksmen who he'd noticed earlier. He knew they were still in there for he would have seen if they'd fled. Keeping low, he scurried from rock to rock, until he had moved several feet into the cave itself.

As he went into the gloom he caught a quick glimpse of a shadowy form moving just ahead. It suddenly dawned on him that he presented a very easy target, standing as he was in the entrance to the cave and silhouetted against the sky, so he moved off to the side where the shadows were deeper. Then, speaking a few words of Zulu that he'd learnt, Harford called for the wounded man to surrender.

At first there was no response so he tried again.

A little to his surprise a figure approached from out of the gloom, shivering in fear and pain and looking very meek. It was the Zulu warrior who had just given him the scare with the gun. He shuffled forward and then squatted down in submission, all the fight gone out of him. Satisfied that he would no longer be a threat Harford turned his attention back into the cave.

By now his eyes had adjusted to the gloom. Several feet infront of him lay a second zulu, flat on his back and clutching at an injury in his stomach with one hand. In the other he gripped an assegai. On hearing Harford approach he lifted his head off the stony ground and peered at him, and suddenly tensed himself.

"Put it down and you will not be harmed. There are many soldiers outside waiting to come in."

The Zulu was too weak to protest. He had been shot through the stomach and had so far lost a lot of blood, making him delerious and unable to think clearly. Moaning softly to himself he threw the assegai away, just wanting the agony to stop.

"Good. Now tell me, how many of your friends are hiding here?" Harford asked.

The Zulu shook his head and waved his arm to the sounds of fighting outside.

"I do not believe you. I know there are others in here. If they do not lay down their weapons and come outside then I will not be able to stop my men from killing you all."

He waited a moment, wondering if this would have any effect. The seconds ticked by. Nothing happened. Harford wondered why it was taking so long for the N.C.O to bring more men forward to give him some help.

Then they appeared. Three dark forms scurrying forward, their hands in the air to show that they carried no weapons. Harford edged away, allowing them to pick up their wounded comrade from the cave floor, then they were outside in the bright sunlight where they joined the first man who was still waiting quietly.

To the amazement of those waiting below Lieutenant Harford marched his prisoners down the slope, having taken the cave single-handed. On the way he picked up his revolver. For him, it had been a grand start to the war!

Once they saw that the cave had been taken the Zulus began a hurried withdrawal from their positions in the cliff-face. Running from cover they scampered towards the back of the V-shaped crevasse, their resistance starting to crumble. The Imperial infantry pushed forward, picking off the enemy here and there or taking prisoners when the opportunity arose. Hamilton-Browne ordered his battalion to try and work their way around the flanks incase any Zulu tried to move against them from either side.

Major Black, who had come out of his scrap with the large warrior with nothing more than a small scratch on his forehead, called for more rifles to come on up and with them he cautiously crept towards the narrow end of the crevasse. Here they discovered that the enemy had escaped up a steep path that led to the top of the cliff, about sixty feet above them. They were waiting for them somewhere up there, a few diehards who refused to give in. So be it, he thought. If they wouldn't see sense and give themselves up then they would have to be killed: there was no time for a waiting game.

But unknown to the British the Zulus at the top had a little surprise waiting for them. They had planned in advance to use this as an escape route and had rolled a number of large, round boulders into position at the point where the path crested the edge of the cliff near the summit of the hill. Now they rushed forward and began to push at them, sending them rolling down the steep drop, a trickle that soon became a small avalanche. They came tumbling down to where the British waited, a lethal cascade descending on the unsuspecting soldiers below.

Major Black had his back to the path as he was giving out the orders to launch a fresh attack. He didn't see nor hear the approaching rockslide. Fortunately for him, Private Metcalfe did. He just had time to scream a warning, aliready throwing himself to one side. Everyone else did the same, including the Major, who dived away with hardly a second to spare. Even so, one rock caught him a painful blow in the backside, and he went slipping down the hill in a very undignified manner, none-the-worse for wear but bright red with embarrassment. He came to his feet and rubbed his behind, a stream of profanity errupting from him.

Despite the narrow shave everyone else all but fell about laughing, the tension of the battle being replaced by the sheer hilarity of the moment. Even Hamilton-Browne saw the funny side.

Once he had recovered his composure Major Black climbed back up to where the 1/24th men and the NNC were waiting.

Several minutes later he had them moving up the path. Once again a fierce firefight took hold.

In the meantime, the mounted units had seen their own share of the action. They had branched off to the right and rode down the stream, heading south where the lower end of Ngedla dropped to the valley floor in a series of gentle slopes. Here the way was easier for the men on horseback. Extending out in skirmishing order, with the Mounted Infantry and Natal Mounted Police over on the left and the Carbineers on the right, they had ascended the hill without opposition, but aware of the fighting taking place out of sight on the far side because of the heavy gunfire they could hear.

As they neared the top a group of Zulus suddenly appeared riding horses along the crest of the hill. They reined in their mounts and as the British watched them dismounted and fled on foot, taking cover behind a rocky outcrop. Major Russell, the overall commander of the cavalry called a temporary halt and quickly got together with his officers. He decided that while the MI and the NMP continued to push forward the Carbineers would be sent further to the right to try and draw fire from this body of Zulus and also to outflank them where they should be able to lay down an e fective crossfire. The move was quickly carried out. Then, Sergeant Methley and four men from the Carbineers, one of whom was Fred Symons, cantered forward towards the rocky outcrop where the enemy had hidden in the hope that they could lure them out into the open.

As they neared about twenty guns were suddenly brought to bear on them, propped up on the rocks and pointing straight at them. Another set of about forty were likewise aimed down the slope towards Russell's position. The Zulus opened up with a surprisingly well-timed volley, causing Trooper Symons' horse to shy and almost throw him, the bullets just passing overhead with a peculiar v-o-o-rrr sound. He somehow managed to keep in the saddle and when his horse was settled again he brought up his carbine and levelled it at the Zulu position, looking for a target. There weren't any. The enemy had dropped down behind the rocks once again. All he could see were their horses which they'd left behind, wandering about and looking for their owners.

Over on the left the Police bore the brunt of the fire and their advance was checked. Inspector Mansel looked around to check for casualties and to his relief saw that his men had got away without a scratch. They were panicked though, for the Zulu fire had been much heavier than expected: they weren't supposed to have this many firearms. What's more, the next volley might be more accurate.

"Mounted Police dismount!" he cried. "Prepare to return fire!"

The whole troop quickly leapt down from their horses, spread out in line, and brought up their guns. He pulled out his revolver too, but held it by the side of his temple and pointed upwards. Slowly he lowered his arm and aimed at the rocky ground up on the crest of the hill.

"Fire!" Mansel yelled, and the whole line errupted with a gout of flame and noise that made the hairs on the back of his neck stand up. Then, "reload, at the double...forward!"

A few of the men looked at him in alarm but they did as they were told, jogging up the slope towards the rocky crest to meet with the enemy.

From their position in the centre the Mounted infantry saw the Zulus break and run. They cantered forward to try and catch them but the ground at the top was hard for the horses and they soon realized that the Zulus would easily outrun them even on foot. They did have time to fire a volley from their saddles at the running figures and were satisfied to see as many as eight or nine of the enemy fall. Pausing to catch their breath, for the short scrap had left them gasping with excitement, the men suddenly noticed a stream of Zulus come pouring up over the edge of the cliffs over to the left front. They quickly dispersed and were soon lost amidst the tall grass on the summit of the hill, escaping to the four winds. Major Russell instantly realized that the men fighting below had succeeded in pushing the Zulus from the line of cliffs that marked this side of the valley. They had obviously climbed up here to get away from them not realizing that in the meantime his cavalry had come up from the south. What a nasty shock it must have been, to see a line of horsemen blasting away just a hundred yards distant and just when they thought they had reached safety!

Drawing out his sword and waving it above his head Major Russell screamed"CHARGE!" at the top of his voice, and with that every cavalryman on this side swept after them at the gallop, the horses hooves thundering over the ground as they gave pursuit.

Trooper Symons and the rest of his companions in the Carbineers saw them go. They did not follow for they had a worrying situation to occupy their minds. A couple of minutes ago several men had been sent forward to round up the loose horses which the Zulus hiding behind the rocks had left behind. These half dozen had just reached the animals and were shepherding them back towards their own lines when from out of knowhere a large body of warriors had appeared and came charging towards them.

Suddenly panic stricken the small group saw the dire position they were in.Hurriedly climbing down to the ground they fixed nine-inch knives onto their carbines, ready for a stand.

Trooper Symons watched the drama unfold. He and the others were helpless spectators. They could not fire on the Zulus for fear of taking down their own men and by the time they rode over to help the Zulus would allready be on them, cutting them up good and proper. All they could do was watch.

Then, at the last moment, the warriors sprinting towards the lonely little group suddenly threw up their arms.

"Nombulwan!" they cried.

The truth suddenly dawned. They weren't Zulu warriors at all. These were men of the Native Contingent. They had climbed up the cliff face from the valley below in pursuit of the zulus but it seemed had then lost their nerve and so had ripped away their distinguishing red headbands to prevent the zulus from attacking them. In the process they had nearly being killed by their own side.

All around there were men taking deep breaths of relief. They all realized what a lucky escape they'd had, not least the six carbineers themselves who came back badly shaken up. At least the fighting at this end of the hill was over for the time being, most of the shooting going on off in the distance where Russell's men were running the enemy into the ground and seemingly having an easy time of it.

The battle had been a hard fought affair. It wasn't quite over yet but they did seem to have broken the back of the Zulus resistance. Now it was just a matter of finishing them off and rounding up as much cattle as possible.

The Mounted Volunteers had handled themselves well and they were fully justified in feeling proud of their performance.

By this time the 2/24th had arrived on the scene having left the camp at Rorke's Drift about two hours after the attacking column. They marched in quickly for they had heard the sound of heavy skirmishing and hoped to be in time to join the fight. Upon arriving they soon learnt to their disappointment that most of the action was over. But there was still the task of dealing with Sihayo's homestead and handling any pockets of resistance they might meet on the way.

Colonel Glyn decided to oversee this part of the operation in person, co-ordinating the movement of the newly arrived battalion with that of Degacher's men who were now up on the heights and preparing to sweep north and move on KwaSokhexe also. Lord Chelmsford expressed a desire to accompany him, and he would also take his staff along.

The battalion marched off the dirt track, shook itself down, and deployed in line for the sweep up the valley. They moved through the tall grass and mealee fields, all the while keeping a wary eye out for any hidden dangers.

Along the way several large flocks of cattle were spotted up the steep slopes, sheltering underneath the krantzes, and men were sent our in small detachments to bring them in together with any herdboys they might find. Chelmsford reiterated that they were not to be harmed. These instructions proved to be unneccesary for several young boys were seen running away as soon as the soldiers came in their direction. The British didn't give chase. From their hiding places high up in the cliffs they watched the column of red-coated white soldiers march past, their fascination overcoming their fear.

When they finally came within sight, and range, of KwaSokhexe they grew more cautious. Moving forward slowly the infantry approached the circle of huts from two directions, dashing from rock to rock. When they were within fifty yards the lead company paused.

"Company will fix bayonets!" came the shout from the C.S.M. "Fix bayonets!"

In perfect unison one hundred men drew out their twenty-two inch long, triangular socket bayonets, and snapped them in place.

"Present arms!"

Up came the guns, the men standing with one foot slightly forward, ready to lunge with them down the throat of any Zulu who came too close.

"Company, on the double, forward!"

161

They jogged forward out of the tall grass and into the open area where Sihayo's homestead was. Moving in groups of three they rushed at each hut, thrust their bayonets inside the low doorways to clear the way, before ducking inside. From but to but they went, ramsacking the interiors, searching for Zulus. Next came the cattle kraal, empty of beasts but with signs that its stone walls had been readied for defense with loopholes knocked out. Then they checked a cave towards the rear of the homestead, which likewise seemed to have been prepared for a fight with rocks placed across its narrow entrance. But of the inhabitants there was no sign. The place was deserted save for a few chickens that ran around in a panic and a black mongrel that snapped away at the soldiers heels. The men, women and children had gone.

The soldiers felt deflated with disappointment.

And to make matters worse they suddenly came to them the sound of voices laughing. In confusion they looked around and tried to pinpoint the source of it. It seemed to be coming from the cliffs above. Then they spotted who was doing it.

High above them they saw the familiar red tunics of the 1/24th, pointing down and unable to stop themselves laughing. Unknown to them at the time, as the second battalion had been cautiously creeping up to what proved to be an empty cluster of huts, expecting to have to storm the homestead, their comrades in the first battalion had been having a good laugh at their expense while watching the show from above.

Thoroughly cheesed off at their foolishness the 2/24th made a pledge there and then that the next time the roles would have to be reversed. One day, they hoped, the first battalion would be caught out. Then they could have the last laugh.

*   *   *

As ordered, KwaSokhexe was put to the torch.

Any plunder that could be had was taken. A number of firearms were found and these were handed in but any loot that the men thought might come in useful they kept for themselves, and the few chickens that roamed about the place were soon spirited away, mysteriously vanishing but only to eventually reappear again plucked, cleaned and spitted at suppertime later in the day. A few souvenirs of the fight were also taken, such as knobkerries, assegais and rawhide shields, which would be taken home as reminders of their time spent fighting the Zulus. When they were done with their rampage of destruction the column set out on the march back to camp.

Behind them, a column of smoke from the burning huts rose into the sky. It was a signal of intent to any Zulus left in the neighbourhood, visible for miles around.

*   *   *

On the way back they were caught in a terrific thunderstorm that drenched the men wet through. The rain sleeted down in long spears, catching them in the open, but there was nothing to do but keep on marching. The weather failed to dampen their spirits. They were in a jovial mood after a successful first fight with the enemy.

This feeling of satisfaction was shared by Chelmsford. He rode at the head of the column and chatted away with his staff and fellow officers, his waterproof pulled tight around his shoulders to keep out the chill.

"Under the conditions, and considering the difficult nature of the terrain, it was a fine display," he was saying, pausing to wipe a water droplet from the end of his nose. "I thought they handled our first set too with admirable discipline."

Those around him nodded their agreement, then Colonel Glyn, who was riding closest to the General, commented, "I'm sure it will give Cetshwayo pause for thought when news of this reaches him. It wouldn't surprise me if he immediately sued for peace."

"Ah, but is that what we wish for Richard?" Chelmsford glanced across and looked at him, one eyebrow raised. "Now that we have started might not it be best for us to finish the job? Rather than wait for a new crisis to rise say in two or three years time?"

"His Lordship is right," put in Crealock, "the only language Cetshwayo understands is that of war and destruction. Give him a bloody nose first and then see what he has to say."

"Yes. This will not be enough to deter him, only being a small affair. Only when we have utterly destroyed his impis will he see sense. Today was only a test for the men."

"But a successful one, I agree," Crealock was quick to put in.

"What pleases me most was the way our natives handled themselves. They may lack the professionalism of Imperial infantry, but for a group of men only recently brought together and with only a few weeks training under their belts I think they did a good job, considering how hard the Zulus fought today. There's no doubt about it, Colonel Durnford has achieved wonders with the NNC. Its also gratifying to see that they heeded my advice for not one of them touched a woman or child or killed a wounded man."

"Yes, their effort was crucial. We must congratulate Commandant Browne and Major Black for the way they led them. It was a sight to behold!"

Everyone murmured their agreement with Glyn's comment. They could see he was pleased with himself and he had a right to be for the assault had gone pretty much according to plan. The fact that the zulus had shown a lot of guts and held on to their positions for quite some time, in some instances being prepared to mix it up with them, was only cause for further self-congratulation.

"Sihayo's men have always been looked upon as the bravest in the country," Chelmsford told them as he urged his horse over the final rise before the track descended down to Rorke's Drift on the plain below, "and certainly those who were killed today fought with great courage."

"They did have the advantage of being in a most difficult spot, my Lord, let's not forget that."

"True Crealock, very true. All the more reason to be pleased though."

Ahead of them they could see the campsite, the line of tents a dim white blur through the heavy rain, the ponts still working to bring more supplies across. He knew that elsewhere in Zululand similar campsites should be in the process of being set up, Colonel Wood's column in the north and Colonel Pearson's at the Lower Drift in the south. So far the invasion was on course.

So pleased was he that Chelmsford made a snap decision right at that moment.

"Gentlemen, the men have had a tiring two days, with the crossing yesterday and the fight today. I think they should have tomorrow as a rest day, with only minor duties to perform. I think you'll all agree that they have earned it."

What a good idea, they all said.

The column marched on through the rain, reaching camp well before sundown.

CHAPTER 17

THE ONDINI *IKHANDA,* KING CETSHWAYO'S ROYAL RESIDENCE.
MAHLABATHINI PLAIN.
MONDAY 13th JANUARY 1879.

Before setting off for the coming fight it was necessary for the gathered *amabutho* to undergo certain 'doctoring' ceremonies. These took place over several days and closely followed the rituals of the *umKhosi* festival that celebrated the nations harvest but in times of war they took on a more militaristic air. Their purpose was essentially the same: to bind the nation together and ensue its strength and invincibility against outside psychic influence. In Zulu belief the shadow-world and the real living-world lived side by side with one another, each effecting the other on a daily basis and therefore forever intertwined. Appeasing their ancestral spirits and fortifying the warriors by the use of *umuthi* medicines to ward off an enemies magic was crucial before the men could wash their spears in an opponent's blood. It was also essential for the regiments to exorcise themselves of any evil agency that might inhabit their bodies, to cast out this badness, in a series of purifying rituals that would hopefully prepare them psychically and mentally for the traumas of warfare. Once the army had thus being 'doctored' the men were said to have entered a different psychic state to the rest of the population and while protected by their ancestral spirits they could have no contact with their families whatsoever. They were prepared to face the dark forces of *mnyama* that might confront them during the hell of warfare and to prevent a risk of contamination they had to temporarily step out of the daily comings and goings of normal society for the duration of the campaign they were about to embark upon. As long as they stuck to these rules the spirits of their ancestors would grant them ascendancy over the enemy and lead them to victory.

On the first morning the regiments that had gathered at Ondini were instructed to go down to the banks of the eNtukwini stream where they were to perform the first of several purifying rituals. Here several holes had been dug into the ground to a depth of about seven feet. Waiting closeby were a number of senior *izinyanga* witch doctors - who had spent the last few days gathering together the ingredients of their *umuthi* medicines. These witch doctors then called the men forward a few at a time and ordered them to sip the medicine, which they kept in pot bowls at their feet, a vile concoction that had the desired effect of making the men sick. Quickly, in twos and threes, they would rush across to the holes and vomit, their whole bodies convulsing painfully as they emptied their stomachs. When they were done the next group were brought forward, then the next, and the next. So on it went, until the stench rising out from the holes was so strong as to be almost overpowering. This made the warriors want to rush and have done with the procedure as quickly as possible, but the witch doctors would not allow crowding. They would stand by the holes to make sure their instructions were followed. One or two men only pretended to sip the medicine and crouched over the holes as if being violently sick, but these were soon spotted and violently beaten, then they had the medicine forced into their mouths.

Mehlokazulu KaSihayo was as reluctant as the rest but he realized the importance of the ceromony and he forced himself to swallow at the concoction. His stomach contents came up so quickly he only just had time to reach one of the pits, which was already about half-full. All around him his comrades were likewise vomiting. Their retching sounds added to the appalling nature of the scene.

When he was done Mehlokazulu stumbled away and flopped down onto the ground to recover, his stomach cramping in pain. All about him his comrades were suffering equally. Then, after a while and once they had recovered somewhat, the iNgobamakhosi regiment were told to return to the Kings kraal for he had need of them. They were grateful to leave.

Back at the stream the vomiting went on all day.

Later, when the last of the regiments had finished, the senior *inyanga* would use a twist of grass to remove a sample of the vomit which would then be taken and added to the *inkatha yezwe yakwaZulu*, *a* coil of grass rope wrapped round with a python skin and which was said to represent the good fortunes and past glories of the zulu people and which also contained items taken from various clans they had conquered over the years. These could include anything from a rival chief's skin to items of psychic potency stolen from another tribe, anything which was a visible reminder of their dominance over all the other clans. By adding their own warriors vomit they would enthuse the *inkatha* with the nation's strength, which in turn would be passed back to the fighting men through their ancestral spirits when they met their enemy in combat. When this was complete the holes were filled in with dirt and carefully covered over with bush and stones and grass to conceal it in order to prevent an enemy from finding it.

The iNgobamakhosi *ibutho* marched quickly back to the King's 'great place', all their revulsion of the purifying ceromony forgotten. They had been chosen to participate in one of the most important parts of the pre-combat rituals, the killing of a black bull with their bare hands, and they felt greatly honoured. They filed back in through the lower gateway, chanting and stamping their feet in marvelous unison, their mottled brown warshields being alternately held low to the ground and then thrust aloft. "Hohho!" they cried, "Hohho! Hohho!"

The warriors were marshalled into the central enclosure by Sigcwelecwele KaMhlehleke and his junior officers. Mehlokazulu led his contingent forward. He felt a kind of rapturous dizzyness take a hold of him as his pride at serving his King swelled in his chest; never before while he had being in its ranks had the iNgobamakhosi being selected to carry out this duty. It would be a day long remembered by the men.

The bull was a brute of a thing. Two or three years old and in its prime, a sniffling-hoof stomping-steaming mass of hatred backed up by solid muscle and horns especially honed for the occassion. It stood in the centre of the ring of warriors, watching them.

They should have been terrified of it but the occassion got to them and a group of men suddenly surged forward, eager to be the ones to bring it down. But the animal wasn't so dumb as to just stand there. It turned and charged and the warriors quickly parted in the middle. One of them was too slow and he was impaled on one of its horns, screaming in pain as the beast shook its head and flung him away. It came in with its head down, thrusting again, and the poor man was brutally gored into the dusty earth, dispatched in an instant.

Several men cried out and turned their faces away. The majority didn't. They ran this way and that, goading the beast first in one direction and then another, playing it a merry dance. Mehlokazulu found himself at the forefront amoungst the group closest to the bull, so near that he could feel the heat rising from its body as it turned to confront them, the blood on its horn glinting in the morning sun. They threw themselves at it, some leaping onto its back like ants, others trying to grab the tail, one brave warrior holding it by the horns and riding the creature. The mens screams and cries filled Mehlokazulu's ears and it took him a second to recognize his own voice amoungst them. "Bring it down!" he shouted eagerly. "Oh, mighty beast, we have you!"

But the bull thought otherwise. Tossing them off its back and trampling them under its hooves, it broke free and careened through the crowd. Mehlokazulu leaped out of its path a fraction of a second in time and rolled away. Quickly he came to his feet and spun. Several of his friends lay prostrate on the ground unmoving, one with a gaping wound in his face. Undaunted, he charged back into the throng.

Another section of the regiment had cut off the bull's escape, standing infront of it in a dense mass so that the others could catch up again. Once again they recklessly flung themselves on it. This time the weight of people became too much for it. Weakened from its exertions the bulls legs started to buckle and it made a loud mewling noise. More men joined in and crowded around and within moments it had stumbled and fallen, forced onto its stomach with its four legs splayed out. A dozen pair of hands grabbed hold of the horns and began to twist. This way and that they pulled until the air was squeezed out of its throat and, its strength now all but gone the bull gave in.

The men sensed their victory. They could see the beasts' eyes rolling in fear and knew the life was fast slipping away, and so they twisted even harder. They broke its neck in two.

Its limbs twitched spasmodically, but the bull was dead.

Overjoyed with their success the men almost did the unthinkable. They wanted to rip the bull to pieces, to tear out its heart and show that they had truly triumphed over this courageous animal. The *izinyanga* quickly managed to prevent this. They fought their way through the crowds, pushing men out of their way, until they reached the dead animal, shouting out that anyone who lay a hand upon it would surely feel the King's wrath. This was enough to make the warriors pull back and give the witch doctors the space they needed.

Using razor sharp spearheads the *izinyanga* went about stripping the hide from the dead bull, working quickly and expertly, ignoring the steam and smell that rose from the carcasse as they cut. In no time at all the task was finished. Then, while the young warriors watched, they sliced off long strips of meat, placing each one on wooden platters that they had put on the ground close at hand. They did not waste any, delving deep into the bloody morass to get at the flesh. Finally they carried these meat strips, known as *umbengo,* over to their cooking fires where they would spend the afternoon roasting them and smearing them with *umuthi* medicine.

The young men of the iNgobamakhosi dispersed and went back to their huts while they awaited the next part of the ceromony. They passed the time by bragging about their courage in bringing the bull down, and about how the king had chosen them to perform this daring deed because they were his favourites.

Meanwhile the purifying rituals taking place down at the stream had come to a finish. The whole army came trotting back over the plain, regiment by regiment, none the worse for wear after their ordeal crouched over the holes but now ravenously hungry. By the time they reached the massive *ikhanda* the sun was dipping below the western peaks, and the mountains cast long shadows across the rolling ground.

When they were all back they were called out into the wide inner enclosure, and they formed a densly packed circle around the witch doctors who had now returned with the cooked meat strips. Mehlokazulu was jostled as the crush of people pushed forward, straining to be as close to the front as possible.

The next part of the ceromony, the aim of which was to pass the bulls strength into them and unite their fighting prowess, then followed.

Taking the strips of roasted meat the *izinyanga* tossed them one by one into the crowd. There was a sudden pandomonium to be amoungst the first to grab one and several men dissappeared beneath a sea of legs, trampled and occassionally seriously hurt. Such was their excitement that several of the younger and older men passed out, overcome by the occassion or from the heat caused by being in the midst of so large a gathering of people violently contending for the meat strips. Those lucky enough to catch a hold of one quickly bit off a piece and then tossed it over their shoulders to the agitated crowds behind. It was soon caught by eager hands for it mustn't fall on the ground, the power of the *umuthi* medicine being lost if this happened.

The meat wasn't to be swallowed. It was custom only to chew it in order to extract the juices of the medicine and then to spit it out onto the ground. But so hungry were some that they could not refrain from consuming the tasty morsels, their tortured stomachs crying out for relief.

To ensure that all had a fair chance the witch doctors cut paths deep into the mass of warriors, tossing the meat this way and that.

Around them the men became estatic. They lost all composure and their mad frenzy reached fever pitch so that their wild chanting rolled across the plain like the thunder of an approaching storm.

It went on like this well into the evening.

So ended the first day of ceremonies

CHAPTER 18

THE KRANSKOP ESCARPMENT.
OVERLOOKING THE MIDDLE DRIFT.
FORWARD STAGING AREA OF No 2 COLUMN.
SUNSET, MONDAY 13th JANUARY.

Colonel Durnford paced up and down inside his command tent, a heavy frown on his domed forehead as he re-read the letter he held in his hand. This wasn't good, he thought to himself. This wasn't good at all.

The letter, with its red wax seal, had been waiting for him on the fold-up desk on his return. He'd spent a long and tiring afternoon inspecting the troops, riding down to Dalmaine's Farm where his official headquarters were and where his column was encamped, before coming back up here to the edge of the plateau where a company of men had been placed on outpost duty. A second company was busy repairing the narrow track that meandered down to the Thukela 3000 feet below and he had intended to ride on to see how they were doing when his Political Officer and good friend, George Shepstone, had politely drawn his attention to the letter. It had arrived that lunchtime. Reluctantly, Durnford had dismounted and gone through the tent flap, young Shepstone at his heels.

The note was from a Bishop Schreuder. As he had read the spidery handwriting a strange chill had passed through him, a sensation not entirely down to the damp clothing he wore - for it had started to rain heavily while he'd been climbing the plateau - a peculiar feeling of foreboding mixed with excitement.

The reason for this was simple.

Bishop Schreuder, a devout Christian who sympathised with the native population of Natal to the extent that he had learnt the language and delivered his sermons in their tongue, a result of which was a remarkably high proportion of his flock were now black, had recieved some disturbing news from within Zululand. For a number of years he had being granted permission from the Zulu king to run a mission station there and he had grown quite popular amoungst the Zulus for his colourful delivery and pleasant manner with children. Even when he was forced out due to the growing tensions between Britain and Cetshwayo, Schreuder had maintained close links with his followers, and it was from these sources that he had been told the following news, which he now passed on to Durnford in the letter the Colonel now held in his hand, pacing up and down as he read.

Schreuder, it seemed, had stumbled upon some intelligence about a Zulu impi that was gathering in the Nkandla forest, opposite the Middle Drift. It consisted of several strong regiments, approximately six to seven thousand men in total, and, most disturbing of all, according to the Bishops "spies" as he referred to them in the letter, they were planning on crossing into Natal some time within the next day or so. Schreuder went on to say that the people who had aquired this news were very trustworthy and as a result of this grave turn of events he thought it best he inform the British waiting up on the plateau with all haste.

If this information was true then it could have dire consequences, thought Durnford. Finishing reading the letter he turned and handed it to his Political Officer.

"See what you make of this George," he said, and stood watching his friend, pinching his lips in concentration.

The young man ran his green eyes quickly over the two pages, running a hand absentmindedly through his hair as he read. When he was done he stood and looked down at his riding boots, sucking air through his teeth. "Interesting," he finally offered.

"This Bishop Schreuder, I've spoken to him on a number of occassions. He's lived in Zululand in the past and doesn't seem the kind to panic easily. If what he says is true then this news places us in a dilemma."

"A rather big one," replied Shepstone.

"The puzzle is, what are we to do about it? Even if this rumour turns out to be false it may be foolish of us not to take some kind of premptive action. We were placed here at the Middle Drift for exactly this reason: to stop a Zulu invasion of Natal." Durnford moved across to the table and dropped the letter down, then lowered himself into his seat. Lifting his head he gazed at the side of the tent, barely noticing it flap in the wind. "His Lordship has granted me a certain amount of latitude in regard to our orders. In his last communication he stressed the importance of maintaining our vigilance and gave me the authority to act with a certain amount of independence if any kind of threat from the Zulus materialized, even to the extent of crossing into Zululand briefly if a situation deemed it necessary. This, to me, seems precisely the kind of scenario he had in mind. Correct me if I'm wrong George."

Shepstone rocked back on his heels and held open his arms. "I share your views Colonel. My only concern is that our own intelligence network has failed to uncover any indication of a Zulu impi hiding just over the river. It seems unusual that Bishop Schreuder comes across this information and we have nothing to back it up."

"Ah, but that does not mean the threat does not exist."

"Very true sir."

The two of them fell silent for a moment while Dumford ran their options through his head. To sit here and do nothing would be foolish on a grand scale but did this threat really warrant such drastic action as marching his column into Zululand, possibly to spend several days chasing shadows, with nothing to show at the end of it? But if the Zulus did invade would he have time to halt them from this side of the river before they reached the nearby settlement of Greytown? The townsfolk wouldn't really stand a chance against a determined attack even from the shelter of the town laager. And from there they was nothing to stop the Zulus from moving on Pietermaritzburg. A massacre of innocent civilians would follow and all because he sat on this information, hesitant, unsure.

No, Dumford decided, he had made one foolish mistake in the past which the colonists had never really forgiven him for, he was damned if he would travel down that same route once again.

He quickly came to his feet, making Shepstone jump a little. Then he explained his decision.

"I shall ride down to the river and see what the situation is there. Maybe the company we have down on the road have more information. When I have seen what the position is for myself, I shall then make a final decision. George, I want you to stay here, but pass word down to the column that they should be prepared to move up here and thence on to the drift at a moments notice, carrying enough rations for two days. Wait for my orders. I shall keep you up to date of any developments. Is all of that clear?"

Captain George Shepstone gulped and nodded his head, taken aback by the speed with which things were happening. His commander was in a very decisive frame of mind. Maybe the possibility of seeing some action was the spur he'd needed to lift him out of the funk he'd settled in over the last few days, Shepstone deduced. Whatever it was, to him Colonel Durnford now seemed to be a changed man, invigorated and hardly able to contain his excitement. He watched him leave the tent, a definite bounce in his step.

Outside Durnford called over Lieutenant Davies, commander of the Edendale Troop, a handful of whom had accompanied him up from Dalmaine's Farm. He briskly explained to the officer that he wished for him and his men to ride down to the river with him, telling him what he had in mind, then Durnford hurried over to his horse and pulled himself into the saddle one-handed.

Within a few minutes they were on their way.

It was a long and circuitous route down from the edge of the escarpment to the sprawling valley below, the ground undulating in a series of twisting and confusing hills. They rode in single file, their figures casting long shadows in the setting sun. It took over an hour for them to reach the small campsite set up by the company of Natal Kaffirs, who had been stood down from working on the track, and it was almost dark by then.

Spurring his horse forward Durnford glanced about for their officer. He saw a cluster of men standing off to one side, lanterns raised and staring at something on the ground, and he rode across.

Dismounting in one fluid movement Dumford strode forward and when the group of white NCOs spotted him they quickly came to attention.

From their midsts stepped a short, somewhat overweight, officer who Durnford recognized as Lieutenant Vetch. He waddled through the long grass and beckoned Colonel Durnford forward, his double chin quivering as he said, "something I think you should see here Sir," in his asthmatic tones.

Distracted for the moment from his reason for coming down here, Durnford followed him back to where the cluster of men had resumed their intense scrutiny of whatever it was that held their attention. They parted for him and allowed him through until he was able to see for himself what the problem was.

Lying in the grass at their feet was the body of a young black man, stark naked except for a red rag tied around his forehead. He lay face up and his stomach was badly swollen, his lips blue. He stared lifelessly up at the ring of faces peering at him, their eyes holding a fascinated glint about them, shining in the glow from their lanterns. Durnford looked around at them, looking for any hint of pity. He saw none.

"One of ours?" he asked Vetch tightly.

"I don't recognize him sir," came the reply, "but then I don't pay too much attention to them."

"There are no reports of any missing fellows from the 1st Regiment," said Lieutenant Davies, who had followed Durnford over, "but he's obviously a member of the NNC. Also, I fail to see any obvious signs of injury." He glanced up at the Colonel who met his eye. "A drowning?"

"It looks that way," replied Durnford.

"Makes sense. He was pulled out of the river about twenty minutes ago," Vetch told them lazily, a bored expression already appearing on his fat face.

Durnford gave the man a stern look, annoyed at his attitude. Maybe a reprimand was in order, but this wasn't the time right now. Instead he looked off into the gathering darkness to where he could hear the sound of rushing water.

The night had come on suddenly and it was impossible to see the river even from this close. Apart from their circle of lanterns and the few campfires the men had started the countryside was pitch black. Durnford stared into the shadows, ignoring the large moths that fluttered in his face, wondering what lay out there on the far bank. Did this darkness conceal a whole Zulu impi, who were waiting their opportunity to pounce on the unsuspecting Colony? Maybe they were over there right now, watching him. It was a disturbing thought.

And this chap lying dead at their feet, where had he sprung from? Had he wandered away from his comrades and become lost in the dark only to be captured by the enemy and flung into the river? Unlikely, he reflected. The state of his bloated body suggested he had been dead for several days. And if that was the case then he could have been washed downriver for many miles to finally land up here on the bank.

Thinking out loud he spoke to the others. "It's my guess that this poor man is probably from one of the regiments attached to the Centre Column. He was probably washed away when they crossed at Rorke's Drift."

"Then he didn't die at the hands of the Zulus we fear are out there," Davies agreed.

"Zulus?" Vetch suddenly looked alarmed and he cast nervous eyes about. "What's all this about Zulus? Have some being spotted?"

"At the moment it's only a rumour," Durnford informed him.

"But they could be out there?" A nervous murmur passed through the men who stood clustered together. "Are we to remain here Colonel, by ourselves?"

Durnford did not reply immediately. He briefly left the small group and wandered several feet closer to the river, but he was still unable to see anything. His small tongue slid between his teeth a minute fraction as though tasting the night air and then he breathed in deeply through his nostrils. Instincts, he mused. Leadership was all about instincts. When to follow them and when not to.

It was his decision.

Durnford turned, his mind finally made up. He marched back to the group. "No Lieutenant," he said evenly, "you won't be staying here by yourself."

Quickly he pulled out a notebook and pencil from his tunic. Leaning forward and using his thigh to rest on he quickly scribbled out a message and signed it, tore the slip of paper off, and then wrote out a second one. Done, he called forward one of the Edendale men, who trotted over, and handed the two messages up to him.

"Solomon. Ride quickly back to the camp and give this first message to Captain Shepstone. Tell him to follow these instructions and bring the column on quickly. Then ride on to Lord Chelmsford and hand him the second one; you'll find him at Rorke's Drift. Now go with all speed my boy...and be careful."

Trooper Solomon Malaza saluted then whipped at his reins, gone in a flash, the sound of galloping hooves lingering long after he had disappeared into the night.

Durnford listened to the sound, sure in his heart that he had made the correct decision.

Suddenly he recalled part of a conversation he'd had with his good friend John Colenso, the Bishop of Natal. It had been several weeks back and the last time he'd visited the Bishop at his home. Standing amidst the flowers in the garden at Bishopstowe they had bid one another farewell shortly before Durnford left to take command of his column. Colenso's parting words had been simply *"God bless you Anthony. Do what is right."*

Then he thought of the Bishop's daughter and he remembered their last meeting.

Durnford reached into his tunic pocket and felt for the tiny fragment of muslin. It felt reassuring to the touch, resting as it did against his rapid heartbeat.

THE BRITISH CAMP AT RORKE'S DRIFT.
SHORTLY AFTER MIDNIGHT, TUESDAY 14th JANUARY.

"What!" exclaimed Lord Chelmsford, the news bringing him instantly awake.

He sat bolt upright in his bed and rubbed his tired eyes, then stared up at his Assistant Military Secretary in amazement. Crealock stood perfectly still and with his hooded eyes lowered to the floor. Slowly he raised them and saw the dumbfounded look on Chelmsford's face, the unspoken question; he nodded the affirmative-yes, it was true.

Swinging his legs off the bed Chelmsford quickly came to his feet, lifting his braces up to his shoulders, a red flush of anger appearing around his neck. "When did the news come in?" he asked urgently.

"Just now sir. By rider, sent by Durnford in person. I read the message and realized its significance so I came and woke you at once."

"Let me see it."

Crealock handed over the thin message slip into Chelmsford's outstretched hand, and the General hurriedly read. His large, hooked nose sniffed in disdain, and when he reached the end he looked to see what time the message had been written, then asked, "what o'clock is it?"

Crealock consulted his fobwatch, squinting in the dim lamplight. "It has just turned midnight sir."

"Four hours," Chelmsford muttered to himself, quickly doing a series of calculations in his head. Maybe they had time to stop all of this nonsense, he thought. Durnford had to be stopped from crossing the river. "The fool! Is he purposefully trying to wreck my invasion plan? My God, one day that man's rashness will be his downfall, you hear me Crealock? It would be like Bushmans Pass all over again, but on a much bigger scale! He must be reined in once and for all. Now. Right here."

He strode across to the desk that had been set up in the corner of his large, spacious headquarters tent, any last vestiges of sleep now long gone, and sat down to begin writing a message of his own. It took him a couple of minutes to complete. Then he passed it on to his Secretary. Crealock, fully understanding the urgency of the situation, hurried outside and gave it to the rider who was still waiting. He instructed him to ride back to the Middle Drift by the most direct route and to take whatever risks he thought worth taking for it was essential the message be delivered as quickly as possible.

Trooper Malaza, not even recovered from the ride out, turned about and set off on the return journey through the night.

THE CROSSING AT MIDDLE DRIFT.
4am, TUESDAY 14th JANUARY.

No 2 Column finally reached the crossing point below the Kranskop escarpement having marched through the night. They arrived just as a heavy mist descended, a whiteness that blanketed the ground and curled in gentle swirls above the fast flowing river.

Durnford and the company of men with him, who had endured a long and fretful night peering into the shadows and expecting the worst, were very glad to see them. Their confidence was suddenly bolstered by the sight of reinforcements and their earlier trepidation was soon forgotten.

The column was chiefly made up of native troops. Durnford had under his command the 1st Regiment of the NNC, which was the largest out of the three formed, consisting of three battalions of infantry. They were well trained for native levies for Durnford had vigorously drilled them himself, trying to instill as much discipline as possible in the short time available, and because some of them had served under him before and knew his ways they soon became a very competent force, enthusiastic and confident. He'd also managed to acquire the best of the available white officers to lead them, Europeans mostly, many of who could speak fluent Zulu. Besides the 1st Regiment he also had five troops of the Natal Native Horse, well armed and brilliant horsemen and who dressed in smart European clothing, totalling about 250 men in all. They were a versatile and flexible body of much needed cavalry, far-reaching and hard hitting, and brave to the last. Finally, there was the three rocket troughs of the Royal Artillery Rocket Battery, led by Brevet Major Francis Russell. With one Bombardier and nine men seconded from the 1/24th, they were the only white unit in the entire column.

Durnford had spent the last few hours while the men were marching down from the heights setting out his plan of action. He felt fully justified in crossing the river and moving to meet this potential threat, in placing his force between the enemy and the vulnerable border as a means of blocking any attack they might launch against Natal. Notwithstanding that, he was aware that this could only be a temporary measure. No 2 Column simply wasn't strong enough to go on the offensive by itself nor to stay in enemy territory for very long without some kind of support. After a day or two they would have to withdraw back to their setting off point. By that time it was hoped that his show of force would persuade the Zulus not to chance their arm by attacking the colony, or if they did then hopefully they could delay their enemy long enough for Chelmsford's force to come rushing to their assistance. It was a risky tactic playing his trump card like this but Colonel Durnford was hopeful that the ploy would work.

By sun-up everything was in place, the men poised and the ponts standing by.

He just wished this damned mist would lift so that he could see the state of the river below them.

Should they wait for another hour and see if the sun burnt it off? Or should they go now?

Seated on his horse Durnford stared into the swirling fog. He made up his mind.

They would cross.

No sooner had he decided then fate intervened and took control of events. A horseman came galloping out of the mist, splashing through the sodden grass and kicking up gouts of mud. Durnford saw it was Trooper Malaza, the same man he had instructed to take the message across country to Chelmsford. But here he was having returned already!

There was something about the agitated expression on the man's face that stilled Durnford's heart and for a split second he felt something very cold and odd pass quickly through him.

Then he saw the dispatch that Trooper Malaza clutched tightly in his hand and he knew, before he even reached out and grasped it, that it was a reply from Lord Chelmsford. And because the rider had galloped through the night with it Durnford guessed it contained urgent, unsettling news.

He was right.

Hd Qr Camp Zululand near Rorke's Drift
14 January 1879.

Unless you carry out the instructions I give you, it will be my unpleasant duty to remove you from command, and to substitute another officer for the command of No 2 Column. When a column is acting seperately *in an* enemy's country *I am quite ready to give its commander every latitude, and would certainly expect him to disobey any orders he might receive from me, if information which he obtained, showed that it would be injurious to the interests of the column under his command- Your neglecting to obey my instructions in the present instance has no excuse. You have simply received information in a letter from Bishop Schreuder, which may or may not be true and which you have no means of verifying- If movements ordered are to be delayed because report hints at a chance of an invasion of Natal, it will be impossible for me to carry out my plan of campaign- I trust you will understand this plain speaking & not give me any further occasion to write in a style which is distasteful to me-*

Chelmsford.

Stony-faced, Durnford sat motionless in the saddle. A hush descended amongst those around him, aware of the sudden shift in his mood, a silence that embarrassed them but one they dared not break.

Then he turned his horse and silently trotted away into the misty dawn. Away from the river. Back to camp.

CHAPTER 19

THE ONDINI *IKHANDA,* KING CETSHWAYO'S ROYAL RESIDENCE.
MAHLABATHINI PLAIN.
TUESDAY 14th JANUARY.

O n the second day of ceremonies King Cetshwayo
KaMpande summoned two of his youngest regiments,
the uKhandempemvu and the iNgobamakhosi, into the
great enclosure with the words "I call you so that I may see what
deeds you will do on the day that you encounter our enemy!"

With this, the two regiments took up their appointed places, seated
in ranks opposite one another and with the King watching over the
isigodlo fence. The time was now for them to begin their challenges,
individuals calling on each other across the wide open space, rivals
bringing up old grievances and proclaiming that they would surpass
this person or that person in the coming battle. The two would dance
in a mock duel, jumping high and thrashing their sticks about
(weapons were never allowed in the presence of the King) kicking
up thick clouds of dust as their exertions grew wilder. But they
never came to blows. It was forbidden. This was known as
giya'ing.

If a person refused to answer to such challenges he was ridiculed
by his comrades and labelled a coward.

But when he came to his feet and responded, then the whole of his regiment would praise him, chanting their warcries.

"Izulu!" screamed the uKhandempemvu at their man's rival. "You *are beaten down by the axe that strikes down! Nhla! Nhla! Nhla!"*

"Tshitshilizi- this sky is dangerous! Hohho! Hohho!" responded the iNgobamakhosi with equal venom.

This was no idle game they played. Each regiment had a rich history of battlefield honours and they wished to uphold their pride and prestige, not to look weak infront of their rivals. When a man made a challenge and boasted of how he would prove his prowess on the battlefield then he was expected to live up to those promises. Anything less and he would bring shame on the regiment.

One of those to come to his feet, to giya and xoxa-challenge-a rival was Mehlokazulu's good friend, Ndlela kaSashangane. He stalked forward, baring his teeth and rattling his stick against the back of his shield, and then leaped high in the air and thrust it forward, as if making to stab his chosen target.

Dilikhana kaBokwe scrambled up and likewise spun and twisted about, feinting a charge before spinning away. His comrades in the uKhandempemvu roared their approval and thrust their own sticks into the sky.

Across the way the boys of the iNgobamakhosi responded in kind, stamping their feet into the dirt from their squatting positions.

The two men called out their boasts while they giya'd, each trying to equal the other.

"My courage, as strong as a leopards, will be greater than yours son of Bokwe!" called Ndlela. "I will stab the enemy first! If you stab a white man before mine has fallen, you may take the kraal of our people, and you may take my sister Nomcoba!"

"Well, if you do better than I do, and my blade will slither unseen like a snake under the white man's heart, then you will take our kraal, and my sister Langazana!" shouted back Dilikhana.

These provocative claims continued back and forth, becoming more florrid in their description, until they bordered on the ridiculous. But in a Zulu man's eyes it was not what was said but how it was said. The more extravagant their delivery the greater their standing in the eyes of their comrades. The men were therefore soon whipped up into a frenzy, a seething and broiling mass of humanity whose sole desire was to unleash their fury upon their enemy. To wash their spears.

It was down to the King to decide who the winner in these contests was. He would carefully scutinize the two 'combatants', his expert eyes and ears picking up on every nuance their challenges contained, until he had reached a decision as to who had shown the greater aggression. Then he would raise his hand and point with the first two fingers at the victor.

On this instance he chose Dilikhana kaBokwe of the uKhandempemvu.

His friends shouted their approval, and he showed his delight by leaping even higher and stamping even harder, a broad grin splitting his countenance as he returned to their ranks.

Ndlela, feeling the ultimate humiliation, shuffled away. Hardly able to look his friends in the eye, he dropped down in his place.

Mehlokazulu saw the disappointment on his face. He leaned in close and whispered into his ear, his words almost lost in the roar as the next challenges commenced.

"It does not matter my friend that you were not chosen," he said soothingly. "The uKhandempemvu have always being full of swagger. They are really fools and their *izindunas* are weak and old. We will show them."

This did little to improve Ndlela's mood. He had been made a fool of infront of his friends and, worst still, his king. He knew that no amount of sympathy could change that. Only one thing would.

"I will stab first! I will show that I am no coward. When we fight the white men my assegai will do much quick work on them! He will be the one who goes home with his tail between his legs!" Ndlela turned to his friend and his eyes were large and imploring. "When will we fight? When will the King send us to eat up our enemy?"

"Soon," Mehlokazulu told him.

"But I want to go now!"

"Soon," he repeated, casting a glance around at those nearest them who were listening to their conversation.

Ndlela still wasn't happy with this but there was nothing he could do. But he couldn't bring himself to watch the remainder of the proceedings, preferring instead to stare miserably at the ground.

For most of the afternoon the two regiments squared up to one another in this way. It was at the King's discretion as to when the proceedings came to an end, usually when he grew tired and retired to his hut. The King himself had also been busy preparing for the coming fight, undergoing rituals since well before dawn in the privacy of his quarters, for it was necessary that he too gained the approval of the ancestral spirits even though he himself wouldn't be taking part in any actual combat. First of all he abstained from eating anything the evening before. Then, in the early morning darkness and in the flickering glow of the small fire that burned in the clay hearth of his hut, he was treated with black *umuthi* medicines. His chief witch-doctors smeared them all over his body to ward off any evil magic their enemies may be trying to cast on the nation, a process that sent him into a temporary psychic trance. While in this semi-concious state his mind was at the risk of contamination and it was dangerous for him to be seen by anyone outside the hut for fear his defences might be breached. No one but the *izinyanga* could be present.

Later they carefully prepared more *umuthi,* a peculiar mixture of soil samples secretly taken from their enemy's territory which were boiled down into a sludge in a potsherd over the fire. When it was ready the witch-doctors went outside, partly to see whether the rising sun was in position and also to clear the *isigodlo* of people. When they were satisfied that the time was right they encouraged the king to leave the safety of his hut, guiding him as they would a blind man for his mind was only partially alert. He was now required to *ncinda* the *umuthi.*

Cetshwayo kaMpande walked around the *isigodlo* with his chief witch-doctor close by his side, holding out a bowl that contained the medicine. Dipping the fingers of both hands into the mixture, he sucked the *umuthi* and then sprayed it at the dawn sun. Time after time he did this, wandering throughout his private enclosure, appeasing the spirits and ensuring the nation was united and ready for war. The warming rays of the rising sun would spread this good fortune throughout the land, to every kraal on every hill, to every man, woman and child.

He was then taken back into his hut and the black medicines were washed off. They were replaced by white medicines, whose properties acted as a further protection for him. Only then was he able to mix with other people, to walk freely amongst commoners, to watch his regiments challenge one another from over the fence.

At the same time that the two regiments inside the central enclosure were *giya'ing,* a third regiment, the uNokhenke, was busy observing their own pre-combat rituals outside the lower gates. As instructed by the King several days earlier they had acquired as many firearms as possible and brought them to the *ikhanda,* as had all the men in the army. For a people with few ties to the outside world the regiments of fighting men owned a surprisingly large number of guns, maybe as many as 20,000. Of these, only a small minority were modern breech-loaders, maybe as few as 500 or about one in forty, the rest being obsolete models, either percussion rifles or old muskets such as flintlock Brown Besses. Inaccurate and as much a danger to the man firing it as the person being shot they were nevertheless very sought after by the Zulu warriors as they made them feel to be on equal terms with their white opponents. The fact that these weapons were sometimes thirty or forty years old and had been discarded by their previous owners to make way for newer, better, models was lost on them. Thus armed they were under the false impression that they would be able to meet like-for-like any threat their enemy posed to them. This mistake would cost them dear in the coming battles.

Their ignorance was what gave the Zulu Army its strength.

They may not have realized just how poor their firearms were but they were still astute enough to realize that these weapons by themselves would not be enough to give them the victory they craved. Other measures would be needed.

Hence the chief *inyanga* was called for.

It was his task to try and ensure the weapons gave them the necessary advantage they needed to hand them their victory. To do this he would need to use all of his knowledge and years of experience as a witch-doctor. Mixing together various herbs and cooking them in a potsherd and chanting a series of fanciful incantations, he called the men of the uNokhenke forward. They filed past, holding their guns downwards over the pot so that the smoke of the medicine contained within drifted up the barrels. The intention was that this heady and powerful *umuthi* would cause them to fire with greater accuracy! So respected was the witch-doctor that the men believed implicitlily that he had the ability to achieve this.

When the regiment, 2000 strong, had finished they were led away by their *izindunas* back to their temporary grass huts that they had built on one of the slopes surrounding the royal kraal.

Throughout the long, hot afternoon, other regiments came one by one, each shuffling past in their turn.

The iDududu, the uMbonambi, the uNdi, the iMbube, the uThulwana, the uDloko, the uVe, the iSangqu, the iNdlondlo, the uMxapho, the iNdluyengwe, the izinGulube, the iQwa, the iSangqu, and many more. Finally the uKhandempemvu and the iNgobamakhosi who by then had finished making their challenges.

Thousands upon thousands, almost too many to count.

CHAPTER 20

TEMPORARY BRITISH CAMP AT THE BATSHE RIVER. 3 MILES
EAST OF RORKE'S DRIFT.
MID-MORNING, WEDNESDAY 15th JANUARY.

As predicted, it took several days to repair the track where it crossed the Batshe valley. Swampy ground here turned it into a boggy morass which would prevent any forward movement of the columns transport convoys and so the company of native pioneers were sent forward to lay down a corduroy surface and to dig out any large boulders that blocked the way. They were under the supervision of Lieutenant Macdowel of the Royal Engineers who also took along several junior officers.

To supplement this labour force Chelmsford instructed Commandant Hamilton-Browne to join them with several companies from the NNC. They weren't happy about it. After their success the other day they were rightly disgruntled at being used in this way. It wasn't surprising therefore that they were slow to put their backs into the work.

As a guard for the work-parties, who were expected to remain out here until the task was finished, four Infantry companies from the 2/24th led by a Major Dunbar were attached to them. It was a job nobody envied, encamped as they were on the far side of the river and several miles inside enemy territory.

They marched out two days after the skirmish to commence with the work.

On the following day, that is the fifteenth, Chelmsford decided it was high time that they started pushing out several scouting parties to reconnoitre the countryside further east. As soon as the track was made passable he would want to move the entire column onwards and so he needed to choose a location for their next temporary campsite. Early indications suggested a place several miles further on past the Batshe would be adequate but he wanted to see it for himself first, so during the morning he set out, taking his staff and a strong mounted escort with him.

Very soon the men labouring on the track saw them approaching over the crest of the gentle rise, their equipment jangling in the still, humid air. Major Dunbar came out of his tent to greet them where they exchanged smalltalk for a moment, and then the General wandered over to ask Macdowel how the work was coming.

Crealock eyed the natives with disdain, his frustration at their lack of progress obvious for all to see. Turning away from them he noticed the worried look on Major author's face, who was hovering about as if he wanted to say something.

"Is everything alright Major?"

"Sir?"

"Are the men not working hard enough? Is that what bothers you?"

Dunbar politely cleared his throat. "They are working as well as can be expected, considering this heat."

"Yes. The damn weather's a nuisance. It's so changeable from day to day."

A few moments of awkward silence. Crealock looked down from his horse, an irritable scowl on his face while he waited. Shifting from foot to foot Dunbar eventually explained what was on his mind.

"Something *is* bothering me sir. I'm a little concerned about the security of the camp. We are very exposed here, as you can see, and all of this thorn bush around us could be used as expert cover for the enemy. The brutes like to launch surprise attacks do they not?"

"Well couldn't you tear it down?" Crealock asked.

"But the men are all busy sir, either working on the track or on outpost duty. I cannot spare them. Plus these cliffs at our backs. If the Zulus get up there then they could fire down on top of us. I don't like it at all sir," he finished by shaking his head from side to side.

Crealock thought about this for a moment and cast his eyes around the camp environs, taking in the lay of the land. Still looking about he asked..."do you have any suggestions on how we could improve your situation?"

"Well ah... it's my understanding that the Standing Orders relating to camps are that we should build entrenchments and the horses placed in a wagon-laager during the night, so with your permis..." Dunbar's voice trailed away when he saw Crealock shake his own head.

"No, no, no, no. Completely unnecessary."

"But the field regulations say..."

"Damn the regulations man!" Crealock snapped harshly. "These are kaffirs we're fighting or had you forgotten? Do not confuse them with a modern, well drilled, European army."

Dunbar stepped back in surprise for the force of the Colonel's words had stun him with their sharpness. He gritted his teeth for he was sorely tempted to reply in kind. Instead he managed to just about keep his cool when he said, "the men would feel more confident if the position could be made more secure. As it is I have to post strong guards throughout the night. Maybe a few reinforcements...sir?"

Once again there was a slow shake of the head. Crealock turned in his saddle and nodded in the direction of Rorke's Drift. "The main force is only over the brow of that hill Major. Men on horseback could be here to support you in less than twenty minutes should you fall into any difficulties."

Dunbar felt himself bristle with anger. He considered pointing out to the Colonel that a determined force of Zulus would be able to overwhelm them in much less than twenty minutes, but he kept this opinion to himself. But when he did speak his voice was tinged with a faint note of desperation. "Then would it be possible for the men to return to the main camp at the end of each day, say at dusk?"

Colonel Crealock could no longer control his temper. He stared hard at the Major and his face started to turn a bright red. He was unused to such insubordination and on the rare occassions when it happened he thought the best way to deal with it was to come down hard on the culprit. Leaning down close to Dunbar he spoke quietly to ensure nobody else heard but his voice, although low, seethed with anger.

"If you are afraid to stay here Major," he said, enunciating each word carefully, "then I can always find somebody to replace you who is not."

Major Dunbar gave an audible gasp. He could not believe his ears! Had Crealock lost control of his senses? He peered at his superior officer and looked for any signs that the reprimand had being said in jest. But no, the Colonel's face was set in concrete, unflinching in its hardness.

At a loss as to what to say or do Dunbar spun and stomped away, muttering curses under his breath.

Chelmsford, who had been deep in discussions of his own with Lieutenant Macdowel, glanced across and watched him disappear into the tent. Quickly finishing the conversation he trotted over to where his Military Secretary was waiting. "Is the Major not feeling well?" he asked. "Has he taken to his bed?"

Crealock's thin lips twitched into a hardly perceptible smile. Reaching forward he stroked his horse around the neck. "Something like that," he replied quietly.

The General did not pursue the matter. It was time to move out, for he wanted to be back at the drift by late afternoon and they had much ground to cover. Bidding the men working on the track farewell the line of horsemen set off, trotting up the gentle slope and heading away from the valley.

The morning was turning out to be blisteringly hot and Chelmsford set a steady pace. Ahead of them the green rolling hills stood out starkly against the deep blue sky, and there was hardly a breath of wind to come to their relief. Beyond the rise the ground dropped and opened out into a wide and undulating vista with a range of hills to the north that stretched away into the distance. These were the Nqutu, a broad band of forbidding terrain that they would need to thoroughly scout as the column moved sluggishly eastwards towards the Zulu capital. Behind them the peculiarly shaped Shiyane blocked their view of the mission station at Rorke's Drift.

A little further on and the track crossed yet another stream, the Manzimyama. This one did not cause much of a problem for it was very narrow and the banks hard and rocky, so hopefully when the advance did resume the wagons and artillery pieces should be got over without a hitch.

Leading the mounted men on Chelmsford urged his horse up a steep hillside, his gaze already on the large outcrop of rock that peeked over the crest to their front. Reaching the top he found himself on the nek that lay between two more hills. The one on the right was large and bulbous looking, its sides strewn with boulders. The one on the left was different entirely. A sheer cliff face at the southern end rose three hundred or more feet into the air, a jagged and brutish jumble of crevasses and ledges and sharp rocky outcrops. Stretching to the north it dropped in height, perpendicular sides that threatened to send an avalanche of boulders crashing down without a moments notice. A grass covered spur joined it to the Nqutu plateau. It was an ugly thing. There was no hill like it for miles around.

Its name was Isandlwana.

ISANDLWANA MOUNTAIN. MID-DAY.

They cantered out onto the plain beyond and looked around at their surroundings. This is what they saw:

Isandlwana loomed over them like some giant, slumbering beast. It ran roughly north to south with its highest point towering above the track where it crossed the nek while the northern end dropped dramatically before gently rising once more in a long spur that attached it to the plateau beyond. Around its boulder-strewn base the land fell away in a series of gradual ledges before flattening out entirely. For three hundred yards or so the plain was more or less level, with only the occassional fold here and there, but then it dipped down towards the first of two dried-up water courses, or dongas as they were known in South Africa, that ran diagonally out to the front in a south-easterly direction. The first of these was only shallow, little more than a hollow line scratched into the earth, but the second one about half a mile further out was more substantial

193

being about fifteen feet deep and forty feet across. The ground between them was covered with a jumble of boulders of varying sizes with the occassional aloe plant sprouting up in several spots. Beyond the dongas the plain stretched on for several more miles flat and uninteresting, only marred by a peculiar conical-shaped koppie about a mile and a half from Isandlwana. Far off on the eastern horizon was the purple haze of more mountain ranges.

Bordering its northern fringes and running parallel with the plain was a steep escarpment known as the Nyoni Heights. This was the jagged edge of the Nqutu plateau, which in turn was an extension to the Nqutu mountain range further north. The spur leading from Isandlwana's tail climbed up the western end of the escarpments face where the ground was less steep, but beyond the trailing edge of the plateau snaked around the back of Isandlwana, the terrain becoming increasingly broken where the Manzimyama streamed through the valley. Along the rim of the escarpment which ran eastwards were a number of notches, which, together with the spur, were the only way up to or down from the plateau. It was from one of these clefts that came the large donga that bisected the plain below.

The view to the south was essentially one of hilly, broken terrain. Much of the land here was unmapped due mostly to its inhospitable nature. Numerous deep valleys twisted through the countryside with dense masses of mimosa bushes covering their flanks, while precipitous krantzes and kloofs gave the area a daunting appearance. Summit after lofty summit marched to the horizon until they disappeared into the hazy distance.

The track to Ulundi weaved its way over the plain. Getting the transports and the artillery forward would take time for the undulating ground and the dongas would slow them to a crawl and they would need to be manhandled along. But essentially the way ahead was clear. Apart from a few deserted Zulu homesteads there was no other sign of life, save for the humming insects and the occassional high-pitched whistle of a bird. The air was hot and still, the mid-day heat stiffling.

With good views all around, the long plain out to their front and Isandlwana at their backs, and with a plentiful supply of firewood and drinking water, it was the perfect location for their next campsite.

James Brickhill, who had accompanied the scouting party in his capacity as column interpreter and who found himself amongst the group of officers clustered around Chelmsford, looked around with a feeling of wonderful excitement.

He could not believe how much his life had changed over the past few weeks. Since joining with the 24th in Pietermaritzburg he had taken to military life with gusto, relishing the prospect of the coming war and enjoying the great adventure unfolding before him. He carried out his duties with a great feeling of fulfillment and knowing that his contribution to Chelmsford's plans was essential. The pay was good, the food-he was an officer-fine, and the companionship marvellous. Basically life couldn't have been any better.

He liked nothing better than riding with the General and Colonel Glyn at the head of the column. Being present when all of the important decisions were made, being in the heart of these historic events. Why, here they were today, deep inside enemy territory, further forward than any unit had thus far travelled. What lay over the next hill? What dangers awaited them around the next bend in the track?

Yes, he thought adamantly, he wouldn't change it for a thing!

It was hard to bring his mind back to what was happening but with a determined effort he tried to follow the discussion Chelmsford was having with his staff. Standing alongside them he was able to listen in to what was being said. Apparantly they were trying to decide whether the area around Isandlwana would make a suitable camping ground.

"Well it is relatively flat and open and is within easy reach of Rorke's Drift," Chelmsford commented. "The ground is a bit on the rocky side but it would only be a temporary site anyway. Right here at the base of the hill would be a good spot to pitch the tents and there's plenty of room for the horse lines and transports. I can't imagine we would find a better location."

"Yes. The hills to the north worry me a little," replied Glyn. "As does the rough ground behind us. They would need to be scouted thoroughly. But yes, essentially it fits the bill."

"Of course I don't think we need worry unduly about being attacked. All the indications we are receiving say that the main Zulu army is still concentrated around Ulundi. We may have trouble with a few small parties of warriors here and there, but as long as our videttes are watchful and give us plenty of advanced warning of their approach, it is nothing we can't handle." Chelmsford glanced back over his shoulder the way they had come. "Lieutenant Macdowel tells me the repairs should be ready in three or four days, so we could move the column up here on...say...the twentieth?"

"And from here?"

"We follow the track east. Sooner or later Cetshwayo's impis must show themselves, so as long as we continue to close on their capital..."

"His Lordship only intends this campsite to be a temporary one. A stay of a few days until the requisite supplies are forwarded from Helpmekaar through Rorke's Drift and on to us. We have in mind a site for our next campsite after this one, which will be a more permanent place."

"Yes, Crealock is correct. What was the name of the hill?" Chelmsford asked, struggling to remember. "Ah... something... what was it? Does anybody know where the map is?"

"Lieutenant Melvill," Glyn called, looking around for the young officer who was seated closeby on his horse. "The map?"

"Sir!" Melvill replied crisply, and trotted over to carefully hand the map over to the General, having already opened it out to the correct section.

Chelmsford squinted down at the mass of contours and rivers, positioning it so that the image on the page was oriented the same way as their view out across the plain. Then he stabbed a finger down on the point he was looking for. "Here it is," he declared jovially. "Siphezi!"

"Siphezi," echoed Crealock.

"It should be somewhere out there," Chelmsford pointed, and all eyes turned to follow his finger eastwards. On the horizon lay a range of purple-shaded hills. "There are so many of them... it is confusing... hard to tell which one."

Brickhill, who had been listening to them discuss matters and could see they were struggling, stepped forward. "Maybe I could help," he offered politely.

"Very good of you Mr Brickhill. I was forgetting you know the area so well."

"If you follow the course that the track takes, you see where it drops to the south and then sweeps back up again before disappearing over the crest? A little further on it curves around a large, sprawling hill? You see the one, the ground around its base is badly eroded? That is Siphezi. About eighteen or nineteen miles away."

"Thankyou," Chelmsford said with a broad grin, "thankyou very much indeed." Brickhill moved away feeling exceedingly pleased with himself.

"That will be our next destination after Isandlwana," Chelmsford informed his staff. "The men will have had a good rest by then. They will be kept very busy after that for I want to clear out the country along the Buffalo and Thukela rivers whilst at the same time constantly probing for the Zulu army. In the meantime our two flank columns will co-ordinate their own movements with ours" He handed the map back to Glyn who in turn passed it on to the ever attentive Melvill.

Turning his horse Chelmsford glanced up at the crag that towered above them. Several possibilities concerning their next actions ran through his mind but one problem remained unresolved, and it had been causing him a headache for quite some time now. Durnford! What should he do about Durnford?

That he was a good officer he had no doubts. One mistake in the past should not mar an otherwise exemplary career. Chelmsford was sure he would go on to great success in the future. But... there was something about the man that worried him. He could not put his finger on what it was but it disturbed Chelmsford. He was sometimes just too quick to take on heavy responsibilities, a characteristic he thought Durnford could not always control. Give him an inch... and he would steal a mile.

Yesterday's little episode only went to prove how right he was.

Durnford may enjoy the unwavering support of the men under his command, to the extent that their devotion to him bordered on a peculiar kind of worship - even from those who rode with him at Bushman's Pass - but Chelmsford did not share their confidence. In his view he had too many flaws to be trusted with an independent command. He would feel much happier having him somewhere where he could keep an eye on him.

"Crealock."

"My Lord?"

"Send word to Colonel Durnford. Instruct him to move on up to Rorke's Drift. He is to bring with him his Natal Native Horse, the Rocket Battery, parts of the 1/1st NNC and the whole of Bengough's 2/1st NNC. Along the way he should detach Bengough at Sandspruit, who may be later required to cross the Buffalo river and strike eastwards to scout the rough ground there. By the time Durnford reaches Rorke's Drift we should have moved on to our new camp here. Tell him he is to wait there for further orders."

Crealock turned away and began to relay the command. Soon a rider was sent galloping back down the track to the drift.

Brickhill, like all of the others, was confident with the way things were going. All they needed now was for Cetshwayo's impis to reveal themselves.

He looked off in the general direction that the Zulu capital lay, some fifty miles to the east across the rolling landscape. What was the Zulu Army doing right at that very moment? he wondered. Preparing themselves for war?

Yes. Of that he was sure.

CHAPTER 21

O n the final day, the King gave his instructions prior to the army setting out.

Throughout the morning the regiments had participated in one final ceremony. Because there were so many of them it was necessary to do it in stages, with the uNokhenke going first. Their chief *induna,* wearing the distinctive lourie-feather head-dress and necklace made of red beads and pieces of bone normally only worn by men of status, gathered them into a large circle on the flat ground beyond the *ikhanda's* wooden palisade. At the centre a senior witch-doctor prepared yet more medicine - called *intelezi* - in a potsherd, boiling it up and stirring in the ingredients. He did not hurry. Like all of the doctoring ceromonies it was important that the procedure be carried out correctly. So the men of the uNokhenke, who pressed in close to watch, waited patiently.

Amongst the dense crush of warriors one man found his attention waver for a moment when he felt someone push him in the small of the back. Mfulandelo kaZibeme turned angrily to see who was responsible. When he saw who it was his anger turned into fury.

Gezindaka kaMadikane towered over him, broad-shouldered and thick-set, a heavy scowl on his face. Both men stared at one another and those around them slowly became aware of the developing confrontation, and so they moved back to allow them room.

It was no secret that both men hated one another. It had been the case for a number of years now, going back to some long-forgotten disagreement between their fathers involving some stolen goats. Their mutual animosity had seethed and bubbled away ever since with the occasional fight taking place. Their friends, although loyal and ready to lend a hand whenever things turned violent, were aware that this rivalry between the two was worsening all the time to the extent that they now preferred not to become involved if at all possible. They feared that ultimately it could only have one outcome and they didn't want a part of that. So whenever they saw trouble brewing they were quick to intervene and drag the two apart before blows could be exchanged.

That was the case this time.

Besides, this wasn't the time or the place; not when in the King's presence.

So Mfulandelo moved reluctantly away at the gentle urging of his companions, muttering threats under his breath. When the commotion had died down the crowd's attention went back to the proceedings.

By this time the *intelezi* medicine was ready. The old *inyanga,* who was wearing his full ceremonial costume which seemed to weigh him down, shuffled forward on his spindly legs and dipped an ox-tail into the pot. Then he called out a command and the whole regiment turned their backs on him. When the men were in position he withdrew the ox-tail and rushed forward, moving surprisingly fast for someone his age, sprinkling the medicine over them. First one section, and then another, moving back and forth and occassionally dipping into the pot for more medicine.

The mixture the warriors were being sprinkled with was said to contain powerful elements. It would instill in them great strength and courage so that they would achieve the victory they so craved. Mfulandelo felt some of it splash against him and a peculiar feeling immediately overtook him, a sensation that he was suddenly invincible. Around him his friends likewise felt themselves grow in stature. They were no longer boys, now they were men! Whether this was all in the mind or not did not really concern them. All that mattered to them was that they were ready for battle.

But before the army could be launched against the white men one last thing was necessary.

When all the regiments had been sprinkled they gathered once more in the large central enclosure and waited for their King.

They waited until dusk.

Waited to hear his words.

Carrying the sacred inhlendla spear in his hand, Cetshwayo kaMpande, King of the Zulu, said, "I have not gone over the seas to look for the white men, yet they have come into my country and I would not be surprised if they took away our wives and cattle and crops and land. What shall I do? I have nothing against the white man and I cannot tell why they came to me. They want to take me. What shall I do?"

He looked out across the concourse at his massed impis, who were squatted before him. For a moment all were silent until, from within their midst, a lone voice called out in answer.

"Give the matter to us. We will go and eat up the white men and finish them off. They are not going to take you while we are here. They must take us first!"

Here and there others cried out their agreement. A ripple of excitement passed through them like a breeze through a mealee field. There was the buzz of a thousand conversations and one or two could not contain themselves and they leaped to their feet in wild exhileration. Only when their King lifted his spear did they fall silent and order was restored.

They watched and waited.

Somewhere in the distance a dog barked.

"There will only be one day of fighting," Cetshwayo told them solemnly, "it will all be over in one day. You will attack by daylight as there are enough of you to eat up the column at kwaJim's; and you will march slowly, so as not to tire yourselves. If you come near to the white man and find that he has made trenches and built forts that are full of holes, do not attack him, for it will be of no use. Do not put your faces into the lair of the wild beasts, for you are sure to get clawed. But if you see him out in the open you can attack him because you will be able to eat him up."

He paused for a moment, choosing his next words carefully, which he delivered with all the regal bearing befitting a King. "You must not cross into the white man's land. Fight them here and chase them away, push them out of our country...but do not cross."

Standing there with his feet planted firmly on the soil, he finished with the simple words... "The matter is in your hands!"

The great impi set out that evening, marching across the Mahlabathini plain in single column. It was, in all probability, the largest force ever assembled by the Zulu Kingdom. A few *amabutho* were sent south to help the local forces gathering near the coast to block a column of white men said to be advancing in that region, and some were also ordered to join the abaQulusi in the north-west to block more of the enemy pushing forward from the mountainous borderland there. The majority, 25,000 young warriors, would deal with the biggest threat approaching from the west. The enemy here had already begun burning kraals and attacking their people and so it was urgent that these be crushed first.

As ordered by their King the regiments moved at an easy pace. Their commanders, the elderly Ntshingwayo kaMahole, a veteran of many a battle, and his younger subordinate, Mavumengwana kaNdlela, set an example by jogging at the front. They moved west into the setting sun and soon they had crossed the White Mfolozi River.

For the first day or two the army would be accompanied by young *udubi* boys who carried the warriors sleeping mats and young girls who carried their food. Herders would also drive cattle which also would go towards provisioning the army whilst it was on the move. But as they neared the enemy these young boys and girls would drop away and from then on each man would need to carry his own belongings, and the regiments would then live off the land, or occassionally forage food from the kraals they passed along the way.

On this first evening the warriors were in high spirits. As they moved away from the White Mfolozi and crossed the emaKhosini valley they sang the great war-songs of Shaka's day, proud of their military heritage. All the young regiments were there, the iNgobamakhosi being led by Sigcwelecwele kaMhlehleke, with Mehlokazulu urging on the company under his command and amongst whose numbers were his friends Ndlela and Mnyamana. The uKhandempemvu, with Dilikhana kaBokwe, still full of himself after his victory the other day, and his younger brother Nzobo. The uNokhenke regiment, Gezindaka kaMadikane and Mfulandelo kaZibeme still glowering at one another after their confrontation. Others came on behind them, regiment after regiment, their young, lithe, well-oiled bodies moving with ease over the rolling grassland.

The impi, a powerful and seemingly unstoppable force, came on relentlessly.

Each stream they crossed and each hill they crested brought them closer to their hated foe.

CHAPTER 22

THE BRITISH CAMP AT RORKE'S DRIFT.
6pm, FRIDAY 17th JANUARY.

When the First Battalion/24th had passed through Pietermaritzburg on its way to the border back in late November, Lieutenant-Colonel Henry Pulleine had been disappointed to hear that he would be remaining behind as new commander of Fort Napier. He had been placed in charge of the Remount Depot to purchase horses for the troops. Chelmsford thought the post was perfect for him, having being told of his excellent administrative qualities and good eye for detail; in his earlier military service he'd held an appointment in the Commissariat Department for nigh on four years followed by a spell as deputy quartermaster-general, receiving high praise from his superiors on both occasions. So he seemed the ideal choice. He obviously had a flair for such work.

Pulleine would have preferred to stay with his regiment. Despite his long career he had yet to command a force in action and when the 24th had been sent up to Natal he had seen this as the perfect opportunity. But now it looked like his hopes were to be thwarted at the last moment.

Ever the professional soldier he had hid his disappointment and set to work at his new duties with typical zeal and dexterity. The work was very important and necessary and Pulleine, as Chelmsford had predicted, found the task a challenge rather than a monotony. But throughout his two months in Pietermaritzburg, despite his heavy work-load and time-consuming duties, he found himself increasingly preoccupied with thoughts of returning to the First Battalion.

Finally, and after reading reports in the local press two days ago of the first brush with the enemy, Pulleine had been unable to keep his impatience in check any longer. He had petitioned the General to be allowed to rejoin his unit.

Reluctantly, Chelmsford acquiescented.

Overjoyed at his good fortune Pulleine had left Fort Napier immediately, taking with him his groom and a spare packhorse. Aware that the Centre Column was planning to push deep into Zululand any day now and possibly meet with the enemy he knew it was vital they reach Rorke's Drift as quickly as possible, and so they had ridden through the night and all of the following day, crossing the swollen Mooi River before climbing the Biggarsberg and finally descending down to the British camp sprawling on both banks of the Mzinyathi. They finally arrived at sunset on the 17th, bedraggled and exhausted.

Despite the arduous journey Pulleine was in high spirits as they rode passed the thatched buildings of the Mission, weaving their way through the hustle and bustle and heading down to the ponts. Along the way he was welcomed by fellow officers and men alike, some of whom he recognized and some who he didn't. Why, over there was Stuart Smith of the artillery, sitting on a box and leisurely smoking his pipe as he watched the sun go down. Pulleine raised a hand and the Major waved back. A little further along the track he spotted the young man he and Colonel Glyn had met in Pietermaritzburg who they had offered the job as column interpreter to. What was his name? Brickhill, that was it. He stopped to exchange a few friendly words with him, asking how he was doing, how his new military life was treating him. He seemed to be in excellent spirits. As was everyone, Pulleine thought as he rode on. The mood in camp was very good with everybody looking forward to the next few days. It was good to be back.

With his young groom leading the packhorse that was heavily laden with his belongings following on, Colonel Pulleine guided his mount along the track to the river a quarter of a mile on from the mission station. A group of men were standing clustered together at the waters edge, waiting to be ferried over to the far bank. The pont, being pulled by native levies, floated towards them across the river.

Pulleine came up behind them. He recognized two of the officers as been companions from his own battalion, and he felt exceedingly pleased to see them.

"Good evening gentlemen!" he exclaimed, making the two men jump.

They both spun around and stared at him in unashamed amazement, mouths agape. After a few seconds one of them, who wore a pair of smart, brown gaiters, managed to say..."why sir, this is a surprise!"

"Not expecting to see me so soon Captain Younghusband?" Pulleine remarked jovially.

"Well...I...uh, not really Colonel," Younghusband stammered, rubbing at his mutton-chop whiskers.

Pulleine glanced across at the other officer. "Lieutenant Cavaye, your friend seems to have lost the power of intelligent speech. I prey the battalion hasn't come down with some fever whilst I've been away?"

Cavaye's face crumpled with restrained amusement and he politely stiffled a laugh behind a gentle cough. "No, not at all," he answered in his soft Scottish burr.

Colonel Pulleine climbed down from his horse and handed the reins to his groom who had likewise dismounted. He slid down the bank and joined them. "I suppose you are both wondering why I am here? Well, I just couldn't sleep from worrying about you fellows, up here without anybody to keep an eye on you. Thought I'd better return at once and keep things shipshape."

The two officers beamed, very happy to have their good-humoured commanding officer back. "Didn't want to miss out on the fun, did you sir?" Cavaye suggested.

"Fancied having a go at these fuzzies?" Younghusband added, having recovered from his surprise.

"I won't deny that that was one of the reasons," Pulleine admitted. "I've come this far and so it seemed pointless in sitting on my backside in Pietermaritzburg while you get all the glory."

"I can think of worse places to be."

"Yes...so can I," Younghusband remarked as he cast a critical eye about the campsite. "What you see is controlled chaos, sir. Bordering on the farcical at times."

"Now, now, Younghusband. Her Majesty's Empire is a well-oiled, streamlined machine as we all know."

"Mmm..."

As they chatted away the wooden pont had finally reached their side of the river. Once the ramp was lowered they, along with several other men going about their various duties, filed onboard. Moments later they were being hauled across the fast flowing water towards the camp that sprawled along the Zulu riverbank. Pulleine and his companions moved over to the side, where they stared down into the muddy flow that passed beneath the decking.

"I'd prefer it," explained Younghusband, "if we were on the move. If we sit here too long a malaise may set in amoungst the boys. They would rather be out there fighting the zulu instead of sitting around with too much time on their hands."

"I'm sure his Lordship has his reasons for the delay. Maybe you should bring me up to date on our state of affairs."

"Certainly. From what I understand the General intends to move the column forward some time within the next two or three days. He has allready scouted forward and chosen the site for our next camp. It is about eight miles in that direction," Younghusband nodded off towards the east, "at the foot of a large hill. A good spot by all accounts. The best for miles around. From there we are to move on the enemy and attack them...once we have located their whereabouts."

"They haven't shown themselves yet?"

"Not in any appreciable numbers. We've come across small groups here and there but they haven't offered much in the way of resistance yet. There are plenty of rumours going around about just where Cetewayo's impis are, but the general opinion is that they are probably still in the vicinity of the Zulu capital. But the truth is knowbody really knows. It's all guesswork."

"That can be dangerous," Pulleine remarked. "We need better, more accurate, intelligence than that."

"So very true," said Lieutenant Cavaye. "It has made for a few sleepless nights, I can tell you."

"They must be somewhere out there. Hiding, or perhaps waiting."

"Like a 'willow the wisp'," Younghusband mused.

The three of them thought about the comment for a moment, each man realizing how apt the description was. Soon after they reached the opposite bank and they stepped off onto Zulu soil, Pulleine for the first time.

"Well, I've much to do, lots to catch up on," he told them.

They both nodded.

"Neither of you would happen to know where the adjutants tent is would you?"

Cavaye pointed off through the maze of tents. "You'll find it along the path that way sir. Just beyond the water cart there."

"Thankyou. It was nice to chat to you both."

The three officers exchanged salutes and Colonel Pulleine, accompanied by his groom, set off briskly, humming a pleasant tune to himself.

The adjutant of the 1/24th, Lieutenant Melvill, was sitting on a small canvas chair just inside the tent doorway, hard at work writing up Captain Degacher's correspondence. Degacher had been placed in temporary command of the First Battalion during Pulleine's absence and was proving a stickler for correctness, demanding that all of the necessary paperwork be in order at the end of each day, a task that fell within Melvills duties. As if he didn't have enough to do. So he would spend two or three hours each evening sitting here working hard, perched on the chair and scribbling away at the books resting in his lap. And to make matters worse his tentmate, Lieutenant Coghill, was fast asleep on his cot, oblivious to the world and snoring to his hearts content. Added to the humid evening which was causing his tunic to stick to his skin and the annoying insects that buzzed around his face, it was a distraction he just didn't need.

He tried hard to concentrate on what he was doing. But the more he tried the louder his friend snored. Eventually he could stand no more.

"Oh, heavens above!" he exclaimed loudly, "do you have to make such an infernal racket all the time?"

Coghill must have heard from somewhere in his deep sleep for he spluttered and stopped and turned over onto his side.

"Thankyou." Melvill went back to work.

A moment later the snoring started up again.

Melvill groaned with resignation and buried his head in his hands, shaking it from side to side. It was no use. How was he expected to work? He'd come in here for a little peace and quiet, but what was the point? He'd find more tranquility in a herd of stampeding elephants. So immersed in his own self pity was he that he failed to notice the shadow on the tent wall of someone passing by outside.

Colonel Pulleine paused and, turning to his groom, put a finger up to his lips. Then, leaning in close he listened through the white canvas side of the tent, a half smile on his lips as he heard Lieutenant Melvill mumbling to himself..." I really don't think we need worry about the Zulus, not with you on our side. All of that din you're making is enough to drive away the bloody crocodiles..."

Crouching by the tent Pulleine half turned and raised an eyebrow at his groom who was waiting patiently with the horses. Coming across, the Colonel told the young man, "I think it wise that we don't involve ourselves with this one, what do you say?"

"Yes sir," he replied with a rueful smile playing across his lips.

"Come along," Pulleine told him, "let us go and find the Headquarters tent."

By early evening he had fully reaquainted himself with proceedings, Lord Chelmsford and Colonel Glyn both quickly bringing him up to date with their plans and how the invasion had gone so far. Soon it hardly felt like he had been away from his regiment at all.

Over the next two days not much happened. The work on the track continued painstakingly slowly and more supplies were forwarded from Helpmekaar to fill up Reverand Otto Witt's church which was being used as a temporary store. On the 19th Chelmsford sent a dispatch to Durnford who was in the process of moving up to the drift from Kranskop - *No 3 Column leaves tomorrow for Isandlwana hill and from there as soon as possible to a spot nearer to the Qudeni forest. From that point I intend to operate against any local Zulu forces in the vicinity if they refuse to surrender... I have already sent you orders to cross the Buffalo river at Rorke's Drift with the force you have and set up camp on the Zulu shore... I shall want you to co-ordinate with me in my move against the enemy...*

Later that same day, which was overcast and cold, the men at the temporary camp in the Batshe valley had their first serious scare. It was only a brief affair but did nothing to improve their already stretched nerves, and it went to show that Major Dunbar's earlier concerns about the position being too exposed were not unfounded.

Just after lunch Commandant Hamilton-Browne recieved word from one of his pickets up on Ngedla hill that a large number of unescorted cattle had appeared down in the valley below them. Intrigued by this development he had gone to see for himself, taking two companies of his Natal natives with him. Upon reaching the top he had joined with his interpreter Captain Duncombe who was the senior officer in charge of the lookouts, and asked him to show him just where these cattle were. Leading him to the edge of a steep drop Duncombe pointed down into the valley which twisted away in an s-shape.

Sure enough, down at the bottom were about a hundred and fifty cattle.

Where they had come from knowbody knew. There was no sign of any herders. It was all very suspicious, the two white officers agreed.

Just then their attention was drawn to a cluster of their own men further away on the ridge top. There were about seven or eight of them, wearing the red rag around their heads, who had been on outpost duty at the southern end of Ngedla. To Hamilton-Browne's dismay they were scrambling down into the valley towards the cattle. No doubt they too had spotted them and seen them as easy pickings, so they had taken it upon themselves to go and bring them in, ignoring the warning signs in their greed.

One of Duncombe's men, an elderly *induna,* also saw the danger. He suddenly came out with a stream of words and waved his arms about excitedly.

"What the Dukes is the old one saying?" Hamilton-Browne asked.

"Good God!" Duncombe exclaimed. "He says it is a trap! Those bushes are full of Zulus! The rascals are luring our men into an ambush."

They both spun their faces around to look down into the valley, their eyes scouring the thickets.

"We must warn them," recommended Duncombe.

"Too late."

The Zulus seemed to appear from nowhere. Coming out of their hiding places they trotted around the bend at the far end of the small valley, about 1500 of them. The Natal natives froze in their tracks as they realized their mistake, turned about, and fled panic-stricken back up the hillside. They were lucky. The enemy did not pursue them, perhaps because they had spotted the two newly arrived NNC. companies up on the crest of the hill.

Hamilton-Browne and Duncombe had withdrawn their revolvers in preparation for a fight, even though they would be able to offer little resistance if the Zulus did push the attack. Thankfully for them and their men, they didn't - for some reason thinking that the opportunity wasn't right.

Then as quickly as they had appeared they disappeared, the ground seeming to swallow them up. And the cattle too, during the few scary moments that their attention had been distracted by the Zulus appearance, had been whisked away. It was as if they had never even been there.

Up on Ngedla the two officers, not to mention the party of Natal natives who had escaped by the skin of their teeth, breathed easily again.

Was this the way it was going to be from now on? they wondered. Looking behind every tree and under every rock for the infernal Zulu Army?

CHAPTER 23

THE BRITISH CAMP AT ISANDLWANA.
MID-MORNING, MONDAY 20th JANUARY.

After the relative inactivity of the last few days the men of the Centre Column were glad to be finally on the move again. Striking camp at Rorke's Drift, they set out along the narrow track leading to Isandlwana. In the vanguard were the mounted units. They led the column forward, probing ahead, feeling their way over the rolling landscape. Behind them came the Imperial Infantry of the 1/24th. Following these were the long, dark lines of the two N.N.0 battalions. The six guns of the Royal Artillery came next, man and beast straining to pull them over the rough terrain, tempers becoming frayed as they toiled away. After these were the hundred or so wagons that carried the supplies, their wheels creaking under the weight, the voorloopers long whips cracking the air like gunshots. Finally came the 2/24th, bringing up the rear.

They made painfully slow progress.

There were frequent delays due to the state of the track, which was still in a poor condition despite a weeks worth of repairs. On more than one occassion they came to a complete stop and the men took the opportunity to take a rest, dropping down into the long grass or finding some shade to escape the burning heat.

Along the way they picked up the men who had been camped in the Batshe valley. Their nerves were still jittery after the previous days scare and they were glad to be reunited with their comrades once again.

Growing impatient at the slowness of their advance Lord Chelmsford rode on ahead with his staff. No firm decision as to the exact layout of the new campsite had yet being made and he wanted to take a second look at the ground they would be pitching their tents on. They arrived about 9am and spent about fifteen minutes discussing the matter. Some suggested that a camp lying at the foot of Isandlwana would be dominated by the large stony hill to the south of the track; it would be better placed further out across the plain, maybe towards the conical hill. Lord Chelmsford disagreed. He thought a campsite running parallel with Isandlwana would be fine as the mountain at their backs would give them ample protection and would also afford them with an unrestricted view out across the plain to their front. Pickets could be placed up on the high ground to the north and south with mounted videttes pushed well out to give them plenty of advance warning of enemy movements.

"Should we laager the camp?" Colonel Glyn had asked.

"It is not worth while, it will take too much time, and besides the wagons will be needed to return to Rorke's Drift for more supplies," Chelmsford had responded."

"So we build entrenchments?"

"On this ground? It is far too rocky. Besides, I only intend staying here for two or three days before we push on."

Turning back towards Isandlwana which loomed over them Chelmsford noticed that several of his staff officers had already started to mark out the positions where the various units might go, making rough tracings in the ground. "There you see," he pointed, "they agree this is an ideal spot. Marvellously efficient chaps, are they not?"

And so, the location of the new campsite at Isandlwana was decided.

While they were waiting for the first wagons to arrive the job of posting the videttes up on the hills got underway. This task fell to Inspector Mansel of the NMP. Riding out with men selected from the various mounted units, who being at the front of the column were the next to reach Isandlwana, he led them up the long spur that connected the plain with the escarpment to the north. The first position he chose was the ridge at the western end of the Nqutu plateau, a spot that would afford the two-man outpost good views down the spur to the camp below and also down into the broken ground behind the mountain. He then picked further spots out across the plateau, on the high hills set slightly back from the edge of the escarpment from where they could view the approaches on all sides, especially towards Ulundi. He informed each pair of men that they were to return to camp at dusk, it being too dangerous to leave them out here through the night. But otherwise they were to remain here and report any enemy movements at once, although they were not to take any unnecessary risks.

It took Mansel until well into the afternoon to finish this task and when he finally returned the campsite was allready taking shape.

The camp was laid out in a long line on the eastern slope of Isandlwana, the tents pitched in blocks according to unit. At the top end was the 2/3rd N.N.C, and just to their south their sister battalion the 1/3rd. Coming down the line and keeping parallel with the mountain was the 2/24th camp, followed by Harness and N Battery, 5th Brigade, Royal Artillery, 130 men in total. Next were the mounted units. Finally, and just over the track at the foot of the stony hill, were the 1/24th. Lord Chelmsford pitched his headquarters tents on the grassy bank behind the Royal Artillery, so that he would have a fine view over their heads. Each unit placed its horse lines and regimental transport behind its own tentage, while the remainder of the transports - when they finally rolled in - would go into the main wagon park that was being established on the saddle just behind the camp of the Mounted men.

The men would be kept busy for the next couple of days. The long and laborious task of bringing in the wagons down the eight miles of dirt track from Rorke's Drift would take all of today. Even by nightfall a number might still not have reached their destination and would have to spend the long hours of darkness out amongst the hills with a strong guard. Then tomorrow would be spent unloading the provisions and camp equipment, then turning them back around to send them back to the border for more supplies.

While the majority of the men worked on setting up the camp several small parties were sent out to collect firewood and drinking water.

The morning stretched on, growing hotter and hotter.

Towards   noon Chelmsford snatched a quick lunch and then selected a few men to ride with him to examine the ground ahead. He was, he informed them, a little concerned about the nature of the broken ground to their south and south-east. It would be easy for a stealthy enemy to use the hilly terrain to mask their approach and sneak up on them, or worse still to slip past them alltogether and launch an attack on Natal. He wanted to take a look around to put his own mind at rest. It would also be a good opportunity to select the site of their next camping ground on their relentless advance to Ulundi.

So they set off just after mid-day, heading out across the undulating plain and making for the distant hills on the south-eastern horizon. They made good progress without the hindrance of any transports to slow them down. Soon, they were several miles from Isandlwana. When they looked back towards the campsite all they could see was a vague white blob in the distance where the blocks of tents were being set up. It was disconcerting, this feeling of isolation,but they rode onnevertheless.

The hills on their right soon closed in. Two large mountains, Malakatha   and   Hlazakazi, dominated the view and blocked off any sight of the Mzinyathi River and Natal beyond, while to their front was another conical shaped hill similar to the one close to the camp. Between this and the mountain range on the right was a low ridge and Chelmsford headed for the gap. Cresting the nek here they rode down into a basin with a circle of hills curving away to their left. Immediately to their front a narrow river meandered across the hollowed out ground, trickling over a stony bed. The group cantered down the gentle slope from the nek and followed the course that the water took, which disappeared amongst a cluster of large boulders a little further on. Chelmsford pushed on ahead of the others.

He spotted the danger at the last moment and just had time to rein in his horse. Quickly he shouted a warning and raised his hand, and his escort likewise came to a sudden halt.

Their hearts fluttering wildly, they took in the view.

Where the river passed through the jumble of rocks the land dramatically dropped away in a sheer precipice several hundred feet deep. The water cascaded over the edge in a majestic waterfall, plunging down the glistening rockf ace into a long and narrow gorge that stretched away to the south, a jagged and ugly scar in the countryside that had almost lured them to their deaths. It was both a terrifying and beautiful sight which drew away their breath. Somewhere down in the bottom they could just make out the river, a thin ribbon of silver that twisted away, soon lost from view.

The small group of riders stood at the edge beside the head of the waterfall, stunned into silence. After a couple of minutes Chelmsford finally managed to utter a few simple words. "Mangeni Gorge," was all he said.

The others nodded their understanding.

They had been fools. Riding hell for leather down the slope with hardly a care in the world, behaving like a bunch of schoolchildren! If they had bothered to look at the map properly, as they did now, they would have seen that the gorge into which they had almost fallen was clearly marked for all to see. They had learnt a valuable lesson today, one they would strive to remember.

As they stared down into the dizzying drop below, one of the officers, Lieutenant Melvill, glanced off to the right and saw something else which made him gasp. "Sir. Would you take a look at that sir!"

Chelmsford and the rest of the party followed Melvill's pointing finger.

Below the gorge the view opened out into a wide valley with mountain after mountain stretching away into the distance. The vista seemed to go on forever. A rugged landscape of broken, hilly countryside, a maze of wild geography the likes of which they had never seen before. Here and there, carefully nestled into the contours, were a scattering of small kraals, while the dark shapes of cattle seemed like nothing more than tiny ants from here. It really was a wild place.

Chelmsford lifted his binoculars up to his face and quickly scanned the broad valley. From this height and distance he couldn't make much out. It was impossible to tell what lay hidden amongst the hills down there. It worried him.

He ordered the men to off-saddle and take a short break, and while the others sat and chatted - with Crealock (who fancied himself as a bit of an amateur artist) actually painting a quick watercolour of the view - Chelmsford wandered away from the group and found himself a quiet spot on his own, lowering himself onto a large rock at the edge of the precipitous drop. He needed to do some thinking.

His earlier concerns about the nature of the land between them and the border, the stretch running from the new campsite at Isandlwana down to the Middle Drift, were, it seemed, well founded. The terrain was infact much worse than he had been led to believe. It was ideal for concealment. He could quite easily visualize one of Cetshwayo's impis making a dash for the border through this very area. Equally they could choose to outflank the Centre Column and sneak in behind them to cut them off from Natal. He wasn't worried about the same thing happening to the north for Colonel Woods column was operating just forty miles away in that direction and should prove an adequate deterrent to stave off that possibility. No. It was here, to the south and south-east where the Zulus were most likely to chance their arm. This was the danger area.

Stiff and robust action would be needed if they were to prevent the Zulus getting by them.

He would need to make some hard decisions in the coming days, Chelmsford mused.

After a half hour break they saddled up and prepared to set off on the return journey. The afternoon was already well advanced and they would want to be back before sunset.

It was decided that they wouldn't retrace their outward route but would ride along the crest of Hlazakazi mountain before cutting back north towards the camp, thus giving them the opportunity to scout as much of the terrain as possible. Once more, Chelmsford took the lead, his small band of officers and troopers following in his path.

Once up on the heights a stiff breeze cutting up from the hills to the south helped to cool the sweating men and horses. In the distance

217

they could easily discern the distinctive shape of Isandlwana while at its base the British camp continued to grow and grow, the white tents shimmering in the summer haze.

A little further on and they noticed a small kraal nestled into the hillside, a collection of four or five huts. From their delapidated state and the absence of any cooking fires, they saw that the place was deserted. They were about to pass on when suddenly one of them, Lieutenant Milne, Chelmsford's naval ADC, called out. He pointed towards the huts, gesticulating wildly.

The others turned to look. Then they saw what had drawn his attention.

It was a chicken, wandering around aimlessly and pecking at the ground. "Ah!" Coghill cried, "Supper!"

Lieutenant Melvill burst out laughing. "Yes please. Let's go and bag the blighter."

The three of them let out a series of wild whoops and set off at the gallop while up on the crest Chelmsford watched, smiling and enjoying the banter.

They raced through the homestead kicking up clouds of dust, chasing after the bird which fluttered madly in its desperation to escape their grasp. It was no easy job trying to catch a chicken, as they soon found out. Amidst an explosion of flying feathers it managed to elude them, dashing this way and that, but the boys enjoyed the challenge for they laughed crazily.

But then Coghill's horse suddenly lost its footing in the dust and slipped over onto its side. The young officer tried to throw himself clear. He only half succeeded. Hitting the ground one of his legs was pinned underneath the horse, which then rolled over and crushed his knee. Coghill cried out in agony and pushed his mount away with his other boot, scrambling clear. But the damage was done. Gripping hold of his leg he stared in horror as he saw that the joint had popped right out of its socket. He beat at the earth with his fists, both in pain and anger.

Milne and Melvill had immediately abandoned their pursuit of the chicken as soon as they saw their friend go down. They galloped across and swung down from their saddles, rushing over to the stricken officer. Chelmsford and the others were soon on the scene.

Melvill looked at the injured leg and slowly shook his head, whistling between his clenched teeth. "Nasty," he muttered, "very nasty."

"I know that!" Coghill snapped.

"Sorry." Melvill looked up at the General, who was leaning down out of his saddle for a closer look. "The knee's dislocated. We'll need to pop it back in right away."

"Can you do that?" Chelmsford asked.

"Yes, I think so."

"Since when were you a surgeon?" Coghill managed to ask in between gasps. "Trust me."

"Do I have a choice? ...just make it quick, will you?"

Lieutenant Melvill smiled through his neatly trimmed moustache, then gingerly touched his friend's leg, testing the joint. "I'll do my best. It's all about pressure and timing, or so I'm told."

"Yes...yes. Just give me some warning before you do...arhhhH!"

With a hideous crack the deed was done, the kneejoint pushed back into place. Coghill screamed in pain, his eyes rolled up into his head, and tears streamed down his cheeks. Melvill, pleased with his work, stood up and brushed the dirt from his hands.

Within five minutes Coghill's cries had subsided into a continuous low moan, and he reluctantly allowed himself to be helped back into the saddle. With the young officer barely concious the small party set off once again. They moved slowly, for every jolt over the uneven ground caused him a great deal of distress. It would be early evening before they were back at camp.

It was an unfortunate ending to an otherwise invigorating day in the field.

*   *   *

Later that evening, whilst the officers of the Centre Column were enjoying dinner in the mess-tent, Lord Chelmsford quietly returned to the privacy of his quarters on the rise overlooking the camp. They were having a jolly time over there, discussing the progress of the war and relaxing after yet another hard day, but he had been unable to put his worries to one side. So he had made his excuses and come back over to his own tent, his mind going over the days events.

219

The observations they had made during their reconnaissance had left a lasting impression upon Chelmsford. The state of the countryside towards the south-east and the many questions it raised plagued him, refusing to let him rest until he had done something about it. So he thought long and hard about their options.

There was no doubt that the terrain would need to be much more thoroughly scouted than they had been able to achieve that afternoon. But if he wanted his Imperial infantry to sweep the area then it would have to wait a few days as they would be busy tomorrow and part of the following day with their work around the camp here and also providing escort for the convoys plying the road too and from Rorke's Drift. Could he wait that long? Probably, yet it wasn't an ideal solution. The alternative would be to make use of his mounted units and native contingents. That made more sense. After all, they were not only more use to such scouting work but they undoubtedly knew the country much better.

Of course it would be necessary to ensure that any such reconnaissance had enough firepower to deal with any threat that they might meet. The N.N.C. were, for the most part, armed only with their traditional weapons of shield and spear. The Mounted units were much better equiped and trained, especially the NMP who were a highly disciplined professional body armed with government issue firearms. So as long as the two worked in unison then they shouldn't have any problems. Plus there would be the added guarantee of being able to rush out two battalions of infantry reinforcements should a serious encounter with the enemy develop.

Chelmsford sat back in his canvas chair and began to formulate a plan based around these ideas. He quickly started to pull together the details.

A short while later and he sent for the commanders of the 3rd N.N.C. and mounted volunteers.

Commandant Rupert Lonsdale and Major John Dartnell arrived quickly, entering through the tent flap and standing before the General's desk. Chelmsford rose and greeted them in his usual polite manner and then set to work explaining his plan.

"Gentlemen, take a look at the map would you?" Chelmsford motioned them forward and together the three of them leaned into a huddle around the desktop. He ran his finger over the contours, describing the terrain features as he did. "This is our position at

Isandlwana, and this is the route towards the Zulu capital cutting across the plain to our front. Now look at these hills here." He pointed to Malakatha and Hlazakazi mountains, the two large peaks that he had noted earlier in the afternoon. "Study them carefully."

He allowed them a few minutes to take in the details on the map, watching their intelligent eyes moving about. When they were done they both glanced up in unison and nodded for him to go on.

"First thing in the morning you are to scout this range of hills. Lonsdale, I want you to take eight companies from each of your battalions and strike south, sweeping around Malakatha until you strike the Mangeni River here. From there you are to work your way up the valley. Give the area a good search and catch whatever cattle you can.

In the meantime Major Dartnell will be patrolling the Hlazakazi heights along this section, working south-east and gradually making towards the Mangeni gorge. Take with you all of the NMP and about half of the volunteers." Dartnell nodded briskly.

"If all goes well you should affect a junction at the head of the gorge. You should be back in camp by noon, so just take a days rations with you. Are there any questions?"

"My Lord," Lonsdale said in his typical gravelly voice, his jowls flapping, "what of the countryside my men will be operating in? How populated is it?"

"For the most part, and from what I could see whilst I was out there earlier, it is very thinly settled. The valley here, leading up towards the gorge, is the one exception. There are a large number of civilian kraals in the vicinity but they are widely spaced apart and as far as we could tell they all appeared deserted, but you had best be on your guard. It seems that the people all across our front have upped and gone, taking all of their possessions with them. Certainly we saw no sign of any young men of fighting age."

Lord Chelmsford strolled across to the tents entrance and lifted the flap, looking out across the camp. It was fully dark and the glow from the oil lamps burning within the hundreds of small tents lent the scene a cosy appearance. A pleasant feeling swelled inside him. He spoke back over his shoulder and the two officers approached so that they could hear him.

"The information we've being receiving suggests that the Zulu Army has finished its preparations and has departed from Ulundi.

Also that it is heading our way. By my reckoning it should be somewhere out in that direction." He nodded off towards the south-east.

"The same area we shall be scouting in the morning?" said Dartnell.

"Yes. So it is possible you may come across them."

Behind him, both Lonsdale and Dartnell exchanged a silent glance.

"Of course, should you become heavily engaged then I shall quickly move out reinforcements to aid you," Chelmsford added hurriedly as if reading their minds. "We have more than enough assets to handle any situation. Not only do we possess our men in this column, but Colonel Dumford's No 2 Column, or at least a large part of it, is lying in wait at Rorke's Drift having arrived there shortly after our departure this morning."

He turned back towards them and granted them a reassuring smile. "We will soon find them," he added, speaking more for his own benefit than anything, "this damn elusive army of theirs, and when we do we will destroy it."

Lonsdale and Dartnell both nodded, hoping that they appeared as confident as their General did. Then they made their excuses stating that they had much to prepare before their reconnaissance in the morning.

Chelmsford watched them go.

Saw them stride down the slope towards the mess-tent, from where he could hear the officers within laughing and talking zealously. They went inside, to pass on the news about his plans for tomorrow.

The sounds of revelry ceased almost instantly to be replaced by a subdued hush. Throughout the camp the night seemed to grow suddenly darker.

CHAPTER 24

THE BRITISH CAMP AT ISANDLWANA.
TUESDAY 21st JANUARY.

It was the early hours of the following morning and still dark, and the two battalions of native levies together with the 120 mounted men chosen for the reconnaissance were paraded on the flat ground before the tents. It was cold at the moment but the day ahead promised to be another gruelling one, and so because they had the furthest to travel - all of it on foot - and their officers wished to avoid the worst of the afternoon heat, the NNC were allowed to leave ahead of Dartnell's party. Shuffling into line they marched tiredly through the camp, some of them waving farewell to their comrades that they were leaving behind.

The 1/3rd led the way south through the maze of tents, with Commandant Hamilton-Browne and Henry Harford riding their horses at the front. They crossed the track that slipped around the shoulder of Isandlwana then passed by the lower end of the camp and made for the hills beyond, which loomed like large shadows in the night.

Just as they were about to leave the camp they both noticed a figure approaching from out of the darkness. Hamilton-Browne recognized who it was and he brought his horse to a halt, a pleased smile appearing on his face.

"Hello there Henry!" he called cheerfully, "you're up and about early. Decided to see us off, did you?"

223

Lieutenant-Colonel Pulleine walked up to them grinning self-consciously. "Yes," he replied, "I thought I'd come and wish you luck. Tell me, how did you manage to work it so that you were picked for this little expedition? You're a load of fortunate fellows, off to fight the Zulu while we remain here in camp."

"You sound envious."

"So I am. You should have a good time of it today."

"Scrambling around in the dust and heat," said Harford, "is not really my idea of fun sir."

"Especially with these blighters," added Hamilton-Browne, indicating the lines of natives marching passed. "They're a slovenly, lazy bunch, and probably not much good in a fight. I don't think today is going to be the picnic you think Henry."

"Still..."

"I'm sure you'll get your chance one day. But unless you have a death wish staying here in the camp is probably more recommended than taking this lot into battle, ha ha!"

Pulleine looked around at the levies working their way through the tall grass beyond the camp area, saw the NCO's cursing them and prodding them on with their rifle butts. They were indeed a far cry from his own highly disciplined and well trained infantry, so maybe Hamilton-Browne had a point. In jest, he lightly cuffed his fellow officer on the sleeve and poked fun by saying... "A lot of you NNC lot will be knocked over today, in that case."

"Mmm," replied Hamilton-Browne, coming back with a quick response, "if that is so, when I return to camp I shall not find one of you alive!"

The three of them laughed out loud, the sound attracting several curious stares from those nearby. Then, with a wave over his shoulder, the commander of the 1/3rd trotted away to take up his position at the front once more, Harford following on.

Behind them, Pulleine went in search of breakfast.

Cutting around the base of the stony hill that lay across from Isandlwana, the two NNC. battalions soon struck the rough country to the south. The land here was torn up with numerous dongas, creating a jumble of broken ground over which it was hard to walk for anyone unused to such terrain. The white NCO's and the officer's horses found it particularly difficult and they were soon tripping and stumbling around, cursing loudly. The natives were not troubled, they feeling totally at home here, and they watched their leader's struggles with great amusement.

A couple of miles further on and they were in hilly countryside. By this time it was daylight, the skies overhead filled with blood red clouds which gradually turned golden as the morning sun rose higher. From the hilltops they were able to look back towards the campsite that nestled at the foot of Isandlwana, the white tents bathed in sunshine. Allready it was hot even though the day was still young. They all knew it was set to be a long and trying morning.

Coming down from the high summits they came upon a beautiful scene. Up ahead there was a steep-sided valley overhung with great kloofs and vines, with birds darting from tree branch to tree branch and filled with the sound of chirping insects amidst a profusion of wild flowers. At the far end a small waterfall tumbled over the rocks, the water sparkling in the sunlight. A narrow stream meandered along the length of the valley, twisting and curling in delicate loops. It was a wonderfully tranquil spot and they stopped to admire the scenery, even the gruff NCO's muttering a few compliments under their breath.

They could not stop for long however and Lonsdale, who was in overall command, soon ordered them on.

He decided to cross the stream with the 2/3rd and sweep the opposite bank while Hamilton-Browne did likewise on this side. Together, but on either side of the water, the two battalions moved along the valley in open skirmishing order, on the lookout for any Zulus who might be lurking in the vicinity.

Hamilton-Browne's men were the first to spot any signs of life. They came across a small kraal situated beneath a large fissure in the cliff-face but as they approached they saw that apart from a few goats that stood about watching them forlornly the place appeared to be deserted. Lieutenant Harford climbed down out of his saddle and carefully routed about, poking his head into one or two huts. He saw a scattering of spilled grain, some meat that looked to have been freshly cooked and up-ended furniture. It seemed that whoever lived here had left in a hurry.

Coming back outside he raised his arms and shrugged. "Nothing," he told his Commandant.

So on they went.

It was soon noticed that the right hand side of the steep valley stretched away towards a high hill that seemed to scowl down on the lines of men moving about below. Its high flanks were covered in dark green scrub, with rifts and gulley's scarring the top. This was Malakatha, one of the features they had been ordered to check.

The regiment was drawn to a halt. After a brief consultation with his subordinates, Lonsdale decided to bring Hamilton-Browne's wing of the contingent over to his side of the stream in order to climb the high ramparts above them. The second battalion, led by Cooper, was to sweep around the foot of the mountain to their right, beating the country on the far side before the two groups met up again somewhere in the valley beyond Malakatha, on the shore of the Mangeni River. They were to catch as much cattle as possible, and to question but not harm any civilians they came across. As for any Zulu warriors, if they showed any signs of resistance then they were to be dealt with forcefully.

Moving to carry out these orders Hamilton-Browne turned to his men who were standing about beside the stream. Cupping his hands around his mouth he yelled to them, making it clear in a few short words what he wanted of them. "Alright you black scum, move your arses up that hill and see what's up there! I don't want any lagging behind! Or you'll get some of this!" He raised his fist and shook it at them.

They seemed to understand him. His was no idle threat, for the rank and file of the 1/3rd had experienced his violent temper on more than one occasion over the last few days. Therefore they had no desire to be roughed up this time. Quickly spreading out the companies began their ascent of the steep hillside.

By now the morning was well advanced and the sun beat down on them. The white officers suffered the worst and they struggled to keep up with the Natal natives, the furnace-like heat sapping their strength and drying their throats. They needed to make frequent stops to quench their thirst and as they slowly climbed and the time ticked away it became obvious that they were running well behind schedule. Yet they needed to complete their reconnaissance of the area no matter how long it took, so there was nothing for it but to push on.

As they neared the summit and the ground became more rocky they came across a number of shallow caves scooped out of the cliff-faces. Hamilton-Browne, who by this stage had found it necessary to dismount and lead his horse due to the steepness of the ground, suddenly spotted several figures scurrying to take cover in one of them. Ducking down and withdrawing his revolver he prepared for a fight, but then he saw that they were only women and children, no Zulu warriors. He halted his battalion and sent forward a dozen men to bring them in.

They came out of their hiding place offering no opposition, for they were trembling with fear at the sight of the armed crowd below. Under orders not to hurt any civilians Hamilton-Browne was furious to see them being manhandled by his own men, and so he angrily marched up to the group and struck the first one hard in the mouth, drawing blood. Seeing this, the group of women and children naturally assumed they would be next to feel his wrath and they cowered away in a huddle. He tried to calm them down but had little success so he called up his interpreter, Duncombe, and told him to explain that they would not be harmed. This he did and soon the group grew quiet.

"Right," Hamilton-Browne breathed. "Ask them what they are doing living up here in the caves."

Duncombe turned and spoke to them in Zulu, listened to their answer, and translated it back. "They say they do not live here sir. When we came into the valley they saw us and fled up here, thinking we would attack and kill them."

"The British Army does not attack civilians despite what they may have been told. I assume that is their home down below, the one we passed before crossing the stream?"

Duncombe asked them. "Yes, indeed it is sir," he fed their answer back.

"So the goats we found must belong to them," pointed out Harford who had been listening in to the questioning. He glanced at the sorrowful bunch of people before them and could not help but feel pity for them.

"Good point. We may be able to use that to persuade them to help us. Duncombe, inform them that I am puzzled as to the whereabouts of their menfolk and why they were not here to protect them. I'd be grateful if they could tell us where they have gone." Hamilton-Browne paused for a moment, then added, "if they can tell us then we can have the goats brought up here and given back to them, you understand me?"

"I do sir."

While they waited for the response Hamilton-Browne found himself a stone to sit on, and he took a swig from his water bottle. His brow was bathed in sweat and two damp patches had appeared on his tunic beneath the armpits. The heat, even up here, was godawful. There wasn't a whiff of a breeze. Around about, he noticed all the white non-coms were in a similar state of near-exhaustion.

"Commandant, this one here says that all of the men left for the Zulu capital a number of weeks ago to answer the King's call. I asked her why, and she told me they went to join the main army that was gathering there."

Still sitting on his rock Hamilton-Browne looked over at the one who Duncombe was indicating. She was young and pretty, he saw, with a high and intelligent forehead. She glanced across to him briefly but when she saw him scrutinizing her she quickly dropped her small eyes down to the ground. Pushing himself back to his feet, he strolled over to her and stood close, looking at her face. Speaking softly so as not to alarm her he asked..."tell me, where is the army now?"

She looked up and managed, only for a couple of seconds, to look into his eyes. She did not seem frightened now. Somehow, she knew to trust him, knew he meant them no harm. When she spoke it was in a whisper, her lips barely moving. She pointed off to the east.

"At the King's *great place* on the Mahlabathini plain," Duncombe translated. "That is where they are, according to her." He sounded sceptical.

"Mmm... she may be telling the truth, in as much as that is what she believes to be the case. It is probably old news by now. Still... I doubt if we will gain much more from her and her companions. This area is on the fringes of their Kingdom and I suspect much of what happens at Ulundi does not concern them a great deal." He continued to look at the girl who waited with her eyes downcast once more. How old was she, he wondered? 13 or 14? Without taking his gaze off her he spoke back over his shoulder. "Harford.

Would you send someone to bring up their cattle. Then see that these folk are left unmolested."

"Sir." Lieutenant Harford turned away and set off.

Hamilton-Browne then reached out and slowly lifted up the girls chin so that she had no choice but to see his face before her. He smiled, and said quietly, "thankyou."

Then he moved away, barking out orders and getting the men moving again.

They reached the summit about twenty minutes later. As they moved across they came upon more cattle nestling in a slight hollow on the top, and as these had no obvious owner they were shepherded along to be taken back to camp later as ordered. At the southern lip of the mountain they had a fine view down to the Mangeni River a mile or two away, and waiting for them were the second battalion who also had captured a large number of cattle. They started the descent down that side.

It was hard work cutting their way through the dense bush that covered the hillside and it tried the patience of the white officers so much that tempers became frayed. They had allready had a tough morning and the next few hours promised much of the same. Plus they were growing very hungry. By the time they finally reached the bottom and wound their way across to the river where their companions were waiting the men were very nearly dead beat. Seeing this, Commandant Lonsdale called a halt and the two battalions settled down for lunch and a well deserved rest.

The mid-day heat settled about them, stiffling and oppressive. Nothing stirred. The only sound was a constant background hum of insects. Finishing their meal, some of them lay back and started to doze.

A short while later and the quiet was broken by the arrival of several men bringing in two prisoners. The party of NNC men had wandered down to the river to replenish their water supplies when they had come upon two Zulu warriors walking along a small tributary stream apparantly unaware of the British partaking of lunch just over a rise and out of sight to them. The two were unarmed and therefore easily accosted, then marched back.

A murmur passed through the ranks as they were brought through the dense crowd, and Hamilton-Browne came to his feet, hands on his hips as the prisoners were pushed forward. Lonsdale joined him. Duncombe was once again summoned and the Zulus questioned.

It quickly became apparant that these two were not going to be as forthcoming with their answers as the women up on the hill had been. Other means of interrogating them would have to be applied.

Hamilton-Browne, who had a knack for this sort of thing, was quick to request permission to carry out the questioning. "With a little persuasion," he told Lonsdale, "I'm sure I can get good results."

Lonsdale huffed and puffed over this for a moment. He wasn't too happy with what his battalion commander was suggesting but he realized they didn't have all day to stand around discussing matters, and so he reluctantly agreed to the idea.

Hamilton-Browne called over one of his European NCO's, a short and heavy set man with small beady eyes and a pug-nose, then indicated that his interpreter was to come along too. The three of them, together with the two Zulus, walked over to a quiet spot out of sight of the others. Here the 'interrogation' began.

It quickly took on a sinister form.

Without speaking a word, Hamilton-Browne turned to the white non-com and gave a hardly perceptible nod of the head. Lighteningly fast, he struck out with his rifle butt, catching one of the prisoners square on the throat. The man went down like a felled tree. He rolled about clutching his neck and gasping for breath, leaving his companion looking on in sheer terror.

Spinning towards the second one, Hamilton-Browne asked the question: where are you from and what are you doing out here, just the two of you by yourselves?

They were deserters from the main Zulu army, who had left the King's kraal several days ago to visit their sick mother.

The NCO stepped over to the man on the grass. Lifting up his heavy boot he carefully placed it on the back of the Zulus head and pushed down, pressing his face into the hard-packed earth. Then he waited for the next question, poised to take whatever action was required to gain the right results.

Where was the Zulu army right now?

The second warrior stared down at his brother, heard his groans of pain and saw the intent in the white mans eyes.

The army was over to the east, out towards the capital at Ulundi.

When was an attack to take place?

The Zulu hesitated.

The NCO slowly withdrew a knife from his hip-sheath, bent down, and grabbed a hold on his captive's ear with the blade pressed close and ready to cut through it.

When the moon was right!

When was that?

In two days!

Afterwards, when the two prisoners were trussed up and tied by their wrists to a rope attached to one of the captured oxen, Hamilton-Browne thought to himself how easy it had been. It all depended on the method of questioning and the people who were been interrogated. Sometimes, as was the case with the women, the gentle approach paid dividends. Other times more robust measures were needed. The results were always the same.

Pleased with his work he passed on the information to Lonsdale.

A few minutes later and their trek through the hills resumed.

They moved up through the wide valley with the Mangeni river racing passed on their right. They were very tired by now. Long overdue back at camp they found themselves fully exposed to the worst of the afternoon temperatures - something they had wished to avoid. In the distance they could make out the occasional Zulu homestead but these all appeared to be deserted so they passed them by; besides which, they did not have the energy to make detour after detour to check them more thoroughly.

Towering over them was the long bulk of Hlazakazi, screening them from any view of the camp at Isandlwana. A cursory check was made of the southern slopes of the mountain but they were keen to push on, dejected and foot-sore, and after a further mile they rounded the end of the plateau and swung north.

Up ahead gaped the jagged mouth of Mangeni Gorge. A strong breeze blew down on them, like fetid breath from a monsters ancient throat.

Binoculars were raised, the officers scanning the perpendicular sides of the massive ravine.

Then a shout went up from one of them. Distant figures could be seen on the edge of the cliffs high above, the sun glinting on field glasses. It was Dartnell's party, looking down on them, no doubt equally delighted to see them.

The 1/3rd and 2/3rd were spurred on with renewed vigour.

*   *   *

Indeed, the mounted Volunteers watching from the brim of the gorge were very glad to have spotted them, for they had had adventures of their own!

Comprising of a large portion of the Natal Mounted Police led by Inspector Mansell and detachments from the Carbineers, the Buffalo Border Guard and the Newcastle Mounted Rifles, the whole force being under the command of Major Dartnell, the cavalry patrol left Isandlwana about one hour after the Native Contingent. They took few rations with them and only the ammunition they carried in their pouches and bandoliers, for this was intended to be only a brief reconnaissance to scout the ground ahead before the column made its next leap-frog movement forward to a new campsite. They rode out from the camp in high spirits, hoping that the day held much excitement for them and keen to get to grips with any Zulus out there.

They followed the dirt track for the first few miles as it slid diagonally across the plain in a south-easterly direction, then where it made a left turn and headed out towards Siphezi they slanted away and continued on for Hlazakazi Mountain, following the route that Lord Chelmsford had taken the day before.

For the next half-hour or so the patrol rode on at a steady canter, the morning hotting up until the sun blazed down out of the deep blue sky. As they drew nearer to the high prominence on their right Dartnell gave orders for the force to be split: he was to continue on with the NMP through the gap between the hills to scout the area above the Mangeni Gorge and beyond the conical hill known as Mdutshana while the rest of the party climbed up to the summit of Hlazakazi to patrol along the heights there. They were to meet again at the point where the river fell down into the deep ravine in what Chelmsford had described as a "marvellously frightful death-plunge".

The two groups of horsemen went their seperate ways, waving a cheerful farewell to one another.

The 46 troopers of the Natal Mounted Police pushed on across the undulating plain. The area was seamed with dongas, a badly eroded, barren looking landscape that slowed them down to a walking pace and it was some time before they eventually slipped over the nek into the wide basin beyond.

Stretching away on their left was the line of hills that Chelmsford had noted yesterday, and Dartnell led them out in that direction. Soon they crossed the Mangeni about half a mile above the waterfall which they could not see from their position. They were riding along in a fairly relaxed mood and had just gone around the foot of Mdutshana when Inspector Mansell spotted something that made his heart miss a beat.

"Good Lord!" he cried, reining in his horse and pointing away to their left.

Dartnell, riding alongside him, drew to a halt and stared aghast. The colour drained from his face and for several seconds he found himself unable to speak.

Spread across the summit of one of the hills ahead of them and watching them quite calmly were between seven and eight hundred Zulu warriors. They squatted there in the tall grass totally still and totally silent, as if they had been waiting.

"Wh-where the de-d-devil did they come from?" Dartnell stuttered, struggling to control his alarm.

Mansell glanced across at his commanding officer and then around at his troopers, noticing their agitated state.

"Steady men," he told them in deep, authorative tones, trying to stop them from panicking. "Keep your heads and stay cool."

His words seemed to have a calming influence on them. However, one man decided this was an appropriate moment to load his revolver, but as he was doing so he accidently discharged it and fired into the ground.

The gunshot exploded in the still air and bounced around the basin of hills, echoing back and causing the horses and men to jump.

Mansell spun in his saddle and looked to see who was responsible, his face turning bright red with anger. "Damn you Parson's you infernal cretin!" he snapped. "Put that thing away or you are going to get us all killed!"

Everyone then looked back to where the Zulus waited, wondering what effect the gunshot would have on them. Would it cause them to launch an attack?

The warriors did not move. As before, they just continued to look down at them in a slightly curious fashion.

"What do you reckon Mansell?" asked Dartnell, his voice now back to normal.

"It's certainly a significant force sir. We don't know how many more of them there are on the far side of the hill. There's too many for us to take on by ourselves."

"I concur with that," Dartnell agreed somewhat quickly.

"I suggest we link up with the others and then come back and deal with these. The NNC. should hopefully be about arriving by now, so we'll have a strong enough force to attack if that is what we decide."

"Yes. But who are these people? Do you think they might be a local group, left behind to slow our advance?"

Mansell thought about this for a moment, then shrugged his shoulders. "Could be," was all he would say.

With the decision made the party was turned around and led away, galloping towards the head of the gorge where they should find their companions. Behind them, the distant figures on the hilltop stared after the departing cavalry.

Meanwhile, as all of this was going on, the group who had been sent to scout the summit of Hlazakazi had spent a fruitless time checking empty kraals during their ride eastwards. They had found not a single soul during their detour much to the disappointment of the men.

Fred Symons of the Carbineers had summed up the mood by saying to his friend and fellow trooper Ted Greene, "all the Zulu warriors are long gone. We are just wasting our time here, wandering around from hill to hill."

"Ah, I'm not so sure," replied Greene, "I think they're out here somewhere, hiding from us."

"If that is the case then why don't they attack? We are not much of a force, us few, and if they are in the numbers his Lordship suspects then what holds them back?"

Symons' brother Jack overheard their conversation and he rode up to them. "Maybe they are under orders not to fight us," he suggested. "They're a wily bunch these kaffirs, not the savages the rooineks think. They'll choose their own time and place to reveal themselves."

"Still," said Ted Greene, "if they do see an opportunity to take us by surprise they might find it hard to resist, orders or no orders. We should be careful otherwise we might just blunder straight into them. Like you've just said, we are pretty weak in numbers, and out here all by ourselves."

"Rubbish!" replied Fred Symons in his ever sceptical way. "They will not attack. I just know it. We might as well return to camp this very minute for all the good we are doing up here."

The other two troopers looked at one another and shook their heads, smiles playing across their faces.

Their attention was drawn away from the matter right then as their commanding officer decided it was high time they descended down the eastern slope and made for the gorge beyond. Their orders had been to rendevous by the waterfall. They pushed on, glad to be doing something more positive than poking around on the summit.

Riding along the crest they reached the hillside overlooking the deep gorge after about half an hour and carefully picked their way down the boulder-strewn slope and then across to the flat ground where the waterfall plunged down into the ravine. There was no sign of either the Police or Lonsdale's Native Contingent and so the volunteers dismounted and broke out their rations to snatch a bite to eat. While they had lunch several of the officers moved to the edge and observed the rugged countryside below them through their binoculars and small telescopes, looking for signs of the N.N.C. who should be on their way up.

They waited for some considerable time and were starting to grow a little worried, thinking that something might have happened to Lonsdale's party, when at last they spotted them rounding the bottom edge of Hlazakazi, the sun glinting off their white shields. The distant line of men slowly made their way towards the mouth of the gorge, moving wearisomely after their tiring day.

The horsemen above watched them approach. The day by now was well advanced and they knew that it would be well after dark before they finally reached camp, the prospect of the long journey back through the night not one they were looking forward to. Even Trooper Symons knew it would be a jittery ride even though he was sure the countryside was empty of Zulus. And just then, as if to emphasise the point, a single gunshot shattered the stillness of the day.

Everyone looked in the direction it came from, waiting to see if more followed to announce the start of a heavy engagement. There was nothing. And although they were not unduly alarmed, the men were ordered to mount up and move around to the far side of the gorge incase the NMP needed any support. They waited, strung out in a loose line, looking for any sign of their companions.

Down below the Native Contingent had come up the gorge and were now beginning the daunting climb up the steep sides, a hair-raising experience made worse because of the large number of captured cattle they had with them. Being fleet-footed and very fit, they scampered ahead of the slower white men who came up on the verge of collapse, gasping and sweating and cursing. Finally they crested the brim, shattered and done in for, and dropped to the ground.

They did not have the chance for a long rest though. After just a few minutes, during which the two groups of men, the cavalry and infantry, brought one another up to date on the days events, it was noticed that Dartnell and the Police were galloping towards them across the wide flats.

Commandant Lonsdale, together with Hamilton-Browne and Cooper, hurried over to see what the matter was.

Major Dartnell quickly told them of their encounter with the Zulu force and how he wished to return and engage them. He was hardly able to control his excitement at the prospect, having conveniently forgotten his earlier panic.

"How many zulus are we talking about here?" Lonsdale asked him.

"Up to a thousand. That's why I waited for you to arrive before attacking."

"If I may say so sir," Hamilton-Browne broke in, "I don't think my men are in any fit state to fight. They've had a very trying day and we have a long journey home. Our orders are to scout this area, with no mention of engaging the enemy."

"Nonsense!" Lonsdale blurted. "They're in fine fettle man!"

A little flustered at his commanders response and hoping he would have his support, Hamilton-Browne struggled to keep his temper in check. "Then I suggest we send to his Lordship for further instructions."

"We do not have time for that. The enemy are there for the taking, now, this very minute. We have to seize the moment." Dartnell turned and raised his eyebrows at Lonsdale, then looked back at the younger man. "Do you not have confidence in your men?"

Hamilton-Browne gritted his teeth at this. He looked straight back at Dartnell, holding his gaze, taking a silent, deep breath. Then he said in a loud and clear voice, "My battalion will attack, if ordered. Have no doubts on that sir."

"Good. The matter is settled then. We move off to attack the enemy." Dartnell prepared to move away but was once more brought up by the Irishman.

"Then I think it wise that we send back the cattle that we have captured. They will only hamper our movements."

"Oh very well," Dartnell snapped petulantly, allready digging in his spurs. "I will leave that task in your capable hands seen as though you have a flair for such things. Join us when you are ready, in your own time of course."

Hamilton-Browne watched the Major ride away. Then he saw the furious look on his own commander's face and waited for Lonsdale to come across, expecting a heavy reprimand from him. Yet he changed his mind at the last minute, perhaps deciding this wasn't the time nor the place. Instead he turned and rode after the Major, shouting out orders and getting the N.N.C. moving.

Twenty minutes later, with the cattle safely on their way to Isandlwana, the British formed up on the eastern end of Hlazakazi. Here, a quick plan of action was hastily reached by the various commanders: the mounted volunteers and Police would move down towards the range of hills where the body of Zulus had been spotted to try and draw them out into the open, and once this was achieved the NNC would come down off the heights to lend support as the attack developed.

A simple idea to what should prove to be a simple, little fight.

They had more than enough firepower to deal with the number of Zulus estimated to be out there, even taking into account the unreliability of the N.N.C's fighting capabilities. The cavalry grumbled that they would have to bear the brunt of the action, and some of their officers agreed, but there was nothing else for it.

Trooper Symons did not join in their protests.

Much to his embarrassment he had been proven wrong with his earlier insistance that they would see no Zulus today, so he kept quiet.

However, inside he was just as apprehensive as his comrades.

By the time the mounted men received the orders to move out the shadows were gathering and the evening drawing in. They cantered forward and cut across the slope, then spread out into a long line at the foot of the hill and headed towards the northeast. The men up on the summit watched them go, tense and nervous. The horsemen reached the line of hills above the Mangeni and urged their mounts up the steep ground, picking their way slowly so as to maintain their positions in line. Several minutes later and they had disappeared over the skyline.

Time dragged, and for the men up on Hlazakazi there was nothing to do but listen for the sound of volleyfire to announce the start of the fight. To their surprise they heard nothing. All was quiet and still.

Lieutenant Harford was about to suggest that maybe the Zulus had retired, and he glanced across to Hamilton-Browne for a brief second. When he looked back down to the hills below he was suddenly struck dumb by what he saw.

The British were racing back down the hillside amid a cloud of dust and shouts of alarm, all order lost as panic seized them. As they manoeuvred their horses over the treacherous ground some of them turned in their saddles to cast petrified looks back over their shoulders. Harford soon saw what frightened them so much.

A dark mass of Zulu warriors spilled over the crest of the hill, charging down after the fleeing horsemen. In a matter of seconds the whole slope seemed to be alive with them. They ran and leaped over the rocks and boulders, hardly pausing in their advance despite spotting the rest of the British force up on Hlazakazi. Lieutenant Harford, Commandant Hamilton-Browne and the rest of the 1/3rd and 2/3rd quickly estimated that there must have been in excess of one and a half thousand warriors, double the number seen earlier. What's more, they were quickly catching the Volunteers and NMP. The Zulus swarmed forward then threw out two flanking wings with superb precision, the men advancing ahead of the main body and making excellant use of cover as they attempted to encircle the horsemen. It was an awesome display of their discipline, which would have been much admired by the men on Hlazakazi had it not so alarmed them.

The cavalrymen were in a dire position. The next few seconds would decide their fate.

Lonsdale immediately spotted the potential for disaster and barked out commands for his Native Contingent to lend them support, but the men did not respond. He raced up and down the line on his horse, screaming at them, but it made no difference. They refused to budge. He came over to Hamilton-Browne and demanded to know why his men refused to obey his orders.

"Because it would be suicidal folly," he told him bluntly.

"Thank the Lord!" blurted Lieutenant Harford beside him, watching events unfold.

The two Commandants turned back to the action wondering what had caused his exclamation.

The Zulus had stopped dead. Just as they were sure to catch up with the mounted men they called off the pursuit, and as quickly as they had appeared they started to pull back, slipping away up the slope. In less than a minute they were gone. Back to where they had come from.

Not for the first time the British had had a lucky escape.

How much longer would their luck last, Hamilton-Browne wondered?

Dartnell and his men came back up to the summit of Hlazakazi, badly shaken after their fright. A few of them tried to crack a joke about it but most were quiet, their faces very pale.

The officers had a brief conference and discussed the suddenly changed situation. That there were far more Zulus out there than first thought had been dramatically shown to them. It was also apparent that they, the British, would not be strong enough to take them on with the force they had. They could return to camp for reinforcements and return in the morning but that would mean losing contact with the Zulus overnight and all of the day's hard work would have been for naught. So they immediately ruled that out. The only alternative was to send back a message to Lord Chelmsford requesting he send out several companies of Imperial Infantry to bolster their numbers before an attack was made, and in the meantime they would bivouac where they were. Then first thing in the morning they could move to engage the enemy.

Yes. It was a good solution to the problem.

His Lordship would be in full agreement with their decision, once he heard that the enemy had been located.

CHAPTER 25

The message reached Chelmsford shortly before two
o'clock the following morning.

It had been a hair-raising experience for the young
rider, travelling through the night alone and knowing the area was
alive with Zulus, and he had almost lost his way on a couple of
occasions. Because of this delay it took far longer than it should have
for him to reach camp but eventually he arrived, greatly relieved
to have made it in one piece. He had gone straight to Colonel
Glyn's Staff Officer, Major Clery, and handed the message form
over, waiting while the Major struggled to read the scrawled
handwriting by the glow of his nightlight. Squinting at the barely
decipherable words and tutting to himself it took the best part of
ten minutes for him to glean the general meaning of Dartnell's
message. Then, thanking the rider and dismissing him, Clery took
the message over to the Colonel's tent. Annoyed at being woken
Glyn had remarked that any decisions about responding to the
request for reinforcements lay with the General and that he was to
take the message to him in person. So, a few minutes later Clery

found himself inside Lord Chelmsford's tent, crouched down beside the bed and gently rocking the General awake.

After a long and circuitous route Dartnell's plea for assistance finally arrived at the right place.

Whispering into Chelmsford's ear and shaking him by the shoulder in as polite a manner as possible, Clery said, "My Lord, my apologies for disturbing you, but there is something that needs your attention."

Without opening his eyes Chelmsford responded in a surprisingly clear and unruffled voice. "What is it Major?"

"A message from Major Dartnell."

Chelmsford's brow furrowed in concentration for a minute, clearly puzzled by this. "Has the reconnaissance not returned yet?"

"No. They apparantly met with a few problems along the way which slowed their progress and made them decide their best option was to form a bivouac and stay out overnight."

Chelmsford said nothing for several seconds. Then, still keeping his eyes shut, he said, "I think you had better read the message."

Clery did as he was instructed. He found it much easier this time, having already worked his way through it once and remembering it all word for word. When he was done he knealt there waiting for the General's response.

With a heavy sigh Chelmsford pushed himself up in bed and swung his stockinged feet to the floor. Rubbing his beard and taking off his night-cap he gathered his thoughts, then climbed to his feet and reached for his uniform which hung on a stand closeby. Major Clery stood at hand while the General dressed, listening carefully to the instructions that Chelmsford quickly rattled off.

"Order the 2nd Battalion 24th Regiment, four of the artillery guns, and all of our mounted troops to get ready and start at daybreak. Myself and Glyn will be going also. Oh, and I think we might need the Pioneer Corps to help clear the track for the guns." He pulled on his uniform, fastening the buttons. "We will leave behind the 1st Battalion, the men on outpost duties can stay as well, as can a section of two guns under Lieutenant Curling and Major Smith. The command of the camp will be in the hands of Pulleine whilst we are away." On went his belt and various accoutrements. "I do not wish to be laden with too much transport so we will only take two ambulance wagons. The men are to only have their requisite seventy rounds of ammunition apiece as I wish us to travel light but inform Pulleine to have a reserve supply standing by to send out should we become heavily engaged." Finished pulling on his clothes Chelmsford smoothed down the uniform and carefully positioned his helmet on his head, lowering its brim to eyebrow level. He stood before a full-length mirror for a moment and studied his reflection. Evidently satisfied with his appearance he turned to Major Clery. "Colonel Durnford is at Rorke's Drift. Have Crealock send him a message to the effect that he is to move up here with his column to reinforce Pulleine. We should be ready to move out to Dartnell's assistance as soon as is feasible incase he has serious problems on his hands, so there is no time to waste." He smiled at Clery, clearly thrilled at this turn of events. "So hurry hurry Cornelius," he addressed him by his first name, "there is much to be done."

Nodding briskly, Major Clery stepped outside and set to work.

He first of all went to see Crealock to pass on the General's instructions concerning Colonel Durnford, and then visiting each of the unit commanders in turn he issued the necessary orders to begin assembling the relief column. Soon the camp came to life. The men began to turn out in good order and gather their equipment. The four guns were limbered up. It was all a well drilled, much practiced operation, and each person knew his role blindfolded, and in no time at all they were ready.

Barely one hour after receiving Dartnell's message the troops were awaiting the command to set out across the dark plain.

Chelmsford was still inside his tent, deep in conference with Colonel Glyn and discussing their plans for the day, and whilst they talked Clery became aware of somebody watching him. He turned to see Pulleine and his adjutant, Lieutenant Melvill, seated on their horses nearby, looks of deep concern on their faces. They obviously weren't happy with proceedings and it took a few seconds for Clery to fathom what was on their minds. Then it suddenly occurred to him that as yet knowbody had issued Pulleine with any instructions. As he was to be in command whilst the General was absent he needed to know what his orders were concerning the camp arrangements, and also his operational status. For some reason the General, in his desire to go to Dartnell's aid, had completely overlooked this.

Clery knew by rights that he ought to go and bring this to Chelmsford's attention, but he had no wish to disturb His Lordship right now, especially as the General had so many other things to take care of. So he made a snap decision. He would venture on the responsibility of issuing the orders himself.

Riding over to them he brought his horse around to stand sideways on to the two men. "Gentlemen," he said warmly.

"Major," replied Pulleine and Melvill together.

"His Lordship is extremely busy at the moment, so I thought I would just clarify what your instructions are to be while we are away from camp. I hardly need to spell them out in detail to an officer with your years of experience, Henry, but it strikes me that you should be aware of what exactly is required."

Clery waited whilst one of the artillery guns rumbled by before going on.

"Draw in your line of defense as soon as the force with the General leaves, that is your Infantry outposts, but leave your cavalry vedettes well out to the front. Act strictly on the defensive. Keep a wagon loaded with ammunition ready to start at once, should the General's force be in need of it. Colonel Durnford has been ordered up from Rorke's Drift to reinforce the camp. I stress again, Colonel, you are to defend the camp. Is that clear?"

Pulleine gave the affirmative, but before he could say more his adjutant spoke up, as forthright as ever. "Are we to laager the wagons Major, as an extra precaution? The General is taking away with him a large portion of the column and I think it might be a wise option."

"No, not at all. This is a strong position Melvill. An all-round defensive formation anchored on the mountain will suffice." He gave a little laugh as he went on, "not that there is the slightest chance of you being attacked, now is there?

Pulleine and Melvill's answer was drowned out by a squadron of Mounted Infantry cantering passed, and anyway, Clery had half-turned away as he prepared to join the General who had just come out of his tent. He threw a final comment over his shoulder before he went. "Not to worry. We will be back this time tomorrow, hopefully with some good news to give you. Cheerio now!"

Watching him go the two officers said nothing at first, each deep in thought. Melvill was the first to speak. "Do you think it is wise Colonel for the General to be splitting his force in two like this?"

"Yes it is a tad cavalier, I agree."

"It is against all the principals of military theory, if you ask me. He rides into the unknown on the basis of poor intelligence. Is he trying to prove something?"

"Ours is not to reason why Lieutenant," Pulleine smiled thinly.

"It should be," responded Melvill, slightly critical of his superior's easy-going attitude to these developments. "What are Colonel Glyn's views on this?"

"I have not spoken to the Colonel since the decision was made, and as he will soon be departing I do not suppose I will get the chance, but I am sure he will fully support the General's strategy."

Melvill gave a disdainful sniff, letting it be known he was not quite as convinced as his superior officer.

"You have something to say on the matter?" Pulleine asked, turning to examine him in the glow from a near-by oil lantern.

Melvill moved uncomfortably in his saddle, his eyes downcast. When he glanced up he looked over to where Colonel Glyn was, waiting by Chelmsford's side. "Well it seems to me sir that the Colonel is...well, no longer in command of the column, and hasn't been since His Lordship decided to join us on our advance. All of the important decisions are being made by the General and his staff. Quite what our Colonel's role now is eludes me."

"His task, Lieutenant Melvill, is to give advice and lend support to the General - the one thing we all should do is support," Pulleine commented pointedly as he gave the adjutant a frosty stare quite uncharacteristic for him. "He is in a difficult position fighting an opponent who has already shown itself to be formidable and unconventional. He only does what he thinks is best in trying to track down the elusive Zulus. We should be grateful we are not burdened with such decision-making ourselves."

"So our policy is simply to do as we are told?"

Pulleine continued to look at the Lieutenant for a moment. One day, he thought, the man's outspokeness would land him in big trouble. The fact that he was used to his ways was probably all that saved him from a severe reprimand on this occasion.

"I have no desire to cross swords with you over this," he said, "so I think we should leave the subject right now. We have more pressing matters to attend to, such as carrying out the instructions Major Clery passed on."

Melvill gave an embarrassed smile as he suddenly realized how close to the wind he had just sailed, and was grateful for the opportunity to withdraw from this difference of opinion with his honour still intact.

As Colonel Pulleine had indicated, they would be better putting all of their energies into seeing to the smooth running of the camp while Chelmsford was away.

Across the way the two men who had been the focus of their conversation had finished making their final preparations and were about to issue the command for their column to set out along the dirt track. Before he gave the word, Chelmsford turned to his companion. "I do not see Lieutenant Coghill. Should he not be with you?" he asked.

"I thought that after yesterday's tumble that it would be better if he stayed here in camp on light duties. I have just looked in on him and he is in considerable pain, so he would be of little use anyway."

"Very charitable of you," Chelmsford said, his attention already drifting from the query. "Are we all ready then? Because if we are I think we ought to get on. I do not wish to keep Dartnell waiting any longer than necessary. He is probably nervously waiting for us."

Together the General and Colonel, followed by his staff, rode down the line of men towards the front of the column.

Several minutes later and they started out, marching purposefully into the darkness. Into the unknown.

SITE OF DARTNELL'S NIGHT BIVOUAC. HLAZAKAZI MOUNTAIN.
12 MILES SOUTHEAST OF ISANDLWANA.
2am-6am, WEDNESDAY 22nd JANUARY.

The men had been arranged into a large hollow square on the bare hillside. On three sides, two companies deep, were Lonsdale's two NNC. battalions, while on the southern face were the mounted men with their horses just inside of them, their arms threaded through their reins. In the centre several large bonfires burned, to warm them and also to lend some relief from the pitch blackness. Further out to the front and across the forward slope was a thin line of pickets.

On the hills opposite and only about two or three miles away to the north hundreds of small Zulu campfires marked the enemy positions. It seemed that their numbers had steadily increased as the night wore on, although it would be impossible to tell exactly how many were out there until first light. In the meantime the British had a long night ahead of them.

It was a lonely and exposed spot.

Their nerves were stretched taut.

Had it not been for their exhausting trek through the countryside the men would have found it impossible to relax. They were so tired however that eventually, just after midnight, sleep started to claim them one by one and eventually a quietness descended.

Even the horses became still.

The night was silent.

Just after two o'clock a single gunshot had them sitting bolt upright, followed almost immediately by two more. For a few seconds there was a hush. Then the night was filled with screaming and yelling voices, and from out of the darkness a horde of running figures charged forward and broke through the front of the square.

Hamilton-Browne leaped to his feet. Mary, mother of Jesus! he thought, they were under attack! He instinctively reached for his revolver but when he couldn't find it remembered that he had earlier unbuckled his belt when he had settled down for the night and the damn thing must have slipped away when he'd jumped up. He dropped to his knees to search for it, scrambling around in the grass with one hand but keeping hold of his horse's reins with the other.

He couldn't find it. He was suddenly seized by panic.

Then he was struck by one of the running figures, a bare foot clipping him across the nose, and he was sent rolling away.

Through blurry eyes he saw that all around people were rushing and fighting, horses stampeding, as a terrible pandomonium spread like wildfire. Why he had not yet being assegaid he did not know, and but for the grace of God he would have been.

247

Somewhere he could hear a voice shouting over and over the same words. "Hold the line! Stand fast and hold the line! HOLD THE LINE!"

They seemed to pay no attention for Hamilton-Browne could clearly see in the light from the bonfires that those rushing by were his own men, obviously too petrified to stay and fight. All that mattered to them was to flee from this spot as fast as possible, whatever the consequences to those they left behind. Angry at their cowardice he came to his feet once more. Picking up a dropped knobkerry he ruthlessly struck out at those nearest him, clubbing at their heads and ranting his fury. "Stay where you are you bloody fools!" he yelled. "Turn back and face the enemy, or we will all die! You black bastards!"

His white non-corns must have heard him through the commotion and they began to beat a path through the melee towards him, and together they tried to kick and punch their men into some semblance of order. They had little success.

Hamilton-Browne temporarily gave up and turned to face the enemy, armed with just the knobkerry in his hand.

He waited for them to come, trying to catch site of them as they hacked their way through his command.

Then he caught a glimpse of Major Dartnell through the flood of running men. He was on horseback and trying to steady himself against the black tide streaming by. Dartnell saw him looking and he forced a path over.

"The idiots!" he ranted. "It's a bloody false alarm Hamilton-Browne! The Zulus aren't even attacking!"

"What?" he answered, not knowing whether to laugh or cry.

"Yes! One of our pickets mistook one of your men for a Zulu and shot the poor blighter! Then his companions fired off a round each and after that all hell broke loose! What a mess!"

Hamilton-Browne could hardly believe his ears. He looked around at the debacle, only now noticing that there were indeed no signs of Zulu warriors in and amoungst the fleeing figures. There were no stabbing assegais. No fighting except his own NCO's beating the N.N.C. back into place.

It was a shambles. Shaking his head he climbed up onto his horse.

Lieutenant Harford joined them, handing something over to his commander. "I found this on the ground sir," he said.

It was his missing belt and sidearm. Thanking his man profusely Hamilton-Browne quickly clipped it around his waist, feeling a little calmer for it.

"Try and get your men in order Commandant," Major Dartnell was saying, "otherwise they'll be spread all over the damn countryside in no time at all the way they're running. I shall take the Carbineers and Police forward and try to strengthen the outposts. Let's hope we don't get shot by our own men! We have to calm the situation just incase the Zulus do make a move."

With that he trotted away, cursing and shaking his head.

When he was out of earshot Hamilton-Browne said to his young officer friend, "I told the fool we should never have stayed here Henry, but he wouldn't listen. These kaffirs would jump at their own shadows so how on earth he thinks they could stem a Zulu attack is beyond me. They're only good for scouting and mopping up, not leading an attack. I prey the General realizes this and sends sufficient reinforcements otherwise come daylight he," and he jabbed the knobkerry after the Major's receeding back, "will lead us all to our deaths!"

Despite the seriousness of the comment Harford had to laugh.

Hamilton-Browne turned to look at him, considered asking whether he was mad, but shrugged the idea away. Maybe they were all a little unhinged. If they weren't allready then they in all likelihood would be before the end of the night.

"Come on," he rumbled instead, "let's sort this bunch of heathens out."

It wasn't easy. A liberal use of force was needed just to stem the flood of deserters and convince them that the Zulus, who they obviously lived in dread of, were not actually attacking. At one stage Hamilton-Browne had to grab a hold of one of his company indunas and, placing his revolver against the man's head, threaten to blow out his brains if he did not get his men under control and back to their positions. This had the desired effect. Slowly the pandemonium levelled out and a semblance of calm returned.

Just to make sure the message got across he loudly informed them, through Duncombe, that the next man who left his post and tried to flee would be bayoneted on the spot and, what's more, the entire company he belonged to likewise dispatched.

The panic now over and the square reformed, the bivouac fell silent once again. For the rest of the night not one of his men made a sound.

They squatted on the ground, staring into the darkness and quivering with fear, casting the occassional look back over their shoulders at their Commandant...who watched them eagle-eyed! At about 5am the sky in the east finally began to lighten.

The 22nd dawned grey and overcast.

The large bonfires in the centre of the square had burned down to just piles of glowing embers which smouldered in the chill air. Then, when it was sufficiently light, everybody looked across towards the hills to the north. To where the Zulus had spent the night, sitting by their own campfires. They were impatient to learn how many had gathered to oppose them.

To the dismay of the British officers but the relief of the NNC. the steep slopes were bare.

The hundreds of fires still belched smoke up into the cloudy sky, but of the Zulus there was no sign.

Quietly, they had slipped away in the night.

Then something new came into view.

Clearly visible on the horizon to the north west could be seen a column of redcoats marching their way, hurrying on over the rough ground. At their head was Lord Chelmsford himself.

He had come to give battle to the Zulus.

But where were they? the men up on Hlazakazi wondered.

CHAPTER 26

RORKE'S DRIFT.
DAWN, WEDNESDAY 22nd JANUARY.

Back in August of '78, when the British plans for the invasion and subjugation of Zululand had been in their early stages, and the war still a distant prospect, Lord Chelmsford had requested that several special service officers be sent out from England to help with their transport problems. Some of them he had asked for by name, from his old unit the 95th (Derbyshire) Regiment. One such man was a twenty year old Lieutenant named Horace Smith-Dorrien, who had sailed out on the *Edinburgh Castle* as part of the few reinforcements London had been willing to allow.

Upon arriving at Durban Smith-Dorrien soon found himself thrown in at the deep end, purchasing teams of oxen and helping gather as many wagons as possible for the forthcoming war, then moving them up towards the Natal/Zululand border. It was demanding work as the country at that time was being ravaged by bovine lung-sickness so that the much needed animals were in short supply and unscrupulous farmers, aware of how much the British needed them, were charging astronomical rates to hire them out. Unlike some of his fellow officers Smith-Dorrien was no fool and he'd seen right through the ploy, refusing point blank to deal with them unless they came up with more realistic figures. His hard bargaining payed off and he very soon earned the reputation of being a first class transport officer, who not only had a knack of getting things done, but under budget as well.

So impressed were his senior officers that he was put to work moving supplies up to Helpmekaar and, from there, on to Rorke's Drift, in readiness for when the Centre Column crossed the Mzinyathi River.

Then, when the invasion began on the 11th January, his tasks became even more important. Now he was required to help keep the convoys running smoothly back and forth as Chelmsford slowly advanced towards Ulundi, ensuing the food and equipment that was essential for keeping an army in the field was allways on hand, when and where it was needed. A tight schedule had to be kept and it was crucial that the timetable worked and so to help with this he had set up a wagon repair facility at Rorke's Drift, replacing broken axles or disselbooms, mending smashed wheels, or making extra trek tows on a gallows he'd constructed.

On the morning of the 22nd, while the column was camped at the foot of Isandlwana and Lord Chelmsford was preparing to take out half his force to chase down a Zulu impi somewhere to the east, Lieutenant Horace Smith-Dorrien was due to return to the drift to carry out some work there when he was unexpectedly summoned by the General's military secretary. Crealock had handed him a dispatch which needed to be taken to Colonel Durnford with all haste, and because he was headed that way he had been charged with guaranteeing its safe delivery.

Following the track from Isandlwana back to Rorke's Drift he arrived at No 2 Column's camp on the Zulu side of the river just as daylight broke. The men were already up and about carrying out their various duties and Smith-Dorrien weaved his way over to Colonel Durnford's headquarters tent to hand over the message.

To his surprise he wasn't there.

Captain George Shepstone came across on seeing him and informed him that Durnford had left to try and gather more wagons from the scattering of farms throughout the region and would not be back until lunchtime, then enquired what he needed to see the Colonel about. Smith-Dorrien explained about the message he carried.

"Let me see it," he ordered politely, holding out his hand.

Smith-Dorrien passed the message slip over and waited whilst he read the message. The expression on the captain's face gave nothing away. Turning, he called over one of his men, a commander of one troop of the Natal Native Horse by the name of Henderson, someone he felt he could trust, and sent him on his way to locate the Colonel carrying the dispatch in his tunic pocket. Then, looking back at Smith-Dorrien, he said..."Thankyou Lieutenant. If you will excuse me..." and then moved away.

Smith-Dorrien thought his behaviour a mite odd, but did not question it further.

He rode on down to the riverbank and waited for the pont to come across, then moved over to the Natal side, chatting to Mr Daniells the ferryman for several minutes as they were pulled through the swollen water. Leading his horse up the steep incline he passed the small tent pitched there by some Royal Engineer sappers who had arrived a few days before to help with the crossing, waving to them as he climbed into his saddle. Then he headed for the mission station a quarter of a mile down the track.

For the next couple of hours he worked on making some new reins, tough leather ropes that needed to be stretched over the top of the gallows and pulled taut with a specially weighted wheel, then rubbed with fat and left to dry. These would replace the trek tows that were forever snapping under the strain of constant overuse, and it was a neverending task that needed his constant supervision.

As he worked his mind kept drifting back to the developments that morning back at the Isandlwana camp. A rumour was going around that a battle was expected sometime soon, henceforth the General's hasty departure. Smith-Dorrien itched to get back there to see what was going on. He had never been tested in battle yet and if a fight was about to happen then he wanted to be a part of it.

From time to time he found himself glancing off in the direction of Isandlwana as he contemplated whether he could make it back and join with Lord Chelmsford's force before it was too far away from camp. Before the battle - if there was indeed going to be one - had been fought.

At about eight o'clock he strolled across to the large pile of mealie-bags that were stacked up in front of the storehouse and awaiting transportation forward, and he sat down to have a short break from his work. Before long he noticed Lieutenant Bromhead coming towards him. Bromhead was the commanding officer of the 'luckless' B Company, 2/24th, who had been left to garrison the post whilst the rest of the column had marched into Zululand two days ago. SmithDorrien had become quite good friends with him, sharing a tent whenever he was around. But on this occassion the sight of a familiar face failed to brighten his day.

"Hot work?" Bromhead asked as he joined him.

"It's monotonous, that is what it is. I'd rather be back with the column."

"Ah, for this fight I keep hearing of no doubt? Tell me, is it true that the General has gone off to search for the enemy?"

"Yes it is." Smith-Dorrien looked up at his friend, then confessed to him, "I'm thinking of hurrying back there."

"Well in that case you should get a move on."

Smith-Dorrien realized Bromhead was right. For all he knew the battle might already have started. Suddenly he made up his mind and came to his feet. What was to stop him? He wasn't like Bromhead who had no option but to remain here guarding the stores. Yes, he would go back.

Before he strode away he asked his friend for a favour.

"I'll gladly help if I can," Bromhead replied. "What is it you want?"

"I'm a little short of ammo for my revolver. You wouldn't mind lending me some of yours would you?"

"I'm down myself, but let's see." He put his hand into the small pouch at the front of his belt.

"Just a few will do, to see me back to camp. It's a long and lonely ride," Smith-Dorrien joked.

"Yes, no problem, I can give you some." He handed a handful over, apologising that this was all he could offer without leaving himself dangerously short - not that he was likely to need to use his gun anytime soon, stuck here on the border as he was.

Smith-Dorrien looked at the cartridges in his palm and counted eleven rounds. "That's wonderful!" he exclaimed merrily, more than happy with the number.

"Glad to be of help. Use them well."

"I surely will. You can count on that."

Bidding his friend farewell Lieutenant Horace Smith-Dorrien hurried away to find his horse.

As soon as the note was handed over Colonel Durnford's first words, after quickly reading it, were...
"Just as I thought. We are to proceed at once to Isandlwana camp. There is an *impi* about ten miles from the camp which the General moves out to attack."

The message, signed by Crealock, read as follows:

Hd Qr Camp at Isandlwana, Zululand
'22nd Wednesday. 2am.

You are to march to this camp at once with all the force you have with you of No 2 Column.
Major Bengough's battalion is to move to Rorke's Drift as ordered yesterday.
2/24th, Artillery and Mounted men with the General and Colonel Glyn move off at once to attack a Zulu force about ten miles distant-

J.N.C.'

Suddenly much more animated, Durnford quickly issued a series of instructions. The task of hiring more wagons could wait for they now had much more important matters to attend to. That Lord Chelmsford had need of them was apparant in the tone of the message he held in his hand, for the words it contained held an urgency which, as Durnford saw it, promised imminent action for him and his men in a co-ordinated move with the force the General had just taken out. An earlier message several days ago had pointed towards such a synchronised attack and the note that Lieutenant Henderson had rode to the summit of the Biggarsberg with confirmed an order Durnford had been anticipating for the last 24 hours. They had no time to waste, he announced. With that he led them back down to the camp at a fast canter.

When they arrived he was pleased to see that the camp was already broken up and the men ready to move out. There was a buzz of excitement about the place for everybody was glad to be finally on the move forward into enemy territory, instead of this pointless waiting.

It would take between two and three hours to reach Isandlwana. They would be slowed down by the wagons carrying their baggage as well as the three troughs and 9-pdr. Hales' rockets of Major Russell's Rocket Battery, which for some reason had been loaded onto pack-mules and made ponderously slow progress over the badly ploughed up roads. However, Durnford was keen to reach the Centre Column's camp as quickly as possible and so he ordered his two NNC companies to escort the artillery and transports in while he pushed on with the Natal Native Horse.

The column set out.

Colonel Anthony William Durnford led his men towards the peculiarly shaped hill known as Isandlwana, clearly visible on the horizon.

He felt sure that today he would have his moment of glory, something he had been striving for his whole adult life.

The 22nd would be his date with destiny.

In contrast to Durnford's bullish mood and desire to stamp his name on history, the new commander of the camp at Isandlwana felt increasingly daunted by the responsibilities that had unexpectedly been thrust upon him.

Since the General's departure before sunrise Colonel Pulleine's nervousness had increased with each passing minute. He could not explain the reason for this. It was not really a crisis of confidence for he knew he was more than capable of handling the routine running of the camp, with all of his experience, but something else worried him...something niggling away at his insides...something he could not put his finger on.

Trying to ignore these misgivings, or at least not to allow them to interfere with the business of command, Pulleine allowed the normal routine of daily camp life to continue unchanged. As soon as it was daylight the mounted vedettes which had come in overnight were sent back out to their positions amoungst the hills north of the camp, and a small infantry picket was placed on the track just behind the shoulder of the hill to watch for Durnford's arrival. Once he was satisfied that all the approaches to the camp were thus covered, he ordered the remaining men to have breakfast. Snatching their mess kits they headed for the field kitchens that had been set up behind each unit's tents, forming lines while the cooks dished out the food.

Pulleine himself did not have much of an appetite right then, he would eat once Durnford had arrived, so he went to his tent to start on some correspondence. He had not long being doing this when a horseman had come riding down from one of the outposts with an unusual report.

He listened intently to what the man had to say.

Apparantly several groups of Zulus had been spotted up on the Nqutu plateau, moving about in sight of the British outposts and occassionally coming close enough to cause them alarm. The size of these individual groups were small, some numbering just a few dozen, one or two of about a hundred or so, but put together they represented quite a large force. Not a serious threat to the camp but enough to gain their attention and make the British think.

This news wasn't what Colonel Pulleine needed.

Now he had even more to concern his already worried mind.

He came to his feet and gathered up his papers, deciding to come back and finish the work later. More pressing matters needed tending to first.

Outside, he saw Lieutenant Melvill hurrying over to see what the problem was. Pulleine quickly explained the situation to him, then added..."I think we had better do the sensible thing. Order Fall In would you."

"Sir. BUGLER!" Melvill turned to shout, "SOUND FALL IN!"

The trumpeting call carried throughout the whole camp and amid groans of disappointment at having their meal interrupted the men put aside their plates of food, picked up their rifles and accoutrements, and dashed down to the flat ground infront of the tents. Here the Imperial companies formed up in column facing out to the northeast, masterfully dressing their lines to the barking commands of their CSM's, their red tunics standing out vividly against the grass. Just behind them the NNC formed a single, long line before the camp area to act as a reserve if called upon while the 1st Battalion band fell in to carry out their dual role as stretcher-bearers, once more if called upon. The whole process took less than ten minutes, a feat that Pulleine felt proud of. His men were excellant soldiers. Of that there was no doubt.

As of yet there was no real sense of alarm in the camp. The boys were in good spirits, Pulleine saw.

He tried to relax. Everything was in order. Until more news came in there was nothing more to be done, he was handling the situation well. Perhaps it was a slight over-reaction on his part having the men fall in like this but he wanted to take nothing to chance.

Now it was just a matter of waiting to see what developed.

Not every single man in the camp was turned out. When the bugle had sounded Lieutenant Coghill had still been resting on his cot nursing his injured leg but the sound of activity had eventually drawn him hobbling to the tent door. He stood there now, watching events.

Soon, he noticed James Brickhill, the interpreter, moving up the slope from the parade ground where the infantry were and Coghill called him across to see what was the matter.

Brickhill told him about the Zulus up on the plateau. "Nothing to worry about really," he added, "but I get the feeling that our Colonel will be mighty glad when Colonel Durnford arrives with his reinforcements."

Coghill nodded. "Well if they need me I'm sure they will come calling."

"Yes, it can't be urgent. There's a convoy of wagons due to return to Rorke's Drift later in the morning and I've just being asked to tell the drivers to gather up their oxen and wait for the order to leave, so an attack mustn't be on the cards. He wouldn't send them on their way if a Zulu *impi* was in the neighbourhood, now would he?"

"No, of course not. You get along now."

Coghill watched him go, then turned back into the tent and hopped back across to his bed.

For over an hour nothing much happened. The redcoats remained in their positions watching the hills to their front whilst Pulleine and the other officers awaited further news from the vedettes. He sent off a quick note to Lord Chelmsford informing him of developments but as of yet there was really nothing to report.

At about ten o'clock a group of figures suddenly appeared on the skyline along the top of the escarpment. Everybody with a pair of field glasses lifted them up to their eyes to take a closer look, and to their surprise they realized they were Zulu warriors. A buzz of excitement passed through the ranks as word of this quickly spread.

The Zulus, who numbered about thirty, made no further move. They simply stood on the hilltop watching the British below.

It was a tense moment.

While this was going on James Brickhill, having readied the wagon drivers as ordered, came hurrying back over. He moved up alongside Pulleine.

"Sir," he said, gaining the Colonel's attention, who turned to hear what he had to say. "The pickets out on the road have just asked me to tell you that they have spotted horsemen approaching from Rorke's Drift."

Pulleine's eyebrows raised hopefully.

"They say it is Colonel Durnford."

Pulleine gave a satisfied grunt and turned back to look at the Zulus once more. But in the few seconds that his attention had been diverted, they had gone, drifting away out of sight.

Well the damn cheek! he thought to himself.

Durnford rode into camp at about 10:30 with his five troops of the Natal Native Horse, moving over the nek between the wagon park and the guard tent and taking up a position in the centre of the camp. Two or three miles further back, with their escort of native infantry, crawled the Rocket Battery and the columns' wagons. Swinging down from Chieftain's back he cast a curious stare out towards the men lined up before the tents and wondered what the reason for this was.

He went in search of Colonel Pulleine.

Pulleine saw him approach and as he went to greet him he tried, but failed, to prevent a look of relief from appearing on his face.

The two men shook hands and exchanged a few friendly words, for they had not seen one another for quite some time, but their talk soon turned to the current state of affairs...Durnford eager to be brought up to date and Pulleine happy to do so.

"You are probably wondering why I have had the men Fall In," Pulleine twittered, "what has called for such drastic measures?"

Durnford noted the hint of sarcasm in the words and quickly realized it was a weak attempt to explain himself, a bad sign in a commander he thought for it automatically told him that here was a man suffering with a lack of confidence. He pretended he had not noticed and kept his response flat. "Tell me Henry."

"Yes. Well, the thing is, our outposts have spotted a number of Zulus up on the hills there." He pointed up towards the plateau. "Only a few. A short while ago some of them came within sight of the camp, standing up there as bold as brass and looking down at us. I think they are probably just some of Sihayo's adherents left over from the fight the other day but I thought it wise not to leave anything to chance and so I..."

"Quite right. I would have done the same myself."

Durnford strolled around for a moment, casting his eyes over the camp and surrounding terrain, craning his neck to look up at the mountain at their backs, finishing by looking up the long spur that connected the plain to the plateau. When he had done he came back over to Pulleine, who had been waiting patiently.

"It seems to me that the immediate danger has passed. Perhaps the men could be stood down? They could quickly finish their breakfasts...keeping their rifles at hand and their equipment still on incase our friends decide to put in another appearance."

Pulleine frowned and once again wondered whether he had over-reacted in the first place. That he had been given command of the camp was a result of His Lordship's confidence in him but it had all come about a little too quickly for him. On top of that the Zulus had appeared in a quite unexpected place, a move that had thrown him somewhat. But now that Colonel Durnford had arrived he was more than happy to allow somebody else to make the important decisions, the officer of engineers being the more senior of the two.

So Pulleine nodded agreement and passed the decision down the line.

"Are you hungry?" he then asked Durnford. "We could take breakfast in my tent if you are."

"To tell you the truth I am ravished Henry."

"Good! Then please be my guest."

The two men strolled away towards the tents while behind them the lines of infantry companies started to dissolve as the soldiers belatedly went back to their cold food.

While breakfast was being served to them the two officers continued their discussions within Pulleine's command tent up on the slope at the back of the camp. Pulleine first of all sat down at his desk expecting his comrade to do the same, but Durnford seemed to prefer remaining standing and moving to the doorway from time to time, breathing in the warm air. Pulleine was therefore unsure whether to come to his feet as well. If he did that he felt sure Durnford would then sit! Instead he thought the best option was to perch on the edge of the table with one foot on the floor.

"A nice decision of yours Anthony," he started saying, "ordering the men to resume their meal."

"It wasn't an order my friend, merely a suggestion."

"Sorry?"

Colonel Durnford turned to look at him with a tiny smile playing across his lips. "I said I did not order the men to do anything. Lord Chelmsford did not ask me to come up here just to assume command of the camp."

"But I assumed, with you being senior, that it would automatically pass to you."

"That wasn't what it said in the message I received this morning. My understanding was that I am to act in a supporting role to His Lordship's move against the Zulu force to the east, not to interfere with your running of the camp in his absence."

Pulleine hesitated. Now this he hadn't expected.

"You should be pleased I am not going to be throwing my weight around," Durnford commented wryly. "You are happy with the situation remaining the same?"

"Oh...um...yes, certainly!"

"You should look on this as a golden opportunity Henry. If you impress Lord Chelmsford enough then who knows where it might lead to."

Pulleine remained quiet, suddenly no longer sure exactly what he felt.

By now their food was ready and Durnford moved to start on his. He took up his plate and carefully balanced it in the crook of his elbow of his injured arm, then with great dexterity he used his right hand to stab at the bacon, so that he could remain standing while he ate. As for Pulleine, he had suddenly lost his appetite, his mind now on other things.

"Tell me," said Durnford between mouthfuls, "what were your orders? What does the General require of you?"

Pulleine glanced up. "He merely asked me to remain on the defensive and to defend the camp."

"Not that it will come to that."

"No."

"It occurs to me though that the situation has changed somewhat since the General left, and if he had forseen a Zulu presence up on those hills he would probably have issued us different instructions."

"Meaning?"

Durnford noticed the worried frown on his fellow officer's face. "Meaning that we cannot ignore the threat - insignificant I agree, but a threat nonetheless - that they pose to us and we may have to take appropriate action to counter this, regardless of His Lordship's orders."

Pulleine gaped at him. He did not like the direction their conversation was taking. "You are saying that we should ignore the General's advice?"

"Not at all," the other answered tetchily.

"Then..." Pulleine shrugged, totally confused by now..."what?"

"Flexibility is the word I am looking for. We should be flexible, as well as adaptable."

Pulleine rolled his tongue nervously around the inside of his mouth, chewing on his thoughts. He could think of nothing much to say, and so the atmosphere inside the tent swelled with a long silence.

Just then Lieutenant Melvill appeared. He squeezed into the tent, instantly noticing the tension within. He glanced from officer to officer. Briefly he wondered what was amiss, but decided it was no concern of his. "I'm sorry to intrude," he said quietly, "but we have further news from our vedettes."

"What do they have to report?" asked Colonel Pulleine.

"They say that the Zulus are pulling away and drawing eastwards across the heights."

Pulleine beamed happily and turned to his companion. "That is good news is it not? I'd say the immediate crisis has passed."

But Durnford was looking at the floor and shaking his head, obviously puzzling over a rapidly changing situation. A crestfallen expression creeped over Pulleine's joyful countenance.

"Moving to the east you say?" the engineer asked Melvill.

The Adjutant of the 1/24th nodded.

"I wonder why? They could be pulling away from the camp, but equally they could be making a move against the General's rear to try and cut him off."

Pulleine and Melvill exchanged a look.

"If that is the case then we must try and stop them."

"You mean go out there after them! Our orders were to defend the camp, not to carry out offensive operations!"

"Those were your orders Henry. Mine were to support the General's advance."

"But...but..."

Durnford ignored his protests for he had already reached a decision. He turned to them both in a flourish to announce it. "I am going to send two of my mounted troops up onto the hills to sweep any Zulus up there to the east, to follow them up and force them towards the end of the plateau. Lieutenant Raw will command the first and Lieutenant Roberts the second. At the same time I will take out the remainder of my horsemen, plus the Rocket Battery with their escort, over the plain and out beyond the conical hill there. Hopefully the men on the plateau will force the enemy to come over the escarpment edge down onto the plain where I can intercept them. I'd like to take with me a couple of your infantry companies as support. Also, it might be wise to reinforce the outposts at the head of the spur, say one company?"

Both Pulleine and Melvill seemed aghast at what Durnford was planning. Not so much what he chose to do with his own command but what he was proposing to do with the force left behind in camp, on strict instructions to remain and defend it. Had the Colonel taken leave of his senses?

"You need two of my companies?" Pulleine asked bewildered.

"I'm sure you can spare them old boy."

"A third of my men though! Is it not a little...excessive?"

"Not if we can prevent the General's column from being attacked in the rear." Durnford could see the strain Pulleine was under, recognizing at once that a further deft persuasive touch was needed to convince him it was the right course to take. "If he see's that you came rushing to his aid I am sure the General will see to it that the right people in the War Department get to hear about it Henry. As I said earlier, a golden opportunity is being presented to you on a plate."

Pulleine opened his mouth to say more but closed it again when he realized that his hand was being forced in a most surreptitious way. He closed his eyes and lightly touched his forehead. Now he had a damn headache coming on.

Eventually he nodded and whispered, without looking up..."very well, if you insist then I'll give you them."

"Thankyou. Do not look so concerned. Everything is under control."

Durnford smiled warmly and placed his empty plate on the desk, then he quietly slipped away to get his men ready.

With his eyes still shut Colonel Pulleine failed to notice the icy glare Lieutenant Melvill gave him. He only heard the swish of the tentflap as his Adjutant went hurrying after Durnford.

Outside, he rushed up alongside the fast-walking Colonel, struggling to keep up with him as he approached the horsemen waiting in the centre of the camp. He coughed politely to gain his attention, but when this failed his stepped infront of Durnford - only just falling short of grabbing hold of him by the shirtsleeve to make him stop.

To his surprise the Colonel grinned broadly, not at all offended by his poor manners. "You do not approve of my decision Mr Melvill?" he asked amiably.

"Frankly sir I think you have overstepped the mark, yes."

"In what way? I did not give Colonel Pulleine any direct orders, merely made a series of suggestions to deal with a fluid situation. In time you will see they are the correct ones."

"You are confident of that?"

"Are you confident they are not?" countered Durnford, still smiling.

"You are stripping the camp of its defences. I really do not think Colonel Pulleine would be doing right to send any men out when his orders are to 'defend the camp'."

"Yes, that would be true - if the camp was under threat, which it is not. The Zulus are moving away from here and towards the

General." Durnford looked passed Melvill's shoulder to where his men waited. He noticed one or two of them edging forward to listen to their conversation as they realized something was up.

"You have to remember sir," said Melvill, softening his tone a little, "that Colonel Pulleine is somewhat inexperienced when it comes to...ah, making decisions under pressure. He is an excellant administrator but he has never commanded men under action. In fact I don't believe he has ever seen action."

"Go on."

"Well I fear he is feeling the strain. He wishes to look after the boys sir. His boys, as he see's them."

Durnford looked at Lieutenant Melvill for a long time. Then, after what seemed an age, he blinked. He suddenly seemed to understand what he was saying. Or trying to say.

It must have been difficult to criticise ones own commanding officer the way Melvill just had. Especially as Melvill very obviously liked the man. It took bottle to do that.

"Very well," Durnford sighed, "it does not much matter; we will not take the two companies on our sortie across the plain. However," and he raised a finger here, "the outposts do need to be strengthened so the idea of sending some infantry up the spur has not changed."

Melvill nodded meekly, not wishing to push his luck.

"If me and my men do, by chance, get into difficulties I shall expect some quick support. With Imperial Infantry. From the camp. Is that clear?"

"Yes Colonel."

"Please make it clear to Colonel Pulleine."

With nothing more to say on the subject Durnford swept passed and strode over to his waiting men.

CHAPTER 27

LORD CHELMSFORD'S FORWARD POSITION. 12 MILES SOUTHEAST OF ISANDLWANA.
MORNING, WEDNESDAY 22nd JANUARY.

After several frustrating hours of low-key skirmishing amongst the hilly country, during which they had encountered only small Zulu forces and not the large *impi* he had been expecting, Chelmsford reluctantly came to the conclusion that he would have to wait several more days for the large set-piece battle he so desired. More mundane work would need his attention instead, such as choosing the site for their next camp.

Before this got underway, and while the British and native infantry and the cavalry were still searching the surrounding terrain and running down the occassional Zulu here and there, he called a halt for breakfast.

It was while they were waiting for the food to be prepared and the large dining table was being laid out under the shade of a sprawling canvas that news reached them of the Zulu presence at Isandlwana. It arrived in the form of a hurried note sent by Pulleine, with very few details.

With characteristic sarcasm Crealock had smirked and given a little shake of his head, giving away his feelings on the matter as he said, "how very amusing! Actually attacking our camp! Most amusing!"

266

Several of his fellow officers gently laughed along with him.

Major Clery, who had handed the note over, politely waited until it was quiet again and then asked Lord Chelmsford what they should do about the report.

"There is nothing to be done on that," the General responded tersly about the message, which he disdainfully handed back. "The camp is under no threat. I feel all they have seen are a few scouts."

"It is just Pulleine being over-cautious as usual," added Crealock. "You would think he had a full scale battle on his hands! Ah, our breakfast!"

As they moved away towards the table Chelmsford nevertheless considered what their next move should be, the news from Isandlwana helping him to come to a decision. He gently steered Crealock off to one side. "Have someone sent back to camp would you, to order the garrison to strike the tents and come here. Then inform Commandant Hamilton-Browne to return there with his men to help with the move."

Hurrying to carry out His Lordships wishes Crealock passed this on.

"If I come across the enemy?" Hamilton-Browne asked.

"Oh, just brush them aside and go on," Crealock replied before dashing off for breakfast.

*   *   *

THE BRITISH CAMP AT ISANDLWANA. 11:15am.

As Durnford rode east, Lieutenant Charles Raw and Lieutenant J.A. Roberts took their cavalry up the long spur that climbed away from the mountain towards the Nqutu plateau. They had with them two troops of native horsemen of the Ngwane tribe, about 100 men in total, who were named Zikhali's Horse after their chief. Armed with Swinburne-Henry carbines, with which they were reputably excellant shots, and combined with their brilliant riding skills, they made for a very professional and well trained body of men.

They moved by the NNC picket and then split in two, No 1 Troop moving to the northeast while No 2 Troop headed directly north. The men fanned out and in groups of two's and three's started working their way over the plateau, searching the numerous gulleys and dongas as they went, constantly on the lookout for the zulu warriors reported to be up here somewhere.

They were soon swallowed up amidst the undulating ground. Within a few minutes they were gone.

Shortly after they left the camp E. Company, 1/24th, led by Lieutenant Cavaye, was ordered to reinforce the NNC picket, as suggested by Colonel Durnford. They marched one thousand five hundred yards up the spur and then deployed in line facing north. Here they waited, watching the ground to their front where it dipped down into a broad and shallow basin surrounded by hills on three sides.

On the horizon a cloud of dust marked the progress of the cavalry.

Lieutenant Roberts' men were not having much success in locating the enemy. They had kept to the ground directly ahead of the native lookouts where the enemy had been sighted earlier that morning but in their eagerness they had ridden further than anticipated, so that they were soon about three miles beyond the edge of the escarpment and now out of sight to the NNC. and Cavaye's men, and also therefore to the camp. So, after about thirty minutes of searching and with nothing to show for their efforts, Lieutenant Roberts swung his command to the right and started out across the plateau in an easterly direction. They now kept parallel to No 1 Troop, keeping a distance of about one mile between themselves and their comrades, both sets of horsemen sweeping across the heights.

Likewise, the native riders of No 1 Troop had also had a disappointing time of it. Captain George Shepstone, who had accompanied them, soon began to realize that the liklihood of finding any Zulus-let alone engaging them in anything more than the odd brief exchange of fire-was becoming increasingly unlikely. There were just too many hiding places where the enemy could easily avoid been discovered, and so if they were to come across any small groups it would only be by chance...or if the Zulus so wished it.

He noticed, as he was sure Charlie Raw had done also, that Lieutenant Roberts' men were working their way closer to them having abandoned their search to the north. It was disappointing as they'd had high hopes of seeing some action, but unless the situation changed soon then they would be returning to camp with the frustrating news that the Zulus had apparantly left the plateau.

Several minutes later the situation did indeed change.

It was fortuitous, as any longer and they would have turned about and retraced their steps to the plain below.

One of the men had been riding slightly to the right of the main body when he had suddenly started calling across to gain their attention and waving his arms frantically. Lieutenant Raw and those around him glanced over to see what the matter was, and then they saw what had caught his attention.

On some rising ground to the front was a small herd of cattle. Running amidst them were two or three young boys, desperately trying to round them up and throwing terrified looks back over their shoulders at the horsemen who had suddenly appeared from knowhere. Crying out and hitting the animals with their sticks they forced them over the crest of the small hill and disappeared from sight.

At last! thought Raw.

Not the Zulu warriors they had been hoping for, but at least their patrol had not been a complete waste of time.

"Our first catch of the day!" he cried triumphantly and drew out his revolver.

Around him he saw a sea of excited faces, the men eager for what should be an easy chase.

Checking that his gun was loaded he waved it above his head, crying out at the top of his voice. "FORWARD, MY BOYS! CATCH THEM!" With that he took off at a gallop, the rest of No 1 Troop close on his heels.

They charged up the long slope, pushing their mounts hard as each man was keen to close with the Zulus first. The ground terminated in a rocky crest and within just a few short seconds they had reached the top, their teeth bared as they readied to storm down the far side. They stopped dead in their tracks.

Each man stared in silence at the scene below them.

What they saw made their blood run cold.

A little way down the hillside the young Zulu herdboys waited with their cattle, scowling up at the them and now no longer afraid. Yet it wasn't this that held the British transfixed. They looked beyond these and into a wide valley that stretched away into the distance.

Here was a sight the likes of which they had never seen before, and it filled them with such a dread that it rendered them speechless.

Here, 25,000 strong, was the main Zulu Army.

CHAPTER 28

SITE OF ZULU ARMY'S BIVOUAC.
NGWEBENI RIVER VALLEY.
5 MILES NORTHEAST OF ISANDLWANA. 11:45am.

If their commanders had demanded it the army could have covered the distance from the Royal Kraal to their hiding place up on the Nqutu Plateau in just two days. It was a feat well within their capabilities. Yet they had been told not to rush, but instead to conserve their energy for the fighting that lay ahead, and so they had travelled at an almost leisurely pace. After spending the first night just west of the White Mfolozi they travelled only about nine or ten miles during the whole of the following day until they arrived at the uSixepi military kraal where they ate and rested. On the third day the *amabutho* split into two columns, travelling parallel with one another, as was customary whenever they neared their enemy. The left column was led by the senior *induna* Ntshingwayo kaMahole whilst the right column by Mavumengwana kaNdlela. They marched up into the table-land near Babanango mountain, covering about the same distance as the previous day, and here they stopped on the night of the 19th. The next day the army continued on its advance but now with greater caution as they were aware that the white men were closeby, and so they kept to the low ground as much as possible and using the

271

terrain to mask their approach. Scouts were sent forward to try and establish the precise whereabouts of their enemy and it became a delicate and risky task to try and avoid the mounted patrols and prevent them from discovering them. Their fourth night was spent encamped on the northern slopes of Siphezi mountain, out of sight of the white mens camp just a few miles away across the plain, and the following morning they carefully began to move northwest up onto the heights of the Nqutu Plateau. They moved in small groups, company by company, regiment by regiment, to lessen the chance of being spotted, with skirmishers sent out to ward off any white horsemen who might wander too close. On one occassion Ntshingwayo felt certain they would be found. Some of the enemy had come perilously near whilst they were making this final move and a body of warriors had been sent to intercept them in the hills to the south, bravely driving them back just in time. They had been lucky. If the white horsemen had come on just another mile then they could not have failed to have seen the vast Zulu army slipping through the valleys and hills, and all element of surprise would have been lost. But they didn't, and the impi managed to reach the Ngwebeni valley undiscovered.

Here they waited, poised to fall upon the white mens camp.

Their plan was to attack two days hence. They had no intention of fighting the day following their arrival in the valley for this was a time of the 'dead' moon - a new moon - and was therefore a warning of ill-omen, and so was no time to go into battle.

Unknown to the Zulus the 22nd would also experience a partial eclipse of the sun. So the forebodings for the following day were not good.

They decided then that they would risk spending the next day and night in the ravine before attacking the white men at dawn the day after. A long wait...and a big risk.

To reduce the chances of giving away their position the *amabutho izindunas* ruled that they would not be allowed to light any campfires through the night, so they ate meals of cold mealies and then slept shivering amoungst the boulders and vegetation that covered the valley sides.

In the morning a few foragers were sent out to several local homesteads, long abandoned, to bring back any food they could find but they were told to avoid all contact with the enemy who were hopefully still unaware of their presence.

A little later and they noticed the dull sound of distant gunfire reverberating around the hills. It being impossible to determine exactly where it was coming from due to the rebounding echoes, a party of warriors from the uKhandempemvu were ordered to carefully move forward to the edge of the escarpment overlooking the white mens camp to see if they could find out what was happening. This they did.

Reaching the southern brim of the plateau they looked down at the camp spread out below them. To their alarm they saw that the white soldiers were gathered in precise lines in front of their tents, their red clothes dazzling in the watery sunshine, facing the hills behind which their impi was hidden. But what was even more disturbing was the sight of a column of horsemen who were galloping in from behind Isandlwana, following the dirt track and crossing the saddle to join their comrades. The warriors stayed and watched events for a short time. They were curious as to the reasons for these strange movements by their enemy, wondering what they were planning, but they did not as yet feel threatened. The sound of firing had died down now, and was in any case not coming from the camp after all, but somewhere out towards the east. It need not concern them.

Satisfied that the white men were still oblivious to their whereabouts they quietly crept away.

The next hour passed uneventfully

The main Zulu Army waited in the valley, the men trying to keep their eagerness for battle under check. In two days they would be unleashed on the hated white soldiers.

Events were to change all of that however.

Just about when the sun was at its zenith a small herd of cattle suddenly came over the crest of the hill immediately in front of the uKhandempemvu regiment, being herded by several of their scouts. Glancing up from their squatting positions the young warriors watched them come down the hill a short distance and then stop and turn to look back.

Curious as to what they were looking at the uKhandempemvu searched the ridge. Then they saw for themselves.

Along the skyline above them a line of horsemen had appeared, the figures hardly more than miniscule specks at this distance. The Zulus could tell, nevertheless, who they were.

They knew in an instant that they had been discovered. They also understood with equal clarity that the battle would, after-all, be fought on this day.

Nothing in the world could stop it now.

CHAPTER 29

NQUTU PLATEAU. 11:45am.

Captain George Shepstone watched as the nearest Zulu regiment rose and came charging at them up the steep hillside. It was a phenomenal sight, and he found himself momentarily mesmerised by it. Unable to tear his eyes away he saw the warriors before him race forward, their dark bodies and black shields sweeping towards the men atop the ridge in an unrelenting tide, moving with a fearful speed and determination. He also saw, beyond and to either side of them, a general movement from the vast host gathered in the valley as more and more of the countless Zulus began to notice that an attack was developing. From one end of the valley to the other, a distance covering several miles, the gigantic impi sprung forward.

For those first initial moments he was unable to snap out of the spell. All he could do was marvel at the spectacle before him. It was only when his horse started to shy away from the approaching horde that the realization of their situation suddenly struck home, and then he cringed in terror.

Quickly recovering his wits Shepstone glanced across to the Lieutenant who was by his side.

"Raw! For God's sake, ready your men!"

Lieutenant Raw turned his massive bulk towards him and stared glassy-eyed and slack-jawed. After a second his mind seemed to

275

refocus itself and in the next instant his training took over as he began to issue a stream of instructions.

"Form half sections! Troop dismount, and prepare to fire! Set for 400 yards!"

With remarkable coolness the men hurried to obey his command, despite the unnerving close proximity of the enemy. Grabbing their carbines they slipped down from their saddles and formed up in loose skirmishing order along the crest of the ridge, each man feeding a round into his weapon and setting its sights.

"Take aim!" came the next command.

Up came their guns, with butts fitted snugly into their shoulders, the barrels pointing down at the Zulus streaming towards them.

"Fire!"

A blinding flash rippled along the line and a thunderous roar announced the start of the battle. A cloud of thin smoke almost obscurred the men's view and they squinted through the grey haze, straining to see the result of this first volley. They saw the whole of the front rank of the nearest Zulu regiment go down. Some were bowled over to fall flat on their faces while others were spun back, their arms flung out amidst sprays of crimson. It was a bloody and brutal image but it filled the Zikhali Horse with a feeling of immense satisfaction, to see their effort show such deadly results.

Yet the Zulus came on without any apparant pause in their charge. Scrambling over the bodies of their dead or dying comrades, they stormed up the steep slope.

The sight of this, and the realization that they had a hard fight on their hands, had an unsettling effect on the native horsemen. They exchanged nervous glances with one another, and had it not being for their professional discipline - not to mention courage - then they might have bolted there and then. As it was, they followed their orders.

Pouring another volley into the zulus the Zikhali Horse quickly mounted up and withdrew to a spot about fifty yards back, where they once more scrambled down to the ground and lined up yet again.

"Fire!"

There came another cacophony of thunder, more dense smoke that flickered with yellow flames from the rifle barrels. Voices calling out instructions, becoming a little high-pitched as the officers tried hard to remain calm. They reloaded and fired, climbed back into their saddles and pulled back again.

Soon, the men of No 2 Troop joined them, their fifty rifles adding to their firepower. They were still a tiny few however, and it was necessary to continue their steady withdrawal across the plateau. All they could do was try and slow the enemy.

Amidst their own volley fire came the occassional shot from the Zulus. Their marksmanship was poor, the rounds tending to go over the horsemens heads, but as the volume of return-fire increased so did the chances that one or two would eventually find their mark, and this did indeed start to happen.

The Zikhali Horse took their first casualty as they were preparing to pull back their line to some high ground to their rear. The men were just mounting up when one of the horses was struck square in the forehead by a stray round, killing it instantly. Unfortunately, its rider was only half in the saddle and as the animal, a beautiful grey now splattered with blood and brain, fell sideways so his leg became pinned under its flank. He tried desperately to pull himself clear but found that he was caught fast and so he twisted his head to call to his comrades for help.

However, they were riding away to their next position, not having realized they had left one of their number behind. By the time they did notice it was too late. All they could do was watch helplessly.

The rider turned back to his front. Coming towards him over the rolling ground sprinted the foremost mass of Zulus. They had seen him fall and seemed almost crazy in their desire to reach him and finish him off, and so in no time at all they had closed the gap.

He just had time to swing the barrel of his carbine around and shoot the nearest warrior at point blank range, screaming his fury, before a dozen assegai blades ripped into his chest, neck and face, snuffing out his whole existence in one instant of sheer agony. Then, even when he was dead, they continued to stab and hack, treating his horse to the same. They split open his stomach as was their custom. They disemboweled him to prevent the contamination of *mnyama*. And amidst the bedlam the Zulus shouted their war-cry "uSuthu!" as they stabbed..."Ngadla! - I have eaten!"

The men of the Zikhali Horse watched this in horror. Some cried out in distress at seeing their friend killed this way. Several fired towards the Zulus in anger and their officers had to quickly get them in order again.

Their withdrawal continued. The maneuver seemed the obvious thing to do. The men had initially been badly shaken by the sudden turn of events, for they had not expected to have a full-pitched battle on their hands like this, but being as well trained as they were they quickly got themselves together and showed great steadyness despite their fearful predicament. Their officers kept a tight fire-control, guiding the mens volleys and instilling in them a confidence they might otherwise have lost. But above all they showed immense courage.

Yet no amount of courage would be enough to slow the enemy advance. There was just too many of them. An endless multitude was pouring over the lip of the valley for as far as the eye could see in both directions, and if the Zulus attacked in their traditional form in the shape of a buffalo's head - with a chest and two huge, sweeping, encircling horns thrown out to either side -then the tide they were desperately trying to stem was in reality only a small portion of the zulu attack. More regiments would be fanning out and taking up their positions to the east and west, deploying beyond the hills there and making to descend upon the unsuspecting camp on the plain below. It was a hopeless task the Zikhali faced.

Captain Shepstone understood this immediately. That they were in dreadful trouble was instantly apparant, but what concerned him even more than their own personal safety was the fact that the men back in camp would have absolutely no idea of the danger they faced. They may have been able to hear the sound of distant gunfire coming from up here on the plateau but they could not possibly know how serious things were. Somehow they had to be warned.

Riding across to Raw's side, who was directing yet more volleys into the Zulu regiments, he shouted into his ear above the din of battle.

"I'm going back to camp Lieutenant! They have to be told about what is heading their way! Pulleine must have time to prepare his men! Stay here and hold them if you can, but slowly pull back towards the infantry at the head of the spur if you have to. They will be able to reinforce you there! Also, pick up the vedettes and outposts on your way, as you will need every man with a gun you can find!"

Lieutenant Raw listened carefully and then nodded. "I suggest sir," he adviced as he looked at the Zulus to their front, "that you ride like the devil!"

"And I suggest that you fight like the devil Charlie!"

Without further ado he turned his horse and galloped away, leaving the maelstrom behind.

At that crucial moment when the initial contact was made with the enemy, Ntshingwayo kaMahole, the senior *induna* and overall zulu commander, had desperately tried to halt the mass attack long enough to issue the *amabutho* their final instructions. He had failed. The regiments had simply streamed by him following the lead of the uKhandempemvu, pouring up the steep valley sides along a front of several miles. The suddeness of the fight had taken them as much by surprise as their foe, but once the moment had come the men were fast to respond. Too fast, for the attack developed spontaneously. In the space of just a few minutes the battle passed completely out of Ntshingwayo's hands, and he was left in its wake, desperate to wrestle back control. Only the reserve regiments heeded his order to halt and these men were in any case to have little influence in the coming battle. To all intents and purposes the young warriors of the Zulu Army were by themselves.

It was a marvelous testimony to their years of drilling and discipline therefore that the attack developed with perfect co-ordination, and precisely as it should have.

Their traditional form of battle was known to the Zulus as *impondo zankomo,* which loosely meant 'the beast's horns', a tactic said to have been devised by the great Shaka and since passed down from generation to generation of young warriors. The men of the more senior regiments would form the chest, battle-hardened veterans of past campaigns who were required to attack the enemy in a full-frontal assault, a task that required courage of steel for it more often than not was these regiments who experienced the bloodiest and most brutal portion of the battle and therefore suffered the heaviest casualties. The younger, fitter, and more agile men would be thrown out in two encircling wings, the horns, who would sweep around the enemy as fast as possible sometimes covering distances of several miles over unforgiving terrain. Their

279

job was to completely surround their foe and then draw in, and thus distract them enough so that the chest could roll right over them and deliver the *coup de grace*. Another section - made up of either the very young and inexperienced, or the older men who would arrive last - would form a reserve, the loins. Usually held back from the main attack they would either be used to reinforce certain regiments who were struggling or if a battle went successfully they might be sent out to mop up any lingering groups of resistance amongst the enemy once their back had been broken by the main assault. It was an effective and bloodily efficient system.

Within minutes of pouring out of the Ngwebeni valley the Zulu regiments instinctively began to take up their positions. The uKhandempemvu and the uMxapho surged forward towards the lip of the ravine to form the chest. Off to their left raced the uVe and the iNgobamakhosi and the uMbonambi, charging out of the eastern end of the valley and up onto the plateau to become the left horn, while several miles in the opposite direction came the iDududu, the iSangqu, the iMbube, and the fiery uNokhenke, sprinting out across the heights in what would become a massive sweep of the right horn. To the rear was the loins, the only men Ntshingwayo and Mavumengwana managed to hold back, made up of the older uThulwana and uDloklo and iNdluyengwe and iNdlondlo regiments. The junior commanders splendidly formed their men up whilst on the move, calling out instructions and jostling the company-sized groups into the correct order. It was a stupendous feat, all the more so for the unexpectedness of it. Even without being under the control of their overall commanders they moved with a perfect fluidity, the chest and horns gliding into position effortlessly.

Even more astonishing was the lead regiments' reaction to the first shots fired by the enemy. The volley of well-aimed rounds ripped the front rank to shreds, all but mowing them down. Men crumpled and fell or were tossed high by the sheer power of the bullets striking home, creating bloody carnage in the wink of an eye, through which those behind had to pass. They ignored their twitching and screaming comrades and wiped their blood from their eyes before pushing on without the slightest pause. Another explosive volley came delivering more death and mutilation, destroying more flesh and bone, spilling blood and gore on the green veldt in copious amounts. But the warriors still did not hesitate. They were committed to battle and they raced on through the hail of lead regardless.

Up the steep valley side came the uKhandempemvu. They pulled themselves up over the rocks and boulders and came streaming out onto the plateau beyond, chasing after the thin line of retreating horsemen.

Of course, for some the battle was over very quickly. Those at the front paid for their enthusiasm with their lives as they bore the brunt of the rifle-fire. Several dozen did not even make it out of the valley before going down and it came as a terrible shock for the young and inexperienced to see their life-long friends killed in such a brutal fashion, right before their eyes. Despite this there was no shying away from those following on. Ignoring the danger they dashed forward to take their fallen comrades' places at the front, their adrenalin overcoming their fear. Some may have called it ignorance while others would describe it as raw courage; whatever it was the regiment came on, and their charge soon gained such a momentum that their early losses did not slow them nor daunt them. There would be time for grieving later.

At the centre of this frenzied attack was Dilikhana kaBokwe. He, like most others in the uKhandempemvu, was experiencing his first taste of real warfare. It was a terrifying ordeal. Accutely aware of his own mortality he cringed at the sound of gunfire, instinctively ducking with each crashing volley and knowing it was pure chance that would decide whether he lived through this or fell dying. His senses danced crazily and he was completely tuned in to every sight and sound around him. Dilikhana's world telescoped in to the here and now as his mind sought to protect itself from the horror. Thus cocooned like this he soon found he was able to detach himself from the mayhem even though he was really a part of it, charging forward with his comrades. Caught up in the whirlwind of battle he became blinkered to its reality, and although he was witness to some appalling things it was as though he was merely an observer and not a participant. In other words, he adapted. He instinctively learnt how to cope.

He ran the gauntlet of fire up the slope and across the plateau, breathing hard.

Somewhere in the crush he had become seperated from his brother, Nzobo, and he found himself looking around in the vain hope that he would spot him, but he quickly gave up. Nzobo was a fine warrior and could take care of himself. He was distracted right then anyway for as he ran on he started to come across the first dead bodies lying in the grass. He leaped over them, trying not to look too closely at their injuries, but a little further on he spotted one man with a particularly horrific wound and one which had not immediately killed him. This man had had half of his face blown away and his lower jaw dangled by a thread. Sitting there on the ground he stared into space and rocked himself too and fro, making a strange mewling sound in the back of his throat. He caught Dilikhana's eye and as he ran past one of the man's hands snaked out and grabbed him by the ankle. He did not stop to help. If he had done so then he might never have regained the courage to carry on. So he kicked the hand away and pushed on, feeling disgusted with himself but at the same time relieved to leave the poor unfortunate behind.

Dilikhana became aware of a sudden crush of people over to his left and he turned to look in that direction, wondering why they had stopped and weren't pushing forward. When he heard their cries of "uSuthu!" he understood. They had caught and killed one of their enemy and were frenziedly washing their spears in blood, hacking and stabbing with their assegais.

This gave him new heart. To know that their foe were not the invincible people some believed them to be. A cry went up and he, along with the rest of the uKhandempemvu, plus all of the other regiments stretching out to either side for as far as the eye could see, charged forward with even greater vigour.

Behind them, more and more continued to pour out of the valley.

An endless tide.

Cetshwayo kaMpande's mighty army, all 25,000 of them, swept over the heights towards the unsuspecting camp nestled at the foot of Isandlwana a scant five miles away.

The position that Lieutenant Cavaye had chosen for E. Company was a good one. Having quickly marched his men up the long spur to the north of the campsite he had lined them up across a gentle slope facing towards the hills that marked the extreme left of the plateau. They had a fine view out to their front as well as both flanks, looking across a broad valley, thus offering them an excellant field of fire. There was no dead ground in which the enemy would be able to gather, if they chose to put in an appearance, and he was also within sight of the NNC. outposts on the escarpement edge away to the east.

There was, however, one drawback.

Because of the nature of the terrain behind them and the distance they had been required to advance to gain a spot from where they could co-operate with the Zikhali's sweep across the heights, to act as a blocking force should any elements of the enemy make a move towards the head of the spur, they found that they were now out of sight of the camp below. It was a little disconcerting being so exposed like this, but then again it would only be a simple matter of sending a runner down the hill to maintain communications with the rest of the battalion. And as there were only supposed to be small groups of Zulus up here anyway it was nothing to be alarmed about.

As an afterthought Cavaye had sent a detachment of twenty-five men several hundred yards to the west, from where they would be able to keep an eye on the broken ground behind Isandlwana. So, with all possible precautions taken, they settled in to wait.

Private Owen Brooks found himself at the far right of the line. Hot and bored he was in no mood to chat like the others despite the best attempts of the man beside him to engage him in conversation. Seeing his scowling face the young soldier soon gave up and left him alone - which suited Brooks just fine.

All of this was a waste of time, he decided. Any Zulus who had been up here were long gone, that much was obvious from this featureless terrain. Once more they had given them the slip just as they had been doing throughout the war, showing their generals up as incompetant fools. This was their country and they knew it intimately. They were probably miles away from here by now, laughing their little black heads off at having forced them to march all the way up here to guard a large, empty hill. They were brainier than they looked, these Zulus.

Shaking his head and mumbling a curse under his breath, Private Brooks unslung his rifle and took a drink from his canteen. A sly smile played across his lips as he drank for instead of water he had managed to slip in some rum when the CSM wasn't looking, and this bit of substerfuge together with the fiery taste improved his mood somewhat.

He suddenly became aware of somebody watching him and he turned to see the man on his left staring hard at the canteen in his hand, his nose twitching, his eyes suspicious. Brookes glowered back and the young private, who was only eighteen years of age and the youngest member of the company, wilted before his eyes.

Carefully replacing the stopper he leaned a little closer and spoke in a quiet, though menacing, voice. "If you have something to say, then say it."

The soldier was now shaking in his boots and his face became deathly pale.

"Well son?"

All he could manage was a minute shake of the head.

"Then mind your own bleeding business."

Brooks watched him shuffle a little closer to the next man down the line, his eyes glued to the ground just in front of his boots. Satisfied that all was well, he shouldered his rifle again and looked across towards the hills in the distance.

Nothing stirred, not even the tall grass on this breezeless day.

All was quiet.

That is, until they heard the distant gunfire from way off, the long and ragged crackle carrying to them on the still air. They all looked up together.

Silence again, and one or two men exchanged the opinion that the mounted men must have had a brief brush with a group of Zulus somewhere. A skirmish that was over just as quickly as it started.

Or that is what they thought, until there came a second volley. Then a third, and a fourth, the gaps in between becoming shorter and shorter.

As the firing went on the men of E. Company gradually became more and more concerned, for the amount of gunfire now indicated that what they were hearing was quite a significant encounter. What's more, the sound of continuous volley-fire was growing louder - and it was coming their way.

Lieutenant Cavaye shared their mounting trepidation. On horseback he rode out along the front of the line and looked through his small binoculars in the direction of the firing, but to his frustration he could see no more of what was going on than the rest of the company. He was just considering sending a man back to camp to report on what was happening and to request for further instructions when suddenly, coming across the plateau towards them and galloping hard, appeared a lone rider. Training his field glasses on him, Cavaye saw it was one of the white officers of the native cavalry troops who had ridden out a short time ago to sweep across the heights. He rode fast, waving his hat above his head, his whole demeanour suggesting that something was very amis.

Before he reached their position the rider veered away to their right, intending to head straight down the spur to the camp, but he passed close enough for him to shout across. His warning cry filled the infantry with dread.

"Zulus! The whole damn lot's coming on fast! I say, the earth's covered in them! "

No more than that. He did not have time to elaborate further, as he needed to take the news to the camp as fast as possible, but it was all that E. Company needed to hear. They watched him go and once he had disappeared over the crest behind them their feeling of loneliness, and the idea that they were all by themselves up here with no support other than a few native horsemen and some poorly-armed pickets, weighed down on them with increased foreboding.

Lieutenant Cavaye was no longer sure of his earlier opinion that he had chosen a good position to deploy his company. Should they withdraw? he wondered. Either to some spot where they could see the camp, or maybe to the camp itself? But to do that would be to foresake their given order to strengthen the line of pickets and vedettes, who would have no chance of holding back a determined Zulu attack by themselves. No, only well trained, steady Imperial Infantry could do that. But at the expense of his company possibly suffering heavy casualties...?

Finding himself in a complete dilemma Lieutenant Cavaye was soon to find that events would dictate their course of action for them.

Quite who it was who spotted them first and called out, no one noticed. All they heard was a cry of "...oh my gawd, would you take a look at that!..." before every single man present spotted what had caught his horrified attention.

They appeared from behind a hill out to their right front, racing into the broad valley before them and moving across the rocky ground from right to left. They did not move in a dense mass for the attack had now had time to develop properly and the Zulus had spread out, making good use of cover and dashing from rock to rock in ones and twos. They were proceeded by several neat lines of skirmishes who screened the main force with brilliant skill, firing towards the line of British infantry who stood watching them in amazement about 800 yards away. Their fire was poor though, and either landed short or passed harmlessly overhead. Nevertheless, it had the desired effect of distracting the British enough to allow the main body of Zulus to pour across the flat ground in a long, dark column, several thousand strong.

The sight chilled the hearts of E. Company, for they suddenly realized the real extent of the Zulu attack. This was no punitive strike but a full-fledged onslaught, and this wing was moving to outflank the British force. They made no attempt to launch themselves against the redcoats, content simply to move across their front in a brilliantly co-ordinated manoeuvre.

It was too much for Private Brooks. Infuriated at their cheek, he quickly loaded and levelled his gun at them.

Before he could pull the trigger the CSM saw what he was about to do and came rushing down the line, screeching at the top of his voice. "You wait for the bleeding order you bleeding imbecile! What the bleeding hell are you thinking of!" He struck down with his sword-bayonet, catching Brooks' rifle and forcing it down, half a second before he would have fired. Then he thrust his face up close to him, his nose almost touching Brooks'. "YOU CRETIN!" he spat.

Private Brooks wanted to answer back, he was in that kind of mood, but to open his mouth would have been to reveal what he had been drinking and so he wisely kept quiet. Inside, he fumed.

The CSM, teeth gritted, snarled under his breath, gave him a once over in a most disparaging way, and then turned away.

He glanced across to where Lieutenant Cavaye waited staring at the Zulu masses, catching his eye once he turned back towards the men. He raised an eyebrow in a silent query and Cavaye nodded in response. It was time.

Turning to the line of men the CSM barked out the necessary orders. Each soldier loaded, brought up his weapon and took aim at the distant figures, and then on the command of "FIRE!" the whole company discharged their Martini-Henry's, the sound of the volley sweet in their ears.

"RELOAD! Set your sights. FIRE!"

They blazed away at the long column of Zulus, each soldier picking his target carefully. Good, steady shots that they were, they dropped a good many, but it hardly seemed to slow them. They continued to flow across the valley floor like a black river in even greater numbers, gliding over the ground from east to west.

Lieutenant Cavaye, still seated on his horse, watched his men fire, every now and then shouting words of encouragement to them.

"Good shooting E. Company!" he would say, "let the brutes take it! That's my men!"

Yet for all their good work he saw that it made scant difference. The enemy were in such numbers that his one hundred men, firing away as they were, could only achieve so much. The simple truth was that the Zulus were able to push on relentlessly. They lost a good number of men but such was their determination that they were able to shrug off their casualties with impunity. If they were to have any real effect in stemming the tide then they needed reinforcements fast.

And every few minutes he would glance back in the direction of the camp, out of sight far below, wondering when help would come.

Growing more and more anxious all the while.

At the same time that George Shepstone was galloping across the plateau carrying the frightful news that the main Zulu Army was fast bearing down on the camp, an unsuspecting Colonel Pulleine had just received the message from the General informing him to strike the tents and to move out to the Mangeni. A new campsite had been chosen twelve miles further on, and as enough time had already been lost Chelmsford wished to resume the advance as soon as possible. Several companies of native levies would be returning to Isandlwana to help with the move and he was to be ready and packed up by the time they arrived.

Pulleine should have been happy that the decision to move meant that the immediate responsibilty of how best to deal with his complex situation was being taken out of his hands. Yet in their way these fresh instructions complicated things even more. A large portion of his force was out either on outpost duty or helping with Durnford's push across the heights, keeping an eye out for the Zulus rumoured to be out there somewhere, and now he was expected to gather up his command and march east - without having determined precisely how many Zulus there were nor their exact whereabouts. Risking a move in those circumstances was a big gamble. On top of that Durnford had already set out on his venture to chase down yet more of the enemy he was convinced was moving against the General - a fact the General was apparantly unaware of. Did the move to link up with the rest of the column include Durnford? Or had Durnford received fresh orders of his own? It was indeed a complex situation...

...about to become even worse.

Unknown to Pulleine, right at the precise time that he was puzzling over the order form that he held in his hands, Shepstone was just arriving at the northern-most part of the camp, breathless and bathed in sweat after his hard ride.

Reining in his horse he quickly looked around, ignoring the curious stares his disheveled condition was drawing from several onlookers, until he spotted a familiar face. Shepstone hurriedly went riding over.

James Brickhill saw him approach and was alarmed at the state he was in, hair awry and his eyes wide with alarm. Before he had a chance to ask what was wrong, the young officer grabbed a hold of his arm, taking him aback.

"Where's the Colonel?" Shepstone blurted, still out of breath.

"You mean Colonel Pulleine?" Brickhill responded calmly.

"Yes, where can I find him?"

"Why, he's at the Headquarters Tent of course. Whatever's the matter?"

"Where the hell is that?"

"Well, there's no need for that," said Brickhill, piqued a little.

"For God's sake, please show me, this is urgent!"

Shepstone still had a hold of his sleeve which he proceeded to shake in a panicky fashion, and it was this, together with the look of fear that Brickhill suddenly noticed in his eyes, that convinced him something was seriously wrong. "Of couse," he said in a whisper. "I'll take you there."

Together they weaved their way through the camp to where Pulleine's command tent was situated. Brickhill noticed that as they went his companion kept glancing up towards the edge of the escarpement as though looking for something there, his eyes swiftly searching the hilltops. He found himself glancing up also, but could see nothing unusual. Nevertheless, there was something about the man's alarmed state that was beginning to make him nervous.

They arrived to find the Colonel deep in discussion with several fellow officers just outside his tent. He noticed them coming and he broke off from what he was saying, taking a step forward and frowning as he saw Shepstone's face.

"Good God Mr Shepstone," he said, "you look like you've seen a ghost."

"I wish it was as simple as that Colonel, sir." Shepstone waited until he had their full attention, and then breathed..."I bring you grave news."

Pulleine and the others looked at one another, the message from the General temporarily forgotten. "Go on."

He raised his hand and pointed towards the plateau way up to the north, and they noticed, worryingly, that his finger was shaking. When he told them the news they began to understand why he was in such a state. "Your Zulus... we've found them... up in the hills... hiding."

There was a long moment of silence. Brickhill looked from face to face, a deep chill spreading through his core, and when his eyes finally fell on the Colonel's he thought for a moment that Pulleine seemed numbed with shock. He saw him struggle to maintain control, and a weak smile half appeared on his thin lips, yet it was not a convincing one. Neither were his next words.

"How many-" he croaked, then had to cough to clear his throat and start again. "How many did you spot?"

Shepstone slowly shook his head and then looked up. "It was the whole damn Zulu army," he whispered.

"Nonsense," Pulleine suddenly blurted as he puffed up his chest and laughed. "You exaggerate surely? The Zulu army is out in that direction, to the east where His Lordship is."

But George shepstone was slowly shaking his head, his patience starting to wear thin, and when he spoke again his words had an edge to them. "I saw them with my own eyes. There are so many that they filled an entire valley from end to end, and my men are struggling to hold them back."

"Your men are actually fighting?" one of the officers asked, alarmed by this news.

"Yes! I'm not an alarmist, sir, but the Zulus are in such black masses over there, such long black lines that you have to give us all the assistance you can. They are now fast driving our men this way!"

Pulleine was at a complete loss as to what he should do. The situation seemed to be changing radically from one minute to the next. He had an order in his hand from the General telling him to move forward to join up with him, yet here was this gentleman informing him that a massive Zulu force was coming their way seriously endangering their camp. He looked down at the message slip hoping that the words written on the piece of paper would contain the answer to his problem, yet he gained no inspiration from them.

Seeing him hesitate, one of the officers – in actual fact he who had brought Chelmsford's orders -suddenly came to his rescue. "Under the circumstances I should advice you to disobeying the General's instructions, for the present at any rate," he said, in a confidential tone. "He knows nothing of this, he is only thinking of the cowardly way in which the Zulus are running before his troops over yonder. Obviously if he knew the whereabouts of their main army, so close to us here, he would not be asking this of you." He nodded at the message.

Pulleine nodded gratefully. "Yes... good point... "

Their conversation was interrupted right then by the first sound of gunfire reverberting down out of the hills to the north. It made everyone jump, for they had not expected the fight to be so close. Everyone except George Shepstone that is. As they all turned and stared up towards the sound, looks of alarm on their faces, he merely informed them in a voice that was now perfectly calm... "that will be Cavaye's company. I saw them getting ready as I rode passed. They'll be hard-pressed too, before long."

Colonel Pulleine, ashen-faced, looked over and wondered how he could remain so relaxed under such circumstances.

The others watched him. They waited for him to speak. They waited an inordinately long time, until eventually Lieutenant Melvill prompted him. "Sir... your orders?"

His stomach seemed to shrivel at the words.

For a moment he held his breath, then let it out through his nose, and found himself talking before he even realized he was doing so, the sound of his own voice seeming to be coming from a million miles away. "We must reinforce him. Lieutenant Melvill, order F. Company to move out and take up position with Cavaye's men."

"Yes sir." He made as if to move away, but pulled up when further instructions came. "You'd better sound the General Alert as well."

"Yes sir, of course."

With Melvill on his way, Colonel Pulleine turned next to the young George Shepstone.

"Your comrades in No.3 Troop have just come in with Colonel Durnford's wagons. I'll send them straight on to support you, as well as some NNC men."

"It won't be enough," Shepstone pointed out matter-of-factly.

"It is all I can spare Mr Shepstone!" Pulleine said harshly, taking those around him by surprise. "My men are already spread very thinly. I cannot dilute the camp's defences any more than that, not until we see the exact nature of the Zulu attack. I'm sorry."

Shepstone wanted to protest further, to get across to him just how serious things were, but he guessed that it would be pointless. Pulleine had made his decision, and his orders were already being transmitted down the line. Besides, he did not have the time to argue.

"I should return to my men," he told Pulleine, who only nodded absentmindedly, his thoughts elsewhere.

So he walked angrily away, shaking his head to himself.

Behind him, Colonel Pulleine gazed up towards the escarpment, his hands by his sides, fingers flexing into twin fists at the sound of each new volley that rolled down from the hills.

As he quickly pulled himself up into his saddle Shepstone glanced down at the young man who had followed him back.

"Do you not have a gun, Mr Brickhill?" he asked.

"No. I am just an interpreter, not a soldier."

"Well if I were you," Shepstone said quietly, "I would find myself one. You're going to need it."

Brickhill stared after him as he rode swiftly away.

CHAPTER 30

1.5 MILES EAST OF BRITISH CAMP AT ISANDLWANA. 12:00pm.

As commander of the Rocket Battery, Major Francis Broadfoot Russell RA. was very proud of the unit under his charge - even if it was on the small side. With just one Bombardier and nine privates furnished from the 1/24th, plus their escort of native levies, it could hardly have been described as powerful, but their main component was of course the three rocket troughs and their 9-pounder rockets, and it was these which provided him the most pride.

Using all of the technology that nineteenth century science had to offer the Rocket Battery had been designed principally to allow a mobile, light, artillery unit to launch ordanance against awkward targets in difficult terrain. Without the large gun-crews and horse-teams normally required to operate the more conventional artillery pieces, like the 7-pounders back in camp, the Rocket Battery was able to take up positions and launch attacks of a nature normally deemed too difficult. With all of their equipment carried on a few pack-animals they were ideally suited for the type of countryside that South Africa had to offer, able to move through the hilly and mountainous land with ease - although admittedly somewhat slowly. Once in position it was just a matter of setting up the firing troughs on their tripods, adjusting their angle of elevation, loading the rockets, and then firing them. They were capable of hitting targets up to 1000 yards away, delivering devastating blows right into the very heart of an enemy force.

At least, this was what the engineers who had designed them hoped.

It was a wild hope indeed. A hope that they would fire with any modicum of accuracy, for they had a notoriously poor record of not landing on target, their flights tending to be erractic to say the least. A hope that they would not turn in mid-air and come screaming back towards their own lines. A hope - and this had happened more than once - that they would not explode on the firing troughs, killing and maiming their crew. For this kind of technology was still in its infancy and the work was extremely dangerous, hence the shortfall of volunteers to man the battery and the need to 'borrow' several men from the infantry battalion. Nevertheless, Major Russell still thought them wonderful.

He had every faith in these new weapons. They were temperamental, true, but as long as they persevered with them and made slight improvements on their design, then he was confident that eventually they would be able to harness this new power and prove their full potential to their many critics. Alheady they were beginning to learn from their early mistakes, improving on the range and accuracy of the rockets to such a degree that he had long since learnt to ignore the ridicule his colleagues at Woolwich cast at him. There was a lot of petty jealousy involved, of that he was sure. Some of the more senior artillery officers, of the old school, were no doubt worried that eventually this new science would fast make their own artillery pieces obselete and that they would be left behind, too old and stuck in their ways to adapt to the changing world of future warfare. Major Russell, therefore, was glad to be at the forefront of these vast advances in weapons technology.

So it was with a feeling of high confidence that he led the Rocket Battery out across the plain, riding at the front of his little command, dwarfed by the landscape around them.

Colonel Durnford and the mounted men with him had soon ridden on ahead, wishing to push on fast while they followed on behind, the pack-animals plodding over the rocky ground at a much more sedate pace. Before long, the horsemen had disappeared from view as they swung slightly north in line with the escarpement on their left, a vague cloud of dust the only visible indication of their progress. Russell and his men found themselves completely alone.

Because of the nature of the ground, strewn with boulders and cut apart with dongas and washed away topsoil, the half dozen animals that carried the firing troughs and the boxes of rockets had almost come to a complete standstill, more intent on chewing on the grass than advancing with their heavy loads. Major Russell, aware that before the day was out they may have to launch their rockets against the zulus at some stage, did not want to be left too far behind, and so in order to press on a little faster he ordered the troughs to be taken down and carried by the native levies instead. Protesting loudly about this the NNC at first refused to obey and further minutes were lost while their white noncoms bullied and pushed them into carrying out the command. Eventually, they resumed their advance.

To save some of the lost time Major Russell steered his men a little to the north-east, intending to cut across the corner of the plain and follow Durnford up towards the end of the plateau. Their new course now took them onto the lower slopes of the escarpment that ran along on the left, and when the men glanced behind them they saw that their view back to the camp was now obscurred by the conical hill. This worried them a little. Yet if they could catch up with Durnford then he felt justified in taking what was, in any case, a minimal risk. So, with the high ground of the lower edge of the Nqutu plateau looming over them, they pressed sluggishly onwards.

When, just after mid-day, they heard the distant popping of rifle-fire blowing down on the breeze from the north, Major Russell decided on yet another change of course. Guessing correctly that the Zikhali had become engaged up on the plateau he quickly abandoned his idea of trying to catch up with Durnford and decided instead that they should move to link up with Raw and Roberts up on the high ground. That was where the fighting was anyway, and they should lend a hand, putting to good use all of the attributes of his highly mobile unit. This was exactly the kind of scenario he had envisaged, climbing up into the hills, into the normally inaccessible areas, to deliver the killer blow to their unsophisticated foe.

Quickly he scanned the steep escarpment lying before them, searching for the easiest route up onto the plateau. He noticed, amidst the broken ground and jumble of rocks, a break in the hillside several hundred yards away to the right, a notch through which he should be able to lead the mules and men that carried their equipment without too much difficulty.

Twisting in his saddle, he looked down at his Bombardier and said, "over there, we shall climb up through that gap." He pointed towards the notch. "Once on the top we should have a good view of what is going on."

Bombardier Gough nodded and relayed the instructions to the men, and the Rocket Battery angled over towards the gap.

They had been working their way up over the steepening ground for a couple of minutes when Major Russell, who had ridden on ahead in his eagerness to join the fight, suddenly drew up with a startled gasp. On the crest of the escarpment above them and spilling down the steep hillside he saw several lines of Zulus, swarming forward rapidly over the boulders and slabs of rock. He watched them come on, frozen to the spot for a moment by their sudden - and unexpected - appearance, then he noticed even more of them racing down the notch towards which he was leading his men, pouring through the narrow gap like a black waterfall.

"Good God," Russell whispered to himself as the realization of their predicament instantly fell on him, crushing his spirit.

The Zulus should not be here. The Zikhali Horse up on the plateau should have been able to hold them, after-all the reports suggested only small numbers of the enemy were in the vicinity. Unless... It struck him that perhaps...just perhaps...the main Zulu Army had sprung a surprise attack against them, having found their way onto the plateau without them realizing it. If that was the case! The consequences did not bare thinking about.

Whatever the extent of the attack one thing was certain; they had to try and hold them here. With his heart thumping in his chest, Russell spun his horse around and galloped back towards his men, who as yet had not noticed the Zulus streaming towards them. He called out to them as he rode, pointing back over his shoulder. "Zulus, we have Zulus up on the high ground! ACTION FRONT!"

Immediately the rocketeers rushed to set up their apparatus. Carrying the three troughs over to a patch of flat ground amidst the rocks, they arranged them side by side, snapping the legs into place and opening the boxes of rockets. It took a couple of minutes to get them ready for it was necessary to fix a friction tube to each rocket as it was loaded onto the firing trough, then to attach a short lanyard. Also, the trajectory was established by means of angle of elevation at which the troughs were positioned, a tricky exercise that required precise calculations as well as a degree of guess-work. So before everything was ready the Zulus had already worked their way down the deep cleft and were starting to spread out at the bottom, racing around the large boulders and over the rough ground towards them.

Russell saw they had no more time to waste. They had to fire now or they would not get the chance to fire at all. Unable to finish his carefull preparations, he called across to Bombardier Gough who stood waiting by one of the troughs, his face pale and tense as he watched the Zulus come closer.

"Fire number one!" Russell shouted.

Gough turned and called back..."but they're not set up sir."

"Fire number one god-damn it! FIRE! FIRE!"

He did as he was told and gave the lanyard a sharp tug. The rocket ignited and screamed away from the trough amidst a hellish blaze of fiery sparks and white smoke. They watched it go, cringing at the high-pitched shriek it emitted, following its erratic course through the air. It twisted this way and that, turning sharply in mid-flight and then falling towards the notch in the hillside, amazingly on target. However, the Zulus had already cleared the area having reached the plain below and they, along with Russell and his men, watched as the rocket exploded harmlessly on the rockface.

Dismayed that their first shot had not slowed the Zulus in the slightest Russell nevertheless gave the order for number's two and three to fire. His men never got the chance to carry out his instruction. A group of Zulus had taken cover in some dead ground when they saw the rocket pass overhead, terrified by its screeching, fire-spitting flight, but once they realized it had come down well to their rear they sprang up out of their hiding place and fired a ragged volley towards the Rocket Battery.

A half dozen men went down, either killed outright or mortally wounded, and all thought of launching further rockets was instantly forgotten as a blind panic took hold. The mules stampeded, kicking their back legs in terror and sending boxes of equipment flying in all directions, and two of them tumbled over a large rock slab to break their legs. Within seconds the nearest Zulus darted forward to finish the poor beasts off, then launched themselves at the British, stabbing and clubbing them into oblivion. The NNC company managed to fire a poorly aimed volley at nothing in particular, then threw down their guns and bolted.

Russell was hit in the face, the round passing through one cheek and out the other, and he fell to his knees vomitting blood onto the ground. One of the redcoats saw him go down and rushed across. "Sir!" he called. "I'll help you-" but then he was dismissed by a single thrust of an assegai through his ribs, screaming and spinning and falling onto the rocky ground, blood pumping, legs twitching.

Russell turned in time to see the soldier tumble away. There was nothing he could do. His men were being butchered around him, the Zulus in and amongst them, taking his command apart piece by bloody piece.

His last thought, before he too felt the burn of a deep assegai stab followed by oblivion, was how disappointingly ineffective his beloved Rocket Battery had proved to be. He'd had such high hopes for it, was determined that one day... one day...

The body of Zulu skirmishes had come down from the plateau ahead of the main bulk of the army, who followed in their wake about half a mile back. Surprised to find themselves confronted by this small force of British soldiers and their black allies, with their strange contraptions, they had soon overcome their initial apprehension and easily over-run them, rolling right through them with hardly a pause in their stride. When they saw the Natal Natives give flight they chased after them, determined that they should not get away. Infact such was their enthusiasm to press their attack that they failed to notice, amidst the wreckage of the Rocket Battery, that one man was still alive. Knocked unconcious by a heavy blow from one of their knobkerries they had left him for dead amongst a pile of bloody corpses.

Trying not to pay too close attention to his dead comrades, whose blood soaked through his uniform and whose spilled insides slithered over his skin, Private Thomas Scott pushed himself clear and came to his feet, groggy from the whack on his head. With some difficulty he managed to stay upright. Fearfully he turned around, looking to see if any Zulus had stayed behind, but to his relief he saw they were some distance off and running away from him.

For a minute or so Private Scott was too shocked and confused to properly take in the scenes of carnage around him. It was probably a small mercy, for had he seen the horrific nature of the spectacle he would in all likelihood have collapsed into a shaking, pathetic, wreck, incapable of anything except waiting for the Zulus to come back and finish him off. Instead, when he had regained a little of his strength and composure, he decided that his best course of action would be to try and make his way across country towards the river, to swim across into Natal, and find a place of safety. As far as he was concerned he was cut off from the camp, and so for him the battle was over. Now it was a matter of saving himself.

Bending down he scooped up a rifle, then turned and started to jog south. Heading for the hills.

CHAPTER 31

THE BRITISH CAMP AT ISANDLWANA. 12:00pm-12:30pm.

Lieutenant Horace Smith-Dorrien turned sharply, startled by the peculiar screeching noise and wondering what on earth it was. He looked out across the plain just in time to see the long white trail of the rocket arc through the sky from beyond the conical hill, but when it dipped and slanted back down to the ground he lost sight of it amidst the broken landscape.

Well, he thought as he stroked his horse's neck, trying to calm it, things must be serious if the Rocket Battery was coming into action. They had only left a short while ago and already they had targets at which to fire at. He waited for more to be launched-and was slightly puzzled when further shots failed to materialize. Perhaps whoever they had been targeting had been scared away, terrified by the sight of this new, devilish weapon. Yes. That must be the reason. Why, for a moment there it had scared him half to death!

Feeling a thrill of excitement, Smith-Dorrien brought his mind back to the events now taking place around the camp at Isandlwana.

It seemed he had arrived just in time.

He had come in fast on the heels of Colonel Durnford's column, having ridden hard from Rorke's Drift. Going immediately to see his superior officer in the transport department, SmithDorrien had made a polite request about joining with Lord Chelmsford's men who had left earlier that morning, on the pretext of needing to

300

organise their supply convoys and to check out the nature of the road ahead. Much to his disappointment he'd been told he was needed in camp to ready a convoy which was required to return to the drift later in the morning, and he had moved off to see to this convinced he would miss out on any fighting. However, within just a few minutes the situation changed dramatically.

Colonel Durnford, acting on reports that a Zulu impi was moving against the General's rear, had left with his force of native horsemen to intercept and attack them, whilst at the same time patrols were sent onto the plateau to scout around. In a little under one hour the first sounds of battle had started to reach the camp. A rumour soon spread that a sizeable Zulu force was moving against them much to everybody's surprise. Smith-Dorrien could hardly believe his slice of good fortune. Instead of the anticipated battle being fought out where the General was it now seemed, remarkably, that it would take place here at Isandlwana. In a strange and peculiar twist of fate it seemed that he was destined to have his baptism of fire after all.

From his position in the wagon park he had watched the comings and goings of the various units as Colonel Pulleine, the camp commander, responded to the threat accordingly. A company of redcoats were sent running up the spur to reinforce the one aliready engaged, the men hurrying up the long slope with a faint air of urgency. He followed their progress with interest until they disappeared from sight over the crest, and a short while later an increase in the level of gunfire indicated that they too had joined the fray. At the same time as this the other four Imperial companies plus the NNC were formed up in front of the tents, for the second time that morning, awaiting further orders. Soon after, Smith-Dorrien noticed some horsemen riding through the camp and heading for the hills to the north, following in the wake of the redcoats, and he recognized them as a troop of Zikhali Horse who had arrived just a short time ago. With hardly time to pause for breath they were being rushed out to aid the blocking force apparantly trying to hold back the Zulus on the plateau. He likewise watched these until they were lost from view amidst the hills. Next, the two artillery guns were deployed on a slight rocky knoll between the two dongas about 400 yards to the left front of the camp, with Lieutenant Porteous' A Company positioned in support to their rear. The gunners unlimbered the two 7-pounders and stood by with their ammunition at hand, their eyes - as were everybodies, including Smith-Dorrien's - on the skyline above.

It was all very exciting, thought Smith-Dorrien.

So much was happening that he could hardly keep up with events.

He could not have known it but right then the situation on the plateau and at the head of the spur was becoming very dire indeed. Had he done, then he might not have been quite so cavalier in his attitude. For with each passing minute things for the men fighting hard to hold back the zulu tide were becoming more and more serious. They were having trouble even slowing the enemy advance let alone stopping it dead.

No sooner had the horsemen of No 3 Troop, Zikhali Horse, and their commander Lieutenant Vause, reached the high plateau than they saw to their dismay their two sister Troops come racing towards them hotly pursued by a dense mass of charging Zulus that seemed to fill the landscape for as far as the eye could see, a terrible sight that hit them in the pit of their stomachs with a sickening crunch. They noticed several of their companions were carrying bad injuries which they had tried to bandage whilst riding back, their uniforms stained dark with their blood. They also saw a number of riderless horses - an explanation for which was not necessary. It became immediately apparant to Vause and his men that Colonel Pulleine had not grasped the seriousness of the situation. The reinforcements he had deployed, which included themselves, would not be enough to halt or divert the Zulus to any significant degree. Yet, good soldiers that they were, they had to try.

Captain Shepstone, still angry after his disagreement with the Colonel, quickly ordered them back. Trying to maintain the integrity of his force and urging them to stay together, he took the Zikhali Horse back down the slope a little and dismounted the men. Leaving their horses in a shallow donga, he quickly strung them out in line and then led them back towards the top of the escarpment once more, in skirmishing order, hoping to catch the enemy as they appeared on the skyline. They waited nervously for them to appear.

Also watching and wondering why they had returned so unexpectedly, Colonel Pulleine soon received his first glimpse of the Zulus. They appeared along the high ground just to the east of the spur and directly above Shepstone's men, first a trickle over the crest, and then an overwhelming flood. He half-cried out loud at the sight and quickly managed to stiffle the sound, hoping nobody had noticed; if they did, then they said nothing, too intent on the Zulus racing down towards the Zikhali. Pulleine watched the drama unfold with his fellow officers.

All three Troops opened up at once, aiming at the groups of Zulus coming down the slope. Their fire, now combined and condensed along a narrow front, had a devastating effect, dropping Zulus by the dozen. All along the escarpment they dropped, caught in silhouette as they came over the crest. Dead and dying warriors soon carpeted the hillside.

Captain Shepstone directed their fire with brilliant skill, leading the men forward in between each volley, taking the fight to the enemy in a complete change to their earlier retreat. He had taken a gamble in withdrawing all the way down the slope but their results started to show as they slowly but surely drove the Zulus back.

Pulleine saw this too. Admiring the way the Zikhali fought, he felt elated at their success. With his spirits bolstered somewhat he called out..."Somebody order Major Smith to open up with his guns!"...to no one in particular, and the order was hurriedly relayed to the artillery detachment on the rocky knoll.

The gunners, one of whom was called Edward Chisolm and whose job it was to use his rammer to shove each round down the muzzle of his gun, sprung into action. Well drilled and highly motivated, they went through their firing sequence with ease. Gunner Number 2 was handed a round and powder bag by the man standing by the limber, which he placed into the barrel. Gunner Number 1 – the short and brawny Edward Chisolm – rammed the projectile home until it butted up against the bottom. Meanwhile, Gunner Number 3, his hand protected by a thick leather glove, would keep his thumb over the vent hole at the breech, waiting until the round – in this case shrapnel – was in place. When it was ready he would shove a wire pick through the vent to prick open the powder bag, then he would stand aside, his task complete. Gunner Number 4 would step forward to ready the powder for ignition. Reaching into a small pouch on his belt he would take a friction primer and insert it into the vent hole, then, taking a nine foot long lanyard of braided cord, attach it to the primer, trail it along the ground, and wait for the order to fire, the whole gun crew taking up a kneeling position. When the command came he would give it a hard jerk, the movement would release the friction primer, which in turn would ignite the powder, thus firing the projectile. With immense violence the whole gun would leap back several feet from the recoil of the blast and the crew would hurry to manhandle it back into position, whilst Gunner Number 1 shoved a dampened sponge down the barrel to put out any lingering embers that might ignite the next round prematurely. Finished, the whole process would be repeated, with the length of fuse on the next round being adjusted according to the range so that it would explode precisely as it landed, causing maximum devastation. A good guncrew could hope to get two, possibly three, well-aimed shots off per minute. It was hard, physically tiring work, and soon the men would be bathed with sweat and grubby with gunsmoke and grease, their ears ringing from the incessant roar of their gun.

The two 7-pounders began firing at their maximum range, lobbing shrapnel over the heads of the dismounted Zikhali at the Zulus massing on the top of the escarpement to their front. At this distance the effectiveness and accuracy of the shots was poor, some falling short or exploding in mid-air, causing one or two of Shepstone's men to cast fearful glances up at the sky whenever they heard the rounds passing overhead. They made a terrible ripping sound as they arced through the air, as though the very heavens were screaming in protest, and it was enough to make these hardened fighters hesitate. Their leaders urged them on though and they pushed on up the steep slope as the artillery continued to belch their fury.

Once at the top Captain Shepstone called a halt to their advance. The guns altered their range a little, laying down more fire onto the flat ground ahead where the Zulus had pulled back to, and a temporary stalemate developed. Both sides fired away at one another, the Zikhali Horse and two Imperial companies on one side, the uKhandempemvu on the other. For a while the Zulus were unable to advance into the withering fire the British were flinging at them. They had allready taken heavy casualties. They simply could not move their attack forward until the regiments behind and to either side caught up. Only then, when they vastly outnumbered their foe, could they make another charge and try once more to press down the slope.

Gradually the rest of the Zulu chest caught up. Lieutenant Raw noticed the Zulu numbers begin to steadily increase, the plateau filling up with thousands upon thousands of them.

"There's too many of them!" he called to Shepstone.

"I know!" He directed another volley towards the dense masses gathering about 300 yards to their front, hardly making a dent in their ranks. "We can't hold them for much longer, not on our own. Our ammunition's starting to run low as well, we'll need to send some runners back for some more soon!"

"If we can find our reserve supply, that is," Raw pointed out gloomily. "Our wagons hadn't even reached camp when we left. They could be anywhere down there."

"Damn!" Shepstone bellowed. Then..."damn you Pulleine, do something quickly otherwise we're going to be overrun up here! Come on, what are you playing at?"

Indeed, many of the men were thinking precisely the same thing. If they were cut off from the camp - and the more hard-pressed they were, the stronger that possibility became - then they would not stand a chance. It was a sobering thought which they tried not to dwell on.

Colonel Pulleine did finally recognize the danger of this as the full extent of the Zulu attack slowly began to get through to him.

It was only when the enemy began to appear on the skyline further away to the east, as far as the conical hill and beyond, that the penny dropped; this was no small advance by a few thousand Zulus but a fully committed, general movement against the camp by the whole Zulu army. Their front stretched from just west of the spur all along the full length of the escarpment, a distance of at least five miles. That could only mean upwards of 25,000 warriors were heading their way.

He could hardly grasp the magnitude of the task now facing them.

How could it have happened? How could so many men evade detection and come within striking distance of their camp without anybody spotting them? How could His Lordship have been so utterly outwitted, and in such a comprehensive fashion? It was just...unbelievable!

Yet it had happened. Despite all of their scouting and all of the precautions they had taken to guard against a surprise attack, the Zulus were about to fall on them with a suddenness and might that was breathtaking. Had the situation not being so dangerous Colonel Pulleine might have admired their audacity and skill, acknowledging the fact that they had completely out-thought them. Yet the circumstances he was now confronted with, as camp commander, meant he did not have time to wonder about the hows and whys, not if he wished to prevent a disaster. Quick and decisive action was called for, a clear head required.

The first and most obvious thing that occurred to him was how exposed the men fighting up on the plateau were. With Zulus starting to appear all along the Nyoni Heights there was the serious danger that if they descended down the escarpment in large numbers then his men might find themselves being outflanked and cut off. He realized at once that they had to be brought back in and reformed closer to the camp, with the rest of the garrison forming a firing line that incorporated the two 7-pounders, the whole force so positioned as to face the threat to the north.

Pulleine turned to his adjutant, and Lieutenant Melvill hurriedly stepped forward. He listened to the colonel's instructions with a worried look on his face, glancing occassionally towards the fighting up on the hills.

"Ride up to where Lieutenant Cavaye's men are. Order them, as well as Mostyn's F Company and the Zikhali, to fall back on the camp with all haste. I am going to form the rest of the men up to cover their retreat and they are to take their place in the line. If we act fast and keep our heads then we need not be unduly alarmed by this unfortunate turn of events."

Melvill was not convinced by the colonel's words but he said nothing.

"We face a hard time Lieutenant, but the 24th are good boys. I'm sure their conduct today will be an example to the rest of the British Army for years to come." He tried to smile but it came out looking more like a grimace. "This is our opportunity to shine! Now go!"

"Sir!" Melvill wheeled away and galloped up the hill.

Lieutenant Smith-Dorrien had been joined by Lieutenant Coghill, who had managed to limp out of his tent to watch events unfold, and the two of them saw Melvill ride away. He cut a dashing figure dressed as he was in his scarlet tunic and navy-blue trousers, his head low against his horses neck, zig-zagging through the tents and then up the grassy spur towards the battle raging on the plateau. A few minutes later they watched as the remainder of the camps force, the three Imperial companies plus the NNC who had been patiently waiting in column in front of the tents, suddenly hurry to take up a new position, aligning themselves into an extended firing line running eastwards and parallel with the escarpment, the companies evenly spaced. The two guns continued to fire while all of this was going on, attempting to hit the Zulus gathering above the camp. The band of the 1/24th once again fell in to carry out their duties as stretcher bearers and Surgeon Major Peter Shepherd, the columns senior medical officer, made his final preparations in the Hospital tents, setting out his surgical equipment on his operating table.

In double quick time everybody was ready.

They waited for the inevitable attack.

When the order to pull back finally reached the men on the plateau they did not need to be told twice. Quickly breaking away from the fight, the two redcoat companies retired first, jogging over the gentle slope to their rear and then down the spur. The NNC men who had been on outpost duty away to the right saw this and panicked. Fearing they would be left behind they sprinted down the hill as fast as they could, losing all of their discipline in the process. One or two took the opportunity to slip quietly away; they tore off their red headbands and sneaked south through the broken terrain, never to be seen again. The Zikhali Horse remained behind for a couple of minutes to pour a last volley into the Zulu ranks, then they too pulled clear.

The uKhandempemvu were elated that they had finally managed to push the whites and their black allies off the ridge. They charged forward, crying their regimental war-cry. "Izulu!" Once at the edge they looked down towards the retreating men. The sight greatly encouraged them and they sprinted down after them, now supported by the rest of the army who had finally caught them up.

Major Stuart Smith of the artillery saw them coming and he quickly switched the fire from his guns, bringing a half dozen rounds down on top of the Zulus in an attempt to blunt their charge and give the soldiers more of a chance. At this range the 7-pounders had more success and they cut large holes in the Zulu ranks, mangling and shredding them beyond recognition and causing enough devastation to make them hesitate long enough for the British to reach the bottom.

All except for Lieutenant Roberts.

Leading his men across the slope to where they had left their horses in the donga, he suddenly found himself losing his footing amongst the rocks and falling headlong into the tall grass. Badly winded, by the time he raised himself to his knee's he saw that the rest of No 2 Troop had left him far behind. He clambered to his feet to catch them up.

He never made it any further than that.

A round of shrapnel fired by one of the guns exploded just feet away, having fallen short from its intended target. It ripped him in two at the chest. The blast tore off the back of his skull and his brain fragmented, killing him instantly.

He did not even know what had happened.

Nobody else realized the mistake either for they had more pressing things to worry about. The two companies of infantry plus the Zikhali made it down, grateful to be back with their comades again. They took up their place in the line.

The Zulu chest followed them up.

In the meantime, Pulleine found himself wondering how Colonel Durnford was faring.

CHAPTER 32

4 MILES EAST OF BRITISH CAMP AT ISANDLWANA.

12:00pm-12:30pm.

Little realizing what was taking place out across the plateau, or that the men of the Rocket Battery were right at that moment fighting for their lives just a few miles behind them, Durnford and his one hundred troopers raced across the plain as fast as they could in their eagerness to intercept the Zulus moving on the General. They could not have known it but this was a mad and futile venture, based on a serious misjudgement of the circumstances. Expecting nothing more than a brief skirmish with just a few hundred Zulus, they were full of high spirits and confidence.

Soon, the line of the escarpment to their rear blocked off all view of the campsite. They swung to the north-east, making for the end of the plain where the plateau levelled out, as this was the obvious route down which the enemy would launch their attack.

They rode on.

This was the moment he had been waiting for, Colonel Durnford thought to himself as he led them further and further away from Isandlwana. His moment of truth. Thwarted thus far during the campaign, and his earlier career, for the chance to prove his leadership qualities, he now felt exhilarated at the prospect of the coming fight. Here was a perfect opportunity to prove once and for all that he had the right temperment and skills to successfully command his men under true battle conditions, against a worthy opponent. Then, and only then, would the cruel gossip and the snide remarks that had been circulating amoungst settler society since the Bushman's Pass affair stop. They would have no choice but to look upon him in a different light. So nothing would take away this chance. He was determined of that.

A shadow of that dreadful time up amongst the Drakensberg Mountains still lingered within him. He would probably never fully shake it off. It had shaped his life ever since. The memories - and often the nightmares - had haunted him on and off for more than five years now, and he carried the constant physical reminder of that doomed fight in the shape of his injured arm. Each morning the pain woke him and never a day went by when he did not glance down to remember how he had recieved the tortuous blow. Sometimes the memories were fleeting and he had learnt to cope with them, burying them under his work and pushing them to the back of his mind. But on other occasions...

The doctors had wanted to amputate. When Chieftain had lost his footing on the steep mountain trail and thrown him, sending him tumbling down the deep gulley, rolling end over end for fifty feet or more and bouncing over the rocks, Durnford had suffered a bad dislocation of the shoulder plus bruised ribs and a deep gash on the forehead. Delirious with pain he had ignored the protestations of his men who urged him to abandon their mission to reach the pass and prevent some renegade natives from escaping and instead decided to press on. Drifting in and out of conciousness Durnford had been unable to stay seated in his saddle, and so the other riders had fashioned a makeshift sling in which they had carried him the rest of the way up the mountainside. Reaching the summit he had finally agreed with their recommendation that he try and get some sleep.

The following morning, and still suffering incredible agony, they had lifted him gingerly onto Chieftain's back. By sunrise they had reached their destination...late because they had lost their way. Angry that most of the natives they had been pursuing had by that time escaped through the pass Durnford had lost his head. Issuing a stream of unintelligible orders, for he was by this time feverish due to his weakened state, he had led them down through the hills to try and round up those still remaining. Things had quickly deteriorated from that point on. Under orders not to fire the first shot Durnford and his men had soon found themselves under attack, with several white riders falling and the rest of his command disintergrating. Durnford was stabbed in his injured arm during the melee, the spear slicing through several nerves and tendons and rendering it useless for the rest of his life, and a bullet had narrowly missed his head, grazing his cheek instead. Riding for their lives the men had been chased down off the mountain, their discipline shot to pieces, with most of them refusing point blank to follow orders from their leader - whom they had lost all faith in.

The column had returned home limping like a badly mauled animal, licking its wounds. Almost immediately the finger of blame had been pointed at Durnford despite his insistance that he had been forced into a hurried operation by his superiors with little time to plan. Grieving for the dead men, the white settlers and townsfolk had shunned him.

Despite the best efforts of the surgeons his arm could not be adequately repaired. It would, they informed him, remain paralysed. The best option would be to remove it, but Durnford had refused to allow this. But worse than his physical injuries was the damage done to his pride. His reputation as a professional soldier had lain in tatters.

Unable to live in Pietermaritzburg because of the hatred directed at him by the population there, as well as throughout Natal - his pet dog had even been poisoned - Durnford had moved into the barracks at Fort Napier, seething with injustice. Determined that one day he would win back there respect.

He patiently waited for his opportunity for five long years.

It finally came on the 22nd January, 1879. At Isandlwana.

As he and his native horsemen pushed on, Colonel Durnford tried not to dwell too much on those bad memories. That was all in the past.

All he cared for was the present. And the future.

Half-turning around he glanced back over his shoulder at the men. He had with him the Edendale Troop, 50 strong, made up of black Christians, and a contingent of Hlubi tribespeople, also about fifty in number. All of them were first-class riders and excellant shots, dedicated and loyal.

It was ironic, Durnford thought as he looked at them. The only men willing to ride into battle with him were coloureds. Apart from a sprinkling of white officers - close friends who had stood by him over the years - all of the other volunteer cavalry units drawn from the towns and farms throughout the colony refused to serve under him, partly through the fact that they thought his loyalties lay too much with the blacks and also because they did not trust his leadership.

Well, maybe after today all of that would change.

For the moment he had to be content with those he had with him at the present.

Turning back to the front Durnford listened to their banter as they talked to one another. Evidently they shared his excitement at the thought of what the day held for them, their confidence sky-high, and he was happy to let them boast and brag about what they would do once they ran into the Zulus.

And run into them they must surely do anytime now.

He was surprised that they had ridden as far as they had with still no sign of the enemy either on the plain ahead or on the high ground to the north. Durnford began to worry that they had allready sneaked by them and were even now attacking the General. Yet that must be impossible. They had left camp at the first reports of Zulus moving eastwards across the plateau, galloping hard to make an interception. The Zulus could not have come this far, so fast.

Whether they had or not they had to push on, either to block the enemy or - if the General was engaged - to link up with him and lend support.

They had gone about four miles and were approaching the Nxibongo river with the low ridge of Quabe away on their right, when Durnford suddenly spotted two distant riders carefully picking their way down the steep escarpment. Taking out his fieldglasses he quickly determined that they were two Carbineers, probably from one of the vedettes. Guessing that they brought news of the Zulus on the plateau Colonel Durnford angled his column towards them.

He was partly correct.

They did indeed carry information concerning the enemy, but not of the kind he was anticipating.

With the rest of the men gathering around he listened to what they had to say.

Apparantly the Zulus were heading their way just as the Colonel had thought, but not numbering several hundred. There were thousands of them! Tens of thousands! The two men, breathless and quite obviously very scared, went on to explain how the whole Zulu army had been discovered and was at this moment charging across the plateau. A part of which was headed right for them.

"You should return to camp immediately or you will be surrounded!" blurted the eldest of the two.

This was ridiculous, Durnford thought, and he felt his lips begin to tremble with rage. "Get a grip of yourselves!" he snapped.

"But they are almost upon you!"

"Listen to me carefully. Even if what you say is true, the enemy can't surround us and if they do, ha, then we will cut our way through them! Return to camp indeed! What of the General? Do you propose we just abandon him?"

The Carbineer was shaking his head, and his tone suggested that he had forgotten that he was talking to a superior officer. "They are not attacking the General. They are attacking the camp."

A long silence descended as the two men glowered at one another and the atmosphere grew razor sharp, Durnford's men hardly able to believe what they were hearing, nor the confrontation taking place right before their very eyes. Durnford finally drew in his breath. He realized it was not proper to show his emotions like this in front of them. Turning away from the Carbineer with a faint sneer on his lips, he addressed the commanding officer of the Edendale Troop.

"Lieutenant, where is the Rocket Battery? Why are they not here?"

Harry Davies nodded back the way they had come, steadying his excited horse. "They are a long way behind sir. Major Russell seems somewhat...cautious."

Durnford gritted his teeth with irritation. This was not the way he had planned things, not the way at all. Sighing heavily he said..."then he will have to catch us up in his own time and look out for himself. We push on gentlemen. With all haste. And you two," he turned to the Carbineers, "will come with us."

"But we have orders to return to –"
"I said you will come with us."
The two, both breathing heavily, said nothing further.
"We have wasted enough time," Durnford announced simply. He jerked at Chieftain's reins with his one hand and used his knees to turn him, preparing to lead on. But he pulled up straight, staring forward towards the end of the escarpment.

At the same time his men gasped or cried out in alarm, fear stealing their composure.

For they, like their Colonel, had seen what was rolling towards them down the face of the escarpment.

*   *   *

The iNgobamakhosi and the uVe, like the rest of the *amabutho,* had joined in with the initial stampede out of the valley, caught up in the heat of the moment and ignoring their commander's pleas to listen to their instructions. Much was at stake here, especially their pride. Seeing their rivals in the uKhandempemvu chase after the horsemen off to the right they had likewise raced across the plateau; they remembered the challenges they had made back at the King's kraal and it was a matter of immense importance to be the first to 'stab' their enemy.

It was left to their *induna* Sigcwelecwele kaMhlehleke, along with his company commanders, to regain control of the hotheaded young men that made up the regiment. As they were on the extreme left and would make up the left horn, sweeping well to the south-east in their attempt to envelop the white soldiers, they had a fair distance to cover before they would join in with the fighting and this allowed the time needed to position them into the correct attack formation. Nevertheless, the warriors sprinted forward much faster than was usual, for they could hear the sound of gunfire from over in the direction where the uKhandempemvu were, and they feared that if they did not close with the whites soon then they would lose out on any of the glory. So they soon reached the lip of the escarpment.

They swarmed down onto the plain below.

Mehlokazulu kaSihayo led his men on. With him were his friends, Ndlela and Mnyamana. The three of them had stayed together so far and as they came down the steep slope, clambering over the rocks and leaping across small watercourses, they saw the line of horsemen gathered just to the front of them. The rest of the iNgobamakhosi noticed them also and they turned that way and charged south to meet them, swinging onto the flat plain and forming a massive curve that gradually turned towards the campsite four miles away.

Racing forward through the tall grass they split into long, even lines, not in a dense mass as this would present too big a target but preferring to charge in open order, one wave following another and making good use of any cover. Keeping their heads down the warriors dodged from side to side, their shields, assegais and rifles held low to the ground and out of sight.

They did not give vent to any war-cries.

They just made a peculiar murmuring sound in the back of their throats, the noise swelling until it became a loud buzzing.

Coming on like this, the left horn launched themselves into the attack.

*　　　*　　　*

Despite the suddenness of their appearance Colonel Durnford immediately felt that he and his one hundred men were more than ready, and capable, of dealing with the Zulus sweeping in their direction. Not for one moment did he consider that they were not up to the task. Even though the situation was much more serious than he had been expecting.

He felt nothing but supreme confidence in himself and his men.

Looking around at the troopers he tried to calm their understandably shaken nerves by speaking in a steady voice, making eye contact with as many of them as possible, trying to instill in them the right amount of self-belief. Those first few moments, the words he said and how he said them, were of vital importance. Battles could be won or lost depending on how a commanding officer led his men and Durnford, knowing all too well what defeat felt like, was determined not to make the same mistakes of five years ago.

Once he was sure that they were ready Durnford quickly issued his first commands. He extended the men in open line so as to cover as much front as possible, the Edendale boys on the left and the Hlubi troop away to the right. Riding up and down behind them he ordered them to hold fire until the enemy were at 400 yards range.

"Wait for it men, let them get in close! Pick your targets but wait for the order!"

The Zulus showed no such restraint. They had opened fire almost immediately, blazing away with their assortment of weapons, and in no time at all the air was alive with a lethal hailstorm of lead. Most of the shots passed harmlessly over the heads of the horsemen, for the Zulus were poor marksmen, so the NNH held their nerve as they waited for the command to return fire.

Durnford held them...and held them...

...until they were in range.

"Let them have it! FIRE!"

Durnford watched grimly as the first volley sent the front line of Zulus crashing into the dirt, dust flying as they rolled over and over. The next line did not pause, but leaped over their fallen comrades and pressed on. Hastily, he ordered his men to reload and fire for a second time; it had the same results, and still the Zulu charge did not falter.

He was left with no choice. They could not hold them, not when they were outnumbered about twenty-five to one. The only alternative would be to slowly fall back on the camp and to try and find a better position from which they might be able to make a more determined stand. It was not an ideal situation but there was no other option for the present.

"Fire by alternate ranks! Thirty yard spacings! Left troop, withdraw first, right troop, lend covering fire!"

Lieutenant Davies immediately wheeled his fifty men about and led them at a gallop to a new position about thirty yards away, whilst the Hlubi Troop raised their carbines and fired once more into the Zulus. By the time the smoke cleared they too had turned and were racing back. They sped by their comrades who were lined up and waiting until their front was clear of any stragglers, who then in turn fired, spun away and made for their next position, leap-frogging by the Hlubi just as they were preparing to fire once more. So on it went, each troop passing the other as they slowly, so slowly, pulled back towards the camp nearly four miles away, withdrawing in stages before the Zulu left horn. Colonel Durnford kept a tight control of the dangerous movement. It was essential that they keep their discipline, for if they retreated too fast then the whole manoeuvre would simply collapse in on itself and then the Zulus would have an open run to the camp.

As they slowly retired Colonel Durnford kept an eye out for Major Russell and the Rocket Battery. They had been left behind about two or three miles back just as they had rounded the conical hill and if they had continued to advance along the same route he and his native horsemen had been following before they had met the left horn then they should be coming up on them anytime soon. They could pick the Major and his men up, maybe even launch a few rockets to slow the enemy advance.

It was Trooper Jabez Molife, one of the Hlubi men, who spotted them first.

Or what was left of them.

He came galloping over to where Durnford was and started to jab his finger towards the lower slopes of the escarpment, talking wildly to get his attention. Durnford saw immediately what had caught his eye. About a hundred yards from where their firing line was, standing frozen to the spot and shivering with fright, was one of the pack animals from Major Russell's command. Lying scattered around it on the ground were half a dozen wooden boxes, some intact and some smashed open, their contents spilled all about. Durnford realized in an instant what the long, dark shapes partially concealed by the long grass were. Rockets!

Quickly he looked further afield, trying to spot the battery itself, but even as he was doing so he knew the chances of seeing them were virtually nil; the mislaid and abandoned rockets could mean only one thing - that Russell and his men, along with their cherished rocket troughs, had been scattered to the four winds. It was just inconceivable that they would have simply dropped their supplies like that and not to have picked them up again. The Major was too fastidious and professional for that to happen.

Durnford felt sickened at the thought of what had happened.

For a few terrible moments all of the bad memories from five years ago threatened to come crashing down on him, as raw and vivid as they had been during that awful time on the mountain. It was only with an enormous effort that he was able to stop them, telling himself that he needed to keep a clear head. For the sake of his men as much for himself. They needed him to remain calm. If he lost control of his emotions... he did not need to complete the thought to know what would happen.

So, for the time being, he ignored the taunting demons in his head.

"Lieutenant Davies, send some men to bring those things in!" he shouted, pointing at the debris.

"What about the mule sir?"

"That as well!"

"I shall get the animal sir," Trooper Molife said immediately.

"Be careful. It's awfully close to the Zulus."

Molife nodded and then dug in his spurs, taking off across the uneven ground. Several more men were hurriedly sent out to gather up the spilled rockets. It was a tense couple of minutes for the Zulu were very near by now, having pressed their attack despite the heavy fire the British were pouring into them. Durnford ordered a brief halt and formed a single line again, massing their guns and letting off several volleys to cover them, watching anxiously all the while.

Eventually, and much to his relief, Trooper Molife and his companions returned safely.

Their withdrawal resumed as before.

Fighting for every inch of ground, and looking for a place where they might make a stand.

CHAPTER 33

LORD CHELMSFORD'S FORWARD POSITION. 12 MILES SOUTHEAST OF ISANDLWANA. LATE-MORNING / EARLY-AFTERNOON.

Once breakfast was over Lord Chelmsford set off to find a suitable location for the new campsite. Whilst they had eaten he had discussed the matter with Crealock, Glyn and Clery, as well as other members of his staff, and after careful consideration they had decided upon an area close to the Mangeni waterfall a little to their south. They would ride over during the afternoon and mark out the sight.

As they had talked things through, their conversation covering the rest of the day's business as well as the general progress of the invasion to date, Chelmsford had frequently found his mind wandering back to the message they had received earlier from Colonel Pulleine. At first he had been annoyed by it. He had agreed with the general opinion that there was really nothing in the reports of Zulus hiding amongst the hills north of Isandlwana, that it was just Pulleine being too jumpy. In spite of this, time after time his concentration on other matters had been broken as a mild doubt had persisted, his thoughts preoccupied by the notion that maybe he had missed something. But what? Try as he might he could not pinpoint what exactly was troubling him.

Still, the disquiet remained; like an irritating itch inside his mind.

The other diners seemed to pick up on his fluctuating thoughts and several discreet glances were exchanged in between mouthfuls of food. Nothing was said. It was only natural that a General in charge of an invasion force would have much on his mind. If he chose to share those worries with them then naturally they would do their utmost to ease the burden and help in whatever way they could. But until he spoke up...it was not their place...

Finishing the meal Lord Chelmsford had departed from the table with a frown on his face, and the rest of his staff had likewise moved off to get themselves ready for their afternoon duties.

A short while later he approached one of his officer's and drew him to one side, where he addressed him in quiet tones.

"Lieutenant Milne, might I have a word?"

The young naval officer, who had a youngish-looking face despite his muttonchop whiskers and slicked down hair, replied in a brisk and attentitive voice. "Of course My Lord."

"There are reports of Zulus threatening our camp at Isandlwana. The information we have is imprecise. I wondered if you would find a suitable place and see what you can make of things there with your telescope, which is much more powerful than our fieldglasses. When you have done so, please come and report to me at once. You will find me down near the gorge."

"Certainly. It will be my pleasure."

Chelmsford returned his salute and watched him go.

He felt a little more at ease now that he had acted on his concerns. Until they had more concrete news as to what the precise situation at Isandlwana was there was little more to be done, from a practical point of view.

In the meantime he had numerous other needs to see to.

Lieutenant Milne casually jogged across to where his groom waited with his horse. When he saw him begin to adjust the saddle he quickly, and in his pleasant way, told him that he would not be needing his mount for the time being. Instead, he slipped his telescope out from its leather case alongside the pummel, and, instructing his man to wait here, he turned and walked briskly away.

A short distance from where the General and his staff had taken breakfast there was a high ridge, on the top of which was a solitary, gnarled-looking tree. Deciding that this would make a fine observation point Milne began to hurry up the steep bank.

It was a much longer climb than he anticipated and soon he was out of breath and clutching a painful stitch in his side, a little indignant at his poor fitness. He stopped to rest for a moment and sat on the dry grass, wiping a handkerchief across his brow. Below him he saw the General set off, heading down through the hills towards the gorge where the new campsite was to be, and the servants soon after started to put away the dining table, chairs and plates. To his amusement he watched as one of them, a boy of no more than twelve, surreptitiously glance around and when he thought knowbody was looking quickly fed a handful of leftovers into his mouth, gobbling them down. Just as secretively he snatched up some more and hid them in his pockets, no doubt saving them for later. Lieutenant Milne laughed gently and gave a pleasant shake of the head.

He carried on up to the flat summit of the ridge.

After ten minutes he finally came out on the top and stepped over towards the tree. It was an ugly, dead thing, stunted and blackened by numerous lightening strikes, the trunk split down the middle. About half-way up there was a thick over-hanging branch which looked strong enough to take his weight, and so he pulled himself up and stretched himself out. Making himself comfortable, he took his telescope and gave the lenses a quick wipe, then rested the end in the V of a small branch at the tip of the one he lay upon, a handy little rest that allowed him to point it towards the distant peak of Isandlwana. Lowering his head he peered through the eyepiece.

The mountain, over twelve miles away, was very indistinct. It lay just beneath the horizon from this position with the hills beyond almost masking it, and a heat haze dulled his vision even further, so that he had to squint and adjust the focus. This still did not improve matters. His view was also partially obstructed by the flank of the next hill over which cut off much of the plain east of the campsite, and also the extreme right of the plateau. What little he could see was blurred.

After a few minutes of looking a few details did come clearer, once his eyes had adapted to the haze. Below the mountain he could vaguely make out the tents, a long, white smudge that ran along its base with no seperation between the different units. Also, behind them and on the nek, was the wagon park with what looked like a large cluster of cattle closeby. Beyond this, nothing. It was impossible to pick out any individuals - or even large bodies of men - at this distance. As for any signs of a battle taking place... it was hard to be totally sure... but to his trained eye, and for one used to using a telescope, it all seemed very quiet and normal.

There appeared to be little untoward going on.

Lieutenant Milne stayed there for nearly an hour, glancing through the telescope from time to time to see if there was any change, dozing in the sun in between. Little happened. At one stage the shadows of several large clouds moved across the part of the plain he could see, and also the spur north of the camp, their massive forms moving slowly in the breezeless air. Apart from this nothing much else changed, the scene a tranquil one.

Eventually, and growing bored, he climbed down from the branch and dropped to the ground.

He leisurely strode back down the hillside to deliver his report.

Out across the plain Commandant Hamilton-Browne and the 1/3rd NNC marched very slowly on, the day turning hot and sultry.

Having received his orders from Crealock to return to camp, he had gone back to his battalion and set out with them on the long hike. The going was tough. The ground was rocky and uneven and the men were tired and hungry. The day before had been spent scrambling around the dusty valleys searching for the enemy and scouting the terrain, and this had been followed by a long and fearful night interrupted with frequent false alarms. Then, during the morning, they had helped with the skirmishing amongst the hills. They had not slept for more than thirty hours, nor had they had anything to eat since leaving Isandlwana the day before. His command was worn out, the black levies and white NCO's foot-sore and irritable, and now they were expected to march the twelve miles back to the camp and help with the move. There was, it seemed, no end in sight to their toils.

As they had advanced Hamilton-Browne had on occassion looked through his fieldglasses at the distant camp, aware of the rumour that large numbers of Zulus had been reported to be moving about in the area in a provocative manner. He was concerned not so much for the camp, for it was well defended with first-rate soldiers who were more than capable of seeing off a large scale attack, but rather he was more worried about his own command. Their morale today was poor; they were thoroughly knocked up after their exhaustive exploits; and they were inadequately armed - he was doubtful whether they would be able to hold back a determined assault, even from a relatively small number of eager Zulus. And so he kept an apprehensive lookout for any signs of the enemy up on the plateau several miles to the north.

They had gone on several miles but were still two or three hours march from the camp when two figures were spotted heading their way over the rolling plain. Hamilton-Browne called a halt and raised his fieldglasses to his face.

He quickly picked them out despite the heat-haze that made the ground ripple. Two black men, each dressed in rag-tag European clothes. They both carried heavy bundles on their heads.

Turning back to his men he explained to the nearest white officers, who waited with expectant looks on their faces. "A couple of niggers from the column. It seems, boys, that they are bringing us some food!"

A faint but only half-hearted cheer went up from those who heard, and several dashed forward to meet the men coming towards them, their stomachs crying out to be filled. Within a few minutes they were back. Placing the supplies on the ground they sorted through them, handing out the meagre but very welcome provisions - bread, some hard biscuits, and a few cold leftovers from the morning's breakfast. And, best of all, two bottles of whisky sent out by some kind-hearted soul. However, there wasn't enough to go around, and so it was decided that the blacks would have to go without, a decision that caused a heated furore amongst them. Yet there was nothing for it.

So there the matter rested.

Hamilton-Browne allowed them a ten minute break while they ate (he himself refused the offer of a share, hoping it would appease the disgruntled black soldiers), the men sitting on the ground under the sweltering sun.

Afterwards, when they were getting ready to continue their long march, one of the NCO's, a short and overweight man with a badly pockmarked face named Turner, suddenly looked up from what he was doing. "What was that?" he asked nobody in particular.

Hamilton-Browne heard the comment. "What was what?"

"That sound sir. In the distance."

He strained his ears and then shrugged. "I don't hear anything Turner."

"There it goes again!"

Irritated that they were wasting time in this pointless conversation, Hamilton-Browne nevertheless asked for quiet. Only then, when the men fell silent, did he finally notice the sound that had caught Turner's attention. He recognized what it was instantly.

"Lord," he whispered in hushed tones, "I do believe that is artillery fire."

It was a faint sound, no more than a soft and intermittent rumble a little like the noise a distant avalanche might make. It did not seem, at first, very threatening in nature but because Hamilton-Browne knew its true meaning (unlike some of the black soldiers who had never experienced it before) a mild shiver of concern went up and down his spine. Taking out his fieldglasses once again, he spurred his horse forward to a slight mound a few dozen yards ahead and peered through them towards the distant camp.

All seemed as before. The campsite, or what he could make of it from this far out, lay at the base of the mountain. The tents were still standing. They dazzled in the bright sunlight. Surely, he thought to himself, if a major engagement was taking place they would have been struck?

But still, the bark of the artillery drifted across the plain.

Then he saw something new. A change to the scene that he only spotted after several minutes' of observation.

Laying across the hills to the north of the camp was a number of large cloud shadows, moving lazily down onto the flat plain. But that was funny. The skies at this moment were clear so how could...? He caught the first puff of smoke, followed immediately by a second, on the escarpment edge. Exploding shellfire. There was a pause, then two more in close succession. Landing right onto the curious shadows there.

It struck him then. The dark marks on the hills were not cloud shadows.

They were Zulus!

A dense mass of them, an entire army, making straight for the camp below.

Hamilton-Browne muttered a curse to himself under his breath. He swept his fieldglasses further to the right, along the escarpement, to see how extensive the Zulu attack was and what he saw was not good. From what he could tell, and the heat shimmering above the baking ground limited his perception significantly, the enemy lines stretched well to this side of the conical hill with large numbers sweeping down from the hills onto the plain, turning towards the camp. It was a magnificent but frightening sight and he could see straight away that Colonel Pulleine would have a tough time on his hands, with only six Imperial companies, a few mounted units and two artillery guns to defend himself with, unless reinforcements were hurried back by the General. Starting with his own battalion - which was allready halfway there.

He turned his horse and rode back to where the 1/3rd waited.

"Turner!" he called, giving his instructions before he had even reined in, "go and find His Lordship! Tell him that the Zulu army is attacking the left of the camp. The guns have opened on them. Inform him that the ground here is good for the rapid advance of mounted men and guns, and that we are pushing on fast to act as support to them. It is vital that he understands the urgency of the situation, do you understand?"

Turner struggled to find his voice so dry had his throat suddenly become.

"Do you understand!"

"Y-yes sir," he managed, his words - like his huge frame - quivering with fear.

"Then don't wait all day! Go man, go!"

The NCO spun away and rode back the way they had come, trying hard to get a fast trot out of his overburdened mare, his large buttocks trembling from more than just the bumpy ride.

Hamilton-Browne turned from the sight, his mind on other things.

By now the rest of his command had also noticed the fighting taking place in the distance, the keen eyes of the Natal Kaffirs spotting their dreaded foe sweeping down upon the camp. A general unease swept through the ranks at the prospect of joining the battle. The white noncoms, always looking for a reason, beat and kicked them into order, snarling at those who continued to protest. Getting them to move forward would be an even harder prospect though.

Thinking fast, Hamilton-Browne ordered his toughest and most reliable company to move to the rear, positioning them behind their more nervous companions with the orders to kill any who lagged behind or showed any inclination to flee. This they did with great gusto for there was much rivalry between the various clans, until slowly the battalion began to move forward once again. Still, the men only moved at a crawl.

Isandlwana shimmered in the distance.

As though the mountain itself shuddered with trepidation.

2 MILES SOUTH OF CONICAL HILL. 12:30pm.

He had not stopped running for the first twenty minutes. With all other thoughts except those concerning his own personal safety banished from his mind, he had fled, sprinting as fast as he could from that scene of devastation. Heading south, he had soon crossed the dirt track that headed further into Zululand, and beyond this the ground had steadily become more broken. It was pitted with dongas and eroded gulleys and strewn with large rocks and further off was a line of high ground that dropped down in a series of rolling hills towards the Buffalo River beyond. And there, across in Natal, lay sanctuary.

So he kept on running.

Occassionally looking back to make sure he wasn't being followed.

Eventually he had to stop and rest otherwise he would drop from exhaustion, and so he clambered over a jumble of large boulders and slipped in behind them, grateful for the cover they provided.

Private Thomas Scott sat on his haunches with his back leaning against a slab of stone, his Martini-Henry clutched tightly in his lap. He peered nervously through a gap between the boulders back towards the conical hill and the plain, his eyes scanning the terrain for any signs of pursuing Zulus. After several minutes of searching he gratefully concluded that knowone had given chase, and he at last allowed himself to relax somewhat. Closing his eyes he rested his head back against the slab, giving a weary, tremulous sigh.

He thought back to what had happened earlier. Up to now he had not had the time nor the inclination to do so, too numbed was he by the horror of it. But now that he had stopped running he began to replay the sequence of events, running them through his mind.

The nightmare images that were ingrained in his memory made him shake. Clutching himself as if he were shivering from some painful fever, the delayed shock of what he had gone through began to hit him. He started to sob quietly to himself. The tears merged into the sweat and dirt and blood on his face and he wiped at them angrily, feeling ashamed that he, a grown man, should be reduced to crying like a baby. But they would not stop. They flowed freely from him, dragged from his body in merciless waves, until he was bowed and beaten by them.

After what seemed an eternity Thomas finally managed to get himself under control again, albeit the tears were never far away. They threatened to return without any warning.

As the shock subsided then he became aware of the throbbing pain in his head from where he had been struck. Up to now it had been a dull ache, so minor that he had paid it no heed, but as he sat there the soreness increased so much that he had to grit his teeth against it. He gingerly touched the tender wound behind his right ear, probing softly, and he winced as the pain flared. Taking away his hand he looked at his fingertips; they were sticky with his own blood.

It was a bad injury but it could have been much worse. His helmet - which he had long since lost - had cushioned the blow to some extent, reducing a brain-crushing, fatal strike into a nasty but survivable blow. The wound needed stitching and he would probably be badly concussed for several days but all in all he had got off lightly. Compared to his friends, who lay butchered in the grass there.

Lucky to have survived or not he was still in a dire situation.

Here he was, all by himself in enemy territory, cut off from the safety of the camp and several miles from the border. Wounded and tired, he doubted if he would be able to defend himself for very long if he was discovered. Perhaps against two or three Zulus he might stand a chance but any more... he shook his head dismally at his chances. No, the enemy were attacking in huge numbers. He could see them in the distance now, a huge column of them sweeping around the conical hill and making a massive assault against the front of the camps defences, with even more broiling down off the plateau to the north. It would be impossible to get back to friendly lines even if he tried. Best to stay clear. He had a slightly better hope of surviving that way, slim though that probabilty was.

The alternative - of trying to make his way to safety by crossing the river, a flight of several miles across hostile country - was almost as unappealing as rejoining his mates was.

Then there was the question of what they would think of him, when the battle was over and the war won. Even though he'd had no choice but to try and escape like this, and even though he had been in the thick of the early fighting with the Rocket Battery, he was sure they would take some convincing that he had not run away at the first sign of danger, fleeing like a coward. A deserter. And it was not just a matter of what his friends thought. His superiors would be wondering the same thing. What was the punishment for deserting? he asked himself. A good flogging at least...possibly a court martial...possibly the firing squad!

He was, he thought to himself with bitter rancour, caught between a rock and a hard place. In a literal sense he mused as he looked around his hiding place.

But what choice did he have?

Very little. Very little.

Weary to the bones, Thomas pushed himself to his feet. He looked around.

The hilly country to the south looked less appealing to his tired body now, and the terrain there was of an unknown nature to him. He did know that the river was at least 10 miles away in that direction, 10 miles of land possibly infested with Zulus. There was a shorter route he knew of. If he cut back to the west and then headed down through the valleys immediately below Isandlwana then he should reach the river much quicker, plus the area there was said to be empty of people for they had passed through it on their way from Rorke's Drift. Yes, that way made much more sense. It would also be taking him further away from the fighting.

Keeping low so as not to be silhouetted against the horizon, he set off again, this time bearing to the west.

CHAPTER 34

COLONEL DURNFORD'S POSITION.
1 MILE EAST OF BRITISH CAMP AT ISANDLWANA.
12:30pm-12:45pm.

"Over there boys!" Durnford cried above the din of battle, "down into the donga!"

They had steadily retired back across the plain for nearly three miles, moving stage by stage, pausing every thirty yards to fire a volley into the Zulus. As of yet, panic had not set in; although they were retreating they felt to be in virtually full control of the situation, drawing the young warriors on to their deaths. Their firing had been good with hardly a round wasted, testimony to their training as well as how they were handled by their leader, and they were confident that as long as they kept their discipline then they would win the day. The Zulu regiments before them would only be able to withstand such accurate and telling fire for so long before their appalling losses would compel them to call off the attack along this section of the battlefield.

As they had come around the conical hill and wheeled towards the camp in the near distance Durnford had noticed the fighting going on there. The whole of the garrison was turned out it seemed, arranged into a firing line facing north, the two guns somewhere in the centre. He could hear them firing over the sound of his own men shooting, the reports of the cannon a deep barking sound, and when he took a moment to determine just what they were firing at he noticed for the first time the dense Zulu ranks storming down from the plateau. The whole of the escarpment, as well as the spur leading into the north end of the camp, seemed to be alive with them, their numbers too numerous to count. And even as he watched wave after wave came surging behind them, pushing on those at the front.

A minute or so later and the Imperial companies opened up too. Soon, the firing was general along the entire line, a sight that to Colonel Durnford was a wonderfully violent tumult of noise and smoke. The grandness of it caught his breath for a moment and brought a lump to his throat, a peculiar emotion to experience for someone witnessing death and slaughter on a huge scale. But to him it was a perfectly natural reaction. He was a soldier who had trained all of his life for this, and it sent pulses of sheer energy through him when he understood that today would be a defining moment for him. The sounds, and sights, of battle were what he craved.

In a short time the accurate fire of the redcoats stemmed the Zulu attack to the north. The black tide, up to now relentless in its advance, was blunted once it reached the bottom of the escarpment. The amount of shots being fired made it impossible for them to charge any closer and they hesitated about 500 yards short of the British infantry.

Gladdened to see this, Colonel Durnford had turned back to his front to continue directing their slow withdrawal. It had begun to dawn on him as they'd pulled back that soon he would need to make a stand somewhere. Although his men had so far fought splendidly, and had slowed down the zulu left horn almost to a crawl, they had not as of yet stopped it alltogether. The simple fact was that they needed to - they could only continue to retreat for so long, and eventually they would run out of space in which to manoeuvre. And the nearer to the camp they came the fewer options they would have, plus less time. So when they were still about a mile or so from the tents he'd begun to cast about for a suitable location from which to hold back the left horn.

One other thing which would have to be a priority, he thought to himself as he levelled his revolver and fired, was that if any stand they made was to be a lengthy one - and in all liklihood it would need to be for the Zulus would not give up easily - then they would need to replenish their ammunition as soon as possible. His men still had a good number of rounds left, and there was no reason to get alarmed just yet, but they had to make sure their rate of resupply kept up with their rate of fire. He would need to send riders back to camp to bring in their reserve soon, to prevent any unfortunate mishaps.

First though...find somewhere where they could set up position. He found the ideal spot a few minutes later.

Ahead of them he noticed a long, meandering line of short trees and bushes cutting across the plain, from the foot of the escarpment to the more broken land further to the south. This, he realized in an instant, was the larger of the two dongas, marked as it was by the green undergrowth which lined its banks. They had rode across it when they had set out earlier and he remembered it as being a dried and rocky riverbed about fifteen feet deep and forty feet across, and about a mile from the nearest tents. It was perfect, he thought. Deep enough to shelter their horses at the bottom while the men lined the eastern bank, the high lip providing them the protection they needed from which to fire behind.

Yes. It would do.

Besides which, they did not have time to search for an alternative.

Durnford bellowed out his instructions, pointing towards the donga with the barrel of his gun, and the native riders responded quickly. Following his lead they galloped across the short stretch of ground and down into the gulley, their horse's hooves kicking up clouds of dust.

"Dismount and line the side," he shouted, "ten yards between each man! Hurry now, we don't have long before those heathens will be on us! Leave your horses at the bottom!"

They leaped down out of their saddles and raced back to the eastern bank, spreading up and down the length of the donga. They threw themselves into the dirt and brought up their carbines, resting their elbows on the lip of the bank and aiming straight out across the plain where the Zulu charge was fast approaching. They waited anxiously for the command to resume firing. Watched as the dark wave of young warriors sprinted towards their new position with renewed hope in their hearts. Sweat beaded their brows. One or two of the Edendale men, all devout Christians, whispered silent prayers to themselves - appealing to their God for protection.

After hastily arranging about a dozen of his youngest men to watch their horses Durnford slipped down off Chieftain's back and handed the reins over, then bounded across to join them.

He signalled to his two Troop commanders, Lieutenant Davies of the Edendale Troop and Lieutenant Henderson of the Hlubi Troop, to begin and he watched as the one hundred men opened up again. The crash of repeated volleying was deafening and soon the donga was clogged with dense smoke.

Durnford clambered up to the edge alongside Trooper Molife to see what effect it had. Standing there with one booted foot on the lip and the other set slightly back to support his stance, revolver in hand and resting on his right knee, he watched the front lines of the Zulu charge falter under the impact of their firing, then crumple to the ground. The warriors behind hurriedly pushed their way over the piles of dead and wounded and pressed on. Their charge was suicidal for they were the next to fall, tumbling end over end as more volleys crashed into them, the bullets blowing away their faces and chests and hands and kneecaps. It was a scene of utter carnage played out for all to see, and Durnford felt intoxicated by it. He was barely able to contain his exhilaration.

"That's it boys!" he cheered madly, "aim low, now! Adjust your fire and aim low, into the grass! Look for them and make each shot count!"

He repeatedly thumped down onto his knee with the butt of his revolver, an expression of immense pride fixed upon his face.

"Keep at it! You're a sight to behold!"

Jabez Molife lay in the dirt beside his commander, listening to each word and drawing great comfort - not to mention resolve - from them. Here was a leader he felt proud to serve. In Jabez's mind, the colonel possessed courage and daring he could only dream of, standing upright as he did despite the enemy fire coming their way, mindless of his own safety in his determination to lead the men. It took a special person to do that. One who was utterly fearless. Jabez felt humbled to be in his presence.

He realized he had stopped for a moment to watch the Colonel, so mesmerized was he by the sight of him standing so close. After a few seconds Durnford turned, having become aware of his scrutiny. The Colonel gave him a friendly wink, his eyes glinting with jubilation. Jabez smiled happily back. A warm feeling coursed through him; a feeling that he could not fully explain.

All he did know was that he would follow the Colonel anywhere. He would do anything. So suddenly devoted to him had Jabez Molife become, that he was prepared to die for him, right here and now if need be.

With such unshakeable determination set in his mind he turned back to the fighting.

Steadying his carbine Jabez lowered his head and nestled his cheek alongside the stock, settling in close and drawing a bead down the barrel to the foresight. Carefully he picked out his next target amoungst the mass confronting them, a powerful looking Zulu who darted forward, staying low behind his black shield, and he waited for the command to fire. When the order came he squeezed the trigger. The gun fired with a sharp crack that was almost lost amidst the sound of his one hundred comrades firing simultaneously, and the recoil thumped into his already bruised shoulder. For a split-second the heat from the shot made the air infront shimmy, and the smoke blew back into his face, but his vision quickly cleared and he had time to look up. He saw his man fall amidst a spray of blood, the black shield tossed high into the sky as he was propelled backwards into the tall grass. Jabez thumped the earth in satisfaction and then ejected the spent case.

"Good shooting Trooper," he heard, and he looked up just as the Colonel reached down and slapped him on the shoulder.

Jabez grinned back once again.

"Keep it up my son," Durnford urged, before he strode away down the line, his voice shouting out encouragement to the others as he went.

As he walked up and down the length of the donga behind the row of prostrate men, he would occasionally find himself being approached by individuals whose guns had become fouled by jammed cartridges. They would trot across, pointing at the breech and waving them about in frustration, and Durnford would hurry to their aid. Taking the Swinburne-Henry's, he would grip them between his knees and then using his one good arm dig out the spent cases with his hunting knife, before handing the carbine back. "There you go, good as new," he would say, or "treat it with care like you would a lady, and they'll never let you down, my lad. Off you go", sending them away with renewed confidence.

The men fought hard. They kept their discipline despite the pressure the charging Zulus were placing them under, following their orders precisely. It pleased Dumford greatly to see this. His earlier opinion that they were up to the job was now being proven beyond doubt.

Every few minutes he would break off from his exhortations to scramble up the side of the donga to see how close the Zulus were, placing himself in the open and ignoring the whizz and zip of bullets flying around his head. After about ten minutes he was elated to see that the Zulu charge had at last being halted. The warriors had flung themselves down into the grass, no longer able to advance into the teeth of such a telling fire that they were being subjected too. In between volleys they would creep forward a few feet only to be driven back once again, leaving their dead behind and dragging their wounded to safety. Satisfied that the left horn had finally being stopped, Durnford was now able to turn his attention towards the problem of their ammunition supply.

Leaving the forward lip of the donga he hurried away to search for his two Lieutenants.

Just then, a stray shot struck a large boulder closeby along the rim of the gulley, ricocheting passed his head and making him duck. A sudden, pitiful shriek had him spinning around. He saw one of the horses in the dry riverbed go down, blood pumping from a wound in its chest where the bullet had hit. It crashed onto the shale, its neck twisting this way and that and its back legs twitching violently, a horrible agonized squeal coming from its yawning mouth.

The sounds of its pain touched something deep inside Durnford, and he flinched.

Without hesitation he rushed across. Even before he reached the stricken beast his thumb had pulled back the hammer of his revolver, already aware of what had to be done. Crouching down he stroked the horse's neck with his fingertips, talking to it in soothing tones. "Quiet my girl, keep still now," he whispered. "I'll stop the pain for you."

He placed the barrel of his gun against its temple.

The animal's eye rolled around to look at him, bulging in fear.

But then, almost bizarrely, it fell quiet. Almost as if understanding.

Durnford turned his face away and pulled the trigger.

Quickly he wiped away the miniscule specks of blood that splattered across his cheek with the sleeve of his uniform and then came to his feet once more. He did not look down at the horse. There was no need. He just moved away, the matter already gone from his mind.

Moments later and he came up alongside Lieutenant's Davies and Henderson who were standing together discussing the fight behind the shelter of a thick branch of one of the trees. They turned as one when they saw him approach, relieved to see him. Davies began to talk quickly.

"Sir, we have a slight problem. My men, as are Mr Henderson's, are running low on ammunition. They only set out with about fifty rounds apiece and our rate of fire is using them up fast. If we are to stop these Zulus then we are going to need more."

Durnford nodded, saying, "that's what I came to talk to you about. It is vital we hold this gully for as long as possible. They can't take much more of this," he added, pointing towards the Zulu left horn. "Soon they will have to withdraw. Victory is coming! I can feel it! But we do need more ammunition, you are right."

They paused as a bullet thudded into the branch just above their heads. Davies and Henderson both shrank away but Durnford hardly noticed this time.

"I want the two of you to return to camp and see if you can't bring in some fresh supplies. Take several men with you to help. It's about a mile or so so do hurry chaps, not that we are going to run out altogether you understand...let's call it a wise precaution."

"But how will we know where our supplies are sir?" asked Henderson. "Our wagons only arrived after we left."

"It shouldn't be too hard. Ask around or if that fails then look for the identification flags on the wagons. A red one marks the ammunition."

Henderson nodded.

"I'll put Sergeant-Major Kambule in charge of the firing whilst you're gone."

Davies nodded.

"Be on your way now," Durnford said cheerfully, "we don't have time to stand around chatting like this is a picnic."

This time the two officers nodded in unison, smiling. The pair saluted and then rushed off. Colonel Durnford raced back to the line.

"Sergeant-Major...to me!" he shouted as he ran.

Being on the receiving end of such merciless fire, Mehlokazulu and his friends, as well as all of the other young warriors in the iNgobamakhosi and uVe regiments, were experiencing a living hell. Their charge across the plain after the fleeing horsemen had been brought to a sudden, and bloody, halt. They lay or crouched down in the grass unable to move forward anymore, piles of dead warriors marking the forward edge of their assault. It was a scene of brutal slaughter, a high-tide mark of death.

Their attack may have been blunted but the young Zulus were still full of confidence. From time to time an individual would try a foolhardy dash forward, recklessly ignoring the warnings of their friends so strong was their desire to 'stab' the enemy, and each time they were riddled with bullets and fell dead. Soon, the ground was carpeted with corpses and the grass dripped blood.

Those with guns were called to the front from where they opened up with a heavy fire towards the gulley where their foe sheltered. Mehlokazulu crawled forward with Ndlela and Mnyamana and together they found a sheltered hole which was deep enough for them to shoot from without any great danger of being hit. As they loaded their old weapons, a difficult task for it was awkward using their muskets' ramrods from a lying down position, Ndlela peered forward through the tall grass, trying to snatch a glimpse of the horsemen. Suddenly he froze, a puzzled expression on his gaunt face. Then he turned to his friend, babbling excitedly.

"I see one, I see one!" he called above the sound of firing.

Mehlokazulu and Mnyamana stopped what they were doing.

"What do you see?" Mehlokazulu asked.

"A white man! *Abelungu!* There, standing by the tree." He pointed towards the line of the gully across the rolling ground.

Both Mehlokazulu and Mnyamana burst out laughing, unable to stop themselves despite their dangerous situation. Ndlela stared back. He looked insulted by their reaction.

"What? Why do you laugh? It is a white man, yes?"

This made them laugh even more.

"I have never seen one before so...so..." He looked forward once again, squinting. "He has skin like milk," he muttered.

Mehlokazulu at last put him out of his misery. "Yes, that is a white man. Now you know why the King orders us to kill them. Because they are so ugly!"

Finishing loading, he raised his gun and aimed towards the distant figure standing atop the gully, brazenly exposing himself. He was either very foolish, thought Mehlokazulu, or very brave. In a moment he would be very dead.

He fired.

His shot struck a branch of the tree just above the white man's head. He cursed, partly out of anger for missing and also because the man did not even flinch. He started to reload once more. Taking his powder horn he busied himself for a few moments. He was determined this time to hit his target.

However, when he looked up, the white man had gone.

Annoyed, he started to look for another target, but could not find one. Their enemy were keeping their heads down. Only their hats were visible above the edge of the gully.

This time it was Ndlela's turn to laugh, although he did so quietly for he did not want to antagonize his friend too much; he had a reputation for losing his temper and resorting to violence; Mehlokazulu did like a fight, now and then.

They continued to exchange shots for a short while, keeping up a heavy fire, waiting for an opening so that they could close the gap once more. They had lost many men so far but their sacrifice had not being in vain for they were now within sight of the camp. Each warrior felt that one more determined rush, one more bold onslaught against the gully, would see them break through the enemies line. Then, then they would show them how a Zulu warrior truly fought.

In the meantime they waited.

Somewhere, one young warrior, watching the line of white and black soldiers firing at them, noticed how the muzzle-flashes seemed to flicker up and down the whole length of the donga. He watched spellbound. Then he called out to those around him... *"Mbane, mbane wezulu, kuyagewazimula"*- "Lightning, lightning of Heaven,

337

see its glittering flash!" Within a few moments the two regiments took up the cry, their throats screaming out this new war-chant.

Sigcwelecwele kaMhlehleke, the elderly pot-bellied *induna* of the iNgobamakhosi regiment, listened as his men cranked themselves up for the next charge. The tension became palpable. Those behind edged forward, creeping through the grass and readying themselves, shield in one hand and stabbing spear in the other. 3,500 men in all, the two regiments reached fever pitch. Their fury broiled over.

Sigcwelecwele saw the moment was at hand.

He jumped to his feet, his clenched assegai thrust towards the enemy. "uSuthu!" he cried. "USUTHU!" his warriors roared back.

The next charge went in.

The whole of the left horn swept forward as one, surging towards the donga about 300 paces ahead of them. A wall of screeching humanity, their pent up blood-lust was finally released and it seemed like nothing would stop them this time. It was a sight to behold. It was, to the young warriors sprinting forward, a charge that even the Great King Shaka himself would surely have been proud to witness.

But like their previous attempts, it was doomed to failure.

The front wave disintergrated once more under the deadly rifle-fire, the warriors falling as though cut down with a giant's sweeping scythe. Some were hit by single gunshots while others were caught by numerous bullets simultaneously, their bodies literally shredded apart. At such close range to the enemy the effect was appalling. Those coming on behind found themselves splashed with the blood and brains of their companions, their feet slipping on spilled innards. They cringed, waiting for the next volley. Expecting instant death or agonizing mutilation.

Their expectations came to be.

Over and over.

Sigcwelecwele threw himself into the dirt and his men did the same. It was no good. He was not willing to see his regiments destroyed right before his eyes, the boys had proven they were worth more than that. No. He could not ask them to keep on charging to their deaths like this. They were the flower of the nation.

He began to think hard, searching his mind for new ideas.

Elsewhere within the iNgobamakhosi regiment Mehlokazulu dropped down beside Ndlela. His teeth were bared and he was breathing hard, partly from the dash forward but also from his frustration that was fighting to be let out. He glanced over to his friend, his eyes mere slits of rage.

When he saw the look on Ndlela's face he froze.

His expression, already long and gaunt, now seemed even more haunted than ever, thought Mehlokazulu. He stared blankly down at the ground with a strange opaqueness covering his eyes, as though he wasn't really seeing what was actually before him but rather at something in his minds eye. Whatever it was frightened Ndlela, for his lips trembled. Mehlokazulu was sure his friend was about to vomit.

He reached over and shook him by the shoulder, breaking the trance.

Ndlela slowly looked around and their eyes met.

Without prompting he said, simply... "Mnyamana is dead"...then looked back at the earth.

For a long while Mehlokazulu could think of nothing to say. He lay in the dirt listening to the shots whizzing by over their heads, the soft snick as they cut through the tall grass stalks, the occassional cry from men being struck. When he eventually did find his voice all he could manage was... "but, he can't be."

Ndlela nodded emphatically. "I saw him fall. His face... his face... he no longer has one..." and he squeezed shut his eyes.

Mehlokazulu let go of his shoulder. He started to shake with anger, and when it suddenly flared inside him Mehlokazulu picked up a rock and flung it uselessly towards the gully. He saw it fall way short. He stared hard towards the line of flashing rifles.

He noticed right then that one of the black horsemen had raised his head slightly higher than was safe, and quickly Mehlokazulu brought up his gun and took careful aim, hatred fueling his resolve. He squeezed the trigger.

This time his shot was true, finding its target.

Mehlokazulu, strangely, did not feel elated when he saw the figure fall back amid a splash of red. Between gritted teeth he whispered... "uSuthu..." to himself.

He waited.

Amidst their dead, who piled higher and higher around them, they all waited.

Trooper Solomon Malaza took the bullet in the throat. He was tossed back from the edge of the donga, his arms pinwheeling, his carbine sent spinning away. A flood of bright scarlet washed down the front of his chest, drenching his uniform even before he had crashed onto his back at the bottom of the slope. There he lay momentarily stunned. When he tried to breathe and found that nothing was happening, his hands grabbed for the wound in his neck, and when he felt the wide opening there, something wet and warm pouring out over his fingers, panic set in.

He kicked his legs wildly and tried to cry out for help. But the sound came out as a horrible gurgling, which terminated in a spluttering cough as blood poured down the inside of his throat. Gripped by a terrible fear he thrashed and squirmed and went beserk, twisting through the dust like a wounded animal. A coldness seeped through him, clinging and working its way through his entire body...and he knew what this meant.

Durnford had just gone passed that section of the line, calling his words of encouragement to the men, when he saw him fall back. In an instant he dashed across. He came down on his knees by his side, horrified by the wound. For a moment he could not stop an appalled expression from appearing on his face, because he too knew how bad it was. And what made things worse was that he recognized him, remembering Trooper Malaza from the other day when he had sent him away carrying one of his important messages to the General. Durnford lowered his eyes, unable to look into his face, knowing the man - a good, kindly person - only had moments left to live.

Solomon stopped his struggles. The coldness in him had gone now, replaced by a peculiar calmness. He still reflexively tried to draw breath but this was a futile attempt by his body to ward off the inevitable, a natural tendency to strive for existence. Inside, deep inside at the centre of his soul, he knew...

...and so he lay still, staring up into his Colonel's face.

Feebly, as he slowly drowned on his own blood, Solomon reached out and found the hand of his commanding officer. He slipped his fingers into the palm and squeezed with all his strength.

Durnford felt this weak grip and he could no longer ignore Solomon's silent plea, a last wish that he not be alone at the final moment, so he looked up.

He gazed steadily into Trooper Solomon Malaza's eyes.

And saw that they were now dead eyes.

Durnford pushed himself to his feet and took a couple of deep breaths to steady his nerves and to compose himself. This was the sad but unavoidable reality of battle, he told himself. In the type of brutal, close-up and vicious fighting of the kind they were involved in they had to expect losses. So far they had got off lightly compared to the Zulus, who had suffered much heavier casualties. Still, the blow was hard to take; no matter how he tried to rationalize it, it always left a horribly empty feeling inside him whenever he lost men.

As he moved away he noticed one or two of those neareby glance down towards their fallen comrade, their faces revealing their shock and dismay...as well as their fear that they might be next. Durnford at once saw that they needed further encouragement and so he once more clambered back up the slope, his words ringing out above the clamour of shots.

"Well done boys, we're holding them! But they'll come again so keep that firing going!"

He reached the top and then strode forward several paces so that they could all see him, fully exposing himself to the Zulu marksmen popping away from the thick grass about 200 yards away. He turned and looked along the line of horsemen who stared at him in amazement, wondering if he had gone mad.

Indeed, that might have been the case.

"Give them thunder!" he roared. "GIVE THEM HELL!" and he turned and fired towards the crouching Zulu masses.

Somebody closeby shouted... "get down, plis get down," in broken English, to which he responded with..."nonsense, what rot, fire away!"

A cheer went up for the men too were caught up in the moment, and they heeded his call to carry on shooting.

At least, most of them did.

341

Durnford noticed that the next volley was not quite as loud as the previous ones and he glanced over his shoulder. Suspecting what the reason for this was he quickly strode back and looked into the donga. He saw that here and there men had stopped firing; they dug deep in their pouches, searching for cartridges, or they tried to beg a few from their neighbours in the line, one man even riffling through the pockets of Solomon Malaza's corpse; several had simply turned and slumped against the side of the donga, unable to play any further part in the fighting - and when they saw Durnford worriedly looking at them they stared back, raising their arms and shrugging hopelessly.

His men, the only thing standing between the Zulu left horn and the exposed right flank of their camp, were running out of ammunition.

He skipped down into the bottom of the donga, much to the relief of his men, and hastened across to the far side. Scampering up the banking he holstered his revolver and took out his fieldglasses, then looked across the mile or so of plain towards the camp, searching for the two officers he had sent back a while ago. They should be on their way with several boxes of ammunition any time now, but he looked for a full minute without success. Giving up, he turned and went to find Sergeant-Major Kambule.

He found him shouting fire-commands and briefly took him by the elbow.

Quickly, Colonel Durnford told him that he was returning to camp to hurry up the search for ammunition and also to bring out reinforcements. That he, Kambule, was in charge until either he or the two Lieutenants returned. He was to hold the Zulus here for as long as possible.

The Sergeant-Major bared his teeth in a brief show of resolve, proud to have been temporarily handed command of the fight.

Durnford looked around for one final time.

Moments later he was on his way.

CHAPTER 35

THE CAMP. 12:30pm-12:45pm.

Colonel Pulleine had arranged his firing line as stipulated in the General's Standing Orders issued prior to the outbreak of hostilities; that is, with the guns and infantry in the centre and the mounted troops and black levies on each flank. These recommendations (for they were subject to a degree of flexibility, depending on local circumstances) had come about as a result of the recent war on the Cape Frontier, where Chelmsford had learnt some valuable lessons regarding African warfare. The centre of the line would allways be expected to be hardest pressed, particularly when facing an enemy who liked to attack enmasse, and it was essential that they place their strongest asset - Imperial companies - in the middle, while keeping the weakest link in the force -poorly trained auxiliaries - as far away from the toughest fighting as possible. In other words, push them onto the wings or hold them in reserve, but do not burden them with too much responsibility for they were regarded as notoriously unreliable.

So, keeping these 'suggestions' in mind, Pulleine hurriedly set up his line at the foot of the hills.

At the moment the threat appeared to be coming from a specific direction - the plateau and escarpment - and therefore Pulleine placed his men to meet it. The firing line ran roughly eastwards, extending from the northern end of Isandlwana all the way out passed the rocky knoll between the two dongas to where the ground gently started to slope up towards the conical hill, a virtual right angle from the blocks of tents, about a mile in length. On the extreme left were the redcoats of Captain Younghusband's C. Company, having been rushed here to cover the retreat of the men fighting at the head of the spur, and as there wasn't time to reposition them here they remained. Next in line running east was a company of NNC, then the three troops of Zikhali horse (minus Lieutenant Roberts, who lay scattered about the veldt) fresh from their exhausting advance up the spur. On their right were Mostyn's F. Company, followed by Lieutenant Cavaye and the men of E. Company, their blistered hands testimony to the amount of firing they had already done. After these came A. Company, under Lt. Porteous, having slipped out from behind the artillery to find a position upon the boulder-strewn crest between the dongas. The two 7-pounders had remained in place so they now continued the line along to Captain Wardell and H. Company. Finally there was the only company from the 2/24th, having being left behind on outpost duties when the General had marched out earlier that morning with the rest of the battalion. G. Company were led by Lieutenant Pope. In echelon to their right rear were placed a second body of NNC, and these formed the final link (although the gap was quite significant) to Durnford's mounted men holding the donga further to the south.

Pulleine was sure the General would have approved of these dispositions. Although this was the first time he had commanded men under combat conditions he was happy with the way he had responded, considering the short time available to him since the attack began. He also had the approval of the officers of the 1/24th, whose advice he had sought when forming up the line. So, all in all, he was comfortably satisfied that this was the best he could do.

This confidence was shared by all, from his adjutant right down to the privates out on the front rank. Although the Zulu attack had developed with surprising speed and in an unlikely location, they felt ready. Some of them were even elated at the prospect of a fight.

As one anonymous officer was heard to remark... "How lucky we are! We shall do the whole thing ourselves, and the others, when they come back and find it over, will be awfully sold!"

*　　*　　*

His brown gaitered boots swishing through the coarse grass, Captain Reginald Younghusband walked up and down behind his men scratching his dense but neatly trimmed beard and muttering to himself. It was an annoying habit he had picked up, running his hand over his chin and talking like this, thinking aloud really, and something he only did at times of stress. And there was no more stressful a situation than being in battle. Some men thrived on it, the occassion bringing out the best in them, but for him it had the gut-wrenching effect of stretching his nerves to breaking point. It wasn't fear, for he was not scared of combat; he had been in these situations too many times and had long since learnt how to conquer such debilitating emotions. No, this was just the anxiety of waiting, those horrible moments before battle was joined. Once the firing began and his company entered the fray he knew he would settle. But the waiting...

Dear God, let's just get on with it, he thought.

The men seemed to pick up on his nervousness and, almost as though it was contagious, they too began to feel it. The constant firing of the two cannons away to the right did not help and with each salvo they jumped, becoming more and more jittery. To calm them down the company sergeant gave them constant words of advice, his thick East-end accent bellowing over the blasting guns.

"Wait for it, wait for it!" he called. "Steady now! They're just a bunch of bare-arsed boys, not the devil i'self! I've seen worse sorts down Silvertown way!" He paced about along the front, stopping from time to time to speak to individuals. "There's noffink special about these, they ain't got two heads or anything. They eat and sleep and fart like the rest of us, so don't you go getting any crazy ideas that they're better than us 'cause they ain't!"

Younghusband listened to him like the rest. And he found comfort in the words...like the rest. Taking out his officer's sword from its steel scabbard he slashed at the high grass stalks, a steely determination starting to creep into his eyes as he ran them over the approaching Zulus.

"We'll send those filthy, stinking heathens running! They won't stop 'till they get back to their mud hut homes! You're the First of the Twenty-fourth, who are you?"

"C.Company, First Twenty-fourth!" the boys shouted back.

"Then show them how you fight!" He stepped back into his position at the extreme right of the line, and shouted the command down the rank. "Mark your targets at 400 yards, take aim!" One hundred rifles came up in perfect unison, the breeches already loaded.

"Fire!"

As he had predicted, Captain Younghusband's last minute bout of nerves evaporated in an instant.

Let battle commense, he thought to himself, and set to work.

Several hundred yards further along the line, out beyond the NNC and Zikhali Horse, Private Owen Brooks and his companions in E. Company had been firing steadily for several minutes now from their new position. After their holding action up in the hills, during which they had expended a lot of ammunition, they had hurried back down the spur in something of a mild panic with several thousand Zulus giving chase. Once at the bottom they had found the artillery lending them covering fire, which allowed them time to regain their composure, and a few minutes later they slotted neatly into the firing line and resumed their volley-fire once more. So, because they had been in action the longest amongst the infantry, they'd had time to settle into a rhythm. They fired steadily and accurately. These were no boy recruits, but war-worn and mature campaigners.

One exception was the young soldier standing in line besides Private Brooks. He had paid him little notice since the fight began, except that he had a tendency to fire too low with his shots striking the ground in front of the Zulus, an indication that his sights were set wrong. Brooks said nothing. He merely smirked as he listened to the lad quietly complaining to himself that there was something wrong with his rifle.

Brooks, like the rest, fired away.

After a while their prolonged firing made the metal barrel and wooden forestock too hot to hold, and those who had not been wise enough to sew small cowhide covers around the barrel in anticipation of this (for previous experience had resulted in many a blistered palm) had to take out a rag and quickly wrap it around their left hand for protection. The rifle-bore also tended to become fouled by a build up of powder, resulting in a nasty kick in the shoulder each time the trigger was pulled. However, there wasn't time to clean them and they just had to put up with this the best they could, ignoring the pain as much as possible.

They lay down a solid field of fire and soon their marksmanship began to tell. At this range the Martini-Henry was at its most accurate, and the Zulu regiment to their front found it all but impossible to move forward. To either side, the other Imperial companies had equal success. All along the line the firing grew in intensity, until dense clouds of smoke rolled forward on the breeze. The noise was deafening, a continuous crackling sound similar in nature to a wild bush-fire.

The Zulu attack was held.

It became inevitable that they would start to take casualties themselves. With the amount of return fire coming back a few rounds were bound, by sheer chance, to find a target. Here and there men fell. Mostly they received just bad flesh wounds of a non fatal nature, enough to bring to an end their part in the battle. They either limped or crawled or were helped back towards the hospital tents by the medical ordelies. Only a very few at this stage were killed outright. The odds of it being you were small. Still, it happened.

Private Brooks lifted his rifle, aimed and fired. He yanked down the lever behind the trigger to release the spent case, and it leaped out to join the dozen or so others that lay scattered about his boots. He reached into his expense pouch at his hip where he kept his spare rounds of .45 Boxer brass cartridges, for he had already gone through two full packets, noticing vaguely in the back of his mind that he had to dig deep to find one. Bringing it out he pushed it into the breech with his thumb and then snapped the lever back home. He waited for the relay of commands to come, his eyes already having picked out his next target. Up came the gun. He squeezed the trigger, the rifle butt thumped his shoulder. He went through the same sequence time and time again with hardly needing to think. He was in the groove and he felt good.

Suddenly he was distracted by a loud yelp close by. Brooks twisted his face around to look.

The young soldier who had been standing several feet away had gone crashing to the ground, a look of complete surprise upon his face. A second later and his expression changed when he realized he had been hit. He sat up and reached for his leg, panic and fear overwhelming his senses when he saw the blood pumping from the bullet hole in his right calf.

"Help me!" he called to anyone who cared to listen. "Please help me!"

Private Brooks watched the lad sway from side to side. He was about to faint. Not from blood loss, for the wound wasn't mortal, but simply from the sight of blood.

"I'm dy...ing. Oh Mammy, I'm dy-dy...ing," he whispered, now close to tears. Brooks shook his head, then reluctantly bent down.

"Shut that trap!" he snapped. "Here, have some of this." He unclipped his canteen and unbunged it, then tilted it towards the boys quivering lips. "It'll stop the pain and make yer feel better."

He swallowed some and the fiery liquid made him splutter and cough.

Brooks laughed. "What did I tell you? Now who's complaining about me having a little tipple on the sly, eh? Eh!"

Right then he saw the CSM come dashing down the line towards them, and Brooks straightened and put away his rum in a hurry, then took up his place again.

"Stretcher bearer!" the CSM screeched when he saw the soldier on the ground. Coming up alongside him, he bent forward and closely examined the injury.

"Looks bad to me sarge," said Private Brooks gravely. He sucked in between his teeth, then said again, "very bad."

"Brooks," replied the CSM, staring at him squarely, "just shut up."

"Is it bad sarge?" the young soldier said in a timid little voice. "Is he right?"

"Stop fretting lad. You ain't about to meet your maker just yet...I don't think." He stood up when the two stretcher bearers arrived and moved to one side while they gently lifted the wounded man onto the canvas carrier, his groans become more and more self-pitying.

They were about to hurry him away to the hospital tent when the CSM suddenly held up his hand. "One moment."

They stopped.

Striding forward, the CSM leant down towards the soldier's face, who lay looking up at him. He sniffed.

"Have you been drinking boy?" he asked in a deathly quiet voice, moustache twitching.

"Me sir?" the soldier asked, all thoughts of his injury temporarily gone. His eyes flicked from side to side and he cringed back into the stretcher and clasped onto the sides, fearing he might topple off in fright.

The CSM looked straight into his eyes. After a moment he pulled back. His gaze never once left him. A muscle in his cheek suddenly fluttered and his face reddened with volcanic anger. His head looked like it might explode.

"Get this drunken mess out of me sight. I don't ever want to see him again." He spun away and stalked off, mumbling various curses under his breath. The lad on the stretcher finally passed out.

They carried him away, leaving a smirking Private Owen Brooks behind.

War could be jolly fun, he thought.

And with this in mind he turned back to the action.

The two fieldpieces of the artillery detachment continued to fire at the Zulus now gathering in the low ground at the foot of the escarpment, the men racing through their drill with clockwork regularity. All those years of hard training were paying off, each man moving fluidly and doing his job with faultless precision, a well-worked routine. The 7-pounders spewed flame and death. The air shook, the ground rumbled, with each round fired. The crews cheered at the gory spectacle of Zulus being smashed and pummelled, watching as arms and legs and heads were scattered to the four winds.

"You're doing just bully my beauties!" shouted Major Stuart Smith to his gunners. "We've stopped them cold, you see? I've never seen such fine work before in all my-ah!"

He jerked back and fell against the side of one of the limbers, grabbing hold of the handle on the ammunition chest to prevent himself toppling to the ground.

"You're hit sir!" cried Edward Chisolm, his face aghast.

"I know I'm bloody hit you fool," Smith gasped through clenched teeth, his left arm dangling uselessly at his side. "Get back to your duties now."

He pushed himself upright and glanced down at the injury. His shirt sleeve was ripped wide open and through the tear he could see the deep gash just above his elbow, blood running down his forearm. Pain shot down to his hand, making his fingers tingle unpleasantly, and soon blood was dripping from the bottom of his cuff onto his dark-blue trousers.

He cursed quietly, more at the pain than anything. He did not think the wound was life threatening.

To slow the bleeding he lifted his arm up above his head, an awkward inconvenience for he had no intention of going to seek help and would stay here with his guns.

Trying to ignore the agony the best he could he paced back over to the crews, some of whom were watching their Major anxiously. He tried to smile. He would be alright, he wanted them to know.

Just then a rider came galloping across, waving to gain his attention.

"Major Smith sir, Colonel Pulleine wonders if you could take one of your guns over to the right a little and lend Durnford a hand. He's hard pressed sir, and could do with a few rounds."

Smith looked over to where Durnford and his mounted men had taken up position down in the donga, their stand marked by a long and ragged line of smoke. Ahead of them the plain seemed to be alive with thousands of Zulus. They poured around the conical hill and charged towards their right flank. He saw at once how serious the situation there was, and he turned and bellowed out a series of commands.

"Number One Gun, limber up and move three hundred yards to the right! Lend covering fire to right flank, shrapnel and case shot! At the double!"

The move was carried out with the same efficiency, the horse teams straining at the reins, and in no time at all they were set up in their new position and firing rounds over the donga in the near distance and hitting targets with sublime accuracy.

For ten minutes they blew great chunks out of the Zulu ranks there. Major Smith watched the shells strike home with pride, his injured arm still in the air, and when he saw the Zulu charges falter and the fighting stabilize he ordered the gun back to its previous spot but ever ready to respond to any other similar requests for assistance.

The men were doing stirling work today, he thought.

But the Zulu regiments ahead of them were no fools. They quickly learnt a harsh lesson about the futility of charging into artillery fire, at a terrible cost.

They noticed how, just before each gun fired, the white men quickly stepped back and knelt on the ground before pulling the lanyards, and the warriors started to take evasive action. With shouts of "uMoya!" ("it is wind!") they threw themselves down onto the ground at the precise moment the guns were fired, so that the rounds whistled harmlessly overhead.

The tactic worked.

And while the English reloaded they slowly crept nearer through the thick grass. Coming closer.

Major Smith noted this with growing concern.

"I don't believe it," said Charlie Noakes of H. Company, shaking his head to himself.

"What don't you believe?" replied his friend Robert Metcalfe.

"They're just standing there letting us pick them off. Why don't they run?"

Robert peered around the large rock that he lay behind, his rifle pointing towards the enemy. It was true, he saw. The Zulus had come to a stop and were making no attempt to close with them. They just waited in the large hollow below the hills making a strange buzzing sound.

It worried him.

They had been firing now for close on twenty minutes and had cut huge swathes through the enemy's ranks, but from what he could see this had not dented their confidence in the slightest. There seemed to be a limitless number of them, the regiments to the rear constantly feeding men forward to fill the gaps created by their volley fire. They did not seem to possess one ounce of fear. They just stood there, waiting, biding their time.

"I don't know!" he called across to his friend. Then in a whisper, "but it don't look good."

H. Company had joined the line to the immediate right of the two guns, on the slight rocky crest between the two dongas and a little forward so that they could fire down into the dead ground where the Zulus gathered. They took full advantage of the cover the boulders provided, the men either laying or kneeling down so as not to create too tempting a target. It was a good spot, with an elevated field of fire. The only drawback was that the camp was almost three-quarters of a mile away, their regimental ammunition supply even further.

But they did not worry about such things. Others would take care of ensuring they did not run short of cartridges.

It was their task to just keep firing away, nice and steadily.

The two friends raised their rifles once again, as did all the other soldiers in the company, and fired. They reloaded, aimed, and fired. Reloaded, aimed, and fired.

"Did you see that?" called Charlie. "The short fellow running along the front? I think he was a chief or something. I just took the top of his head off!"

"You lucky swine."

"If you look closely you can sometimes see their brains fly about. It's like shooting ripe pumpkins!"

"Yes...thankyou."

"We're giving them a jolly good beating. I thought you said these Zulus would charge home? Ha, they ain't the demons you think Robert Metcalfe!"

Robert looked over at him and saw the wide grin on his face, his eyes shining with excitement. He was a good pal was Charlie, but there were times when his over-enthusiasm worried him. If he was ever to fall in battle then Robert thought he would never be able to live with himself, for he had promised Charlie's mother that he, being older, would look out for him. These days that was proving harder and harder as the boy's recklessness grew. But there was only so much he could do to stem his over-zealous nature. If the going became tough, and as of yet it did not look like that would happen, then he might not be capable of keeping Charlie out of harm's way.

Robert tried not to dwell on such thoughts. To take his mind off them he raised his rifle again and pulled his trigger on command.

He saw the Zulu warrior he had aimed at go down, his chest expanding in a cloud of blood-spray where the bullet struck.

He had lost count of the number he had killed. Over a dozen so far, surely.

352

How much longer could this go on? he wondered. Before the Zulus chanced their arm? And if they did, and managed to get to within stabbing distance, what then?

*   *   *

Ntshingwayo kaMahole and Mavumengwana kaNdlela, infuriated at their warriors' refusal to hold back and hear their instructions, had raced after them across the plateau in the hope that they could regain some kind of control of the battle. They had acted like impetuous children! Without their wise words of advice, garnered from numerous successful military campaigns, then the King's regiments would surely be bloodied and mauled, the fight all but lost in those first few crazy moments. The attack should not even have taken place that day, for it was a day of the new moon, *olumnyama usuku* - 'the dark day', when dark forces were said to walk the land. It had been Ntshingwayo's intention to wait until the following morning and then to launch his well planned attack at first light, in 'the horns of the morning' when the horns of their cattle could first be distinguished against the lightening sky. That was the best time to go into battle.

Yet it wasn't to be.

The moment they were discovered the attack had developed spontaneously, the warriors' minds already made up.

The young fools would pay for their impatience in blood.

But all was not neccessarily lost. If only they could catch them up.

The two *indunas* reached the crest of the escarpment just as the stragglers from the slower regiments were dropping over the edge. They immediately hurried over to the highest point, an exposed patch of cliff known as the iNyoni rocks that overlooked the plain, and they clambered up and inched forward towards the steep drop on the far side. They looked down.

Things, they immediately saw, did not look promising.

From here they had a perfect view of the battlefield; the mountain, the white tents of the enemy camp, the red lines of soldiers; the whole scene spread out before them. Far away to the right they could see the *amabutho* of the right horn starting to slip down behind Isandlwana, trying to stay hidden in the contours of

353

the land, sweeping forward unhindered, their objective being to fall upon the enemy from the rear and taking them by complete surprise. They were moving rapidly and so far, successfully. However, the left horn, which had poured around the eastern end of the escarpement, had been dramatically halted infront of the large donga that cut the plain in two, the men unable to advance further, and the chest likewise had stopped short in the broken ground immediately below them, having come under the heaviest fire from the white soldiers. They were suffering horrendously, rank after rank falling, their dead piling higher.

It seemed that Ntshingwayo's worst nightmare was coming true.

The King's grand army, entrusted to his leadership, was being put to death before his very eyes.

*   *   *

The first requests for fresh ammunition came from the two Imperial companies longest engaged thus far, Lieutenant Cavaye's and Captain Mostyn's. They were still firing solidly and had sufficient quantities to last for some time, but the two officers thought it wise to bring forward extra supplies so that they could maintain their rate of fire uninterrupted. The battle had all the signs of being a long one. They were merely showing the right kind of prudence, and they were in no way over-concerned.

The regimental reserves for the First and Second Battalions were stored on several mule carts parked immediately behind their units tents, thirty boxes per cart and six hundred rounds per box. These were heavy crates of solid mahogany, fitted with a sliding lid fastened down with a single screw, and two copper bands on each end further strengthened the boxes. Once the top panel was removed, either with a screwdriver or by delivering a heavy blow to the side to snap the shallow screw, there was a tin lining that needed to be ripped aside before the ammunition packets-of ten rounds each-could be removed and doled out. Opening the boxes was relatively easy as long as a person remained cool and unflustered. Then runners, either buglers or bandsmen, would hurry to the lines carrying the cartridges in their helmets or haversacks, to hand them to the soldiers. It was an efficient system. The quartermasters oversaw the whole operation with their customary professionalism.

Elsewhere, there were similar supplies for the NNC and Mounted Troops, who were expected to arrange their own distribution.

In total, there were well over 400,000 rounds in camp, in addition to those the men carried in their pouches. More than enough to handle any scenario.

As the reserve supply for the Second Battalion had earlier being made ready for departure out towards the Mangeni gorge as requested by Chelmsford, Quartermaster Bloomfield was at first reluctant to start opening his precious boxes once the calls came in for more ammunition. In truth he was only responsible for the 2/24th, only one company of which had remained in camp, so when the companies along the line sent runners back he at first had to turn them away. They should draw from their own supply, from the 1/24th camp over five hundred yards to the south. After a while however, when the single company from his own battalion started queuing up at their carts, he had had no option but to open several boxes and start distributing packages. Soon, it became impossible to determine who was from which battalion, and in the confusion ammunition was no doubt being handed out to the wrong people. Yet there wasn't time to question each and every man. The important thing was that the soldiers out fighting on the firing line be kept well supplied.

For the runners drawing extra rounds from the First Battalion camp the problem wasn't one of convincing over-zealous quartermasters of their genuine need for further cartridges, nor of opening the boxes quickly enough - which was an easy enough task anyway - but rather one of distance. From the companies out on the line back to the 1/24th's camp they had to cover over half a mile just to reach their ammunition carts, then another half a mile back laden down with packages; and all of it over bumpy ground. A relay they had to repeat over and over again. To speed things up the two battalion quartermasters decided to shorten the distance by moving out with their mule carts towards the firing line. Also, as many spare men as could be found throughout the camp, such as cooks, officers' servants, artillerymen in charge of spare horses, the sick, etc, were collected to help carry the ammunition to the soldiers.

This temporary change to the normal procedure was a result of the tremendous pressure the Zulus were applying.

It did not give them cause to panic, they were just being flexible to a changing situation.

And it worked. Once the initial confusion was overcome, the distribution of extra ammunition was sufficiently fast to cope with events. The soldiers firing at the Zulus got their cartridges and the fight continued unabated.

Still, the two quartermaster's did become more and more irritable as the requests became more and more demanding.

Smith-Dorrien had moved down from the wagon park to help, having no other role to play. He'd hurried over to the 2/24th camp and had taken it upon himself to lift down one of the crates from a cart, and had started to try and open the lid by kicking at it with his heel when Quartermaster Bloomfield had noticed. He came dashing across with a dismayed look on his face.

"Stop that! Stop that at once young man!"

Looking up, Smith-Dorrien continued to stamp down on the lid. "I'm taking it out to the line," he explained.

"For heaven's sake, not that box, it's part of the supply the General asked for!" "I think our men are in more need of it right now."

"But it's for the Second Battalion!"

He kicked down once more, and this time the sliding panel came free. Smith-Dorrien said, "Hang it all, you don't want a requisition now, do you?" before kneeling down and ripping back the tin lining and delving inside for a handful of packages. He stood back up and looked squarely at Bloomfield. "Now really isn't the time to quibble, is it?"

Flustered and somewhat taken aback by the young man's forthrightness, Bloomfield went bright scarlet. "I'd rather you asked first, that's all."

"Well alright, I'm asking now. May I?" he said, lifting the packages he held and looking meaningfully towards the sound of firing.

"Oh I don't have time for this," snapped Bloomfield. "But mark my word, I shall be discussing this later."

With that, he turned and hurried away.

Smith-Dorrien bent down and took a couple more ammunition packages and then he too spun away, hastening towards the firing line.

Bloomfield went over to where one of the battalion ammunition carts was being made ready to go out to the firing line. He pulled himself up onto the back and started to count the boxes, making the occasional note on his inventory, and trying his level best to concentrate on the task at hand. A scowl remained on his face though, annoyed that his meticulous organisation was being hampered by the ebb and flow of battle, as well as by impertinent fools like the young man he'd just had words with.

Just then, something made him stand up straight and swivel his head around. It was as though something had caught his attention, but when he looked to see what, there was nothing of obvious cause. Funny, he thought to himself, and gave a shrug.

About to call down to his Quartermaster-Sergeant that all was in order and that they could move off, he never heard the sharp crack of the stray round that struck him. Nor did he have cause to wonder how he could be so unlucky to be hit this far from the firing line.

All he knew was, it was the fortunes of war.

Or in his case, the misfortune.

The fine line between life or death, at best a fickle thing, could be resolved by the strangest of occurrances.

The bullet hit him just behind the right ear and exited through the top of the scalp, totally destroying half of his brain. His dark blue Glengarry cap went flying with part of his head still in it, and Quartermaster Bloomfield fell slumped over the ammunition boxes, his neat and tidy handwriting on the inventory obliterated by blood. He twitched just once, but he was already dead, and thereafter he moved no more.

Colonel Durnford cantered into camp yelling at the top of his voice, "Carbineers to me! Form up, quick as you can! Hurry and follow me! Come on now!"

One or two of the Carbineers noted the excitement in his voice, the red flush in his face, and it filled them with dismay. They remembered a time, five or more years ago, when the Colonel had ridden into battle with a similar death-or-glory look about him, for they had been there that foggy morning in the mountains when they had been forced to leave several of their comrades behind, only to return later to bury their corpses. They instantly recognized the signs in his demeanour. It stole away their breath. Chilled their blood.

This was unexpected. None of them had anticipated the Colonel to come looking for them. Durnford, of all people! Had the man no scruples? Did he think they could just forget the past like that?

He was obviously caught up by the exhileration of combat, possibly thinking that they too wanted to sieze the moment and make a name for themselves. To temporarily put their grievances to one side and ride with him once again.

The Carbineers stayed rooted to the spot. They looked at him with hard stares, their jaws working silently.

Durnford saw that they were not responding. "Come on!" he repeated with indignation. Still they refused to obey.

The Colonel trotted forward into their midst. "What are you waiting for?" he demanded to know. "Look. Do you not see the pressure my men are under?" He pointed towards the line of the donga in the near distance, with the awesome sight of the Zulu left horn building up before them. "Our flank will be turned and the enemy will be through our defences if you do not help."

They followed his outstretched finger and a quiet murmur of unease built up when they saw the seriousness of the situation, that he was not exaggerating. Their horses became skittish as though they picked up on their disquiet.

"I ask you again Carbineers! Follow me! Help us to hold the line!"

One or two gave barely perceptible nods, hating themselves for agreeing but realizing they had little option. More followed suit, until eventually they had all acquiescented.

Durnford breathed a silent sigh of relief.

He led this motley collection of troopers through the camp, calling out for more men to join them. A group from the Newcastle Mounted Rifles came across offering their assistance, then the Buffalo Border Guard. Other individuals came in dribs and drabs, some whom he knew, but several were complete strangers to him. Until eventually there were about seventy men gathered around.

It wasn't much of a force but it would have to do.

Whether it would make a difference remained to be seen.

Durnford turned his horse and spurred away, heading back towards the fight. They followed.

Colonel Pulleine had noticed his return to camp, thinking that he'd come back to take overall command of the battle as was his duty as senior officer present. When he saw him gallop away again with a handful of reinforcements just a few minutes later, he realized he had assumed wrong. The man was an enigma! What was he thinking of, taking more men away from the camp and spreading their defences even thinner? Was he so obsessed with seeking glory for himself and his men that he was prepared to endanger the camp still further, all as a means of proving his worth?

Trying to bite his tongue Pulleine allowed his gaze to drift out towards where the mounted men were headed.

He saw with alarm how open their right flank was. There was an enormous gap between Lt. Pope's G. Company and the men fighting in the donga, with only a few NNC loitering about nervously. They would be of little use if the Zulus tried to exploit this opening, as they surely would any time now.

Pulleine remembered his promise to Durnford that he would support him if he ever got into difficulties. Now, it seemed, was the time to keep his word.

Somehow he had to plug the gap.

He swung about in his saddle and beckoned forward one of his junior officers. "Take the following order to Lieutenant Pope. He is to drop south a little and rotate his company to face east. Tell him to extend his line with ten yard spacings and to try and link his right up with Colonel Durnford's left. The NNC will anchor on Captain Wardell's company. Is that clear?"

The messenger repeated the order back word for word.

Satisfied that everything was taken care of, Pulleine sent him away.

CHAPTER 36

Whereas the Left Horn had been brought up short before the wide donga, their repeated charges so far having come to nought, the Right Horn in contrast was making rapid progress down the back of Isandlwana. 'The beast's horns' attack formation required that one wing remained hidden, taking advantage of the terrain to move undetected upon the enemies rear while they were distracted by the chest and remaining horn, then closing in for the kill from this unexpected direction. To achieve this took great skill from the regimental commanders, as well as speed and discipline from the warriors themselves. One slip up, one mistake by an over-eager, keyed up company, was all it took to lose this element of surprise. The success or failure of an attack could hinge on this turning movement alone, and so it had to be carried out with expert precision.

On this day the warriors of the Left Horn excelled themselves.

The iDududu, the iSangqu, the iMbube, and the uNokhenke *amabutho* had raced quickly across the plateau in a dense column before splitting into their various sections, each regiment following the contours of the land and trying their best to remain out of sight. At one stage the uNokhenke had briefly being detected and fired upon by a small group of white soldiers in a broad valley at the head of the spur, and for a moment it appeared that their ploy to envelope the enemy would fail right at the outset. But the warriors had pushed on, refusing to be drawn, and they bypassed them, disappearing into the broken ground further west. To their relief the white soldiers did not pursue them; by this time the Zulu centre had been rolling over the escarpment, dragging away their attention, and thus helping the Right Horn to pull away without further incident.

After about another mile they had dropped down into the valley behind the mountain, the other three *amabutho* doing likewise away to their right. Even further west, the Zulu reserve - the loins - swept around in a majestic curve and slipped through the hills to cut the road to KwaJim's where they hoped to catch any white soldiers who managed to slip through the net closing around them.

The ground at the back of Isandlwana was riddled with donga's and small tributary streams, and numerous small hills covered in boulders and tall, thick grass, all of which aided their attempts to remain concealed as they hurried south. Keeping as silent as possible, talking in low voices, their bare feet whispering over the ground, they made quick progress.

Beyond the high crag that soared above them they could hear the sound of fighting. It was strangely faint from here, even though it was only a mile or so away, the tall rocky ramparts cushioning the noise. It gave the warriors a peculiar feeling of isolation, a not altogether unpleasant sensation.

But they all knew this was the calm before the storm.

The Right Horn closed in.

With deadly accuracy the trap was being sprung.

*   *   *

Mfulandelo kaZibeme noticed it first.

A dimness about the sky, a general gloom that suggested twilight was upon them.

Yet they were only part way through the day and the approach of evening was still some time off.

So it must have been a bank of clouds covering the sun, having skimmed quickly across the sky.

361

He glanced up as he ran along, and to his surprise he saw that the sun was not obscurred. He stared up at it for several seconds before realizing that this in itself was unusual, for normally at this time the glare would have blinded him, the brightness of the sun hurting his eyes and making him quickly look away. Not today. Today he could stare at it with no discomfort whatsoever.

Mfulandelo paused. He stood still, his neck craned back, mouth agape.

He felt suddenly cold even though the day was humid.

"What are you looking at you fool?" he heard somebody closeby growl, and he did not need to look for he recognized the voice.

Gezindaka kaMadikane, large and imposing, strode across to where he stood and looked at him like he would a dumb and useless beast. "The white men are in that direction, not up in the heavens."

"Look," Mfulandelo replied, ignoring the jibe. He pointed up. "Look!"

"Ah!"

"The sun is turning dark! Something ail's it!"

"You are mad. Crazy." Gezindaka shook his head.

"But look. It is growing fainter."

Gezindaka did not look up. He was convinced he had lost his mind and he stepped away, fearing he too might catch whatever madness was in the other's veins. With one final hateful glance at him he hurried on, leaving Mfulandelo behind.

The rest of the regiment passed him by also, hardly noticing his odd behaviour. They were too intent on joining the fight.

Mfulandelo kaZibeme did not understand that what he was witnessing was infact a partial eclipse of the sun, a perfectly natural event. To him it was a sign of bad omen, proof that the supernatural forces of *umnyama* were abroad that fateful day. It filled him with dread. He found himself wondering what lay in store for them.

Eventually he rejoined his comrades, jogging through the tall grass as they snaked their way south down the valley.

Every now and then he would peer nervously up at the sun.

And each time it seemed to have grown that bit darker.

As though the light was being sucked out.

CHAPTER 37

COLONEL DURNFORD'S POSITION. THE NYOGANE DONGA.
1 MILE EAST OF CAMP. 1:00pm-1:15pm.

Durnford noticed the change at once, how much things had deteriorated in the short time he'd been gone.
When he had left the fight under the capable hands of Sergeant-Major Kambule most of the men had still being firing regular volleys, only a few having finished off their ammunition. Now, riding back with his meagre reinforcements in tow, he saw that roughly half of his command had run out. They crouched in their positions, feeling useless, either hoping fresh supplies would reach them or waiting until a few rounds became available as more men went down, killed or wounded. Several, anticipating the worst, had fixed short knives onto the ends of their carbines. All around he saw faces deeply etched with fear and dread, everybody realizing the moment of truth was fast approaching.

As soon as he had positioned the new arrivals, placing them carefully to plug any gaps in his line, Durnford dismounted and went across to where Kambule was directing the fight.

"Sergeant-Major, where in God's name are Henderson and Davies? They should have been back long since!"

Simeon Kambule turned around as he loaded his last few rounds into his revolver, his face caked in dust and his lips cracked with thirst. He shook his head. "I do not know sir," he replied in a voice gone hoarse from shouting orders, "I thought they would be returning with you."

"I didn't see them in camp."

Kambule could only shrug helplessly.

"They must still be searching for our supply wagons," Durnford thought aloud.

"Well sir...without more ammunition my men cannot hold back another determined charge like the last one."

Durnford merely nodded.

"Also, the Zulus are moving further south. I think they mean to slip by and come in behind us."

The Colonel looked to where the Sergeant-Major was indicating, seeing for himself how a large body of the enemy were sweeping away to their right and keeping out of range as they probed the donga in that direction.

"And there. Some are getting through on our left."

Durnford swivelled to the north, spotting the danger Kambule was pointing out. There was an enormous break in the line between himself and the nearest redcoat company nearly half a mile away. Some soldiers were at that moment dashing down to fill the opening, but it was probably too little too late for even as he watched groups of Zulus, in tens and twenty's, were already sneaking through.

Things looked bleak.

Almost out of ammunition and in too exposed a location, they were been outflanked on both sides.

Durnford understood what needed to be done to prevent them being overrun. They had to fall back on the camp and take up a position closer to the tents. Not just his own command, but the whole camp force. It wouldn't be a retreat, for the situation was not irretrievable, but simply a withdrawal to a stronger location. Once there they could close their ranks or even form squares and fight with their backs to the mountain, with their ammunition supplies at hand, and hold off the Zulus indefinately. It made perfect sense. Was, in truth, their only realistic option.

Yes.

"Sergeant-Major, order the boys to mount up!" he shouted.

"We are leaving now, yes?" Kambule asked hopefully.

Durnford affectionately patted him on the shoulder, then said in what he hoped was a good-natured voice, "yes, but only as far as the camp. Our day's not over yet Simeon, far from it. All is not lost!"

Kambule was certain he detected a fair twinkle in his leaders eyes as he climbed back onto Chieftain's back. Was the man excited? he wondered. Or mad?

Ignoring the question for the time being, he shouted the necessary orders at the top of his voice.

They were on the move again.

Their stand in the donga was over.

THE CAMP. 1:20pm.

Colonel Pulleine quickly raised his binoculars and trained them on the line of retreating horsemen, the full implications of what he was seeing slow to register. When they did they hit like a bombshell. He felt the blood drain from his face and his knees went suddenly weak.

Beside him, Teignmouth Melvill noticed him sway. He made to grab for him, thinking his Colonel was sick, but something stayed his hand and he glanced eastwards across the plain instead.

"Good God," he whispered after a second or two, "what has the fool done?"

Without warning, their entire right flank suddenly became exposed. Durnford pulling back like that opened up the whole of that end of Pulleine's firing line, with only Lieutenant Pope's company and a group of NNC left to oppose the enemy's Left Horn. The redcoats who had been in the proccess of dropping down to fill the large gap realized that with no horsemen anchored to their right they would be immediately surrounded if the Zulus charged forward, and so they turned eastwards to meet this attack if it came. For the moment they had a few minutes' grace.

A ripple of sheer terror passed through Pulleine and the officers clustered around him. He quickly regained control of himself. He set his jaw grimly and waited to see what happened.

Growing increasingly concerned that their attack had stalled along the entire centre and left, Ntshingwayo had watched the battle develop with trepidation from his spot up on iNyoni Rocks. A few moments ago he had sent down one of the uKhandempemvu's sub-chiefs to try and stir up his regiment and get them moving forward again. He waited anxiously to see whether this had any results. If it failed then there wasn't much more he could do. There was no sense in sacrificing his men for no gain.

It pained him to even think it, but if they did not break through the white soldiers lines soon then the King's regiments were facing a humiliating defeat.

Events were not yet out of control, Pulleine realized, but if he did not act fast then they would very quickly be facing a spiralling disaster. The right of the firing line was buckling with Durnford's withdrawal the main catalyst, and the NNC. company there - never the most reliable at the best of times - was starting to disintergrate as half of them simply threw down their weapons and fled.

He looked across at his adjutant, hoping for some much-needed advice, but Melvill was too busy staring towards the Zulu masses with an almost spellbound look upon his face. Clearing his throat, Pulleine tried to keep his voice steady. Not easy when his heart was beating fast.

"Bring the line in. Form them up before the tents. They must close up, they're too extended."

For a second or two Melvill seemed not to hear.

"Mr Melvill, I said bring the line in!" he snapped.

"What...? yes." Melvill spun around. "Bugler, sound the Recall!"

As the order was relayed to the men, the strident noise of the bugle seeming to stab at his conscience, Pulleine preyed that he had not left it too late.

The firing along the entire line ceased at a breath and, in one fluid movement, the white soldiers together with their native allies turned about and pulled back.

It took the Zulus completely by surprise.

366

The last thing they expected.

The sub-chief sent down from the heights by Ntshingwayo, having just arrived, immediately saw his opportunity. He sped forward through the ranks of crouching and lying warriors and danced about before them, waving his staff above his head. It was a moment of sheer drama, one that would take on legendary status over the years to come.

"What is this?" he cried, leaping and stamping down with his foot. "Our King *'the little branch of leaves that beats out the fire"* did not order this! They run! While you cower, they run! Go after them!" He pointed after the retreating white men.

Hearing him call out their King's praise name, the uKhandempemvu leapt to their feet as one. Waving their shields in the air and shouting "Izulu!" they charged forward.

The sub-chief led from the front, imploring them not to stop this time, that this was the moment they had been waiting for.

Then he fell dead. Shot through the temple.

But history would remember him.

Elsewhere, the iNgobamakhosi *ibutho* watched enraged as their rivals poured towards the disintergrating line of enemy soldiers. One of their own *indunas* decided to act quickly, to likewise spur the men of the Left Horn on.

"Never did his Majesty the King give you the command to lie upon the ground! He told us to toss the enemy into Pietermaritzburg! What was it you said to the uKhandempemvu?"

The warriors remembered their challenges made at the King's 'Great Place' to the other regiment.

"There are the uKhandempemvu going into the tents. Stop firing. Go in hand to hand!" Their response to his words was an almighty chant of "uSuthu! uSuthu!"

The Left Horn stormed in.

Following their example the rest of the Zulu force grasped their chance. Lurching to their feet they dashed forward in one huge concerted effort. They fell upon the British.

CHAPTER 38

THE CAMP. 1:20pm-1:35pm.

"**F**ix Bayonets, and turn and meet them!" roared Colour-Sergeant Wolfe.

H. Company hastily did as he said, the men snapping their bayonets into position, and they faced the front once again. Some of the men cried out in terror at the sight that met them, for racing towards them fast were a densly-packed mass of charging Zulu warriors, their voices raised together in a single-throated war-cry, assegais beating against their shields. The nearest were just a hundred yards off, having closed the gap in a few terribly short seconds. This time, they would not be able to stop them.

The line of infantry wavered but held, the men hurriedly jogging backwards with their Martini-Henry's thrust forward. Away to the right the company of NNC. had caved in completely, most of them running for their lives, several of their European NCO's doing likewise; a few hardy individuals remained, and these started to angle towards H.Company thinking this would give them sanctuary. In the opposite direction, to the west, the gunners in the artillery detachment were racing to limber up their guns, their usual discipline gone as pandemonium reigned supreme. Beyond them came more Imperial companies, these too falling back towards the tents. Here and there voices called out, imploring them to remain steady, to keep firing until the last possible moment.

H.Company managed to fire one more volley at virtually point-blank range, dropping the nearest group of warriors. Then they barely had time to reload before they were inundated.

"Independent, fire at will!" cried Captain Wardell in desperation, levelling his revolver and blasting at a Zulu charging straight for him. The warrior went down, his stomach opened up by the shot, his guts spilling out between his fingers. He shrieked in agony but his death cries were lost within the tumultous sound of mayhem all about. Wardell looked around for another target and found one, this time picking a Zulu who was stabbing viciously at one of his men closeby. He pulled the trigger and the Zulu fell back into the grass, his assegai still sticking out of the infantryman's shoulder blade. Wardell dashed across to see how badly hurt he was. Reaching down, he pulled him back carefully by his arm and rolled him onto his side. The soldier was barely concious, moaning feebly, and the whole of the front of his tunic was awash with blood where the blade of the spear projected out of his chest. Wardell saw at once that he was beyond help and he reluctantly let the man go, trying to ignore the pangs of guilt he felt inside. He stood upright again.

He failed to notice the warrior coming racing up behind him, stabbing spear poised to strike at the back of the Captain's neck.

Private Charlie Noakes spotted him at the last second. Without thinking, he let out a scream of rage and sprung forward, lunging with his bayonet towards the warrior's waist. The 22 inch blade sliced straight through, meeting no resistance, and the momentum of his charge carried the Zulu clear. He seemed to squirm on the end of the razor-sharp point for a second with a look of outright anger on his features. Then he fell to the ground, spreadeagled.

Charlie pushed down hard with his rifle to drive the bayonet in even deeper and then he gave it a brutal twist, listening with a sick kind of relish to the sound of ripping flesh. The Zulu buckled and jerked, grunted...then went still.

Only when he was certain that he was dead did he pull his bayonet clear. At first it wouldn't come free, wedged as it was between the Zulu's ribs, and he had to stand on the corpse with one boot in order to prise the blade out. When he turned to look at Captain Wardell, he saw instead the surprised face of Robert Metcalfe, his eyes wide with shock at what his friend had done.

Behind him, Captain Wardell gave a quick nod of thanks for his help, and then he disappeared into the whirl of fighting.

Robert quickly snapped out of it and he grabbed hold of Charlie's accoutrement belt, yanking him backwards. "Come on, we have to get clear. Keep moving."

"I am!" Charlie yelled. "I am!"

The two of them, side by side, rifles held at the ready, continued to retreat.

The rest of H.Company did the same. They fought every foot of the way, parrying at the Zulu warriors in fierce hand-to-hand combat, desperation lending them the strength of character they required.

One unfortunate group were too slow to respond to the order to fall back. This party had formed the link between their company and that of Lieutenant Pope's, on the right, but once Pope had moved to the south to take up his new position nearer to Durnford they had found themselves holding this end of the firing line, with only a group of native levies in support. They had also being set slightly forward from the rest so that they could fire down into the shallow ground below the rocky knoll. All of this meant, therefore, that when the order to retreat was given - coinciding with a fresh Zulu assault - they took the brunt of the attack in the side.

The Zulu charge, when it came, was preceded by a shower of thrown spears. They cascaded down upon the British infantry, falling right amongst them and breaking up their formation still further, and about twenty men suddenly found themselves seperated from their comrades amongst the rocks. Colour-Sergeant Wolfe saw them and he went racing over.

"Stay together men! Keep with us!"

But it was no use. As soon as he reached them, more Zulus had closed in behind, completely surrounding them. He turned back to call for assistance but the rest of H.Company were already scampering back towards the distant tents, and they could not have reached them even had they tried.

For about half a minute the small group he was now with made a brief rally. They drew around their Colour-Sergeant as if gaining courage from him, and then turned to fight. Standing back to back they met the charge with the points of their bayonets.

Stabbing, and thrusting, and clubbing, and punching, they made short and bloody work of the first Zulus to reach them. Yet behind these came more and more, crashing against them like black waves against a tiny island of red.

And one by one they fell.

Swamped by overwhelming numbers they were brushed easily aside.

Colour-Sergeant Wolfe was stabbed first in the thigh, but he ignored the wound to pin his assailant through the neck with his bayonet, then managed to get off a quick shot into a second Zulu. Then he felt something thud into his chest, and he dropped his rifle to pull the assegai clear, and used it to hack at a third warrior, stabbing him over and over in the face. But he could fight them off no longer, grievously wounded as he was. The Zulus swarmed forward and he went down under their thrusting blades, ripping his body up, skewering him to the ground, Wolfe still calling for his men to rally on him.

"Bloody Hell!" Charlie Noakes cried. "They've finished the Sarge off!"

"I know!" responded Robert.

"The bastards!" He was about to go charging back, hell-bent on revenge, when he felt himself hauled back yet again by his friend.

"Don't be a fool!"

"But they just killed our Colour-Sergeant!" he cried back.

"Yes, and you getting yourself chopped to bits ain't going to bring him back!"

"Christ, I think I'm going to be sick!"

"Well," said his friend, ignoring his constant blaspeming, "I don't care what you do just as long as you keep running." And he shoved him hard, back towards the direction of the tents nearly three-quarters of a mile away.

Not far away a desperate attempt was being made to save the two guns.

The gunners of N Battery, 5th Brigade were, like all artillery detachments, mighty proud of their guns. To lose them in battle was a matter of great shame and men would willingly give up their lives in order to extricate them from the midst of disaster and take them safely away from a battlefield. They must not be allowed to fall into the hands of the enemy, whatever the cost.

And so when Major Smith heard the order to retire and saw the Zulus respond by pouncing forward along the entire front, he quickly bellowed out the order to limber up. Growing weak from his injury, he still managed to haul himself up into his saddle and drew out his sword, watching as his men swarmed around the two 7-pounders. A handful of them broke away and moved to engage the Zulus who were fast bearing down on them, hoping to give the rest the chance to harness up the horse teams. With few weapons available (there were only two carbines per gun, fastened onto the limbers) they grabbed whatever was to hand and formed a semi-circle across the front of their position.

Edward Chisolm snatched up the rammer just as three Zulu warriors came sprinting through the tall grass in his direction. He swung it crazily in a wild arc causing them to flinch back and he almost lost his balance, but managed to right himself in time before one of them ducked and tried to sneak forward. He thrust out this time, catching the warrior square in the face, crushing his nose and sending him toppling back. The other two hesitated, alarmed and not sure what to do. It cost them their lives.

Major Smith spurred forward and hacked down with his sword onto their heads, killing them in two deft strokes. They crumpled to the earth, lifeless.

Gunner Chisolm was about to offer his congratulations on such a brilliant display when a warning shout from the Major stayed his words.

"Behind You! Watch out sonny!"

He spun his head around to see yet another Zulu coming out of the melee. With barely time to react he somehow managed to swing the rammer once again, but this time in a definate swipe at his opponent. The hard, wooden butt on the end of the staff caught his man on the side of the head, sending him staggering sideways in a daze. Gunner Chisolm ran forward and leapt onto him, still holding the rammer, and the Zulu fell under his weight, shield and assegai dropped from his clutch. Once they both landed on the hard ground he bore down with the long staff across the Zulu's throat, trying to crush the breath out of him, to choke him. Applying more pressure, he brought up his legs and kneeled onto the rammer either side of the warrior's blue face, to free his hands. Then he pummelled him hard, striking over and over with his balled fists straight into the gasping, gaping mouth, until his knuckles were red from the Zulu's blood.

Breathing hard, Edward Chisolm stood up. He held the rammer across his chest, waiting for another attack.

Briefly, he stole a glance over his shoulder to see how the guncrews were fairing.

To his horror he saw that they had already set off, the drivers urging their horses on, scores of men clinging to the sides like ants, the few survivors from the mad scuffle chasing after them and trying to grasp the outstretched hands of their friends. Chisolm looked around to his front again.

He took one look at the rampaging mob of Zulu warriors heading his way, threw the rammer aside, and went racing after the guns.

Luckily for him the ground here was very rocky and the horse teams were forced to weave in and out between the boulders, slowing them enough for him to catch up. Plus, fear lent him the speed he needed to keep just ahead of the chasing Zulus.

Running alongside one of the guns he made a grab for the hand of a fellow gunner clinging onto his seat by one of the wheels, and to his relief he felt himself being hauled onboard. The only space available was on the trail behind the barrel and he quickly slithered down between the two seats, holding onto the elevating screw for dear life, the constant bucking and jolting threatening to toss him clear at any second.

He looked back to see if any of his mates needed help, but they were already being caught. They turned and fought, whilst still trying to flee. A few made it, either by jumping onto the limbers or by outrunning the Zulus; but most were stabbed and dragged to the ground, their screams terrible and haunting.

Edward Chisolm closed his eyes against the trail of destruction they left behind, whispering a quiet preyer to himself.

He wept silent tears.

Similar scenes of groups of men in flight were being played out across the entire front of the camp as the British line desperately tried to retire. The redcoat companies strived to draw together as they backpedalled across the flat ground, but they had been too widely spaced apart and the Zulus were able to drive deep wedges between them, disintergrating their formation still further. The Zikhali Horse to the north managed to reach the tents below them, but only by galloping hard, but for the men on foot it was a terrible trial as they sought to fend of the thousands of warriors who poured after them.

Lieutenant Pope and his men had been granted a brief lull before the Left Horn pounced, allowing them the opportunity to reach the roadway. Once there, they paused to regain their breath and settle their nerves. Not far away they noticed Colonel Durnford and his mounted unit riding hard for the camp and they called across for them to stop and help, but the basuto's had problems of their own; coming after them fast, suddenly free from the gunfire that had so far held them in check, were the young warriors of the uVe and iNgobamakhosi. Fired up with hatred and thoughts of revenge, they rolled onward towards G.Company.

Quickly they formed two ranks across the road, the front line kneeling, the rear standing and positioning themselves between the interstices. They opened fire in alternate volleys, with each line passing back through the gaps of the men behind, slowly leapfrogging backwards. They kept this up for several minutes, gaining valuable time and dropping a good many Zulus, but the young warriors were not to be denied this time. Slowly they closed on this puny force. Eventually, the British had to resort to the bayonet.

In the fierce hand-to-hand fighting that followed no quarter was given and none expected. It was a simple matter of kill or be killed.

Unable to fire by ranks any longer, each individual fought his own private battle, stabbing and thrusting out with their rifles. To the best of their abilities they tried to stick together, forming a dense pack and fighting back to back as they slowly shuffled along the roadway. But occasionally men became isolated, cut off from the rest. Hemmed in, they didn't stand a chance.

This happened more and more as the pressure around them became unbearable, so that soon they were losing men every few yards.

Lieutenant Pope, his monocle glinting each time he fired his revolver, battled with them. He had lost his hat somewhere, blown off when a stray shot had clipped it, grazing his scalp; a thin trickle of blood ran down the side of his nose and around his mouth, dripping off the bottom of his chin. So fervently did he fight that he did not even notice.

Alongside him, one of his men suddenly buckled and collapsed. Pope almost tripped over his body but he managed to keep his feet, and he reached down to pull the soldier back up.

The man gave a loud, agonized moan, as he clutched at his stomach, trying to stem the bleeding. His face was deathly pale.

"Keep going!" Pope screamed in his ear. "If you stop they'll finish you off!" "I can't! Oh my, the pain!"

"Lean on me then." He wrapped the soldiers arm around his own shoulders. "I'll take your weight, but try and help me as much as you can."

He did as he was told, trying to walk backwards on trembling legs. His head lolled from side to side as he fought the agony in his gut.

"That's right, you're doing fine," Pope encouraged. "We'll get you to the hospital tent and the surgeons will see to you there."

He glanced back over his shoulder towards the blocks of tents.

Oh mercy, he thought to himself, they were still a long, long way off.

Why, oh why, had they been sent so far out? What had the Colonel been thinking of?

Then he looked down at his companion, seeing that he was gazing ahead towards the Zulus pressing in on them, a look of sheer terror on his face. Lieutenant Pope shared that fear. His hopes...along with the soldier's life...were fading fast.

One company that did manage to retire in good order was Younghusband's. Holding the left of the line, they had been furthest from the initial breakthrough a mile or so to the east and therefore just had time to react before the Zulu regiments to their front reached them. They hurriedly closed ranks and refused their right flank, swiftly stepping backwards towards the mountain to their rear. Keeping the steep slope to the left, they moved down behind the lines of tents which afforded them some protection on that side, continuing to volley-fire with remarkable discipline.

Younghusband himself, his earlier nerves long since forgotten, controlled the men brilliantly. Barking out orders in a deep, booming voice, his steady display set a perfect example for the men to emulate and they responded with the guts and tenacity he had come to expect of them, all thoughts of flight banished from their minds. They stuck with him all the way, losing a man here and there, but mostly keeping their fighting cohesion.

Backwards they went, the ground gradually sloping upwards as they climbed the flank of Isandlwana, until they were above the camp on a rocky ledge that ran down the side then around the shoulder of the mountain. It was a strong position, with the rocky fastness on their left and a deep drop away to their right making it extremely difficult for the Zulus to reach them. As long as they kept up their fire, or used the bayonet to good effect, inching back all the while, then they should be able to hold the enemy back indefinately. Their only weak spot was their rear, for they could not spare any men to guard their backs; as long as they were not attacked from this direction, then they should last out.

Praising his men for their efforts, Captain Younghusband allowed himself a moment to turn and scrutinize the rest of the battle which was raging below them. From here, he had a good view of the rest of the line shrinking in towards the tents, fighting a desperate rearguard action as they retired. The signs looked bad. Already several companies were being swamped. The speed of the Zulu's final rush had taken many completely by surprise and everywhere he looked he could see breaks appearing where the enemy were rushing through. In the tents below he could pick out members of the NNC company which had been positioned alongside them rushing to the rear, too panic-stricken to attempt making a stand, and an entire legion of warriors gave chase, spurting forward into the heart of the camp. Still further out, on the broad, flat ground to the front of the tents, more redcoats were hastening to reach safety, yet these had to take the full force of the Zulu charge as well as having the furthest distance to cover. They fought bitterly for every foot of ground they gave, taking heavy casualties in the process.

Younghusband spun to the front again just as the Zulus attemted to make one more charge. His men's rifles crashed out, sending them falling back in heaps, and those behind cowered down behind the bodies of their dead comrades, whilst still more rushed up the slope. This time they succeeded in reaching them, and a nasty skirmish of hand-to-hand fighting developed on C.Company's flank. Younghusband joined in, slashing and cutting with his sword which soon dripped with blood and gore. Some of his men were dragged clear from their stand, spreadeagled, and disembowled before their very eyes. But there was nothing the rest of them could do, but fight, fight and fight.

Soon, the rocks and ground about were covered with the slain and injured, both white and black. Men roared with rage and hatred, or screamed in pain. Guns fired, bayonets and assegais stabbed, swords flashed in the sunlight.

For several minutes the fierce tussle went on. It looked like the Zulus would finally overwhelm them. Yet the infantrymen refused to be beaten; they simply would not allow it. They pushed the Zulus back over the edge, kicking them away and breaking open skulls with brutal strikes from their rifle butts. The defences held and the black tide subsided, unable to gain a foothold upon the high shelf.

But the respite was but brief.

Almost immediately a fresh wave of eager warriors pushed through their beaten comrades, screaming their cries of "uSuthu!" as they clambered up the slope. They grasped at the line of bayonets that came up to meet them and tried to yank the soldiers off their precarious perch, or they threw their spears at close range to distract them so that they could rush in. A few even used the bodies of fellow warriors as human shields.

The battle had reached a stage of pure savagery now.

This was Hell.

And Hell knew no bounds.

*   *   *

Though it only took about one minute from the time he had ordered the withdrawal to the command being issued to the companies out on the line and the men to execute the move, something happened to shatter Colonel Pulleine's resolve in that minute.

He saw, in an instant, that it was a combination of two things.

The distance the men had to cover to get back to the tents - for which he was singularly to blame, having stretched his line too thinly and pushed them too far out - and also the sheer speed of the Zulu response. Even before his men had begun to turn and run back the lead Zulu ranks were charging forward, covering those last few hundred yards seemingly in the blink of an eye; then they were throwing themselves onto the men's backs, stabbing with their long-bladed spears and bludgeoning down with their knobkerries.

Pulleine watched in horror as his battalion promptly fell apart.

He felt completely helpless. The full extent of his failure was being bloodily played out before him, his men paying with their lives for his shortcomings as their commander.

He wanted to change things, but it was too late.

Wished he could issue fresh orders to retrieve the situation, but it was too late. Too late to salvage any personal honour or to save his battalion.

Was this how it would end? he asked himself. Nigh on twenty-five years service in the army, a career that had seen him reach the rank of brevet Lieutenant-Colonel, President of the Remount Depot in Pietermaritzburg and commander of Fort Napier, all brought short beneath this peculiar crag called Isandlwana? Crushed into the dirt by...natives! Armed with...spears!

This, his first action.

Was defeat to be his only taste of combat?

Right at that moment Colonel Henry Burmester Pulleine had never felt so alone, despite the many thousands of men fighting it out closeby.

Nobody spoke to him, not even his good friend Lieutenant Melvill who stood by his shoulder. He was sure that he, as well as the other officer's with him, shared his sorrow.

But ultimately the responsibility had been his.

Words could not express how he felt.

A silent sob, from deep within, made Pulleine's shoulders tremble.

CHAPTER 39

5 MILES SOUTHEAST OF CAMP. 1:35pm.

As the 1/3rd NNC neared Isandlwana the view across the plain opened out and the heat haze gradually cleared, visibility becoming better with each stride. The camp could be made out in more detail now, and it was therefore possible to determine something of what was going on there. That there was a major engagement taking place was beyond doubt for they were now close enough for even those without the aid of binoculars to see the fighting raging around the whole northern perimeter. Individual redcoat companies could be distinguished, firing in volleys towards the Zulus spreading out before them, while fighting alongside them were the various mounted units and their fellow NNC, indicating that the whole of the camp force was turned out and battling hard. The sounds of combat, the massed firing and the thud of cannon, carried on the bakingly still air.

Hamilton Browne, growing more and more unsettled at how grave things looked, urged his small column on, almost begging the men to march faster. But they were in no hurry to join the fight. Even his white NCO's seemed hesitant, no longer lashing out at those who hung back, their gaze concentrated on the scenes up ahead.

He could not blame them for their reluctance. Even had they pressed on and reached the camp in time to add their numbers to the garrison he doubted whether they could make much of a difference anyway. First of all they would have to fight their way through the zulus who were quickly encircling the camp, a difficult enough task even for well-trained British infantry; for his inadequately armed and poorly disciplined natives, who had the shameful tendency to cave in at the first signs of danger, it would be a nigh on impossibility with only one probable outcome - a bad mauling, and maybe even total defeat, for his battalion. So it was hard to motivate the men, to stir any fighting spirit into them.

As the battle ahead raged on Hamilton Browne angled his men slightly to the left, with the intention of approaching the camp from the south, hoping this would be the enemy's blind spot. Maybe the sight of reinforcements would frighten them off anyway, long before they entered the fray. Maybe... but not likely.

A sense of gloom seemed to permeat the air. Men spoke to one another in gruff, off-hand voices, everybody seeming to be ill-tempered. The tension built as they came nearer to the fighting.

Strangely their feelings of foreboding seemed to be shared by the countryside around them, for a peculiar stillness seemed to have descended. There was no breeze, nor any sound of birdsong or insects buzzing. And the sunlight appeared to be curiously despondent, a general haze that bleached the skies even though the afternoon was cloudless and hot. There was a dimness about it similar to that of early twilight, which was odd since it was only shortly passed noon.

Trying to shake off sensations of imminent catastrophe, the commandant led his column across the plain towards the mountain just a few miles to their front.

After about another mile he brought them to a halt.

Being this close to the camp they were now perilously near to the Zulus descending down from the eastern end of the escarpment. A whole body of warriors swept across their front just the far side of some hollow ground, maybe a mile and a half away, forcing them to stop. The NNC wavered and for one awful moment Hamilton-Browne thought they were about to run away in pandomonium, but luckily for them the Zulus did not notice them. They were too intent on attacking the campsite to check their rear. He watched them charge forward towards the tents instead.

Suddenly he saw the whole massed impi launch a massive attack. In one fluid movement, and in perfect co-ordination, they poured forward enmasse as though at some secret signal.

He raised his binoculars and watched, terror-struck, as the assault developed with amazing and deadly speed. Nothing could withstand such a charge, not even the finest infantry in the world. Sure enough he saw the British line crumble. They were simply swept away in the flood of Zulus.

"Oh my word," he whispered to himself. "Lord have mercy on them."

But no amount of preying would make one jot of difference. He saw that with crystal clarity. Things had simply gone beyond the point of no return.

He also realized that there was now nothing to be gained by them continuing to press on towards the camp, for the battle had gone beyond the stage where they alone could possibly influence matters. Only if the General rushed back with the whole of his force could they perhaps salvage something from this God-awful mess, and even then it would be but a slim hope.

He continued to watch through his binoculars for several minutes, and then he turned back to his men.

Issuing fresh instructions through his white officer's he ordered the 1/3rd to face about and retire to a slight knoll about a mile to their left rear, from where they might make a better defence should they be attacked. The men hurried to comply, suddenly energized and shaken out of their earlier stupour. As they marched - or in some cases ran - Hamilton-Browne cast frequent glances back towards the battle raging around the foot of Isandlwana, his keen eyes taking in more dreadful details. What he saw bleached the colour from his face and made the hair on the back of his neck stand up.

Sickened to the pit of his stomach he tried not to dwell too long on the sights and sounds, concentrating instead on readying his own command for a fight, if it came to that.

They made the knoll without too much incident, allthough it was difficult to prevent their retreat from turning into a flight for he felt sure that some of his natives wanted to keep on running. Once there he formed them up into a ring and placed his white NCO's in the centre, and they waited to see what happened.

381

It seemed the nearest Zulus had still not noticed them. Or if they did then they made no move in their direction. Hamilton-Browne and his men breathed a little easier.

The next thing he did was to despatch another messenger, urging him to find the General and to pass on the terrible news of what was happening here.

"Tell him...tell him that for God's sake he must come back, the camp is surrounded, and things, I fear, are going badly!"

There was nothing else he could do.

For the time being Colonel Pulleine was by himself.

MANGENI GORGE.
12 MILES SOUTHEAST OF ISANDLWANA. MID-AFTERNOON.

Dismissing Lieutenant Milne, Lord Chelmsford watched the young naval officer trot away with a satisfied look on his face.

The report that he had just spent the last five minutes listening to generally supported his own views, more or less. It seemed that earlier rumours about a battle taking place back at Isandlwana were false, no doubt as a result of bad intelligence and too many people with vivid imaginations. If any kind of action had occurred then it was probably no worse than a skirmish, possibly between Pulleine's scouts and small parties of Zulus; certainly there was no indication of a major engagement, according to Milne. All was now quiet. The cattle had been gathered into the centre of camp, and he assumed this was Pulleine getting ready to move out to join him, as ordered. So there was nothing to worry about.

Having had his mind put to rest Chelmsford turned his attention to finalising the layout of his proposed campsite on the flat ground above the Mangeni waterfall, and to posting his vedettes on the surrounding hills. A large part of his column was still out chasing groups of Zulu warriors and trying to round up any captured cattle, but with the help of the Natal Mounted Police and some Volunteers he had been able to mark out where each unit would pitch their tents as well as segregating a seperate area for the cattle and wagons. All that remained now was for the rest of the men to join them from Isandlwana. At his estimation, if Pulleine was almost ready to set off then he should reach the new camping ground some time early this evening. By this time tomorrow they should be ready to resume their advance towards Ulundi.

Accompanied by several members of his staff Chelmsford rode around the perimeter of the marked area, giving it one last check. He was in the process of doing this when a rider was spotted approaching from the far side of the river, obviously bringing him information. Chelmsford led his small party across and they waited whilst he trotted through the shallow water and up onto their bank.

"Ah, Lieutenant Harford!" Chelmsford exclaimed. "Do please tell me you bring some *interesting* news!"

Henry Harford smiled self-consciously as he saluted the General, but then shrugged and sighed apologetically. "Well that depends, my Lord."

Pursing his lips Chelmsford said, "go on, what is it?"

"I've just been given a curious message from one of Commandant Hamilton-Browne's men. The chap was very excitable, babbling away as though he had sunstroke."

"Really? So what has 'Maori Browne' got to say?"

"Well... apparantly there is a bit of a problem back at the camp. Pulleine, according to this man, is under heavy attack."

Chelmsford blinked slowly and then raised his face to the heavens. "Not again," he murmured to himself.

"I'm sorry?"

"I keep hearing constant stories of this mysterious phantom battle, with no concrete evidence."

"I beg you pardon my Lord, but whether or not it's true this fellow was very graphic with his information. Said he had seen it for himself, the fighting that is. He told me the camp is surrounded and struggling to hold the enemy back, and that if you don't return at once then Colonel Pulleine might be in serious trouble."

"I've never heard so much ridiculous nonsense," sneered Crealock from his customary position at his General's side.

"It's all bosh!" somebody else was heard to cry.

"During the Cape Frontier War large bodies of Xhosa quite often gathered close to our camps, without ever actually attacking them. This is no different - if the enemy is there at all. Perhaps they are seeing mirages, ha ha!"

383

"Yes, thankyou Crealock," Chelmsford said thoughtfully.

This wasn't helpful. Here he had two quite contradictory reports concerning events at Isandlwana, from two varying sources of reliability. On the one hand, an eyewitness description of shaky credibility, while on the other a confident assessment from a trustworthy officer of his own staff. He knew which he preferred to believe.

Still... an element of doubt had returned to his mind.

And when in doubt...

Better to be sure.

"We shall ride to the top of that ridge and take a look for ourselves," he announced to those assembled around him.

They followed in the General's wake as he led them up the gentle hillside, leaving the Volunteers and NMP behind to continue their work on laying out the new camp. Once at the top they spread out to either side and brought out their binoculars. From here they had a fairly unobstructed view back across the plain, with the hump of Isandlwana resting on the far horizon. For several minutes they gazed towards the distant camp.

"It's not very clear," Chelmsford conceeded.

"Murky somehow," added Crealock.

"If only this haze would lift for a moment we would be able to see... more exactly... what is going on. Damn!"

Chelmsford lowered his fieldglasses and put them away.

"Gentlemen," he said in a strained, annoyed voice, "it appears that the only way to settle matters is for us to ride over there and see for ourselves, much though it bothers me to be wasting valuable time on what will probably prove to be a pointless exercise."

He scowled heavily, his staff duplicating the expression.

"Lieutenant Harford, would you be so good as to go and inform Colonel Glyn that we are returning to Isandlwana, tell him why, and that he is in charge whilst I am away. We shall not be long, I am certain."

Henry Harford saluted and rode briskly away.

Chelmsford turned his horse and cantered down the far side of the slope, the others close behind. Then they set out on the long journey across the plain.

Back to Isandlwana.

THE ONDINI *IKHANDA,* KING CETSHWAYO'S ROYAL RESIDENCE.
MAHLABATHINI PLAIN.
MID-AFTERNOON.

Since the time of Shaka, founder of the Zulu nation and the greatest of all their King's, one person only had been appointed sole guardian of the *inkatha,* the Sacred Coil of the Nation - Langazana, his father's fourth wife.

For sixty years she had watched over the small ring of python skin, seeing Kings come and go, through war, pestilence and famine, growing old and feeble but never relinquishing her role as custodian to the kingdoms most prized possession, this tiny and fragile thing that symbolised the Zulu peoples pride and nationhood. Her status as guardian granted her enormous privileges normally only reserved for a king's 'Great Wife'. She was revered throughout the land by all generations.

Langazana, with the *inkatha,* did not reside with the King at Ondini. She lived instead at the esiKlebheni royal homestead south of the White Mfolozi River. Only at times of national gatherings, such as the *umKhosi* festival or when the army mustered for war, did she bring it to the King's *ikhanda.* It would be taken into the *isigodlo* and hidden away inside a special hut known as the eNkatheni, placed on the ground at the back where it was believed the ancestral spirits gathered. Cetshwayo would enter the hut whenever he needed to discuss important matters with his inner council, or during the great feasts that celebrated the nations harvest, where he would bind himself with the *inkatha's* enormous mystical powers and communicate with the spirits of his forebears, to seek their advice or approval. Langazana herself would remain outside, denied permission to enter, and she would wait anxiously for him to finish; this would be one of the few times when she would be out of sight of the *inkatha.* She would fret, she would hold her head in anguish, but she dared not intrude.

On this day, the day of the 'dead' moon, Cetshwayo had disappeared into the hut for much longer than usual. Earlier, runners had brought him the first news that his warriors were attacking the white men's camp at Isandlwana, and at the urging of his chief izidunas he had gone to seek strength from the *inkatha,* to increase the fighting prowess of the army.

In the huts dark and shadowy interior Cetshwayo squatted over the coil, his eyes aglow with reflected firelight from the glowing embers of the cooking fire. On the clay floor before him lay the inhlendla spear.

Concentrating his mind, he allowed himself to be absorbed into the darkness. He could feel the strength enamating from the *inkatha* in waves, washing over him like warm air.

He breathed slowly. Cleared his mind. And waited patiently.

CHAPTER 40

THE CAMP. 1:35pm-1:55pm.

As the killing and bloodletting went on at the base of Isandlwana, British soldiers and Zulu warriors struggling to overcome one another in those final, desperate moments, as the battle reached its zenith, nature seemed to sit in judgement of those locked in deadly combat. The moon slowly glided across the face of the bright, dazzling sun, temporarily blotting out the ball of fire. Indeed, as one African folk-tale would one day proclaim: God closed his eyes, for He could not bear to look on the horrors that mankind was inflicting upon itself.

With Major Stuart Smith and his second-in-command Lieutenant Curling cutting a path for them through the throng of Zulus, the two cannons somehow managed to reach the camp. They had lost several men along the way, either thrown clear or dragged off and stabbed, and only a handful of gunners remained; they clung on with all of their strength, their bodies soon bruised and bleeding from the violence of this crazy dash to safety.

Edward Chisolm thought it would never end. Each bump in the ground, each rock they passed over, each dip and gully, sent painful jolts through his body like he was being hit in the ribs. He did not know for how much longer he could hold on. His hands and arms seemed to vibrate from where he gripped the metal screw behind the gun-barrel, and his knuckles bled where the skin had been rubbed off. Vaguely, he was aware that he was yelling. But so too were those around him. The noise of the wheels bouncing over the ground, the grinding of metal hinges protesting, the clattering of the limbers and the pounding of hooves all came together in one horrendous clamour, so that his whole world became a wall of sound interspersed with brief glimpses of the fighting raging on around them.

At last they broke through the mass of struggling men and entered the lines of tents beyond. The two cannons careered through the camp, smashing through equipment and snapping tent lines, ripping down white canvas and dragging all manner of things in their wake. Cooking fires were sent flying, their burning embers scattering in all directions. Here and there tents caught alight causing further alarm and panic. Sacks of grain and flour were torn to pieces under the wheels, boxes of supplies crushed. Mens personal possessions, clothing, smoking pipes, trinkets, letters from home, were wrecked or lost forever. The trail of destruction caused by their passage was endless.

The drivers tried to direct the horse teams towards the nek, realizing that they had to make their escape along the road to Rorke's Drift, the only route back to the border. Controlling the animals took all of their skill and expertise for the horses seemed to be infested with fear, charging headlong away from the carnage. Just ahead of them Major Smith gave immeasurable assistance by finding the easiest path through the congested campsite, shouting out at anyone who blocked their way to make room. Flashing his sword above his head, and with blood slipstreaming from his wounded arm, he led them around the tents and then between the maze of waggons on the saddle below Isandlwana's southern ramparts. They finally made it to the road, turning westwards. The two guns raced over the small rise over the nek. They picked up speed on the flatter ground beyond having finally left the fighting behind.

Or so they thought.

Just when they were sure the worst was over they were struck another terrible blow.

The dirt road back to Rorke's Drift meandered away through the rolling hills ahead of them, twisting and turning around the contours of the land. The valley immediately to the rear of Isandlwana was high and stony, cut up with numerous donga's, and it was here that a dreadful sight awaited them.

Moving down towards them was the awesome spectacle of what could only have been the Zulu right horn, thrown out secretively whilst their attention had been focused on their front. It was a chilling sight for Major Smith and his men. They quickly calculated that in only a matter of minutes the lead warriors would be coming charging around the southern tip of the mountain, sneaking in through the camps unguarded rear, to ultimately fall upon their comrades from behind. Yet they did not have time to warn them. To turn back now would mean the end.

Even worse than this they could see that one Zulu regiment had allready cut the road where it swung a little to the north, blocking off their planned escape route back to Natal.

The Zulu net was about to close in. And if they did not hurry, they would be caught, spiked on the two horns.

There was only one option left. The river, thought Major Smith, lay approximately six miles south west of the camp as the crow flies, and as they could no longer escape via Rorke's Drift then they would have to force their way over the hilly landscape along an alternative route. It would be a nightmare of a journey, trying to take the two guns over such formidable terrain, but it was either that or be butchered.

So, without once stopping, he pointed his sword away to his left indicating their new course.

"TO THE RIVER!" he roared, and turned his horse off the track, galloping hard and glancing back to see them following him.

They swept down the flank of the broad stony hill this side of the roadway, the going underfoot difficult for both mounted men and footsoldiers. Allready there were a sprinkling of other men fleeing from the fighting, mostly black levies but with a few white waggon conductors -civilians who saw it as their right to leave whenever they saw fit, not being tied to any particular regiment like the Imperial Infantry - amoungst them. They ran in headlong flight down the rocky slopes, tumbling and falling occasionally but quickly picking themselves up again. Through this mayhem, this frenzied stampede, came the two artillery guns.

They managed to get over the first rise and found themselves in a shallow gully, and the drivers, following Major Smith's example, followed its course as it snaked down through dense bush. Riding on ahead once more the major forced his horse quickly on, shouting over his shoulder for his men to keep up.

Suddenly, the ground underneath his horse's hooves gave way. Major Smith saw to his horror that the shallow channel had unexpectedly opened up into a deep chasm some twenty feet deep, the edges of which were hidden by the undergrowth. He cried out and flung himself clear of his saddle.

He landed in the dirt, his uniform ripping as it snagged on a branch. Scraping for a purchase with his heels he just managed to stop himself before he went over the edge, a cloud of dust rising around him. His horse was not so fortunate.

He watched as the animal disappeared from sight, listening to its high-pitched cries as it tumbled into the deep cutting, ending in a loud crunch of dislodged rocks and splintered bone. There was no need to look over the edge for he knew the horse was dead, or beyond help, and besides which he did not have time. Instead he jumped to his feet and turned, desperately waving his arms to warn the guns coming on behind.

Too late.

The second team just about had time to react, their driver pulling the lead horse aside to avoid disaster, but in doing so the limber and gun crashed into a large boulder and their right hand wheels went flying. The wooden frame of the limber disintergrated and the gun carriage snapped around ninety degrees, breaking off at the lunette to go spinning away in spectacular fashion. The men clinging on were flung free, dashed onto the rocks, some to be killed outright while others left dazed and semi-concious. The horses were hit by debris from the limber and they too suffered horrible injuries, the driver crushed underneath their flaying hooves.

Just in front of them, the first team were carried forward into the chasm, the momentum of their flight contributing to their misfortune. Major Smith watched helplessly as the whole mass of men and horses and precious equipment went arching through the sky in a brief moment of breathtaking, gravity-defying flight, before they crashed down into the chasm. The sound was horrendous; the earth was surely being ripped asunder?

Still clinging onto the elevating screw, Edward Chisolm barely had time to whisper a farewell to the world before he saw the opposite rockface come racing at him.

After that all was black.

Back at the camp Lieutenants Davies and Henderson had finally succeeded in finding more ammunition. Sent back by Colonel Durnford earlier, they had wasted an awful lot of time searching for their own supply waggons but because they had not arrived until long after the NNH had departed across the plain knowbody knew precisely where they had been placed. First of all they looked for their tents, thinking the ammunition would be there, but these had not yet being pitched and so next they went off towards the waggon park. Still having no luck, they rode towards the carbineers camp, and here, amidst the camp equipment, they eventually came across a discarded ammunition box. It had allready being opened and now contained only about two hundred rounds, an inadequately small amount for their men; but it would have to do.

Yet all of this hunting around had taken a long time.

When they were eventually ready to ride back out to the donga they saw that the line was allready falling apart, men racing back into the camp hotly pursued by the Zulus. Everybody was becoming intermingled, no single unit maintaining its cohesion apart from a company of redcoats up on the lower slopes of Isandlwana. Reigning in their horses, the two officers and the black horsemen with them looked around for their commander, hoping to rejoin Durnford. But the situation was deteriorating fast. Even had they been able to reach their comrades the pitifully small supply of ammunition they had acquired would not last long.

They decided instead to stay where they were and see if they could create a rallying point for others to converge upon. Quickly, Davies led them south across the dirt track and up onto the side of the stony hill above the 1/24th camp. From here, they began to fire over the tents below them, giving whatever assistance they could. They noticed a group of Imperial infantry trying to retreat along the dirt road surrounded by a thick mass of Zulu warriors, the white soldiers obviously attempting to draw in towards the camp.

Lieutenant Davies directed their fire down upon the Zulus there, his men carefully picking off targets. It was all they could do.

A few minutes earlier he had seen the two artillery guns come racing through the tents, and now he saw following in their wake the dark, bulky shape of the ambulance wagon. He watched it briefly come flying down the track and up onto the nek with twenty or so Zulus charging after it, and what he saw next was so gruesome that he thought he would be sick.

Surgeon Major Shepherd had seen that the game was up. For him, it became brutally clear when he saw the Zulus break through and begin pouring into the tents, stabbing at the wounded laid out on the ground infront of the hospital tent. Without the slightest hesitation, he ordered the ambulance wagon to be quickly loaded up with as many patients as possible, and his ordelies in their panic unceremoniously shoved in a half dozen men with a variety of injuries, ignoring their groans of agony. Then shouting at the driver to ride as fast as he could go, and choosing one of his senior medics to go with them, Shepherd sent them on their way.

They followed the artillery guns, but being so overloaded they were soon left behind, and it was as they were cresting the nek that the chasing Zulu warriors caught them.

The uMbonami *ibutho* had been the first into the camp and so elated were they at this success that they ran amok amoungst the tents, stabbing at everything that moved, be it man or beast. When they saw the strange looking cart start off they went racing after it, determined that none should escape. Running alongside, one warrior threw his spear at the young driver, and his aim was true. The blade sank into the man's ribcage, causing him to cry out and sit bolt upright. He let go of the reins as he tried to pull it out, his teeth gritted. When the assegai finally came free with a horrible sucking sound he flung it back and then reached down for the reins. But they had disappeared down underneath the horse's hooves, and he just could not reach them.

The Zulu warrior saw his chance. Leaping up onto the canvas side of the ambulance he struck the driver with his shield, knocking him senseless. His body sagged, and then slithered off the seat to be crushed into a bloody morass beneath the wheels.

More Zulus dashed forward, freshly emboldened by his daring. They attacked the horses, stabbing and slashing at them mercilessly, bringing them to a slithering halt on their knees. They quickly finished the poor animals off, cutting their stomachs wide open in an orgy of violence.

Then they turned their attention to the patients inside.

One of those cowering within was the young soldier shot in the calf while fighting alongside Private Brooks a short while earlier. He had been stretchered back unconscious, coming too whilst in the middle of having his leg stitched and still protesting his innocence about the accusation of being drunk. Still bemoaning his fate, for he knew he would probably be up on a charge after the battle was over, the lad had suddenly found himself being virtually thrown into the rear of the ambulance with several others. Not quite sure what was happening but guessing they were being taken to the rear where they could be better cared for, he had heard the sudden commotion outside and then felt the wagon slew to a halt. For several seconds they all stared at one another, their various injuries (some serious, some, like his, not so serious) temporarily forgotten. Then the tall and lean medical orderly who was with them moved towards the flap at the rear to see why they had halted. Bending over to avoid the low roof he pulled back the canvas.

To be confronted by several spear-wielding Zulus who crowded the entranceway, jostling one another to peer inside at those within.

The orderly moved to block their way, a look of outraged indignation upon his face. "What in blazes do you think you are doing?" he asked in English. "These are wounded men-"

He never finished the sentence.

One of the Zulus struck out at him with a heavy knobkerry, cracking open his skull and splattering the canvas walls with his brains. The medic fell back spreadeagled on the wooden deck, one of his legs twitching spasmodically, his eyelids fluttering.

There was sudden pandomonium from the patients. Screaming, they flung themselves against the far wall as the Zulu warriors poured in, their assegais stabbing fast. But there was knowhere for them to escape. They were trapped.

Within seconds the inside of the ambulance wagon resembled an abattoir, hot steaming carcasses piled high at the back. The young soldier crawled into the furthest corner and tried to hide beneath them, but they still found him.

He pleaded with them to spare him. "No, no, no, NO! PLEASE NO!"

But they still killed him.

They slit open his stomach.

"Ngadla!" they cried triumphantly - I have eaten!

Lieutenant Harry Davies, watching from his position up on the stony hill, spun away appalled at the sight. He glanced down towards the fighting going on all around the base of Isandlwana, and he witnessed countless other scenes of similar brutality. He looked across to his friend, Lieutenant Henderson, who caught his glance and looked back.

"It is over I think!" he called. "There's nothing left to fight for here! What shall we do?" Henderson followed his gaze down into the maelstrom below, then back to his companion. He gave no answer.

But his silence spoke volumes. In unvoiced agreement, the two officers silently turned and galloped away, taking their few men with them. They rode south. For the river.

Lieutenant Coghill, seated on his horse beside the road, watched the small party leave the battlefield. For one moment he thought about calling out and ordering them back, surprised that they were going while the fighting was still raging, but when he saw the Zulus sweeping through the tents to the north he too came to the conclusion that this battle, if not the war, was all but lost. And, after all, they were volunteers; they had their farms and their families to think of and could not be expected to stay until the end. Not like Imperial soldiers.

Blinking away sudden tears which had embarrassingly appeared in his eyes, Coghill trotted into the 1/24th camp, ignoring the jolting pain in his knee. As of yet his injury had prevented him from joining the action directly but he saw that things were now so serious that it was his duty to lend a hand, limited though his contribution would be. First however there was something he had to do.

The noise of the battle was deafening as he rode in between the tents, his eyes searching for somebody. More and more men were running passed him, making for safety, and he had to force his way against the flow in what became an ever increasing struggle to control his panicky horse. After a few more moments he reached down and grabbed one of them, one of the 24th's company cooks.

"Tell me, have you seen the Colonel's groom?" he asked.

"Let me go, the black heathens are almost on us!" the man blurted back.

Coghill gave him a violent shake. "Get a hold of yourself, you're still a soldier you hear! Now tell me, Colonel Glyn's groom? Do you know where he is?"

"Fighting somewhere. I saw him... I think."

"Show me."

"But-"

"SHOW ME!"

Reluctantly, the fat cook led Coghill through the maze of tents, his eyes large and wild with fear, his body reeking of sweat. Eventually, they came upon a group of men standing atop one of the wagons and firing towards the Zulus working their way forward. Amoungst them was the man that Lieutenant Coghill was looking for.

He called him over and then addressed the two of them.

"Men, things look bad, I won't deny that. The camp is in serious danger. Yet despite that certain duties have to be adhered to, and it is my responsibility to see that the Colonel's belongings, his personal effects, do not fall into enemy hands. We must try and save what we can whilst we have time. I want the pair of you to pack his tent away in that wagon, and his things too. His chest, his mirror, his bone-handled cutlery set, and his private letters. You do not have long I fear so dispense with tidiness, just get them loaded up. Is that clear?"

The two men nodded.

"Good. The Colonel will be much gratified by our kind consideration, I'm sure. Keep your chins up you hear. You're British soldiers of Her Majesty's Army. I shall be back shortly to see how you are getting on."

He spun his horse away and the men set to work immediately.

Sitting upright in his saddle, Coghill pulled out his revolver and rode into the smoke and dust of battle.

By some miracle Lieutenant Pope and the remnants of G. Company had made it back to the tents on the forward slope of the nek. There were now pitifully few of them left, having been reduced from a reinforced company to little more than a platoon. Bloody and bowed and so exhausted that they could barely stand, they fought resolutely on, still not beaten. They had long since run out of ammunition and now only had their bayonets and clubbed rifles and fists with which to fight.

A few minutes ago the soldier that Lieutenant Pope had been supporting had died. His life had simply trickled away with his blood, his body sagging and then going limp, and he had gently laid him upon the ground. Standing erect again, Pope had momentarily stared at his shaking hands. They were red and sticky. Quickly he wiped them on his tunic. He breathed heavily, trying to expel his revulsion and get a grip. Now was not the time to go to pieces.

Back in control of himself he had continued to take his dwindling command backwards along the roadway, edging closer and closer to the tents. To him and his men they represented a place of sanctuary, a goal for them to reach, an illogical notion that if they could only get into the camp then all would be fine; yet even as they told themselves this they were aware that this was a futile hope, a stupid and unrealistic thing to think. Yet it was the only thing that drove them on. To have abandoned these thoughts would have been to go against the most primal instincts of human life - to strive for survival, no matter what it took.

In its way this was their final defence.

They fought on with redoutable courage and tenacity. It seemed to the Zulus who strived to overcome them that these men were not human, but were white devils, the way they stood firm and looked death in the face without flinching. The warriors had them completely surrounded but still could not break them.

After what seemed an age the rag-bag group of survivors reached the lines of tents and they joined with their fellow companies who had converged to the same spot. There were a sizeable number of men here putting up a stout fight, their officers showing great skill in keeping them together. Nevertheless, they were still in a dire, dire predicament.

H. Company had managed to maintain their discipline during their withdrawal from the rocky knoll, despite losing their colour-sergeant and twenty men. With Zulus to their front and right they had retreated up the gently sloping ground before the camp, angling towards the nek. Once there they had used the cover that the tents provided to reform their line, their flanks turned back and anchored on the base of the stony hill, and poured a heavy fire into the enemy again. The Zulus were brought to a sharp halt, their charge broken up by their accurate marksmanship, and this allowed more groups of redcoats and mounted men to come in and bolster their stand. Colonel Pulleine was with them, standing up in his stirrups and looking over the heads of his men, pointing out weak spots here and there and plugging them with any spare men such as servants, wagon conductors, bandsmen, shoesmiths and such like as he could find. He had overcome his earlier moment of panic although the pain of seeing his battalion destroyed before his eyes was still there. Maybe he, like the rest of the men, had accepted their fate, and once he had come to terms with this his mind seemed to clear. Whereas before he had been hesitant and slow to respond, unsure of his own abilities, now he began to show his true colours. Cool-headed and issuing brisk, clear orders, he was at the pinnacle of self-control.

To Lieutenant Melvill, and Lieutenant Coghill, to James Brickhill the interpreter and Smith-Dorrien the transport officer who had somehow found their way through the scrum to join their stand, to Captain Wardell and the other men of H. Company, including young Charlie Noakes and his friend Robert Metcalfe, to the few survivors of Lieutenant Pope's company and Mostyn and Cavaye's boys of F and E. Company, Owen Brooks amongst them, and to all the other men and officers who fought alongside him, professional soldiers and civilians alike, he was simply magnificent.

When he returned to camp for the second time, this time with the Edendale and Hlubi Troop's in tow, Colonel Durnford could not believe that their whole defensive perimeter had collapsed so quickly. His own retreat from the donga had been unavoidable for the Zulus had been on the point of outflanking him, but to his alarm this had precipitated a panic-stricken withdrawal by the whole camp force. Instead of bringing in his companies stage by stage, with one covering the other, Colonel Pulleine had apparantly ordered a general retreat which had soon developed into a rout. Even before they could reform with their backs to the mountain the enemy were intermingled with the infantry, and their formations lost all their shape.

In an instant he recognized the magnitude of the disaster about to befall them. A tight knot suddenly formed in his stomach and the inside of his mouth felt very dry.

The battle was beyond rescue. The camp would fall. He knew there was nothing they could do to change this. Yet there was still a chance that a large proportion of those still alive might be able to extract themselves, to get through this hell and live to fight another day. If only they could fall back to a stronger position where they could rally and laumch a counterattack, or await the arrival of reinforcements, then they should at least salvage something of their honour and stop an invasion of Natal. It was the best they could hope for. But in order to do this he and Colonel Pulleine had to co-ordinate their movements, to gather in as many men as possible and form a united body. So first thing he had to do was to find Pulleine and confer with him.

"Sergeant Major!"

Simeon Kambule was by his side in moments.

"Keep your men together the best you can. I must find the Colonel, but whilst I am gone you must get that ammunition we desperately need. Try our own camp but don't spend too long looking around, just get some from somewhere. Quartermaster Pullen or Quartermaster Bloomfield should be able to spare some."

He did not wait for a response but turned and galloped through the crush of men, leaving the Sergeant-Major and his men behind.

When the lines of men had come in those on the far left, with the exception of the NNC, had retreated in good order, keeping up their fire as they fell back. Younghusband's company had been helped by the steep and rocky flank of the mountain which acted as a natural bastion from which they could blunt the enemy's first rushes, and they made the most of their good fortune even though they soon started to take casualties from the Zulus' sheer persistance. The horsemen of the Zikhali Troop, led by Lieutenant Raw and Captain Shepstone, being further out where the ground was flatter, had to put their trust in their mounts to get them to safety. They raced in towards the tents at that end of the camp, weaving in and out between the fleeing native infantry who were running pell-mell in a blind panic. Turning every thirty yards to fire a volley they succeeded in stopping the first zulu wave just long enough for them to make it down to the roadway in one piece.

Pausing to glance around, George Shepstone was numbed by the scale of the Zulu breakthrough. It seemed that nothing would stop them. Everywhere he looked, regiment after regiment was lapping around the edges of their campsite, squeezing in like some giant fist. The Zulu chest - or the *isifuba* as he knew the correct term to be - was charging after the redcoat companies in the centre, in some places catching and overtaking them. Further away along the dirt road, and below it out past the stony hill, came the left horn; it swept forward mercilessly, engulfing all before it. And the right horn... he turned in his saddle to look for it...

The Zulu right horn? Where was it?

One wing of an attacking Zulu force was always thrown out secretively, he knew. It was a tactic that had worked time and time again, their enemies fooled into turning to meet the chest and remaining horn whilst they sneaked up on them unsuspectingly, usually from the rear.

Good God Almighty!

The truth, when it struck, shook him to his very core.

There was only one place that it could be and that was behind the mountain. Masked by its large bulk they had almost sprung their trap to perfection, the two horns about to meet below the camp and trap them all within their enveloping arms.

If that happened... not a single man still fighting amongst the tents would get out alive.

He looked back over his left shoulder towards the steep southern shoulder of Isandlwana, half expecting to see this new Zulu assault come charging in, but as yet there was no sign of it. He knew that they only had a few minutes to act. He also knew that whoever volunteered to act as this blocking force, placing themselves directly infront of this charge, would have very little chance of pulling through. It was, he understood even as he made up his mind, a suicide mission.

But for the good of the remaining survivors, to give the rest of the force a slim hope of getting clear - and now it was just a matter of trying to save as many people as possible - he knew it had to be done.

Quickly he called for as many men as possible to accompany him, a mixture of Sikhali riders and fleeing Natal native infantry, although it was hard to bring the latter under control; many of them simply ignored him and ran on. When he had approximately one hundred men with him he led them back through the wagon park and up over the crest of the nek, around the rear of the mountain where the ground was steep and strewn with boulders, wild aloe plants and thorn bushes.

"Spread out men! Find yourselves a good spot and keep your heads down! Don't cluster together! Let them come on!"

Nervously they did as he told them, the horsemen reluctant to dismount but doing so dutifully, the NNC looking terrified and shivering in their fear.

They settled into their positions, guns and assegais raised, and waited.

They did not have long before they got their first glimpse of the Zulu right horn. They heard it first, the peculiar swishing sound of a large body of men running through tall grass, coming closer and closer. Craning their necks, Captain Shepstone and his small band peered forward. A moment or two later and they finally saw them.

They came on fast. Several lines of skimishes screened the main bulk of the charging regiment, making excellant use of any available cover, snaking through the grass and slipping around the rocks with superb discipline. It seemed that they grew out of the very ground. Carrying their large shields - black with white spots - and an assortment of rifles, spears and knobkerries, they were soon within range of Shepstone's men. As of yet they did not seem to have spotted them, hidden as they were in their commanding position high up on the slope, and when the British opened up it came as a shocking surprise.

Suddenly, unexpectedly, the uNokhenke *ibutho* found itself under heavy fire. Their advance down the back of the mountain had been completely unopposed so far but when they heard the sound of bullets striking the rocks around them, and warriors began to go down, they came to a crashing halt. For a few moments they crouched down in complete bewilderment, looking this way and that, the shock of this sudden ambush robbing them of all reason. Yet they were quick to recover. Within seconds their chief *induna* had pinpointed the source of the firing, noticing the tell-tale puffs of smoke amongst the boulders on the high ground above them.

He called forward several companies of his best warriors and directed them to dislodge the enemy soldiers, to get amoungst the rocks and finish them off. They could, he told them in his fiery way, not afford this delay; not if they were to join the main battle raging on the far side of the mountain, and to complete their encircling movement and prevent the enemy escaping.

These words, together with their first opportunity to prove their worth, were enough to spur them on. They crept forward and began to move up the banking.

Shepstone saw them coming. So too did his men, and those armed with rifles began to carefully pick them off. Firing his own carbine he was satisfied to see that the native infantry were for once holding their ground. Even those only armed with their traditional weapons kept to their positions, waiting their chance to join in. He saw one group of three or four lay low until several zulus had crept within their midst, utterly unaware that they were surrounded, and then they leapt on them with astounding speed to club and stab at them ruthlessly. Others copied them, a tactic that worked many times. He wondered at this new-found courage they displayed, asking himself why they suddenly stuck by him when all of their comrades were fleeing. Yet the answer eluded him. All he could think was that something in their nature had changed in the blink of an eye, their own boldness spawned by the countless acts of selfless courage taking place around them. Perhaps they felt a new bond with their white officers, a brotherhood that spanned race and creed. Whatever the reason, Captain George Shepstone felt touched by it.

If courage and guts alone were enough to stop the Zulu charge then they would easily win the day. Yet their ammunition, already depleted after their long spell of fighting, was on the point of running out completely. He noticed as he reached for another round from his bandolier that he only had enough left for about seven or eight shots, and that elsewhere several of his men were allready turning to their comrades to borrow a few. When their pleas came to nought they threw their carbines aside and drew out their hunting knives, holding them at the ready or sharpening them on the rocks, a steely determination in their brown eyes.

Shepstone loosed another shot at a Zulu warrior leaping up the slope towards his hiding place, and watched as he jerked back like some crazy marionette to go tumbling down over the slabs of granite leaving a trail of blood behind him. He snapped his lever down to eject the spent case and pushed a new round into the chamber.

Around him, the level of firing began to trail away in a feeble splutter as more and more men fired their final shots.

Shepstone knew they did not have long to go.

As the Zulus moved closer.

Under the cool guidance of their senior NCO, Sergeant-Major Simeon Kambule, the Edendale men searched high and low for a fresh supply of ammunition. First off, they hunted about amongst the tents of their fellow mounted colleagues in the area of camp just above the road but failed to find any, just as Henderson and Davies had struggled earlier. Also, by this stage the fighting was raging hand-to-hand closeby and the Zulus seemed on the verge of overrunning the defenders here, and so he decided to lead them across the dirt track and try their luck at the 1/24th's reserve supply instead.

Within the chaos and confusion of battle, the noise, the dust, the whirlpool of running figures, they eventually came across a single wagon set apart from the rest near to the officer's mess tent. Here, standing guard over the stockpile of wooden ammo crates, was a young drummer boy. He fidgeted from foot to foot anxiously and wrung his hands together, his tiny features pale and sickly looking.

Simeon Kambule rode up to him quickly.

"Your bullets... my men need them... you give me some now?"

The drummer boy craned his neck and shielded his eyes from the muted but still bright sun. He took one look at the coloured NCO, noting his uniform and unit, and then shook his head.

"I'm sorry sir but I can't," he squeaked.

"But we need some to fight."

402

"I cannot sir," he repeated steadily, "Quartermaster Pullen told me that only soldiers from our battalion could draw fresh supplies from here."

Sergeant-Major Kambule thought about pushing the boy aside and helping himself to the crates, of using his domineering presence and rank to good effect. But he only considered this for a brief moment. Despite the obvious difference in age and seniority it was completely against all military etiquette to force this youngster to disobey a direct order from his own superior, and what's more, it just wasn't right for a black man to exert any kind of authority in a situation like this- even over a boy of fifteen or sixteen.

"I will be in all kinds of trouble if I let you, the Quartermaster was in a fearfull mood when he left me," the drummer boy offered by way of an apology.

Sergeant-Major Kambule waved the words away, thinking fast. He noticed that lying in the grass were a number of loose rounds apparantly dropped whilst several boxes had been opened. It seemed that they had not being missed by anybody and so he ordered his men, in their native tongue, to quickly pick them up. As they hurried to obey he turned his attention back to the drummer boy.

"I am taking my men away. This battlefield belongs to the Zulus. Look, others try to escape also, there is no point in remaining here to die. Come with us boy. It is foolish to stay. You have done your duty well."

But the drummer boy shook his head once more. He stood up straight and puffed out his chest like a model soldier. "My Quartermaster has not told me to leave my post. He will be back soon with fresh orders."

"What fresh orders? The camp is destroyed, but our Good Lord has granted us a chance to escape. Save yourself."

This time the youngster did not look back. He glanced off to the side, simply repeating... "He will be back soon..."

Sighing heavily, Kambule shook his head and turned to inform his men that they were leaving. They had fought well, he told them, but sadly the time had come to try and save themselves... they would, he assured them, get another chance to defeat the enemy. But not on this day. They would still have to show immense courage and discipline to escape in one piece so it was essential they stick with him and follow orders closely. With God on their side they might make it.

He led them away then, leaving the drummer boy behind.

He doubted if he would ever set eyes on the poor mite ever again.

At the same time that the Edendale men were leaving several other individuals also decided to get out while the going was good. One of these was the young transport officer Horace Smith-Dorrien. He had given up the task of doling out ammunition packets to the men on the line the instant the retreat had been sounded, hurrying back on his tired horse, and by the time he had turned to regain his breath and reorientate himself the defences were allready buckling under a fresh Zulu attack. What followed had been one nightmare after another as the fighting had whirled around him, ulus, British redcoats, their native levies and mounted volunteers all mixed up together. Somehow he had reached the lower portion of the camp, gravitating towards what appeared to be a sizeable stand led by Colonel Pulleine, but it had quickly dawned on him that the fighting had by then taken on a more desperate nature. All thoughts of actually winning the battle seemed to have evaporated in the space of just a few minutes. Now it was simply every man for himself.

These sentiments were echoed by the words of one of his friends in the transport department, a civilian wagon-driver who fought alongside him on foot. In between firing his hunting rifle he looked up at him, saying out of the corner of his mouth, "the game is up. If I had a good horse I would ride straight for Maritzburg," before winking a farewell and launching himself into a fresh melee of tussling bodies.

It was this bleak appraisal of the hopelessness of their position that spurred Smith-Dorrien into making the decision to leave. Others, he noted, were already doing the same, some on foot and some riding horses. It occurred to him that only those mounted on good, strong animals would have any real chance of reaching safety, which probably cut down his own odds of getting through alive for his horse was quite exhausted allready after more than twenty-four hours of almost non-stop riding too and fro. Still, he thought adamantly, he should at least give it a go.

Taking one final glance around he dug in his spurs and galloped towards the nek.

As he passed over the low rise, revolver in hand, he rode around a shallow hollow in the ground where he noticed Surgeon-Major Shepherd crouched amongst several wounded men. Busy dressing their injuries despite the bullets flying just overhead he stole a quick glance up as he heard Smith-Dorrien's horse go thundering by. For the briefest of moments their eyes met, and then Shepherd gave a jaunty little salute and nodded, a slight and somewhat sad smile on his face, before returning to his work. Smith-Dorrien wanted to shout out, to urge him to try and escape too, but his charging horse had already taken him beyond earshot and he knew it would have been no use had Shepherd heard him anyway; the surgeon was a gentleman and a professional to the end and would not even contemplate leaving the field whilst there were still wounded men needing his skills.

Smith-Dorrien urged his horse on even faster, his gritted teeth setting his face in a rigid grimace.

Just beyond the nek he saw that the roadway ahead was already swarming with Zulu warriors, with even more moving down immediately behind the mountain. There appeared to be some kind of fighting going on here as though somebody was making a last ditch attempt to hold this new attack back, but Smith-Dorrien - his mind already filled with morose thoughts of defeat -was convinced their effort would end in failure. He veered away from this action, partly to avoid being drawn in by it and also because the way to Rorke's Drift was now blocked. Instead he forged on through the broken ground to the south, his horse - like he himself was - seeming to be drawn towards the distant river that lay somewhere out there.

Following close on his heels came James Brickhill, the interpreter.

For him, his dreams of going off to seek his glory, to find adventure, had come crashing down around his ears. Oh, what his brother would say! He had warned him how foolish he was being, imploring him not to leave on some damned stupid crusade just to prove that he had come of age. He had always showed too much recklessness, he'd scoffed. Not thinking things through. How right he had been!

Brickhill had been so full of confidence over the last three months since leaving home to join the war, finding good employment with the British and making many fine friends, more

405

than happy with his lot in life. Army life had certainly been more exciting than those dreary years spent working at Knox's store and many times, usually at night when he was curled up in his tent, he had told himself that he would never go back, not when the war was over, not ever. This kind of existence, marching across enemy territory, fighting a fierce and worthy opponent like the Zulu, was just too appealing to give up.

But today everything had gone wrong.

A morning that had begun with so much promise (for they had been waiting for a chance to give battle to the Zulu Army like this) was quickly turning into an afternoon of sheer hell.

And it galled him to think it, but right now he wished he were back home with his brother to protect him.

If this was what warfare was all about... then he no longer wanted a part of it.

All around was death, and carnage, and wanton butchery, and noise, and fear. Men fighting or running or pleading with the enemy for their lives.

There was a sudden increase in the level of the battleground din as yet another Zulu charge rolled in and Brickhill watched the shrinking British lines pushed even further back through the tents, the men using their bayonets freely now. He could clearly hear the chants of the nearest Zulu warriors over the sound of fighting. "It is beaten!" they teased. "They are running! KILL THE PIGS!"

Brickhill rightly decided that it was time to get out.

He followed the example set by many others and joined the stream of fugitives heading along the road over the saddle, fleeing back the way they had come. It was fast becoming a rout as panic was starting to set in, the men casting aside all unnecessary equipment that might hinder their progress, only keeping a hold on their weapons. Brickhill found himself possessed with the same fear and soon he was at the heart of this blind stampede, shouting for his horse to ride faster, his hat blown clear and his blond hair streaming behind.

At the crest of the nek he noticed a group of Basuto riders firing steadily back into the camp, retreating in between each volley, slowly backpedalling down the slope below the road. He admired their pluck for showing such fortitude while others ran in headlong flight, and he saw at once that they were trying to gain a little time for those attempting to escape. One of which, he realized with shame, was himself.

Just then a riderless horse bumped into him, almost knocking him clean off his saddle, and he reached over and snatched up its reins to control the animal. When he had it calmed Brickhill looked swiftly around.

Closeby he saw a soldier come limping along. He turned every few feet to glance behind, a look of horror on his deathly-pale face. Brickhill waved his arm to get the man's attention.

"Here soldier! I have a horse for you! Climb up, or they'll be on top of you in no time!"

The infantryman came hurrying across, out of breath and very distressed but now with a faint glimmer of hope in his tearful eyes. "Thankyou my friend!" he panted in a quaky voice as he took the bridle. He hauled himself unelegantly up onto the horses back.

And promptly fell off again as his face exploded in an eruption of blood and bone and grey brain.

Brickhill felt himself being drenched in warm, sticky matter, specks of red splattering his spectacles. He cringed back in shock and shielded his face, and his spooked horse bolted away taking him clear of the terrible sight of the soldier's featureless corpse. He let the animal go and held onto its mane for purchase, all thoughts of stopping to offer assistance to others gone in a trifle.

"Oh God... sweet Mary..." he whispered to himself as he rode away from Isandlwana.

When Lieutenant Coghill returned to the wagon beside the officer's tents he was disgusted, though not surprised, to see that the fat cook had scarpered. He had left Colonel Glyn's groom to pack the column commanders belongings by himself, which he had dutifully done despite the fighting going on all around. Coghill saw that it was mostly loaded up with only the Colonel's tent needing to be struck and folded away.

He admired the soldier's dedication.

A pity, he thought bitterly, that it had all been for nothing.

Riding over he leaned down from the saddle. "Very good work private. You've done well, yet it seems we might have to wait a while before we make a move. Don't bother with any more. You had better return to your mates now."

The soldier looked up, knowing full well what he meant.

They exchanged crisp salutes, these two men from very different classes but caught here in the same nightmare, sharing the same emotions, and probably the same fate. Coghill then dismissed him and watched him jog away back to the fighting.

He had noticed more and more men fleeing over the last few minutes, taking a last gasp opportunity to leave. First a trickle, now a flood. It was understandable. There came a point in any battle when a cause was very obviously lost, when to stay and fight would achieve nothing but further losses for the defeated side. Then, when that moment was reached, there was no shame in leaving a battlefield.

Coghill's mind was a turmoil of thoughts right then as he considered his own destiny. He guessed that all around, hundreds of other men were struggling with identical private battles in their hearts, each man coming to his own decision. Whether to stay and die or leave and save oneself.

It was a very personal and lonely decision. Lieutenant Coghill made his.

He turned his horse and rode clear.

George Shepstone and his men were dead.

Their heroic attempt to hold back the tip of the Zulu right horn had only lasted for less than ten minutes, but this proved just long enough to allow those who recognized the danger early on the opportunity to break through and slip away, before their escape route was closed shut. History would not recognize their gallantry for over a hundred years, but many of those who survived this terrible day owed their lives, plus their futures, to this brave stand. So their sacrifice was not in vain.

Shepstone was the last to fall. He had used up the last of his bullets, and as several Zulus had closed with him he'd used his rifle butt as a club, swinging it against the lead warriors face. Turning, he'd managed to scramble up over the rocks to a higher spot just underneath the sheer krantz and here he turned to meet them, his hunting knife slashing from side to side, teeth bared in a fierce snarl. The Zulu warriors hesitated for they had already seen many of their friends fall at this man's hands.

Gezindaka kaMadikane, seeing his colleagues cowering, sneaked forward through the boulders until he was just a dozen feet away. Keeping low he raised one of his throwing spears and drew back his arm, holding his breath. Then he powered his shoulder forward and released the wooden shaft.

The *izijula* spear whispered through the air with a faint hiss and thudded into Shepstone's midriff. He dropped his knife as he was propelled backwards against a large stone slab, and he lay there for a brief moment staring up at the blue sky above, arms flung out to the sides as though nailed on a cross. He felt nothing.

The spear embedded in him did not kill Shepstone immediately, but it distracted him just long enough for the other Zulus to pounce. They leapt forward and finished him off.

Colonel Pulleine knew that the final moments of defeat were almost upon them. His battalion was dying around him, and like the mortally wounded thing that it was, it seemed to twitch spasmodically in its painful death-throes, instinctively fighting to its last gasping breath. He knew his own fate was sealed for even given the opportunity to escape he would not have taken it, not when so many of his boys had already fallen. It was his duty to stay. Similarly, the infantrymen of his five companies, plus the one attached company from their sister battalion, seemed reluctant to leave. They preferred to stand by him.

So, he thought with a peculiar warm flush inside, they would die together.

But before the end there was one further duty that needed taking care of.

Breaking away from the heart of the tempest he led Lieutenant Melvill back through the camp to the battalion guard tent. Ordering his friend to wait outside, Pulleine dismounted and ducked through the flap.

On a small table at the back was a small wooden plinth with an ornately carved stand lying on the top. Its purpose was to hold the battalions two cased Colours, the Regimental and the Queen's. On this day the Regimental flag was absent, having being left behind at Helpmekaar before the invasion had begun, but the Queen's

Colours were still there. The black leather case with its brass clasp at the end rested horizontally on the stand. As though lying in state.

Almost reverantly, Colonel Pulleine reached forward with both his hands and lifted it free. The Colours, rolled on its wooden staff in the protective case, was quite heavy. It was cumbersome to carry with all the weight at one end, the whole being maybe four feet in length.

Pulleine stood still for a moment and closed his eyes, ignoring the tumult outside, feeling totally calm. He breathed in deeply.

Then he turned and walked back outside.

Lieutenant Melvill watched him approach and his face became even more solemn, his eyes intense.

Stopping before his friend Colonel Pulleine passed the Queen's Colours up to him and Melvill took a hold of the case, lying it across his saddle and making himself as comfortable as possible. He already knew what was required, the reason for all of this, but he listened carefully as Colonel Pulleine gave him his instructions.

"Carry them away from this place Lieutenant. They must not fall into enemy hands. Ride hard for Natal and find sanctuary there."

Melvill did not need to respond. He just nodded.

"And Godspeed my friend."

The two of them saluted. Then Lieutenant Melvill jabbed his heels into his horse's flanks and galloped away, winding through the maze of tents.

Pulleine watched him go for several seconds.

Then he climbed back into his saddle, and went to seek his fate.

*　　　*　　　*

Durnford had been unable to find Pulleine in all the confusion. With the camps defenders now split into several seperate widely spaced fragments, and being driven back through the tents towards the nek, his movements were restricted. He had found it impossible therefore not only to reach the large stand south of the road where he was sure the Colonel would be but also to make his way back towards his own mounted basuto's. Instead he headed towards the closest body of troops, who fought back to back on the gentle slope below the saddle, a mixture of infantry, mounted Volunteers and Carbineers.

It was ironic, he thought momentarily, that his final moments should be spent with the very same white horsemen who so despised him after the debacle of Bushman's Pass. These troopers who had vowed never to forgive him, never to acknowledge his leadership. Odd too how they now appeared to gather around him at this time of great destiny. Was it his imagination or did their countenances hold expressions of appreciation rather than hate? Was he to be finally accepted as a worthy commander, now, at the very end? If so then it was the ultimate endorsement. How better could they express it than to rally around him, to fight with him, and to die alongside him?

Their respect of him, if that is what it was, had almost come too late. He would have but minutes to delight in it. But Durnford would carry it forward into infinity.

For the briefest of moments the white troopers paused, looking at him for guidance. "Now, my men," he said in a loud and vigorous voice, "let us see what you can do!"

CHAPTER 41

THE CAMP. 1:55pm-2:10pm.

It was the pain in his face that woke Gunner Chisolm. He jerked into conciousness with a loud groan. Something was crawling across one cheek, setting off the fiery agony there, and he swatted at the intrusive insect feebly. The tips of his fingers scraped against the bridge of his nose and a split second before the pain suddenly intensified to excruciating levels he realized the skin on that half of his face had been peeled away right down to the bone. And so his scream was a mixture of the torture and horror this caused.

After a few seconds the agony subsided to a more bearable level, and he then opened his eyes. His vision through one of them (on the same side where the injury was) seemed distorted as though he was gazing through red, splotchy water, and it also felt to be lower down somehow, near the level of his cheek. He dismissed this as unimportant right now, for to have dwelt on it too long would have revealed that it had infact being torn out and was dangling at the end of its nerve tendril. Instead, he glanced about to get his bearings.

He appeared to be lying at the foot of a steep and rocky crevasse, wedged in between two large boulders, and staring skywards. Piled all about were pieces of wood and iron, as well as several bloody red lumps which he did not at first recognize. Only when he stared harder and saw a slither of steaming intestine did he understand. Then it all came back to him.

Once again Edward Chisolm groaned, but this time from the horrible memories that came flooding back into his now lucid mind. He had no desire to think about them for too long and so he shut them out and turned his thoughts to more constructive things. Like, how long had he been here? How long had he been unconcious?

Not for very long, he quickly realized. Nearby was a part of the gun carriage, upended amoungst the boulders, and he saw that one of its wheels was still slowly turning after having come to rest at the bottom of the deep chasm. So, a few minutes, no more. Which meant that the chasing Zulus would not be far behind.

This suddenly spurred him on into moving. If he could just get to his feet and climb out of here then he might still have a chance. The injury to his face was bad, he would probably be disfigured for the rest of his days, but it wasn't necessarily life-threatening.

Before he made a move a noise above him caught his attention. Puzzled, Edward glanced straight up the rockf ace behind his head. What he saw there horrified him.

Dangling above him, whinnying in terror, were the half dozen horses that had pulled the gun and limber. Somehow their traces had caught on a protruding rock during the descent, snagging fast and saving them from being killed on the jagged boulders below. But now they hung there kicking their legs helplessly, caught and unable to free themselves.

It was a pityful sight made worse by the knowledge that knowbody would be able to help them, not soon enough to make a difference. Such was the cruelty of war. And he did not have time to ponder the matter further.

Edward hauled himself up into a sitting position and then grabbed the rocks to either side to hoist himself to his feet. And with a second agonized scream fell back.

Spasms of pain shot up his left leg, so bad that he almost blanked out. He gritted his teeth against it, the torture this caused in his jaw puny in comparison, and for a few seconds all he could do was gulp in lungfuls of air as his yell trailed away in a breathless shudder. Edward waited until the shock of pain fell away and then he craned his neck up off the ground to see through his one good eye what was wrong.

He saw that the skin just below the knee was split wide open, the cut deep and gory with blood pumping down his ankle to swill

413

about inside his boot. A slender piece of white bone showed through the mess, sticking right out from the gash where it had splintered on impact, and the skin to either side was shredded and tattered, as was his trouser leg.

The implications of this sickening wound were instantly apparant, and he cried..."no, no, no..." to himself in resignation.

So, this was it then.

Trapped at the bottom of a deep chasm, his leg broken, unable to climb out, waiting to either bleed to death or be assegaid when the Zulus found him here, his face crawling with flies and bugs. Not a nice way to go, he thought bitterly between the pain. It would have been better if it had been instant, not this prolonged and drawn out affair.

Unless...?

He saw the figure of a man high above, silhouetted against the sky on the edge of the gully. He appeared to be looking down at him. Waving. No, gesticulating, urging him on.

Encouraging him to give it one last go, to pull himself hand over hand up the steep gradient.

Perhaps he had a spare horse, Edward considered. If he could just get to the top.

Ignoring the pain he pulled himself onto his front and began to crawl upwards.

The cries of agony and despair had drawn Major Stuart-Smith towards the lip of the chasm.

He'd been about to set off on foot across country towards the river but instead when he'd heard the voice calling out woefully, followed by what sounded like a man weeping, he had stumbled across the rocky ground to look down into the deep gully. At first he could not pick out the source of the noise amidst the wreckage and dead bodies that lay scattered at the bottom, but then a slight movement caught his attention and his eyes fell upon the figure of a crawling man.

From up here Major Smith could not tell how badly injured the artillery man was. He noticed the way he dragged one of his legs, and that his face was a mask of red (preventing him from recognizing this man as the same one whom he'd shouted a warning to during the earlier melee) but the simple fact that he was still alive and able to move meant that as his senior officer, Smith had a duty to stay and help. He could not - would not - turn his back on one of his young charges.

He looked around to see if there was anybody nearby who could lend a hand, but there was knowone. Lying in the dirt not far away was his bent and battered sword, twisted out of shape, and he bent down to retrieve it. When he straightened again his gaze happened to drift across to the far side of the chasm, and here he saw, coming down off the dirt track, the first of the pursuing Zulus. He gasped aloud.

They were headed straight for them.

Smith realized that there wouldn't be time for him to climb down to the bottom and help his man, like he'd been intending. It would have taken several minutes just to pick his way down and then he would have been faced with an uphill struggle with a wounded man weighing him down. No, to do that would mean certain death for both of them for the Zulus would close with them before they made it back up. It would be better for him to climb up as fast as he could while he waited at the top.

Major Smith leant forward and called down into the dark rift in the earth.

"Climb faster man! Climb faster!"

All the while he kept one eye on the approaching Zulus.

Edward detected the barely restrained fear in the major's voice, and half guessing what was wrong he made the mistake of looking back over his shoulder. Just as he did the first Zulu warriors reached the brim directly overhead, and so alarmed was he by their closeness that he cried out in fear and lost his grip. He slid back down several feet before he regained a secure purchase again, but the slip sent fresh waves of agony through his entire being forcing tears from his single eye. He fought through the pain and pulled himself forward again, babbling incoherently to himself. He knew without looking that the Zulus had seen him for he heard their triumphant yell, just as he knew they would be clambering down the side of the chasm to reach him. Edward managed to haul himself another six feet up the sheer rocky slope before exhaustion and dismay overcame him.

It was no good.

He couldn't go on. The pain - and uselessness of it all - was too much to bear.

He sank down into the rocks, burying his bloodied face in the dirt so that he wouldn't have to see them coming, and waited for the Zulus to get him.

They soon did.

Their assegais stabbed furiously.

In the end it came as a relief.

"Bastards! Bloody butchers!" Major Stuart-Smith screeched as he watched the Zulus ritually disembowel the artilleryman. He kicked out at the ground in fury, sending pieces of shale cascading down the steep side of the fissure.

The Zulus crouching around the body, as well as those others busy stabbing at the other bodies lying about, looked up at him. They slowly came to their feet.

He noticed even more of them racing across the terrain from the direction of the camp just over the stony hill, charging after the fugitives. They saw him standing there - maybe his shouting aloud had drawn their attention - and a large number veered his way.

Major Smith backed up.

He lifted his puny and twisted sword in defence, then realized what a futile gesture this was. Throwing the useless weapon aside he turned and ran on.

*   *   *

The Zulus finally managed to overwhelm Pulleine and his men only after they had killed a great many of them by throwing their assegais at close range. Kept at bay by the soldiers thrusting bayonets, they had nevertheless forced their square through the tents and over the nek onto the slope beyond, killing them one by one.

Lieutenant Pope and a companion from G. Company tried to shoot their way out with their revolvers, but both of them fell dead doing so. Seeing his friend go down from a gunshot wound, Pope

416

emptied his sidearm at the nearest Zulu, grazing him on the side of the neck. Then he charged forward and threw himself bodily onto his opponent.

A sharp burning sensation in his chest made him leap back in surprise and Pope looked down to see a spear sticking into him, and so he dropped his gun and tried to pull it clear with both hands. With a supreme effort he almost succeeded in tearing it free, but then he dropped to his knees from the agony this caused, and the warrior darted forward and pushed it home with a fierce yell. Lieutenant Pope did not rise again.

All around men fought for their lives. The two horns of the Zulu Army had almost closed in behind them, very nearly cutting off their path to freedom. Now only a few managed to slip through the net. For the rest there was simply nowhere to go. Trapped here, they died here.

At the end there was nothing glorious about it.

It was ugly, it was foul, it was squalid.

Charlie Noakes and Robert Metcalfe were amongst the few men of H. Company who were still alive. Their commanding officer, Captain Wardell, was with them and his reassuring presence was priceless even though they knew the end was near. He kept glancing across at his dwindling command, winking and smiling at them. Mixed up with these were the survivors from all of the other companies who had succeeded in fighting their way over, bonding together and temporarily forgetting their fierce rivalry's

From somewhere within the crush appeared a familiar face. Robert Metcalfe watched in amazement as Private Owen Brooks scrambled towards them on his hands and knees, his uniform ripped in numerous places with blood seeping through from various cuts and abrasions. He had lost his rifle somewhere but had managed to find a bayonet, and he gripped it in one hand, grinning madly. Once he reached them he held out his free hand.

Robert hesitated for half a second, then pulled him to his feet.

"Thankyou!" Owen Brooks growled as he took his place alongside them.

Then, with undiluted ferocity, he proceeded to stab at any Zulu who came near. He pinned them through the neck or face, turning this way and that, and above the tumult of screams and gunshots Robert could clearly hear him laughing aloud.

He raised his gun and dropped a warrior coming forward through the clouds of dust and smoke, and the body fell onto the piles of dead building up infront. Next to him, Charlie used his rifle butt as a club, breaking a neck here or smashing a face there.

The fighting was relentless with the protagonists just feet apart.

Just behind them Colonel Pulleine paused to reload his revolver and it was as he was doing this that he was struck by a wild shot that caught him in the dead centre of his chest. With a gargled cry he crumpled forward, staggered, then went down into the grass. His lungs seemed to deflate as all of the air rushed out where they had been punctured, and his strength rapidly left his body, leaving him weak and still.

He tried to push himself to his knees but hardly got six inches off the ground before he keeled over onto his side.

Funnily, he felt no pain. Just a numbness all over.

Then the shadows crept in...

"The Colonel is down!" somebody shouted, and all of those still alive - whether on their feet and fighting, or lying mortally wounded - turned to sneak a quick look as if unwilling to believe this unless they saw for themselves that it was true. A ripple of shock and anger passed through them all. They each spun back to face the Zulus with renewed determination.

It seemed that the warriors knew they had killed somebody of great importance, that their enemy were now leaderless, and they guessed that their moment of total victory was upon them. So they charged forward again, ready to swamp the British square.

Owen Brooks bent low and picked up Colonel Pulleine's revolver and then fired point blank at a Zulu warrior's face. It disintergrated in a red spray. He fired a second time, but missed his new target, and was about to pull the trigger again when Robert Metcalfe ran his bayonet right through his shield and impaled the man for him. Not pausing, Brooks fired three shots in quick succession at a third Zulu, the rounds making a diagonal line across the warrior's stomach and chest. He went down flat, like a felled oak tree.

He looked from side to side to pick out where his next, and final shot, should go. But there were too many. They were being overrun.

They were finished.

Not even needing to think twice he raised the gun, placed the barrel against his own temple, and pulled the trigger.

Standing so close to him both Robert Metcalfe and Charlie Noakes were drenched with blood and brain. They stood there dripping with gore and shocked immobile for a second. They gasped in horror.

Then the Zulus reached them.

Ndlela kaSashangane and Mehlokazulu kaSihayo and the rest of the iNgobamakhosi poured through the piles of dead and twitching bodies and smashed into the line of white soldiers. Ndlela was still seething with fury and heartache after the death of his close friend Mnyamana and was becoming increasingly reckless in his attempts to 'stab' a white man. Upon reaching the tents his frustrations had been so severe that he found himself stabbing at anything, the tents, dead oxen, even sacks of mealie. Only a severe clip around the head by his chief *induna,* Sigcwelecwele kaMhlehleke accompanied by a barked command to keep charging, brought him to his senses. And so he pushed on. Soon finding himself at the forefront of their renewed charge with Mehlokazulu at his side.

Just as they finally reached the British square Ndlela saw one of the white men put a gun to his head and blow out his own brains. He cringed, more out of disgust than pity for several specks of blood splattered across his face. When he wiped his eyes clear he saw the young soldier with the blond hair immediately to his front hesitate and Ndlela, seeing his chance, sprang forward. Using his shield to hook the soldier's rifle upwards, throwing him off balance, he thrust his spear straight into the man's ribcage.

With his face just inches from that of his enemy Ndlela stared straight into the young man's eyes, seeing the fear and pain there. He twisted his spear. Warm blood splashed onto his hand as he pushed the blade in even deeper.

"uSuthu! Ngadla!" Ndlela was ecstatic.

Robert Metcalfe watched on in horror as his best friend twitched and bucked on the end of the assegai blade, mouth stretched wide in agony, eyes rolled back in his head. Charlie gave a loud grunt and coughed out a large globule of blood, then ever so slowly slid back off the spear and lay gasping on the ground.

"NO!" Robert screamed. "NO! PLEASE, NO!"

He leaped forward towards the warrior who had delivered the lethal strike and hit him in the jaw with the stock of his rifle, sending him reeling backwards. Robert followed through with a vicious kick to the man's solar plexus, felling him. Standing over the Zulu he used the tip of his bayonet to hook the bloody spear out of his hand, so that it went spinning away, and then he thrust down hard straight into his chest. The bayonet sliced straight through flesh and bone, piercing vital organs on the way down, and came out the back and into the ground beneath, pinning him there. Leaving the rifle thus impaled in him Robert went rushing back across to his friend and knelt down at his side.

Charlie was dying. And he knew it. So did Robert.

He stared down at Charlie, wanting to help but knowing there was nothing he could do. The wound was too bad, a jagged hole which pumped dark blood. Robert placed his hands over it and tried to stem the bleeding but it still seeped between his fingers and soon they were covered in red. He shook his head, not knowing what to say, and hot tears trickled down his cheeks.

Then Charlie smiled. He reached out his hand and took a hold of one of Robert's, and actually smiled. He opened his mouth but his lips could not create any words, so he simply lay there on the ground and stared up into Robert's eyes. He blinked languidly, content it seemed just to have his friend with him. He died a smiling man.

Weeping uncontrollably, Robert Metcalfe leaned forward and buried his face into his bloody hands and lay over Charlie's corpse.

He failed to see the knobkerrie that came swinging down towards the back of his head, and so instant was the deathblow that he did not even register the pain. In a fraction of a second it was over. He pitched forward, his life snuffed out.

Mehlokazulu barely gave the two corpses a second glance. Hefting the knobkerrie in his hand he went looking for further victims.

But by this stage, with the last pockets of enemy resistance caving in, there were precious few left.

CHAPTER 42

THE CAMP. 2:10pm-2:25pm.

Captain Younghusband still had perhaps forty men of C. Company with him. It was astounding that they were alive and continuing to fight after this long, when all about them had been overrun and scattered, trodden bloodily into the earth. But the position he had chosen - tight under the cliff face of the mountain, on a shelf of rock overlooking the camp - was a naturally strong one to hold, and so they were able to stand up to repeated charges for some considerable time. So they fought on long after most of the other stands had crumbled.

From up here they had an excellant vantage point from which to witness the destruction of the camp and its defenders.

In between fending off the almost continuous zulu rushes with exhausting hand-to-hand fighting, chiefly concerned with events to their immediate front, their own tenuous survival constantly hanging in the balance, they nevertheless managed to snatch brief glimpses of events taking place amoungst the wagons and tents below. They saw their fellow soldiers gradually draw in towards the nek where Pulleine had tried to organize a sizeable defence, men from various units seeking safety in numbers. They watched the return of Colonel Durnford with his horsemen and his consequent attempts to hold back the Zulu left horn. They noticed a group of native levies and basuto riders rush by just below and disappear behind the mountain, then the sound of heavy gunfire signifying that they were engaged with more Zulus there. Younghusband and his men witnessed all of this and much more.

At one stage he contemplated making an attempt to link up with Pulleine in the camp just the other side of the roadway, partly to reinforce the Colonel but also to improve their own chances of surviving. Yet no sooner had Younghusband thought this than these last pockets of resistance began to fall one by one, the pressure on them now too much to bear. Men were fleeing hell-for-leather over the saddle, further disintergrating the defenses, and the Zulus rushed in to chase after them and to finish off those brave enough to hold their ground. First one stand fell, then another, and another. Colonel Pulleine's men were swamped and in less than a minute they ceased to exist. Almost simultaneously with this there appeared a new wave of charging Zulus coming from the far side of the mountain, indicating that the gallant endeavour to put in a blocking force there had also failed. Durnford managed to stall the left horn for a little longer but the result of this struggle could only have one outcome too. Still, his bravery - and that of the Colonial Volunteers with him- made it possible for a few more men to get away, mostly in one's and two's and sixes. Only one substantial body of men were able to escape together, half a company of redcoats who retreated down into the broken ground between the road and the stony hill. They were, Younghusband realized, making a dash for the river; a last-ditch attempt to reach safety. Good luck my boys, he thought to himself, a sentiment shared by his men who gave a hearty cheer of encouragement to them.

But for C. Company there would be no such escape.

They were now hemmed in on three sides with the mountain at their backs. Their ammunition was gone with no access to fresh supplies, many had lost their rifles in the struggle and now fought with knives or rocks or their bare hands, and all of them had sustained injuries of one sort or another. Their numbers were dwindling by the minute while in contrast the Zulus seemed too many to count. They might be able to hold out for a while longer, stubbonly holding on until the last man fell.

But for what? It would achieve no purpose.

Their deaths were now an inevitable certainty.

So why prolong things?

Younghusband jumped up onto a slab of rock that overlooked the drop below and slashed down with his sword, skinning a Zulu's face and making his companions draw back. To make sure they kept clear he cut the air from side to side, shouting wild profanities, then when he had a moment or two's breathing space he turned back and yelled to his men.

"C. Company, you're the damn finest soldiers in the world! Oh God, my boys, you've made me so proud! But now it's time to end this, LIKE MEN! ARE YOU WITH ME?"

"YES!" went the cheer.

Younghusband spun his sword above his head in splendid fashion, so that it flashed in the sun, then he pointed it straight down into the host of enemy warriors. "CHARGE!" he screamed at the top of his voice, then again and again. "CHARGE! CHARGE!" and he leaped down off his rock with the remainder of C. Company sprinting hard after him.

They ran down the steep slope straight into the very jaws of death. Bayonet clashed against spear and shield, body against body, the line of redcoated soldiers pouring out of their bottleneck like blood from a severed artery. Immediately the Zulus rushed in on either side, while others got in behind them, and their wild chants of "uSuthu!" merged with the soldiers' defiant cries. Here and there they went down; a sudden crush of dark bodies and flashing assegai blades, together with jets of scarlet lancing high into the sky, marking the spot of each man's demise. The scent of blood tinged the dusty air.

Several managed to reach the bottom of the slope, the momentum of their charge taking them right through the Zulu ranks. Captain Younghusband almost got as far as the roadway. Almost.

Then he, along with those few men still with him, were finally brought to earth. They did not die easily.

*   *   *

A few men were still alive amongst the tents and in the wagon park, fighting with a desperate rage. They battled on either singly or in pairs, with their backs to a rock or a tree or an overturned cart. One soldier, grieviously wounded, crawled underneath one of the supply wagons and lay with his head resting on a saddle and with a tarpaulin pulled up over him, where he died quietly. Closeby a giant of a man, from the pioneer corps, was seen charging forward towards the enemy holding a huge axe above his head, screaming like the devil, while just through the tents a young sunaltern sat on the ground with his face in his hands, rocking gently backwards and forwards. Another soldier was finally overcome close to the Headquarters tents, the Zulus ignoring his pleads for mercy and pinning him to the ground by thrusting his own bayonet into his mouth up to the socket, stilling his words mid-sentence. Lieutenant Milne's servant, a fellow sailor from H.M.S. Active, fought on while backed up against a wagon and hacking away with his cutlass at any Zulu who came too close. He was eventually killed when a crafty warrior sneaked up from behind, crawling through the grass to stab him through the spokes of one of the wheels. Several soldiers tried to play dead by lying amongst the corpses of their slain companions but as it was normal practice for the Zulus to go around disembowelling all of those killed they were quickly found out and hurriedly dispatched. Still more sought sanctuary by hiding inside the tents, but the Zulus chased in after them and butchered all those they found within, then set the canvas alight. One civilian conductor actually hid himself inside an officer's travel chest and would have escaped had the Zulus not heard his soft whimpers and preyers; opening the lid they bludgeoned him into an unrecognizable pulp with their knobkerries.

There was simply nowhere to run and nowhere to hide.

*   *   *

Colonel Durnford and the Volunteers had dismounted and had either sent their horses away or they shot them dead with great sorrow and used their bodies to shelter behind. He himself had handed Chieftain's reins over to his servant, a friend of the Colenso's, and instructed him to try and get clear; whether he succeeded or not Dumford could not tell, for he soon lost sight of him amidst the swirling gunsmoke.

He formed his last stand on the uneven ground before the stony hill just south of the dirt road. The men who had gathered around him were a mixture of horsemen, infantry and camp casuals who were able to fight their way over, both white and black. There were about fifteen Carbineers, maybe twenty Mounted Police, a few of the Newcastle Mounted Rifles and Buffalo Border Guard, as well as a handful of survivors from the 24th and the NNC. Amongst their number were several wounded who they sheltered at the centre, protecting them the best they could.

Durnford did his best to keep them under his tight control and it was both a credit to his leadership qualities in these dying moments and their sudden willingness to follow his instructions when they could have tried to break out instead, that he was able to partially achieve this. Over the incessant roar of close-quarter combat his voice could be heard, shouting out his orders and adding words of encouragement. To some, had they taken the opportunity to scrutinise his conduct right then, he might have appeared to be a madman ranting and raving, with a lunatic glint in his eyes. And who knows whether this was the case or not?

Some might think he was completely insane...

While others would prefer to say he was a genius at the zenith of his powers... There was a fine line between the two.

But one thing was very clear. To those who stood with Durnford at the end, and fell with him, he was the man they most wanted to be with.

From a personal point of view, Brevet Colonel Anthony William Durnford felt no fear or regrets. He was in full control of himself... whatever 'control' actually meant.

"Fire!" he roared. "Make your shots count my men, make them tell! Reload! Fire! Ha, Ha, that's right! Praise the lot of you!"

Another Zulu rush came in and this one carried away part of the line, so Dumford sprang forward and blazed away with his revolver, his example encouraging a handful of others to storm forward and plug the gap.

"Independent fire!"

Just then a giant of a Zulu appeared right before him almost filling his entire vision with his massive bulk. Durnford fired twice, one shot passing right through the warrior's throat and clipping the man behind while the other blew a hole in his stomach the size of a fist. The Zulu stopped dead for a moment as if unsure what had happened and then amazingly ran forward again and

Durnford flinched as he saw the Zulu's spear come flashing towards him.

But at the last second one of the Carbineers next to him leaped forward and grabbed the Zulu's throat with both hands and squeezed. The assegai went into the troopers side and he gave a gutteral cry but did not let go, and the two of them went down together. They rolled over and over, the Zulu shoving the blade in even deeper and the Carbineer trying to throttle the life out of the big warrior, each man unable to overcome the other. Eventually both their struggles slowed down as they grew weak from their injuries. A moment later they lay still, their bodies grotesquely entwined in deaths cold embrace.

More of his men were being swept away all around and Durnford knew that they would not survive this assault. Drunk with bloodlust he threw the empty revolver away and reached for the hunting knife strapped at his waist.

He never succeeded in drawing it clear of its sheath.

From somewhere he felt a shot find him. He did not hear the explosive blast, just became aware of an excrutiating pain in his heart. Quickly he looked down at his chest and saw blood pumping out of a ragged hole there, and even as he considered whether the wound was fatal or not his vision blurred and he collapsed to the ground. For about half a minute - although it seemed much longer - the agony was unbearable and he lay there convulsing spasmodically and clutching at his chest. He was dimly aware of the Zulus running by for their bare feet kicked and trampled him, and the sound of fighting was now strangely muted, echoing through his mind as though coming from afar. Time seemed to slow down.

Slowly the pain eased off, just enough for him to regain his senses and become fully aware of his surroundings. Durnford glanced around.

To his left and to his right lay the dead bodies of his fellow soldiers and troopers, with a number of Zulus amongst them. Some had been mutilated whilst a few had hardly a scratch on them. All lay perfectly still.

Durnford sighed silently to himself, and waited.

Suddenly he remembered something and reached into his tunic pocket with his bloody fingers, rummaging about. Panic almost overcame him when he at first failed to find what he was searching for and he started to whimper fretfully, almost like a frightened little boy. "Oh no! No, no, I can't... where is it..? Please, oh no-" Then his fingers touched the tiny piece of folded muslin and he carefully pulled it out.

Durnford held it in his palm and watched as it slowly unfolded like the petals of some spring flower. Inside was the golden lock of hair that Frances Colenso had given to him just before he'd left to join his unit. Looking at it now he recalled that day and how gloriously happy they had been, and he felt tears well up in his eyes at the memory.

Weakly he lifted his hand and brought it up to his face. He breathed in, smelling the hair. It still had her scent even after all this time. It reminded him of... what?

Flowers. Yes, a profusion of flowers.

Like the ones in the garden at Bishopstowe.

Oh, how they had liked to walk together along the path, amidst the beautiful colours and aromas of a hundred different varieties of flowers. The exquisite red George Lily, the spectacular crane flower, an abundance of daisies: Ursinia, Cotula, Arctotis in every shade of blue, white, orange, yellow ochre, cream and magenta. The flowering coral trees flushed with trusses of scarlet. And Fanny's favourite, the rare disa orchid known as the 'flower of the gods'.

Yes, he could smell them all now as he lay quietly dying in the tall grass on that bloody battlefield.

Funny how this scent overrode all of the usual smells of conflict; the smoke, the pungent aroma of spilled blood, the acrid tang of gunpowder. Almost as if it was inside his head.

Durnford sank softly into unconciousness, and death.

His clawed hand slowly fell back down to the soil, and the tiny piece of muslin fluttered in the breeze. A soft draught caught the golden hair within and blew it away, so that it was lost forever.

CHAPTER 43

THE FUGITIVES' TRAIL.
SOUTHWEST OF ISANDLWANA. 2:25pm.

Not long after leaving the camp together Henderson and Davies had split up, each going his seperate way. Davies continued riding in a southerly direction, hoping to strike the river a few miles below Rorke's Drift, but his colleague had galloped off across country taking a number of surviving men from his troop with him, shouting back over his shoulder something about warning the British garrison at the drift. Then they were gone, leaving Davies by himself for the time being.

He lost no time by contemplating matters further and dug in his heels, directing his horse down the long slope below the road. The start of his intended path was fairly easy-going but after a few hundred yards the amount of bush and small trees increased so much that they began to impede his progress and he found it necessary to weave his way in and out of the rocks to find the best route. Occassionally he glanced about to see whether he might spot any other survivors likewise escaping, but the ground was becoming more and more broken with numerous gullies and donga's and small valleys in which a hundred men would quite easily be able to hide, and he saw knowone. He pressed on, pushing his way through dense branches.

Suddenly a Zulu warrior appeared out of nowhere directly infront of him brandishing his shield and spear, and rushed forward towards Davies. Cursing, he barely had time to react. He snapped his reins sideways and brought his horses head quickly between himself and the attacking Zulu before he had a chance to plunge the assegai blade into his thigh. Finding himself blocked by seven feet of horse muscle the Zulu stabbed at the animals shoulder instinctively, and then darted around to the side.

But Lieutenant Davies was ready for him now. He lashed out with his heavy boot, catching his foe square on the jaw and sending him crashing to the ground. At the same time his horse shied for it was startled by the sudden pain caused by the assegai stab, and then it sprinted away to take Davies clear leaving the zulu rolling about in the dirt with a broken jaw.

He tried to control his horse the best he could at the same time as watching out for any low-hanging branches that might unseat him, and it was only as they approached a scree of loose shale that he slowed enough for Davies to calm him.

"Easy boy," he whispered close to its ear and patting it on the neck, "nice and easy."

Davies leaned forward to inspect the wound and was extremely happy to see that it was only superficial, no more than a nasty cut that only bled a little. Sighing with relief at their lucky escape he glanced back the way they had come. The Zulu did not appear to be following. But if there was one, Davies thought somberly, then it was almost certain that there would be many more out here, lurking in the undergrowth and waiting to pounce.

Nervously he encouraged his skittish mount on.

After a short while they emerged from the dense thicket and came out into the open again.

He then saw, some way ahead, another horseman. Davies recognized him as one of the Carbineers but could not recall his name and he assumed that he must have left the camp around about the same time as he himself had done. He trotted across to join him.

The rider gave a half-hearted smile through his thick beard. "Am I glad to see you, my friend," he said gruffly.

"Likewise," Davies responded.

They shook hands.

"I should warn you that there are Zulus around here. I just had a brush with one back there a moment ago. Shouldn't we press on?"

"Yes, but look ahead," the carbineer said motioning forward with his carbine. "There's a nasty chasm in the ground, you see it?"

"Why yes. It's almost hidden by the bush. Thankyou for warning me otherwise I might have gone riding straight into it."

"That is precisely just what happened a few minutes back. Both of the artillery guns fetched up in there, with the horses and limbers and the lot. They went straight over the edge without stopping."

"Good grief! Did anyone survive?"

The carbineer shrugged his huge shoulders.

"Then let's take a look," replied Davies.

Riding forward together they both approached the edge and looked down.

It took less than a minute for them to see that nobody could possibly have gotten out of there alive, for wreckage and dead men lay scattered everywhere. Even the horses lay slain in their traces part way up the steep chasm side, their stomachs slit open and steaming. The two men absorbed the terrible details of carnage and slowly shook their heads.

"Come on. We should get away. There might still be Zulus around."

They both turned, then stopped dead.

Further away along the lip of the chasm they saw a body of enemy warriors come racing over the scrub in hot pursuit of somebody. The half dozen men leaped and bounded over the rocks and bushes, chanting their warcries. Davies and his companion quickly looked around to see who they were after.

Davies spotted a flash of red amongst the boulders up on the low rise just to their left and he pointed it out. It was an infantryman with his scarlet tunic showing clear against the brown earth as he ran away from the chasing zulus, and a second or two later another joined him. Somehow they must have escaped from the fighting on the nek just in time before the two horns met and had made their way towards the deep cutting in the ground, only to be discovered by this roving band of Zulu warriors. Flushed from their hiding place they made a second dash for freedom.

But by this stage they were nearing exhaustion point and they soon used up their last reserves of energy. The Zulus quickly closed with them. At the last second the two soldiers turned and tried to ward off the Zulus with their bayonets, and one of them managed to get off a quick shot, but he missed and did not have time to reload. After that it was over quickly. Both men fell under repeated blows from either knobkerries or assegais and they did not get up again.

Davies and the carbineer cringed, then felt their heckles rise in anger. Pulling out his carbine Davies looked at his companion. "Come on!" he instructed, then galloped forward.

With the trooper following close behind he charged the group of warriors. So busy were they with opening up the two soldiers' stomachs as was part of their belief they failed to see the two horsemen until the last moment, and when they did they tried to scatter in panic. Not before the men riding down on them each fired a single shot, dropping two Zulus, and then Davies and the other man were riding straight through them and out the other side. They did not stop but rode on leaving the other four warriors running about like panic-stricken chickens.

Davies was about to give a triumphant cheer when another Zulu - who had remained hidden just below the lip of the chasm - jumped up and sprinted out of the shadows. He did not try to stab his opponent but instead he grabbed a hold of the horses bridle and tried to pull the horse down, but was yanked off his feet and thrown onto the grass. Davies reined in then lunged down with his carbine on the end of which was fixed his hunting knife. But the Zulu saw it coming and managed to dodge the blade then snatched the stock and pulled hard. The rifle came clean out of Davies' hands.

For a second he looked on in amazement, unable to believe that he'd lost his gun. Then, and with an air of indignation, he loosened his holster strap and pulled out his revolver. The Zulu quickly dropped the carbine and threw one of his spears but missed his target by a good foot.

Slowly, with cold calculation, Davies levelled his gun and fired point-blank at the warriors head. And watched with grim satisfaction as the top of his skull erupted in a geyser of scarlet. Then saw the warrior topple backwards and disappear over the edge of the chasm.

Catching his breath and wiping a smear of blood across his forehead, Davies looked around for the carbineer. He was nowhere to be seen. He must have made it through unscathed and decided enough was enough and rode on whilst the Zulus were distracted. Glancing back he noticed the remaining four warriors were rallying again and starting to creep closer. This was not the time to be hanging around he told himself. Nor was there time to dismount and pick up the fallen rifle.

With a loud yell he dug in his spurs and rode away.

Slightly further back, up on the top of the small hillock and shielded by a large slab of rock, Smith-Dorrien watched the skirmish with detached fascination. An almost joyous feeling did swell inside his chest however when he saw the two riders finally break through and ride away, leaving the group of frustrated Zulu warriors to go running after them. He followed their progress until they were out of sight where the ground dipped. Waiting for a further minute to make sure the way was now clear, he walked his horse slowly down the slope towards the chasm.

He stopped about halfway down.

Something had caught his attention on the flatter ground on the far side of the chasm and he gazed across to see exactly what.

There was a small group of horsemen there working their way in single file on a course that would bring them out more or less directly opposite his own position, a mixture of officers, mounted infantry and Volunteers. Smith-Dorrien counted about eight or nine, but his eyes were drawn towards one man in particular riding out infront. He wore a distinctive scarlet undress frock which immediately identified him as Lieutenant Melvill of the 24th, and he seemed to be carrying one of the cased Colours across his saddle. The others seemed to follow him as though they had drawn together seeking safety in numbers and it occurred to Smith-Dorrien that this might indeed be his only chance of survival, for to ride alone would be extremely hazardous. If he could link up with them...

But to do that would mean backtracking some distance in order to cross the gully for it was too wide at this point.

Was it worth the risk when there were obviously Zulus in the vicinity?

A moment later and his mind was made up for him.

For a few hundred yards behind the party of horsemen came a fresh Zulu regiment, having worked their way down off the road behind Isandlwana. These, he thought horror-struck, must be the same ones he had seen earlier blocking the way to Rorke's Drift. They had been delayed temporarily when they had skirmished with some men placed to hold them back, but after just a few minutes it seemed they had easily brushed these aside and then resumed their advance south. Perhaps their intention had been to attack the rear of the camp but on seeing some of their enemy escaping they had decided to set off in pursuit instead. It appeared they had not yet noticed the riders to their front, for the lay of the land blocked their line of sight, but Smith-Dorrien knew that this state of affairs could only last a few minutes. Once they spotted them then the chase would begin in earnest.

Taking only a moment to make up his mind he continued down the slope, and once at the bottom followed the line of the chasm on this, the near, side. Unless a better opportunity presented itself for him to join them, or another group of survivors, he would stick by himself.

As well as Lieutenant Melvill, whom Smith-Dorrien had correctly identified, within the small group of horsemen were several officers from various units, a few civilians attached to the camp as conductors or guides, and a couple of footsoldiers who had managed to find stray horses. Lieutenant Coghill was there, having being slowed up by his painful knee during the ride across the difficult terrain, and so was James Brickhill the interpreter.

They made the best progress they could on their tired horses. Each of them was in a near state of shock after having come through the hell back at the camp by the skin of their teeth. And what's more, their ordeal was far from over. From Isandlwana to the Buffalo River was a distance of about six miles, six miles of high country bisected with deep valleys, numerous donga's and gullies, and dozens of small streams and tributory's, the land rocky and covered in dense vegetation - all of which would by now be infested with hundreds of Zulus intent on catching as many survivors as possible. So they would have to keep their guard for every foot of the way, continuously on the lookout lest they be surprised and slaughtered like their comrades back at the camp.

Brickhill was riding immediately behind Lieutenant Melvill. He noticed how the adjutant of the 1/24th was struggling to force his way through the thickets of bush and aloe plants for the Queen's Colours which he carried was unwieldy and awkward to hold and it kept snagging on the branches, impeding his progress. Melvill would shout out a curse or two every few yards, his face strained and covered in sweat, his hands grimy and scratched. The black leather case had been partially pulled loose and was hanging down at the end and a part of the standard was just visible.

Their way was already strewn with pieces of equipment and kit, marking the 'path' already taken by others who had escaped ahead of them, and they followed this bizarre trail. They passed dropped shields and assegais, empty ammunition belts tossed aside, a hunting rifle with a smashed stock. On a rock here was a grey blanket, while hanging on a branch a tattered slouch hat. Saddles lay about in the grass, somehow kicked loose by frightened horses. A riding boot standing upright on a boulder as if purposefully placed there. Revolvers, items of clothing, tins of meat, and a dozen other things, all abandoned in flight. That the retreat had quickly descended into a confused, panic-infested rout, was blatently obvious, those fortunate few who had slipped through the Zulu trap running headlong for safety. Yet here and there Brickhill spotted signs that not all had successfully escaped. For occcassionally they would pass a dead body partially hidden in the bushes, or spots of blood marking where an individual had been run to ground and attacked. Once he noticed a riderless horse standing still amongst a jumble of rocks and he called across to try and persuade the animal to come over, but it refused to budge and he quickly realized why. For lying there at its feet was the bloody remains of its master, quite obviously disembowled, the horse refusing to leave his side. Brickhill shook his head in pity and ran a weary hand over his face.

A little further on and they came out alongside a deep gully. They turned to follow it southwest, riding very close to the edge, glancing down at the wreckage of the artillery gun at the bottom but not stopping to investigate. They grew more and more nervous, their eyes constantly searching for Zulu warriors. Somewhere in the near distance they heard a single gunshot followed by a blood curdling scream, then silence. The tension grew.

After another half a mile or so the terrain gradually became progressively worse and it grew difficult to find a safe passage, the ground covered with loose rocks and hidden obstacles that threatened to unseat the riders or send their horses tumbling. They started to look for a way across to the far side.

At the rear of the party one young man, a member of the Mounted Infantry, grew impatient at their slow progress. Being at the back he was fearful of any chasing Zulu sneaking up and cutting him off, and he watched their rear with growing trepidation. "Come on chaps!" he called from time to time. "Get a move on. Things are a little dicey back here!"

But they could only go so fast.

Several minutes later he decided to take the matter into his own hands.

"Dash it! I'm getting to the other side! You men can join me if you like, or you can stay this side and suffer the consequences!"

And with that he backed up his horse, steeled his nerves, then charged forward towards the lip of the chasm.

The others watched on in amazement as he jumped the wide gap, their hearts in their mouths as both horse and rider sailed through the air, striving to reach the opposite side... ...and closed their eyes in horror as he fell far short.

The man screamed in terror as he realized his mistake, the sound of his yell echoing off the rocky walls of the chasm.

It ended in an abrupt but muffled grunt as man and beast met their bloody fate on the rocks below.

"Fool," Coghill murmured. "His brain must have been half-baked to try that."

"If anybody else wishes to chance it then go right ahead, but I wouldn't recommend it," added Lieutenant Melvill, before turning away and trotting on.

The others followed him.

There was still no sign of any Zulus but they all knew they were out there somewhere, working their way nearer. It was only luck that they had not yet being found, and since they had suffered a singularly short supply of good fortune throughout the day they now made the most of it by putting as much distance between themselves and the destroyed camp while the going was (relatively speaking) fairly good.

A hundred yards further on and Providence shined on them again, for Melvill at last spotted a dip in the land where the gully narrowed enough to allow them to carefully pick their way down to the bottom and then back up the far bank. He led the way, carefully sliding his horse down the earth slope, along the bed of the dry donga for several feet and then up the opposite side via a series of steep, rocky ledges. James Brickhill followed him closely, whispering a silent preyer that his mount didn't loose its footing and break a leg, for he knew that to be stranded out here on foot, miles from nowhere, in hostile country, was as good as signing ones own death warrant. Coming up the rocky steps he leaned forward and linked his arms around the horse's neck to give as much assistance as possible.

"Come on, a little further, that's right, we're nearly at the top," he whispered in its ear.

As if understanding the meaning of his words, (or maybe it just sensed the danger for itself) the horse gave a final heave and cleared the last few feet in a quick bound, bringing him out behind Lieutenant Melvill.

Taking a moment to regain their breath they both waited until each of the others had successfully cleared the obstacle, wiping the sweat from their brows.

Lieutenant Melvill suddenly put his hand down towards his scabbard and then turned to look down at the ground behind them. "Mr Brickhill, have you seen anything of my sword back there? I seem to have lost it coming out of that hole."

Brickhill wearily glanced back and gave a quick cursory check of the steep banking, but he was too exhausted to search properly and did not fancy dismounting and scrabbling about amoungst the rocks so he looked back to the officer and shrugged his shoulders. "Sorry."

"Damnation! My own fault. Can't be helped though, I can always buy a new one."

When the others were ready he led them on.

From this point on the ground became very bad. They could see the land rolling away into the distance in a series of progressively steeper hills, reaching all the way to the southern horizon. Brown and green scrub and short, stunted trees, their branches gnarled and twisted together, covered the landscape as far as the eye could see. Somewhere out there in one of those twisting valleys lay the Buffalo River, with Natal beyond. They were allready exhausted, bathed in sweat and grime, their flesh and uniforms scratched and torn, but they still had several miles to trek before they could even consider themselves safe. Even when - or rather, if, - they crossed the border there was no guarantee that the zulus would not follow them in an invasion of the British Colony, their confidence sky high after their astounding triumph at Isandlwana. To cut a long story short, each of them thought they might never reach the end of this nightmare.

Certainly for those who would survive their lives would always be haunted by the memories of this day.

Gradually their route started to descend down towards a deep river valley, not the Buffalo but one of the many watercourses that criss-crossed the area. Just a few minutes later and they were stopped short by a sudden drop, the way ahead following a precarious course along this steep slope. Melvill dismounted and contemplated their next move.

"We can't go back," he said almost to himself, "that would be suicidal. So we go on." Brickhill, who had overheard his ruminations, said, "you go first sir while I hold the others here. One at a time I think, otherwise somebody will end up in a pile at the bottom."

"Thankyou."

He carefully led his horse along the narrow pass, testing his footing all the way down. Twice he almost slipped. His balance wasn't helped by the weight of the Colours, which he carried resting on one shoulder. It was slow, tricky work, but there was no way he could be rushed.

Meanwhile the others queued up behind Brickhill to wait their turn.

At the back somewhere was Lieutenant Coghill. From there he could not see the hazardous drop down to the left, all he saw was his friend Melvill slowly leading his horse on whilst the others bunched together and watched him. He tried to raise himself in his stirrups to see what the holdup was but his knee was too painful, and so he figdeted in his saddle, tutting to himself. After a minute he could hold his frustartions in check no longer.

"Get on your horse there Mr. T, this is no place to be leading a horse with all these Zulus about!" he cried. "Mount up you fellows in front and get a move on!"

Someone, Brickhill did not know who, shouted back vehemently, "get off yours, this is no place to be riding one!"

"My dear friend, without my ride I would be helpless! I can't walk!"

"And neither could we with broken legs!"

"Did you hear that? The bare cheek of him..." Coghill objected, but nobody was listening anymore and so he fell into a moody silence.

By now Melvill had successfully reached the end of the narrow track and Brickhill set off next. Taking extreme care to watch his footsteps he too made it down in one piece, and he set off after Melvill who had not stopped to wait. Behind him the others likewise worked their way down, a sense of urgency starting to grip them. Lieutenant Coghill had the worst of it for he had to manoeuvre his way on horseback for his leg was too weak to properly support his weight, but with a touch more good fortune - plus a bit of guts - he was soon catching them up as they snaked their way through the vegetation.

At last the chasm opened up as it joined a narrow stream in the valley bottom. This, those who'd had a chance to study maps during the campaign knew, was the Manzimyama blackwater.

They pulled up on the top of the high bank and stared down at the dreadful scenes below.

The actual stream itself, they noticed, was very shallow, running along the centre of the wide and flat valley bottom and hardly much of a problem to cross. But to either side was a broad band of wildly scattered rocks of every shape and size imaginable, piled upon one another in a crazy and uneven layer. Very difficult for a man on foot to traverse but incredibly perilous for somebody seated on a horse. Yet it wasn't so much the nature of the land which chilled them but rather the slaughter taking place there. And slaughter it was.

Every person who had managed to escape from the camp had it seemed passed through here, their various routes ultimately bringing them out along this same stretch of the stream. Men on foot and men on horseback, white and black. And here the rocky terrain had slowed them up allowing the Zulus to catch up and launch a fresh attack.

There was perhaps two dozen men still alive, floundering and tripping amongst the rocks and bodies of their fallen comrades, with horses and mules charging about in panic which added to the disorder. While dashing in and out and stabbing furiously, swarming like angry bees, were several hundred Zulus.

Brickhill watched the fighting with a cold feeling in his heart, for he knew the men down there didn't stand a chance. They must have been exhausted after their long trek over the broken landscape, coming immediately after the gruelling battle, especially those on foot. Perhaps a few of the mounted men - and he spotted several desperately trying to force their way clear of the skirmish - might be lucky enough to get away. But the rest...

Then another equally disturbing thought occurred to him.

They, this small band of dishevelled riders new on the scene, would have to fight their way through if they wanted to reach safety. The Buffalo River was still several miles away and to reach it they had to cross this stream first. And there was no time to waste for more Zulus might be on them any second now.

It was every man for himself from here on, he realized.

Lieutenant Melvill was already on his way, and so were one or two of the others, then, after a heartbeat's hesitation James Brickhill charged forward into the fray.

He would never quite know how he made it. Luck, dash, recklessness? Or a combination of all three? Whatever, he seemed to find a clear path straight through the centre of the maelstrom with knowbody paying him much notice. The Zulu warriors seemed to be paying particular attention to the soldiers wearing red tunics for these were the real prizes, the most prestigious opponents to overcome, the bravest combatants to take on. Imperial soldiers. Their true enemy, who lay waste their land and killed their people. Was this why he got through unmolested? Or were other more mysterious forces at work, such as fate, destiny? He would ponder these unanswerable questions for years to come and never come up with a satisfactory conclusion.

But right then he wasted no time pondering on it. He was just grateful to come throughalive.

Brickhill reached the stream and splashed through the shallow water, kicking his horse's flanks to urge it out onto the far shore. He did not pause but hurried on across the treacherous rocks, his horse's feet slipping and sliding but mercifully it stayed upright.

Just then a voice cried out nearby. "Hey mister!"

Brickhill glanced around.

From behind a rock appeared a soldier of the 24th, flapping his arms and limping towards him, his hair wet and matted to his forehead.

"It's, ah... Gamble isn't it?" Brickhill shouted back.

The soldier nodded. He looked to be in a state of shock, shivering uncontrollably and his eyes wide and unblinking. The paleness of his skin added to his terrified appearance. In one hand he held a large stone, his only weapon, and in the other his scuffed and dented helmet. His mouth was bleeding and Brickhill thought most of his teeth seemed to be missing.

Suddenly he tripped and went down with a curse, and now Brickhill had a clear view of what had caused him to leave his hiding place. Two Zulus were running after him, each brandishing a knobkerry and shield.

Gamble saw how close they were and he once more came to his feet.

"For God's sake give me a lift!"

Yet Brickhill knew that to stop a moment longer would mean certain death. Besides, he quickly rationalized, he doubted if his horse had the strength to carry an extra load. So far it had got him through all that had been thrown at them. He dared not ask too much more of it.

He gave a regretful shake of his head and wondered if he would ever be able to live with himself for what he was about to do.

"My dear fellow, it's a case of life or death with me. I'm sorry."

He smacked his horse's rump with the flat of his hand and sped away up the steep hillside in front, away from the fight.

"Damn you sir!" came Gamble's hoarse cry. "May God have mercy on your poor soul!"

CHAPTER 44

THE MANZIMYAMA STREAM.
2 MILES ALONG THE FUGITIVES' TRAIL.
SOUTHWEST OF ISANDLWANA. 2:35pm-2:45pm.

So far Private Thomas Scott had managed to evade detection. Once or twice during his escape he had almost been discovered; each time any Zulus had come too close he had quickly gone to ground, holding his breath and keeping as still as possible until the danger passed. Once, whilst hiding in a shallow cave at the foot of a small cliff as he waited for a group of Zulus to go by, he thought one of them had seen him. The warrior had stopped dead only thirty yards away and looked straight in his direction, his eyes seeming to pick Thomas out. He had waited for the inevitable, his whole body quivering with dread. But then, to his amazement, the Zulus' gaze had drifted on by as he searched the rockface further away. Thomas had ever so slowly drawn back into the shadows so that when he did turn towards the cave again this time he was out of view.

The Zulu had hurried after his comrades.

Waiting for a good five minutes before making a move, Thomas had slowly slipped out of his hiding place and continued heading west.

Over the last hour or so he had slowly come to the conclusion that changing the direction of his escape route westwards towards the river rather than sticking to his original plan of hurrying directly south from the site of the rocket battery's demise had been a big mistake. Rather than taking him away from the worst of the fighting he had if anything made matters worse, for the countryside hereabouts seemed to be swarming with Zulus. And the sound of battle had progressively grown louder with heavy gunfire echoing off the hills and krantzes all about. It seemed that the fight had shifted from the camp, about two miles away by his reckoning, to these very same hills and valleys he now found himself in. So, he thought bitterly, all the time he'd assumed he was moving further and further away from danger he had instead been running straight into the very heart of it!

Because of this, and the ever-present threat of a bunch of marauding Zulus stumbling across him, he was making little headway. Leaving the safety of the cave Thomas had climbed up through a narrow notch in the cliff, using the branches of a stunted tree at the top to pull himself up the last few feet. From here he had made his way along the crest until the land dropped down the far side in a series of deep granite shelves, what he presumed was the course made by a long-dried-up waterfall.

At the bottom snaked a shallow donga, the sides screened by vegetation, and he carefully moved forward down the centre, keeping crouched low all of the time.

After about a couple of hundred yards the gully he was in split into several smaller tributaries and he chose one to follow at random, hoping he was still headed in the right direction. A little further on and this eventually ran out and he was confronted by two enormous slabs of rock which eons ago must have come tumbling down from the hillside away to his right to block the small stream, thus causing it to dry out. There was a narrow gap between the two and Thomas squeezed himself through.

On the other side he stopped and listened.

Somewhere closeby he could hear fighting. A few shots at first, then more and more, growing steadily in volume. The hills caused the sound to bounce around and it was hard to tell exactly from which direction it was coming. But it seemed to be getting closer.

Thomas looked around nervously and checked the hilltops to either side and to the front, searching for Zulus.

He saw nothing.

Yet the gunfire came steadily nearer.

Thomas realized of course that these signs of fighting meant that somewhere in the vicinity were fellow soldiers who like him had escaped, but were now being pursued again. And from the level of firing it must be quite a significant group. But he thought it wise to remain vigilant and so until things became clearer he decided to stay out of sight and backed up into the gap between the stone slabs.

From time to time he carefully peered around the corner.

Now he could hear voices yelling, shouts of desperation, and cries of determination. He was positive they were speaking English.

One more glance confirmed the suspicion that had started to creep into his mind. For now he could see coming towards him in one compact body a large group of redcoats, slowly backing their way over the ground as they fought to hold back several hundred Zulu warriors who pressed after them. They fired steadily and accurately or used their bayonets superbly, keeping their opponents at bay, buying themselves a few more yards, moving slowly, slowly backwards.

Thomas watched them and as he did he came to a snap decision.

He knew as sure as night follows day that if he chose to escape alone he would be dead in no time at all. So far being by himself had worked to his advantage, but once these zulus passed him and put themselves between himself and the river he would have a heck of a time trying to sneak through. Their course would take them right by him and the chances of them not spotting him were so low as to not even be a possibility. No, his one real hope lay in joining with this band of survivors and making a joint fight of it.

It might also help him to redeem some of his lost honour for the fear of being branded a coward was still predominant in his heart.

Thomas slipped out from between the rocks and hurried over to join them.

*   *   *

They belonged to F. Company.

Their commanding officer, Captain Mostyn, was already dead. He had been killed when the order to retire on the camp went out to the firing line, falling as they reached the tents above the road.

443

Therefore the next most senior officer had taken charge, drawing the men back over the nek as the fighting had raged all around them. Somehow they found themselves being squeezed through the narrow gap between the two Zulu horns, the shoulder of the stony hill affording them some degree of shelter. Retreat along the road to Rorke's Drift had proved impossible and so they had followed in the path of the other fugitive's, heading southwest through the dongas. They kept up a heavy fire upon any zulus who appeared on the hill to their right, preventing them closing with them at first, but as the nature of the ground worsened the zulus chasing after them were eventually able to sneak up in large numbers under cover and launch a series of fierce charges that the redcoats struggled to hold back. Several times it had seemed certain that they would be swept aside but just when they were on the point of breaking through the zulu attacks had faltered, and the warriors pulled back to regroup and prepare for the next charge. And on it went. For two miles.

Lieutenant Edgar Oliphant Anstey had a broad and pleasing face with a receeding hairline. Popular amongst his fellow officers for his conscientious and kindly nature he was a quiet and shy young man who held high moral views on life, a stout supporter of family values and the welfare of the poorer classes. Born in South Australia, then educated at Rugby, he'd gone on to pass through Sandhurst before joining the First Battalion of the 24th Regiment in March of 1873. From there he had proceeded to Gibralter and on to the Cape, taking part in the Ninth Frontier War of 1877-78. Frequently mentioned in despatches he was one of the Regiments rising stars and it seemed that the war against the Zulus would only accelerate his rapid advance through the ranks.

But of course all of that changed at Isandlwana.

Here he found himself unexpectedly in command of the survivors from F. Company, and at the heart of their fighting withdrawal away from the camp.

He led from the front as they repulsed the latest Zulu assault. Earlier a thrown assegai had slashed open one of his cheeks and the skin hung down in a bloody flap by his neck, bleeding profusely so that the whole of that side of his face was red with slick blood. He seemed to hardly notice. Infact, the majority of the men had sustained an injury by this stage but they carried on regardless,

444

limping or stumbling backwards, or supporting each other. Their predicament meant that they could not pause to tend to their wounds (the Zulus were not sporting enough to allow that!) which meant that they were growing progressively weaker from a combination of blood-loss and sheer exhaustion from their long flight. And each attack left more and more of them dead, so that their nmbers were dwindling all of the time. Lieutenant Anstey doubted if they could keep going for very much longer; certainly not long enough to reach the Buffalo River.

When they were joined by a lone soldier who seemed to appear from out of nowhere, as though suddenly materializing out of thin air amongst their ranks, they at first paid him little attention. All of the extra pair of hands they could find were at that stage very welcome and they made room for him. Only when they pushed the Zulus away and were able to run down the sloping ground for a few minutes in between attacks, trying to put as much distance between themselves and the enemy, did one or two breathlessly ask who in blazes was he?

"Private Thomas Scott, 623, C. Company," he introduced himself as they ran down into a wide valley at the bottom of which was a small stream.

"Well, wherever you came from you came at just the right time... or the wrong time more likely," one of the soldiers answered back.

"Where are the rest of C. Company? What happened to them?"

The soldier glanced across and then looked at one of his comrades before turning back to Thomas. "C. Company don't exist anymore."

Thomas stared aghast. Barely able to register what the man had said he wondered if he'd heard right. The soldier running alongside saw the shock, then puzzlement, on his face, and he offered more in the way of explanation. It made for grim listening.

"They were wiped out lad. Those bloody Zulus caught us on the hop and were right into the camp 'afore we knew what were happening. It were a right shambles." He shook his head pityfully. "The whole Battalion gone. And the artillery, and the horsemen. Wiped out!"

Thomas felt chilled inside and his heart hammered against his chest. Good Lord, could it be true? The camp taken and all of the defenders - apart from a lucky few who had escaped -killed?

445

"Those blasted Zulus ain't finished with us yet neither. They're hungry for more blood." Yes, thought Thomas. Our blood.

The body of men stopped once again and turned about to meet the next assault. In a daze he glanced around at their surroundings.

They were on the rocky banks of the small stream he'd spotted a moment ago, with the high flank of a large hill overshadowing the valley on the far side. He noticed several horsemen galloping up towards the summit, the riders widely spaced apart as though choosing to make their own way on the final leg to the Buffalo. Down here by the side of the stream there had obviously been some nasty fighting for laid all about over the boulders were the bodies of dozens of dead soldiers and Zulus. The sound of gunfire just around a bend in the valley indicated that some were still battling it out nearby. The ground underfoot was extremely hazardous he saw as he stumbled backwards towards the waters edge, and he guessed that the fugitives who had been killed here had probably been slowed up by the terrain long enough for the Zulus to reach them. This place was a death trap.

Thomas did not have time to ponder things further for right then the Zulus next attack came in.

The Zulus poured down the grassy bank onto the shore from several points and then charged forward as the British opened up with their Martini-Henry's. The first line of warriors fell to their accurate fire but the main bulk of them quickly closed the gap whilst the soldiers reloaded, and Lieutenant Anstey barely had time to order a second volley. They fired again just as the Zulus reached them. Fearless of this point-blank fire they darted towards the British to engage them hand-to-hand.

Private Thomas Scott was in the thick of it. All around him men cried hoarsly. It was hard to see too much for the pall of white smoke that hung in the breezeless air obscurred everything except that to his immediate front, but he could hear the discordant sounds of assegai clashing against bayonet, the occasional shot thudding into shields or ripping through soft tissue, and the brutal smack of rifle butts and knobkerries smashing bone. A Zulu came at him and instinctively Thomas lunged with his bayonet but his opponent was too fast and he side-stepped his thrust. Quickly he grabbed a hold of the blade with one hand and pulled even though it cut into his palm. Then he dropped his shield and used both hands. Thomas heaved back, and they proceeded to wrench each other too and fro in a bizzare contest of tug-of-war.

Realizing that it was of paramount importance that he keep possession of his rifle Thomas let go with one hand and threw a left hook. The Zulu, caught off guard, lurched backwards under the blow, allowing Thomas to reclaim the rifle. Quickly feeding in a round he aimed into the warrior's chest and pulled the trigger. With a loud shriek the Zulu fell to the ground and lay there twisting and turning in his own gore.

The fighting flowed back and forth, at one moment the Zulus seeming to have the upper hand and then the next the British. Amid the chaos Lieutenant Anstey shouted out in desperation.

"Keep intact! Close up your ranks, fill the gaps and hold them back! HOLD THEM!"

He turned to look towards the right, spotting an opening there, and he leaped across to fill the empty space between two of his men. They slowly backed up towards the stream and then were stepping through the ankle deep water, tripping and faltering over the slippery rocks. From here they had a clearer view up and down the stream to the left and right but what they saw heading towards them was enough to knock the fight out of them. For coming down the centre of the stream from both directions were more Zulus, racing to attack them in the flanks. Having finished mopping up the fugitive's elsewhere they had headed towards the sounds of fighting closeby, and when they saw this pathetic band of redcoats there for the taking they broke into a charge.

Now under attack from three sides the compact group of soldiers started to buckle. So far they had managed to hold the Zulus at bay during the retreat, for small groups of warriors had constantly broke off from the attack to chase after other escapees thus reducing the number of Zulus they'd had to contend with, but now that these other knots of resistance had finally being dealt with they could now concentrate on finishing off this last stubborn group of redcoats. Suddenly reinforced, the Zulu attack soon overwhelmed them.

Men fell in quick succession, bludgeoned or stabbed to the ground. Others lost their footing and did not have time to get up again before several Zulus were on them. One soldier had his face forcibly held under the shallow water until his struggles ceased, and just to make sure he was dead his attacker assegaid him ten or twelve times then opened him up from sternum to groin. Soon the stream ran red with blood.

Thomas saw the soldier who had briefly befriended him parry with his bloodied bayonet towards a cluster of warriors closing with him but whilst his attention was diverted another Zulu attacked him from the rear. Thomas bellowed a warning but his voice was drowned out by the sounds of combat and he could do nothing but stand and watch as the soldier disappeared under the crush of Zulus.

He spun around just in time to see Lieutenant Anstey take a shot to the head. The bullet blew away the top of his skull in a white mist, and after remaining on his feet for the briefest of moments the officer's legs crumpled and he fell to his knees then toppled over onto his side in the stream.

Unable to hide his horror of these appalling scenes of carnage, Thomas Scott started to scream at the top of his voice. Standing at the centre of this slaughter he wailed and cried unabashed, his mind now unhinged and incapable of coping anymore.

A few seconds later he felt an overwhelming pain in the back of his neck, so severe that it blossomed throughout his entire being in one white-hot instant of agony.

Then it was over.

CHAPTER 45

THE VALLEY OF THE MZINYATHI (Buffalo) RIVER.
SIX MILES SOUTHWEST OF ISANDLWANA. 2:45pm-3:00pm.

James Brickhill pushed his horse hard as he rode up the steep flank of the large hill, trying to ignore the sound of ricocheting bullets as the Zulus below fired after him and the other horsemen. He flinched with each report and waited for the thud in his back which would tell him he'd been struck. But the expected agony did not come. Luckily for him the Zulus sniping away were poor shots and their aim was either too high or too low. And as he neared the summit and went out of range they eventually gave up alltogether; after all, there was plenty of killing to be had on the banks of the stream in the valley bottom. After several minutes he reached the top and paused to glance back.

There were still several individuals alive down there he saw but all of the larger groups of soldiers had been overwhelmed. Their bodies lay in clusters, either on the rocks or in the bloody red water. The Zulus were busy hunting down the last survivors amongst the tall reeds that lined the bank further down, allowing them no respite, finding them and killing them. Briefly, he wondered whether the soldier named Gamble was one of them, but when the lingering echo of his final pleads reverberated around inside his head he turned sharply away and rode on.

Up here on the broad summit it was a different world entirely. The noise of the fighting soon died away, to be replaced by a strange tranquility. Birds sang softly, accompanied by the pleasant buzz and chirp of insects in the long grass. A multi-coloured butterfly fluttered on the air, dancing merrily towards a stand of small trees. So peaceful Brickhill thought. So inviting.

He trotted through the long grass stalks and allowed his horse to move at its own pace now that the worst of the danger seemed to have passed. Brickhill breathed a little easier and allowed his frayed nerves to settle. Leaning forward, he patted the animal reassuringly on the neck, then sat upright and took a long and grateful swig from his water bottle.

Boy oh boy!

Please let that be the end of this terrifying experience. All he wanted was to safely cross the river into Natal and reach home in one piece, he thought. Then there would be no more adventures, no more wars, just a normal and mundane life working with his brother again. What bliss that would be! Yes, just a few more miles.

A few more miles.

His route took him around the eastern shoulder of the hill and from here a splendid view of the rugged countryside opened up for him. About two miles off in this direction he noticed the brown walls of a narrow gorge slicing through the valleys and Brickhill knew that somewhere within lay the Buffalo River, twisting its way between the hills and krantzes. If he continued on his present course across the summit and then down the far side he should come out - hopefully - at the waters edge. Then it would just be a matter of forcing his way across before setting out for Msinga, and home.

So intent was he on thoughts of getting safely back, of warmly embracing his brother and then sitting down to enjoy a stiff drink, that he failed to notice the boggy, swampy ground underfoot until they had ridden half way through it. He cursed quietly. The land here was marshy, with water seeping to the surface from underground springs to create a thick layer of mud beneath the tall grass. His horses hooves sank down several inches with each step, and it struggled to lift them clear again, tottering from side to side. Soft squelching noises marked their progress.

Brickhill looked around for some dryer land but the marsh seemed to spread right the way across their front and when he turned

450

to glance behind he saw that the ground back there was the same. Damn! It served him right. He should have been paying more attention instead of daydreaming like that.

Having no option but to press on he carefully sought to find the best path through the deep quagmire, his teeth gritted in concentration.

A little further on and they found themselves well and truly stuck.

With a loud whinny his horse came to a stop, its feet planted firmly in the oozing mud, and refused - or was unable - to budge.

Sitting in the saddle Brickhill lifted the reins and gave them an encouraging flap, then a click of his tongue. Still his mount remained stock still.

"Come on now," he ordered.

The beast had made up its mind. It had had enough.

"Don't do this to me, not now. Just a little bit further and we'll be home."

But his words had no effect. They both sank further down into the mud, which looked cold and very uninviting.

Brickhill lost his temper. "Well we can't stand here all day!" he fumed. "You sullen little mare!" And with that he dug in his spurs into its sides.

Giving a loud protesting call the horse suddenly reared up onto its hind legs nearly unseating him. Brickhill cried out and hugged its mane to prevent himself slipping off the saddle, briefly wondering just how deep the marsh was should he go tumbling down. Then his spectacles flew off.

The horse came back down onto its front legs and strode clear of the clinging quagmire.

In a panic he peered down into the grass and tried to spot where the spectacles were, but now everything was a blur to him and he failed to find them. He had to get them back, he thought; without them he was virtually blind. Plus they had been damned expensive, bought from an upmarket gents store in Pietermaritburg three summers back. So he slipped one foot out of its stirrup and swung his leg back over the saddle.

He got no further.

Just then a shot cracked out from nowhere. The round struck a tree nearby, sending fragments of bark spurting out. A bird took to the wing and went screeching away in anger and fear.

Brickhill's head spun around this way and that, a fresh wave of adrenalin and alarm gripping him. Well, he told himself, the Zulus were up here after all. He couldn't see any but they were no doubt hiding in the tall grass and intent on pressing the pursuit all the way to the river. This was no time to be lingering and searching for his lost spectacles. Their loss was a serious blow but he could manage without them - just. They could also be replaced later. They were not worth risking his life for.

Now compelled once again to get over the river as quickly as was humanly possible James Brickhill did not hesitate for a moment longer.

Neither did his horse. It needed no further bidding to keep moving as well.

About two miles ahead Lieutenant Davies carefully guided his horse down the far side of the hill, into the deep valley where the Mzinyathi lay. The river glistened like a silver ribbon at the bottom, the water moving at a heck of a rate from west to east for it was in flood from all of the heavy rain of late. It sluiced over the rocks and boulders, sending up clouds of spray, tearing down the valley before being squeezed between a narrow gorge further downstream. Even from up here he could hear the dull roar of its passage. To Davies it sounded like some great beast breathing fire and brimstone, an angry monster of a river.

To get to the Natal bank he had to get across - somehow.

Several men were already trying. He saw them on the nearside moving up and down alongside the waters edge looking for the best place to cross, bracing themselves for the ordeal. And they did not have long to make a decision for already the advance parties of Zulus had caught up with them. He watched them dart forward from time to time to attack individual horsemen, growing bolder and bolder as their numbers were bolstered by more arrivals. The British were trapped with the surging river to their front and several hundred Zulu warriors to their rear.

A few plunged into the water knowing that they had but one chance to escape. Only about half made it to the far side. The rest were swept to their deaths. Davies counted about a half dozen bodies go racing away, dashed onto the rocks, or tossed high out of the violent river. It was sickening to watch. Those that did somehow reach the opposite bank pulled themselves exhausted out of the water, every inch of their tired bodies bruised and battered, and here they paused just long enough to regain their breath before riding away towards the hills in the distance, hoping to lose themselves in the rugged landscape.

Just then, as Davies reached the bottom of the hill and approached the large rocks that lined the bank, he spotted a large group of riders clustered together on a piece of high ground that overlooked the river on the Natal side. Their uniform and the colour of their skin identified them as the Edendale Troop, his own unit. Hardly able to believe that he was nearly within touching distance of them Davies lifted his arm and waved. He thought several of them saw him for they pointed back but their attention was distracted by something else then for they raised their carbines and fired a volley towards the top of the hill behind him. Davies turned and saw about a hundred more Zulus come pouring down over the brim of the hill straight towards him, a timely reminder that he should get a move on.

Finding a place to cross was hard. But the worst thing was steeling oneself for making the plunge into the water. Down at the edge of the river the roar was deafening and it was terrifying to look out across its raging, angry surface towards the shoreline just one hundred feet away, aware of just how close he was to safety but knowing he might die right at the very end, not at the hands of the zulus but from drowning in the unforgiving torrent before him.

He moved further upstream where the flow seemed a fraction slower. All the time he kept a sharp eye out amoungst the boulders and thorn bushes that lined the riverbank, expecting to be attacked at any time. Across the water the Edendale men continued to fire away steadily, lending as much assistance as they could. They must have escaped and got over in one body, Lieutenant Davies realized, before deciding to remain behind and keep the Zulus at bay for as long as their ammunition lasted. That could not be for much longer he thought. Little did he realize that they were in fact down to their last two or three rounds per man, for the small number of cartridges that they had picked up off the ground back at the camp were fast running out. Soon they would make the decision to pull clear, their duty done.

Davies halted his horse and faced the flow of rushing water. He could not put it off any longer. This was it.

Before he went in he happened to turn and look down into a cleft between two large rocks closeby. Here lay a man's body. He had been stabbed a number of times and had his stomach opened up so that his insides were tumbled out into his lap, and steam rose up out of the wide slash to indicate the killing was fresh. Davies felt bile rise up into his throat and he quickly covered his mouth with his hand and fought back the urge to vomit. Breathing deeply he got himself back under control.

Lying on top of one of the rocks he noticed a Swinburne-Henry carbine, obviously belonging to the dead trooper. Remembering that he'd still had a few rounds left in his bandolier before he had lost his own gun earlier Davies decided to take the weapon; he had his revolver but that was only good for close up fighting, while the carbine would enable him to keep any zulus off at a safer distance should some attack him. So he leaned down and scooped it up, now trying to ignore the butchered man staring up at him with a faintly disgruntled look in his lifeless eyes.

"Sorry," Davies offered weakly, "but I need it more than you now my good chap."

Then he spun away and put himself and his horse to the river.

Immediately the flow grabbed them. The river's power was awesome and in just seconds his horse's feet were being swept from under it, and both of them struggled to keep their heads above the surface. Davies swallowed a mouthful of the foul-tasting water and he gagged and coughed until his lungs ached. Keeping hold of the reins with one hand he strived to hold the carbine above his head with the other, whilst at the same time he gripped his horses flanks with his knees to stop himself being torn free of the saddle for he knew that would be the end of it if that were to happen. His mount swam valiantly but they were still being carried downstream very fast and Davies remembered the narrow gorge. They had to reach the far shore before they were swept between the steep walls for there was no telling for how far the gorge went; careering from rock face to rock face and with no way out they wouldn't stand a chance.

Midstream they started to twist around. They turned two full circles and Davies could feel his horse starting to lose its strength. He saw its head slip under the water and he had to lift it clear by pulling up on the reins.

A moment later and he felt his leg strike a rock. Suddenly the gravelly bottom of the riverbed was under his feet and he gave a desperate push upwards, and in the next instant his horse was rising clear of the water and heaving itself towards the far bank having successfully made it across.

They came out onto the Natal shore more dead than alive, dead beat. Lieutenant Davies sagged forward and lay his forehead against the horse's mane, his shoulders heaving from exertion. For a full minute neither man nor beast were able to move. They stood there shivering on the rocky riverbank, grateful that the ordeal was over.

It was only when the sound of shooting reached his ears that Davies glanced around to take in their surroundings.

They had been swept several hundred yards downstream and had clambered out just short of the beginning of the gorge. The bank here was covered with dense bush which eventually led up towards a high hill beyond that overlooked the river. The sound of firing came from his right and he remembered the survivors of the Edendale Troop that he'd seen off in that direction. Evidently they were not out of the woods yet for the Zulus were still pursuing the fugitives right up to the Mziyathi and several of the more daring ones might even try to swim across after them. They would have a better chance by joining with as many of the survivors as possible - what's more, it was his duty as their commanding officer to lead his Troop again, to organize their fighting retreat and to create a rallying point for any other men who managed to get over the river.

Wearily, Davies worked his way up the riverbank towards the source of the fighting.

Aware of just how close the chasing hordes of zulus were, in his desperation to reach the Mzinyathi young Horace Smith-Dorrien galloped over the lip of the final hill and down the other side so recklessly that he almost failed to spot the steep precipice ahead. Luckily for him his horse did, and it reined in at the last. He gave a cry when he saw the perpendicular drop and the hairs on the back of his neck stood up when he realized how fortunate he'd been; another few feet and he would have gone plummeting down there onto the rocks below.

Quickly pulling out his revolver and checking that it was loaded (those rounds he had borrowed from Lieutenant Bromhead of B. Company had proved to be his salvation on a number of occassions during his flight, he reflected) he climbed down out of his saddle and led his horse forward. At the edge he glanced down.

Lying at the bottom of the rockf ace on the bush-covered sloping ground that led towards the riverbank were the corpses of two or three fellow fugitives and their horses. He grimaced as he visualized how they must have gone tumbling to their deaths, their bodies striking the rocks like rag dolls on the way down. He could clearly see a series of white scratch marks on the side of the precipice made by the horseshoes as the riders and their horses had gone sliding down to the bottom. He shuddered at the awful sight.

Trying to close his mind off from this latest horror Smith-Dorrien started to pick his way down an alternative route alongside the edge of the precipice, keeping several feet back incase he should lose his footing on the treacherous ground. The path he took snaked through the undergrowth along a circuitous course that cost him valuable time but now that the river - his final obstacle-was now in view he started to feel a little more confident that the end was within reach.

Just then he heard a loud moaning sound. He came to a halt and raised his sidearm.

Holding his breath he waited.

Then the sound came again, longer and drawn out now, the noise of someone in pain. It ended with a blasphemy and a whimper.

"Who's there?" Smith-Dorrien whispered.

There was a moment of silence and then a quiet voice answered back. "Help me, please. Thank God someone came. Don't leave me."

"Where are you?"

"Here by the rock."

Smith-Dorrien crept towards the sound and came upon a large boulder partially hidden by a screen of aloe plants. Sitting with his back against the rock on the far side was a soldier in his thirties, dressed in the uniform of the Mounted Infantry. He was gripping his upper arm tightly where he had been stabbed and blood seeped between his fingers and ran down his wrist to drip in a puddle of the ground. The man looked up at him with pleading eyes. His face was deeply lined with pain.

"Please help me. My arm is badly hurt, I can't stop the bleeding. He crept up on me and stabbed me before I even knew he was there." He nodded towards where a dead Zulu warrior lay at his feet, flies buzzing around a gaping hole in his stomach. "But I managed to shoot him before he could finish me off. I've been here ever since, waiting for someone to come along. You're the first person I've seen who didn't end up going over that drop at the top. Don't leave me. You'll stay and help, won't you?"

"Of course," Smith-Dorrien told him as he dropped to his knees beside the wounded man. "But you must keep quiet as there are still Zulus around. And you should save your strength too. So no more talking, you understand?"

The Mounted Infantryman nodded and then rested his head back against the rock. Smith-Dorrien set to work.

Even though he was no surgeon and had no medical expertise he knew the basics of first aid. Taking out his riding crop and a white hankerchief he started to fashion a crude tourniquet in order to stem the bleeding. Wrapping the makeshift bandage around the wound and tying in the riding crop he twisted it several times and then secured it firmly. Within a few seconds the amount of blood seeping out was reduced to a thin trickle. Satisfied that this temporary measure would do he helped the man to his feet.

"Keep your arm above your head," he instructed, "and hold onto my belt. I'll get you down to the river."

Threading one hand through his horse's reins and holding out the other to maintain his balance, Smith-Dorrien gingerly led him down the steep hillside. It was tough going for the man was very weak. He just barely had enough strength to hold on to his bandolier so that he dragged Smith-Dorrien down. One false step and they could both go tumbling over the high precipice.

Ahead of them he caught brief glimpses of the river through the dense bush-cover and thought he saw several men trying to swim across to the other side, but the water seemed to be flowing very fast and the tiny figures were soon lost from his view as they were washed downstream. Faintly he could hear distant cries and shrieks. Were they coming from the men struggling to get over? he wondered.

They were about halfway down the hillside and he was trying to work out a way for them to get to the far shore when a sudden shout from behind startled him.

"For God's sake get on man, the Zulus are on top of us!"

They both spun their heads around together to see Major Stuart Smith come leaping and running down from the top of the hill, white as a ghost. He was badly injured they saw for his dark blue uniform was drenched with blood, and he seemed to stumble as though on his last legs, but something terrified him enough to keep him running despite his debilitated condition. He glanced back over his shoulder in fear and Smith-Dorrien followed the Major's gaze back up to the crest of the hillside just as the first Zulus appeared.

A knot of about twenty or thirty warriors carrying black and white shields came bounding down after Major Smith, chanting and rattling their spears excitedly now that they realized they had their prey trapped hard up against the fast flowing river with nowhere else to run to. More swept down further away to the left to cut off their flight in that direction, fanning out as they charged down the hill. Some swerved towards Smith-Dorrien and the Mounted Infantryman.

"Oh God," whispered the soldier, and he sagged to his knees in hopelessness, all thoughts of survival now gone.

Smith-Dorrien disentangled himself from the man's weak grip and let go of the reins as he backed up. He watched the Major come racing towards him, but he was too weak to outrun the young Zulu warriors and when a thrown assegai struck him in the back he pitched forward onto his face. They were on him before he had a chance to pick himself up, shoving the spear in deeper and clubbing the life out of him with their knobkerries in a mad frenzy. Several paused to slit him open but the rest rushed forward towards the soldier who was still on his knees, and he likewise disappeared beneath their onrush. Smith-Dorrien's horse panicked and instead of running for safety it instead went vaulting up the slope into their midst and he watched in horror as they brought the petrified beast down. But still the Zulus came on.

He knew he was next.

He fired two quick shots with his revolver into the charging mass but did not wait to see whether he hit anybody. Instead, with a passionate hope that fates guiding hand would come to his aid, Smith-Dorrien turned and leaped over the edge of the precipice.

His feet hit the hard-packed dirt side of the slope and crumpled under him so that he went spinning forward down the almost sheer drop. He bounced from rock to rock as he curled himself up into a tight ball, his back taking the worst of the blows, and his whole world became a crazy kaleidoscope of light and dark, of sky and earth. Then he felt himself crashing through dense undergrowth that slowed his descent momentarily before his body freefalled through mid-air for two or three heart-stopping seconds. A moment later he hit the river in a spectacular splash and the freezing cold water closed over his head.

It took less time than a heartbeat for Smith-Dorrien to realize what had happened and when he burst through the surface he let out a yell of thanks towards the deep blue sky, hardly able to believe his good fortune.

Yet his joy was shortlived for now he was racing downstream at a tremendously fast rate, the flooded river sweeping him away like some piece of driftwood. He kicked his legs furiously to stay afloat. He was twisted this way and that and while he was spun around he was granted a brief glance back towards the Zulu bank. The group of Zulus watching him there were receeding so fast that they quickly became tiny dots lining the side of the river, and then they were gone altogether as he was pulled under.

Somehow he heaved himself up and gasped in a lungful of air. He was about midstream now and at the mercy of the river, the flow too powerful for him to make any headway towards the far bank. It took all of his strength just to prevent himself being dragged under as his waterfilled riding boots and heavy clothes weighed him down. Through the spume and spray he saw the occasional body go spinning passed, as well as items of equipment and rifles. He'd kept a hold of his own revolver through sheer instinct but whether the water had damaged it beyond repair was impossible to know.

Suddenly he felt something large and solid thump him in the back and he was brushed aside as a large and powerful horse went swimming towards the Natal shore. Smith-Dorrien made a grab for its tail and through sheer luck rather than good judgement he managed to get a firm hold. He thought the horse might lash out with its back legs but it either failed to notice him hitching a ride or it was too intent on getting across for it continued to make steady progress through the torrent.

Smith-Dorrien held on grimly.

A minute later and he was being dragged over the large rocks that lined the opposite bank, and utterly exhausted as he was he could keep a grip on the horse's tail no longer. He slumped into a shallow pool at the rivers edge and watched as it galloped away.

His body ached all over. He thought his nose was broken for blood poured down his chin, and the skin on the hand which had been holding the horse's tail was lacerated with dozens of tiny scratches. But... it could have been so much worse. At least he was alive.

Alive but so tired.

He had never felt so weak before in all his life. He would have given the earth just to lay here for a while and have some rest. To sleep the nightmare away. To gather his strength for the long hike to the nearest settlement. Yet even as these self-indulging thoughts entered his mind he knew this was not to be, that he was not yet safe, and the end was not quite in sight. So he pushed himself up to his hands and knees and dragged himself onto one of the rocks nearby to take a look around.

His instincts proved correct. Further upstream along this bank - on the Natal side - he saw a body of Zulus running around to try and cut him off. They must have crossed elsewhere (presumably they knew of safer crossing points) and on seeing him drag himself clear of the water they set off at a run down towards his position.

Smith-Dorrien set off at a jog in the opposite direction, tired beyond belief but unwilling to just sit down and wait for the end like the wounded soldier had done. He hauled himself up a small hill that overlooked the narrow gorge, using rocks and branches to pull himself to the top. Every few hundred yards or so he turned to fire a round towards his pursuers (thanking the Lord that his revolver did indeed still work) and he was satisfied to see that with each shot more and more Zulus abandoned the chase, deciding to return to the crossing point for more easy pickings. However, a small handful of about eight or nine did stick with him. For a couple of miles they followed him down the river valley but for the most part they merely shouted insults after him or threw the odd assegai. Soon after this their pursuit peetered out. They had had their fill for the day.

Lieutenant Horace Smith-Dorrien cut across country to set out on the twelve mile trek to Helpmekaar.

At the same time that the young transport officer was making good his escape, James Brickhill was trying to pluck up the courage to enter the water himself. He had managed to get down the steep, brush-covered slope with little incident and found himself several hundred yards downstream of the main crossing point. Here the course of the river swept around a jagged outcrop of rock, slowing the flow somewhat before it entered the high sides of the narrow gorge. He could see the waters there stirred up into a wild and frothy maelstrom where it flowed over a shelf to create a miniature waterfall, and spinning around and around, trapped in its merciless grip, were three or four struggling horses. Brickhill looked away from the awful sight and thought it wise to choose an alternative spot to cross, further upstream.

But he stopped dead when he saw the mass of Zulus descending down towards the fugitives gathered on the bank. The soldiers and horsemen who had got this far suddenly found themselves fighting for their lives once again, turning to meet the Zulus who charged out of the high grass and vegetation. With most of their ammunition long since used up they used their bayonets or cavalry swords, fighting with sheer desperation. Many fell on the mudflats or amoungst the jumble of rocks. Others turned and threw themselves headlong into the river. A large proportion went under and did not surface again. Yet even for those who did manage to successfully get across the ordeal was not yet over, for by now several hundred warriors had also swam to the far side and here they waited, ready to stab them as they emerged from the water.

Brickhill knew right then that he had little choice but to take his chances and take the plunge right where he stood. To hesitate would only increase the likelihood of discovery. He had to make a move whilst the enemy were distracted.

Forcing his way through a gap in the vegetation he plunged in, holding on tight to the reins.

His horse began to swim surprisingly well, moving quickly towards the middle of the river in the shelter of the jutting rockf

461

ace. But once they cleared the calmer waters and entered the stronger currents where the flow was squeezed towards the mouth of the gorge then the going became harder. He urged it on by shouting words of encouragement. He assisted the best he could by kicking with his own legs. About halfway across he realized it was going to be too much for the animal to swim with him seated in the saddle and so he slipped off its back and clung on to one of the stirrups and swam alongside, guiding the horse as much as possible. It took the best part of five minutes for them to navigate the treacherous river, and more than once Brickhill nearly went under, feeling the currents tugging at him, but the sight of the horses swishing about in the seething pool just twenty feet away injected a last boost of resolve into the two of them. They finally emerged choking and spluttering onto the Natal side, both of them shivering from the cold water and barely able to stand.

Brickhill allowed himself and his horse no respite. Quickly checking that neither of them had sustained any serious injuries he wearily pulled himself back into the saddle.

His long hair was plastered to his face and slick with brown mud and he scraped it free of his eyes so that he could take a hurried glance around. Without his spectacles everything was a vague blur which he thought probably wasn't a bad thing; he had no desire to soak in too many details of the fighting raging away upriver, for the sounds alone were distressing. He did note a body of horsemen firing away towards the Zulu shore but there was a large group of Zulus between them and himself. Some had even moved downriver and were running up towards a hill to his front as though chasing after someone there. He waited until they passed out of sight, then he firmly urged his tired horse on, heading away from the Mzinyathi valley.

Keeping to the dense undergrowth as much as possible he made towards the southwest. Towards the settlement of Msinga.

And home.

When Lieutenant Coghill reached the riverbank the skirmishing had moved on. By that stage the fugitives attempting to cross over had either being caught and killed in the shallows or had thrown themselves bodily into the water to either drown or - if they were lucky - to survive the crossing and clamber out on the far side to ride away. A few had turned back when confronted with this final obstacle and had tried to hide, but the Zulu warriors hunted them down one by one, a task which drew them away from the crossing point. Those warriors who had followed the escapees to the Natal side likewise had plenty to occupy themselves as they converged on any horsemen in their determination to stop any breaking through. So by the time he found himself stepping up to the waters edge the way seemed clear, the riverbank deserted except for the numerous corpses lying all about.

For a moment Coghill balked at the thought of entering the rapidly-moving river, wondering if he should find an easier place to get over. Yet would he get a better opportunity than this? he asked himself. He had a chance to cross unmolested whilst the Zulus were busy elsewhere. He should take that chance.

His mind made up, Coghill prompted his horse forward.

Before they entered the flow he looked back over his shoulder towards the top of the hill behind. Just as he did he saw Lieutenant Melvill appear on the crest, still clutching the Queen's Colours across his lap, and he watched his fellow officer begin the dangerous descent down towards the river. Waiting until he was halfway down, and satisfied that all seemed well, Coghill turned back to the front and then plunged in.

He gasped aloud, partly from the cold water but mostly from shock at just how powerful the current was. After just ten feet or so they were being pulled off course, his horse struggling to keep going with any forward momentum. And the pain in his knee-joint became so bad that he felt sick to the pit of his stomach as his leg was wrenched this way and that. Through clenched teeth his groaned aloud and his eyes squeezed to mere slits as he fought to overcome the agony.

At one stage his horse sank almost up to its eyes as it struck an object beneath the surface, perhaps a boulder or a submerged corpse, and Coghill clung on as they both nearly went swishing away. He lost his hat as the chinstrap snapped and his blue patrol jacket was half wrenched free by the force of the flow, but with a loud whinny the horse reared up and struck for the far bank with a renewed effort.

Then, as they reached the shallower waters again the strength of the surging river subsided enough for them to gain a foothold on the sandy bed, and they emerged drenched and half-drowned onto the Natal bank.

"Thankyou Lord, thankyou," Coghill managed in between coughing up great mouthfuls of water, his strength all but gone, and the whole of his leg on fire.

Pausing only to shake the water from his eyes and to pull back on his jacket he pressed on towards the steep hill to their front.

Back across the river Lieutenant Melvill briefly glanced up to see his friend riding away, wished him luck, them snaked his way in between the boulders that led down to the water. Somewhere closeby he could hear shooting. Occasionally a round passed by overhead with a peculiar whirring sound, causing him to duck reflexively, but he did not think that he was being directly targeted. Still, it was only a matter of time until the Zulus (wherever they were fighting) noticed him and decided to pay him a visit. Therefore he followed the route set by Coghill and the many others before him and charged straight into the river, keeping tight hold of the precious Colours.

He found himself in difficulties right from the offset. Like those before him he was physically spent even before they were confronted by this final obstacle that was the Mzinyathi River. Coming over the crest of the final hill to see the wild, seething waters below, and knowing that they had to cross over if they were to have any chance of surviving, was a heart-rending experience. This last blow was too much for many to take and they preferred instead just to sit down and wait for the Zulus to catch them. But Lieutenant Melvill, charged with the task of escaping with the Queen's Colours, did not once contemplate giving up. His responsibility towards the Regiment, towards salvaging the pride of Her Majesty's army as a whole, meant that he had to find the willpower to go on, to never even consider failure. Whatever the personal cost may be. And it was this determination to carry out his duty, to take the Colours to a place of safety, that gave him the strength of character to push on.

Once in the water the weight of the standard seemed to quadruple. He pulled it from off the saddle and held it above his head but this soon proved too awkward and so he clutched it tightly to his chest in the crook of one arm whilst he tried to steer his horse with the other. But already the flow was turning them over and Melvill scrambled desperately to stay in the saddle.

It was no good. The long ride over miles of difficult country, coming immediately after the hard fight, then this Herculean attempt to swim a flooded river just proved too much for his horse. With a sudden jerk it craned its neck back and rolled its eyes, then sank away, dead from a burst heart. Melvill nearly went with it for his boots were caught in the stirrups but with a twist and a kick he managed to thrust himself clear, only to be tossed about by the wild river.

Rolling over and over he was sent swirling away, his heavy boots and empty scabbard dragging him under. Every few seconds his face broke the surface allowing him to snatch brief gasps of air, but he knew this was only delaying the inevitable. His strength was going fast now. He had lost all sense of direction for he lived in a crazy place of cold water, dark shadows and body-breaking rocks. It was all he could do just to hold the cased Colour aloft and hope the end would come soon.

Ahead of him he caught sight of the top of a large boulder just breaking the surface and he considered whether he could struggle towards it, but he knew that his present course would take him right on by. He tried to turn his body and propel himself closer but he was being swept downriver too fast and in two or three seconds his chance would be gone. He wouldn't make it. And once he entered the mouth of the gorge a little further on, with its steep walls, there would be nothing to get a purchase on.

Just when he thought all hope was lost Melvill suddenly felt a hand grab hold of him and drag him in towards the rock. Not understanding what was happening he felt himself smack against its hard surface so hard that the Colour was nearly jarred loose from his grip. He grunted from the force of the impact but managed to keep hold of the slippery rock. Yet the staff was falling away and he grappled with it in terror. Then the other person who was also clinging on came to his aid again and helped him to pull the Colour back until it was safe in between their bodies.

"Get around the side!" he heard somebody shout into his ear above the roar of the water. "Keep out of the flow or you'll be pulled off!"

Without thinking Melvill did as he was told, happy to let somebody else be in charge until he got his bearings again.

Gasping for breath and wincing at the various aches and pains from the numerous injuries he'd sustained during his brief race down the river it was a full minute before he eventually looked up to see just who had saved him.

The man who looked back at him across the surface of the dark boulder had an oldish face, thickly bearded and covered with several old scars from many a fight, and with deep-set, wise eyes. Yet his voice suggested he was relatively young for it had a youthful tone, full of vigour despite his weary appearance.

"The name's Higginson, Lieutenant Higginson of the NNC," he introduced himself with a crazy half smile.

Melvill stared back thinking he was completely mad but he nevertheless told him his own name.

"Nice to meet you Mr Melvill, although I wish it was in better circumstances! I won't shake your hand otherwise this damn river will have you again!" He laughed out loud.

"Good idea!"

Melvill pulled himself higher up the rock so that he could take a quick peek around. They were about midstream, with water gushing around both sides of their perch. Their 'island' seemed very precarious and exposed, a lump of stone just a few feet wide from which they could so easily slip off. If they did then he doubted they would survive for very long for just a hundred yards downstream a small waterfall fed the river into the narrow gorge, and the water there was whipped into a fierce maelstrom as it flowed over rocks and boulders of every shape and size. If they didn't drown then they would be dashed mercilessly from one gorge wall to the other before being spat lifeless out of the far end a mile or so on. Already several men had met their grisly end there for he spotted their bodies being pummelled on the rocks. Trying not to think about this possibility too deeply he twisted his head to see how far away the Natal bank was. At his rough estimation he reckoned about sixty feet. Sixty feet of raging water seperating them from safety. It might as well have been sixty miles.

"You have my heartfelt thanks for saving me Higginson," he told his companion, "but what do we do now?"

"Prey?"

Melvill scowled heavily, not liking the answer.

Then, and just when they thought things couldn't get any worse, the water around them started to explode in little geysers as bullets began to strike the surface. "Good Lord! Haven't they had enough!" balled Higginson as they both ducked down.

Melvill spotted a new group of Zulus gathering on the riverbank, those with guns firing wildly in their direction, the others leaping up and down and stabbing the air with their spears in excitement. A second bunch higher up on the hillside joined in, lending even more fire. Soon, from the amount of shooting going on, every now and then a round would come dangerously close with several actually striking the rock they were clinging to and sending up sharp splinters of stone. They seemed to pay particular attention to his red tunic, he thought miserably as he pressed himself flat against the boulder. Yet they could do nothing about it. Trapped in the middle of the river they waited until one of the rounds found its mark.

On the Natal side Lieutenant Coghill was a third of the way up the first hillside when he heard this new bout of firing, and he paused to look back. He saw the two groups of Zulus taking potshots down into the raging torrent and he quickly scanned the area below to see who they were aiming for.

"Oh no," he murmured to himself when he spotted the two figures clinging on to the rock, one of whom who he recognized as Lieutenant Melvill. A sudden fear gripped him with an icy claw, not just a natural concern for his friend's safety but also because of the very real possibility that their Colours might be lost and destroyed for ever should Melvill be hit. It filled him with dread more so than the fresh memory of having witnessed the virtual annihilation of six full companies of regular soldiers from the 24th, even to a larger degree than his own life coming to a premature halt. Those things were bad... but to loose the Queen's Colour...

That Melvill and the other man, stranded as they were, needed help was instantly apparant to him. He could not leave either them or the Colours to their watery fate.

Turning his horse Coghill galloped back down the steep hillside.

The newly arrived Zulu warriors, part of the iNdluyengwe regiment of the right horn sent to mop up any survivors at the river, noticed him come back towards the bank and several of them switched their fire to him. Their aim, as usual, was poor, a combined result of old and obselete guns, homemade bullets, and inadequate training, and they mostly blazed away with little discipline. But one warrior was better than his companions and he patiently rested his musket on some rocks and carefully aimed at the horseman across the river. He waited until the rider slowed as he approached the water and just when the horse was stepping into the shallows, he fired.

He missed his intended target, the white officer, but hit the horse square in the forehead instead. The shot blew out its brains. The animal faltered and then its legs gave way.

Coghill felt himself being pitched headfirst into the river. His mouth instantly filled with water and he came up coughing and retching, then turned in time to see his horse's lifeless body go floating away, turning the river crimson.

For a second he was too shocked to do anything but when he felt the currents begin to tug at his uniform he quickly snapped out of his rigidity and started to swim out towards the boulder, his injured leg trailing uselessly behind him. Straining against the flow and trying to turn his head so that it pointed downstream, breathing heavily, he slowly approached the two men who were now watching him with incredulous looks on their faces.

More debris came washing down the river, saddles, helmets, empty bandoliers, a pair of riding boots, knocking against him and hindering his progress still further. Coghill fended them off with one arm but he was still hit several times about the face and upper torso. He saw a pack-horse fully laden with boxes strapped to its back go sailing by, its petrified braying echoing off the steep hills along either bank. Several lifeless bodies; white colonials, black native infantry, Zulus. They all swept passed like so much flotsam.

He swam through it all, trying to stay focused on one goal, one destination - the rock. Eventually he fetched up against the side, panting and shaking.

The three of them clung on, tired, bedraggled and bleeding, but not yet beaten. "Coghill, you should have got away whilst you had the chance!" Melvill shouted above the din.

Coghill wearily shook his head. "Had to... come back... to help you," he managed to gasp. "But we won't make it over! Not with the Colours, they're too heavy!"

"We might do... with all three of us carrying them."

"Those bloody Zulus will hit us the second we leave this rock!"
"They bloody well will if you stay as well! We must swim! It's our only chance!"
"I'm too tired! I've nothing left!"
"SWIM, DAMN IT, SWIM! OR YOU'LL DIE HERE!"
They stared at one another for several tense seconds, eyes burning angrily, until Higginson intervened.
"He's right Melvill, we don't have a choice! Come on! One last go!"
Coghill snatched up the black leather case containing the Colours. He noticed it was torn near the end, with the standard showing through. In all liklihood it would be ruined anyway by the time they crossed to the far side, the water destroying the material inside, but it wasn't just their physical possession that counted. It was the symbolism of saving them no matter what their final condition. That was the true source of their motivation.
"Alright, I'm with you!" Melvill finally said. He too took hold of the case.
Higginson came around to their side and gripped the end of the wooden staff.
Then they pushed themselves away from the rock and struck out for the riverbank.
Instantly the level of firing increased. The air above their heads was filled with lethal shot, whizzing passed their ears and striking the water. They swam harder than ever. Shouted words of encouragement to one another. Bunched together like this they were aware that they presented an easy target but it also helped them make better progress for they could propel their mass through the strong currents. For a few brief moments they began to believe that they might actually succeed.
Then their luck ran out.
As they reached the shallower water Coghill's bad leg struck a pile of boulders and he screamed out in agony, his hand releasing the case as he gripped his knee. Melvill and Higginson, startled, fell back into the deeper water and the Colour was snatched from their grasp by the current. They both lunged after it but were not quick enough. It went spinning away down towards the gorge. Floundering in the water all three of them watched as it disappeared over the small waterfall into the white rapids beyond.

"No, no, no," wailed Melvill dejectedly. He dragged himself up onto the rocky bank and lay there shaking his head.

Lieutenant Coghill saw the look on his friend's face and he came hobbling across, then shook him by the shoulder. At first he got no response so he did it again. After a moment Melvill glanced up. His eyes, he saw, were blank and empty voids as though all purpose had gone out of him. "We got across. The Colours are gone, so forget them. We did our best. Now let's try and save ourselves."

Melvin buried his face in his hands. He looked totally deflated, physically and mentally spent. Coghill gripped him under the shoulder and heaved him to his feet despite the agony in his leg, and then spoke closely into his friend's ear. "We have to get a move on. Some Zulus have crossed higher up and they are heading this way."

Lieutenant Higginson, who had also pulled himself from the river and moved higher up the banking, overheard this and he glanced towards the spot that Coghill was indicating, seeing the Zulus for himself. "They're coming on fast!" he called back down.

"Prey, we might still get to Helpmekaar, but only if we hurry. If you stay here you will never see your family again."

This last bit at last provoked a response from Melvill. He straightened himself and the fog that had been shrouding his eyes cleared. He gave a small nod of the head. "I'm alright now," he whispered hoarsly.

"That's my man."

The three of them then set off up the side of the large hill that led away from the valley. Higginson moved ahead to find the best way, turning to call back and guide the other two from time to time. Melvill and Coghill, near to total exhaustion, one still demoralized after failing in his duty to save the Colour and the other a virtual invalid who was unable to walk unassisted, came on behind helping one another forward. They stumbled over the uneven ground, pulling themselves higher and higher and forcing their way through dense brush. They spoke very little, their breathing coming in loud rasps.

The roar of the river although still dominant fell away as they climbed towards the top of the first rise. Near the crest was a large stone slab which leaned out crazily as though about to roll down and crush them, and they angled towards it hoping to lose themselves on the far side.

As they entered its cool shadow, escaping from the suns heat, Coghill caught a movement out of the corner of his eye. He flicked his head around and saw about a dozen Zulus darting towards them out of the long grass.

"Here they come!" he shouted.

Higginson, without a weapon, panicked. "For God's sake fire," he yelled, "you both have revolvers!"

Melvill and Coghill pulled out their sidearms and together they fired at the charging mob, dropping a Zulu each. Higginson crouched down and picked up a rock with which to defend himself with if they were rushed but then saw the other warriors flinch back, their nerves suddenly wavering. They dropped down into the grass just twenty feet away.

The three officers slowly backed up towards the slab of rock.

Suddenly, Lieutenant Melvill seemed to sag as though somebody had cut his strings and he fell to one knee, mouth agape, jaw trembling with fatigue. "I'm done up, I can't go any further," he groaned.

Alongside him Coghill slumped back against the slab. The colour had drained from his face. He could hardly hold his gun so weak was he. "Me also."

Higginson looked from one to the other, then back to the Zulus who had crawled several feet closer. A cold sweat broke out on his brow. He found he could hardly breathe for this throat had closed up and when he tried to speak all he managed was a weak croak. Without further ado he turned and fled.

Heart pounding in his chest he scrambled up the side of the large stone slab and then darted towards the crest of the hill just a few yards ahead. He did not look back.

Once at the top he ran down the other side into a shallow gulley and then sprinted away to the right, keeping himself shielded by the top of the hill. A couple of hundred yards away a second ridge began, this one higher than the first but further back from the valley, and he made for the thick vegetation that covered its flank. Before he reached it two horsemen suddenly appeared near the base, waving him over, and Higginson veered towards them with a feeling of immense relief. But also a tinge of deep shame.

The two riders were both basuto's and they seemed as pleased to see him as he was to see them. He came to a halt beside them and leaned forward to get his breath back.

Closed his eyes as the guilt came down upon him in a great avalanche.

Coming to a decision he straightened again. "Quickly men. There are two officers who need our help. We must go back for them."

Stepping up to one of the horsemen he pulled himself up onto the saddle behind him and pointed him in the right direction. Without hesitating they both galloped towards the hill-crest, drawing out their carbines and loading them even as they rode.

At the top they halted and looked down. Higginson saw the slab of stone below but Melvill and Coghill were on the far side and hidden from view. He could see the group of Zulus hiding in the grass very clearly. It wasn't too late, he thought. The Zulus still had not rushed them.

But even as he thought this the body of warriors leaped to their feet and sprinted forward with a single synchronised war-cry, brandishing their assegais. He watched them converge on the rock from several sides at once.

There was the sound of a brief struggle, then two high-pitched screams, followed by more excited chanting.

Lieutenant Higginson closed his eyes and slumped his forehead against the basuto's back, shivering inside.

It was finished.

CHAPTER 46

ISANDLWANA. 3:30pm.

The fighting was at an end and the orgy of destruction had begun.

The victorious Zulu army moved through the camp and methodically slit open the stomachs of all the enemy dead. This was not to ensure that all had been killed, but was a part of their ritual to ward off the evil spirits of *mnyama* the 'darkness' - that would otherwise contaminate them when they returned home. Once an opponent fell in battle his body would quickly begin to swell in the African heat, an indication that the person's soul was trying to escape from the corpse, and if the warrior who had delivered the fatal blow did not help it on its way then this spirit would haunt him, cause his own stomach to swell, and ultimately send him mad. So to release it he must open up the body's stomach from sternum to groin, to *qaqa* his enemy. Once this was done the warrior must then wear an item of clothing taken from the corpse until such a time that post-combat ceremonies could be performed by their witch-doctors, and they were not allowed back into normal society until they had thus been cleansed. Each warrior who had killed - and even those who had simply stabbed an enemy soldier after he was dead, *homulaing* him repeatedly in order to share the glory of having overcome a worthy foe - was considered to be polluted following violent combat. They were said to be "wet with yesterday's blood".

They went around stripping the corpses, sometimes leaving on their trousers or just their boots, disemboweling each of them one by one.

When it was done the Zulus turned their attention to the campsite itself. With wild abandon they set about destroying or looting as much as they possibly could. The tents were torn into strips for the canvas was much prized by the Zulus and their contents ransacked and smashed. Travel chests were upended and the clothes and personal items within either taken as booty or thrown to one side. Any food was quickly devoured by the famished warriors and bottles of spirits broken open and greedily swallowed. Several of the younger men broke into the camp's medical supplies and found numerous bottles containing foul-smelling liquids of various colours, but so thirsty were they that they did not stop to think what these might be and they foolishly drank the lot. One of them contained carbolic acid. Within seconds several warriors were rolling about on the ground clutching their throats in agony.

The dozens of wagons situated on the saddle were plundered of all their goods. Ammunition boxes were kicked open and those Zulus who had managed to snatch up a much sought after Martini-Henry rifle took handfuls of cartridges whilst those who had older weapons, such as obsolete muskets or hunting rifles, tore off the brass bases with their teeth and poured the gunpowder into their powder horns. Sacks of mealie and foodstuffs were ripped to shreds once they'd had their fill and the contents scattered about; flour, sugar, tea, biscuits, tinned meat, and so on. The Officers mess was burnt to the ground, so too the Headquarters tents, the flag outside pulled down and ripped to shreds. Any animals that were found were brutally slain; horses, mules, oxen, officers' pet dogs. Nothing was spared. The devastation was total.

Soon a pall of dense, black smoke from the numerous fires they had lit hung over the camp like some somber funeral shroud.

Amongst these scenes of rampant destruction attempts were made to recover their own dead. Hundreds were dragged away on their shields or loaded into several wagons which were then hauled clear of the camp. They were taken out towards the dongas that scarred the foot of the escarpment and pushed or rolled in. They were not buried for in Zulu culture it was a dead man's spirit which mattered and not his body, and all that was required was to quickly dispose of their fallen comrades in the most convenient spot. Some were tossed into the grain pits of some nearby deserted kraals, whilst a few were unceremoniously shoved headfirst into ant bear holes. But many, either unnoticed or unclaimed by friends and relatives, were left on the field.

Here and there single Zulu warriors strolled amongst the wreckage and debris of battle looking to see if they could find lost companions or family members. They poked about amidst the corpses for in places the dead, both white and black together, were piled high. It was grisly work and usually they gave up after a while. Not always, though.

Dilikhana kaBokwe continued to search for his brother, Nzobo, long after the fighting had stopped.

Although he had not seen him since the beginning of the battle, having become separated from each other during the confused rush out of the valley, he knew in his heart that he was dead. He felt a great empty void inside as though a part of him were somehow missing, torn out by some merciless hand, and it left Dilkhana weak with dread. Walking amongst the corpses and searching face after face, trying not to slip on the blood and gore that covered the ground, he steeled himself for the inevitable. For sooner or later he was sure he'd find him.

He moved down through the camp area, ignoring the looting and disruption taking place all around him, his mind set on this one task. He crossed the dirt track and found himself close to the nek where the fighting had been fiercest, the ground carpeted with bodies. He worked his way through the piles of dead, the air thick with the smell of spilt blood. One large knot of corpses caught his attention and he wandered over, his gaze roving quickly over them so that he would not dwell on their horrific injuries. Searching. Always searching.

Until he finally found his brother.

Nzobo lay on his back staring sightlessly at the sky. His mouth was open a fraction and a thin trickle of dried blood had run down his cheek. Below this his throat had been ripped open by a gunshot wound, taking away so much of the neck that his brother's head was barely attached to the body. Another bullet had hit him in the chest. Either one could have proved fatal.

Just to one side was the corpse of a white man. An assegai was sticking out of its ribcage, and one of Nzobo's hands still clutched the shaft, defiant to the end.

At his brother's feet, another dead soldier, this one an officer. He had long, grey whiskers that stretched all the way to his collar bone, Dilikhana saw. And, most bizarrely, he appeared to have only one hand, for the man's left sleeve was tucked into his tunic. The other arm lay stretched out to the side, the fingers curled into a claw as though he had been holding something.

Dilikhana stood there for a long time looking down at the poignant scene. His face was expressionless, his mind blank. There were no tears, no cries of despair. He felt strangely calm within.

The feelings of heartache and loss would hit him later, and he would mourn in the privacy of his home, but for now he easily accepted the stark truth that was revealed before him.

That his brother was dead, but that he had died a warrior's death.

Victory was theirs, Dilikhana thought, yet it had come at such a high cost.

He crouched down then and pulled Nzobo's war shield over his body, covering him up the best he could, deciding to leave him where he had fallen. It was a fitting resting place.

Then he walked away.

CHAPTER 47

5 MILES SOUTHEAST OF CAMP. 3:30pm.

The waiting was the worst part, Commandant Hamilton-Browne thought to himself.

Waiting for His Lordship to respond to his warnings of imminent disaster. Waiting until reinforcements arrived so that they could hurry back to the stricken camp and hopefully rescue any survivors. Waiting here in their exposed position and wondering whether they would be next.

Waiting. Unable to do anything to help the camp's defenders in their hour of need.

His feelings of uselessness and frustration, shared by all of the 1/3rd NNC, was enough to make him want to drop to his knees and beat his fists against the bare earth. What could be taking Chelmsford so long? At least three hours had elapsed since he had sent his first messenger off to carry the news that Pulleine was under attack, plenty enough time for him to organize a relief column and come racing back across the plain as fast as was humanly possible. So why was there still no sign of them? For what seemed the hundredth time he ran his binoculars across the range of hills that lay to the east, searching for the tell-tale clouds of dust that would indicate the approach of a large body of cavalry and infantry. Once again he saw nothing. Cursing quietly under his breath he turned around and looked once more towards Isandlwana.

The fighting was over. The Zulus had carried the camp's defenses some time back, bursting though into the tent area and sweeping all before them. All was now quiet. There was just the occasional celebratory gunshot fired into the air. Here and there several fires had been lit and thick plumes of smoke rose into the sky, to hang there as though in silent witness to the carnage that he imagined lay beneath. Large groups of Zulus still loitered at the base of the mountain; no doubt they were looting what they could and destroying the rest, savouring their incredible victory.

Hamilton-Browne could hardly bring himself to dwell on the details.

Whilst he and his men had waited on the low ridge, urging Chelmsford to rush back in time to lend support, the camp had been overrun.

He cringed inwardly at the sheer totality of the disaster.

Of course there was a slim chance that all was not necessarily lost, he told himself halfheartedly. Perhaps a large proportion of the garrison had managed to fall back to Rorke's Drift still relatively intact. If the remainder of the Centre Column that was with Chelmsford could fight their way through the Zulus and reach them then it might be possible to regroup and counterattack, or at least secure the border from an all-out Zulu invasion. Yet they could only do that if and when Chelmsford returned, and the longer it went on...

The afternoon passed slowly away. The men could do nothing for the time being so they sat or lay on the ground resting, knowing that soon they may be called upon to retake the camp. They had no food, just a little water which was tepid and =refreshing - they drank it anyway. The sun blazed down on them for the earlier gloom had lifted and with no shade in which they could shelter they suffered under its boiling heat, adding to their misery.

A little after three-thirty somebody towards the back called out the news Hamilton-Browne had been waiting an eternity to hear. "There's a group of horsemen approaching from the rear, sir. I think it's the General."

At last!

His spirits raised somewhat by this - for they might finally be able to do something positive instead of all of this hanging about - he wearily brought out his fieldglasses and lifted them up to his eyes again. After a quick scan across the plain he picked out the approaching group.

It was His Lordship indeed. He could easily distinguish his dark blue undress uniform against the green earth as he rode at the head of the small party. With him were his staff plus a cavalry escort, perhaps thirty men in all. They must be the advance guard to the remainder of the column, Hamilton-Browne assumed, and he searched behind them for the welcoming sight of heavy reinforcements.

His heart sank.

All he saw was mile after mile of empty countryside, the plain rolling gently away towards the distant range of purple-shaded hills that rested on the far horizon. Of the force that had marched out that morning with Chelmsford, as well as the 2/3rd NNC who had accompanied Hamilton-Browne's battalion on their reconnaissance on the twenty-first, there was absolutely no sign whatsoever.

Where were they? he asked himself. What was His Lordship thinking of by not bringing them with him, despite his messages - his pleads! - for urgent reinforcements?

He dropped his fieldglasses in dismay and they swung against his chest.

Their one chance of rushing to Colonel Pulleine's aid had all but slipped away. By the time Chelmsford's men did join them, a march of seven miles followed by the five mile advance from here to Isandlwana, then the return trek along the road back to Rorke's Drift where any survivors might have gathered, it would be too late to make any difference.

With a nauseous feeling in the pit of his stomach Hamilton-Browne rode out to meet the General. As he approached the group he saw them hesitate on seeing him and they exchanged a few quick remarks with one another, nodding in his direction. Then they cantered forward, and as they came together Hamilton-Browne saw the heavy frown on Chelmsford's brow.

He gave a lazy salute which the General failed to return.

"What are you doing here, Commandant Browne?" Chelmsford asked in a surprised tone. "You ought to have been in camp hours ago helping with the move."

Hamilton-Browne stared back incredulously. Had he heard right? he wondered. The way the General was talking it was almost as if he had no knowledge of events at Isandlwana whatsoever. "Did you not receive my messages?"

Chelmsford pursed his lips before replying. "Yes. Some vague report of a heavy skirmish involving some of Pulleine's scouts, and that bodies of Zulus were gathering in his vicinity. However," he added with a glance over Hamilton-Browne's left shoulder, "all seems quiet at the camp now."

"That, My Lord," he muttered through gritted teeth, "is because the camp has been taken."

There was a moment of stunned silence from the riders gathered around them, as well as one or two horrified looks being passed too and fro. All of them then glanced off towards Isandlwana. Except for Chelmsford. He sat there stock still with his features set in granite. In the shadow beneath his hat's brim his eyes burned fiercely.

"How dare you tell me such a falsehood?" he snapped savagely, making them all jump. 'I left more than one and a half thousand men behind to guard the camp! More than enough to beat back the entire Zulu army! Taken indeed! What do you take me for?"

He leaned forward and glazed at Hamilton-Browne, continuing with his tirade.

"I ordered you to return to assist Colonel Pulleine to strike the tents and load up his baggage and to move forward to our new position. Instead I find you sitting here like you are on some kind of jaunt, unwilling - or too scared, I hazard - to advance because of a... a rumour... that the enemy has been sighted! You and your men are a disgrace! An embarrassment! Now you get them into line at once and move forward, or I shall have you court-martialled!"

Hamilton-Browne looked straight back at the General, his gaze steady as a rock. He said nothing. Slowly he took off his slouch hat and ran a hand through his thinning hair, then put it back on, pulling it down low to his eyes. Then he turned around and trotted back to where his command waited, curbing any response.

He got the battalion back to its feet and issued a stream of orders and within two minutes they had resumed their march towards Isandlwana, precisely as ordered.

Chelmsford, his staff, and their escort, fell in beside them.

For about one mile they trampled over the undulating plain, losing sight of the camp from time to time whenever the lay of the land dipped, but with more and more details coming into view the closer they went. An uneasy murmur passed through the black infantry for their keen eyes could see more of the true nature of the state of affairs than their white officers or the Headquarters staff could, but they dared not halt for they had seen the General's fury, and it was a wrath they had no desire to see again.

Soon they reached the track and now were able to advance more quickly.

Half a mile further on and the truth was plain for all to see. Chelmsford called a halt.

Quietly, almost furtively, he brought his horse up alongside Hamilton-Browne's, who at first refused to look at him. Speaking now in a mild-mannered way, for his demeanour had changed dramatically since his earlier outburst - something he was acutely ashamed of -Chelmsford asked, "On your honour, Commandant Browne, is the camp taken?"

Waiting several seconds before he turned to appraise his superior he glanced across at him. His anger at being painted a fool, no, worse than that, a coward, evaporated in a flash as soon as he saw the pained expression on Chelmsford's long and gaunt face, the look of a haunted man.

In an equally kind way he replied in a soft voice.

"The camp was taken at a little after one-thirty sir, and the Zulus are now burning some of the tents." He looked meaningfully at the clouds of smoke that hung over the base of the mountain and then back at Chelmsford.

"That may be the quartermaster's fatigue burning the debris of the camp."

"Quartermaster's fatigue do not burn tents, sir." He took out his fieldglasses and leaned across to offer them to the General.

Chelmsford waved them away and said dully, "hold your men here."

Hamilton-Browne watched as he turned and trotted over to where his staff waited in a lonely little cluster, looks of dumbfounded shock on their pale faces. Orders were passed on and a moment later a single rider went galloping away to the east.

Too late, Lord Chelmsford was bringing the rest of his force back from the Mangeni.

THE TRACK TO ISANDLWANA. DUSK.

By the time the remainder of the column joined them the sun was starting to dip towards the western horizon. The sky turned a vivid red as the end of that traumatic day approached. Stretching out across the plain, the shadow of Isandlwana hid the horrors that lay along its base, and the men gathering together and preparing to return knew not what to expect.

With all hope now extinguished their misery had been replaced by a dread of what lay out there coupled with a growing sense of anger at what had happened to their friends. Vengeance was in their hearts. It gave them the determination they would need if they were to retake the camp by force.

Now that he had his reinforcements Lord Chelmsford, after allowing the new arrivals to slake their thirst at a nearby stream, strode forward on foot to address them. In the dim light the men could see that his face was ashen and he appeared distracted, as though his mind was far away. His eyes were red-rimmed from where he had been constantly rubbing them. He cast a shambling and forlorn figure.

In a barely audible croak he told them the news... and his intentions.

"Whilst we were skirmishing amongst the hills in front it appears that after a hard fought battle the Zulus have taken our camp." He paused as a ripple of gasps and moans of despair passed through the ranks, their shock as sharp and deep as that which he felt in his own heart. When they quietened again he continued. "There are ten thousand Zulus in our rear where we were this morning and twenty thousand to our front; we must win back our camp tonight, secure the track, and cut our way back to Rorke's Drift tomorrow. There can be no retreat. No man must retire."

He ran his eyes over the ranks. Every single man aligned up in front of him was looking steadily back, some muttering quietly to themselves, others weeping silent tears that stained their dirt-grimed but determined faces. Chelmsford wondered what thoughts were passing through their minds. Hatred was certainly one of their emotions he surmised, but was it directed at the Zulus or at himself? How did they regard their General now, after this terrible calamity?

As if to seek the answer to this he turned and looked towards Colonel Crealock who was standing just off to one side.

But his Military Secretary could no longer bring himself to look him in the eye. His face was downcast, staring at his own boots.

Feeling abject pity throughout his entire being Lord Chelmsford scratched and tugged his beard.

Just then, something quite remarkable happened.

From within the silence that had followed his little speech the men began to cheer. They gave a hearty shout and in unison they raised their helmets and waved them high, or some just shook their fists or their guns or their shields and assegais. It was a spontaneous thing which came from the heart. Not an endorsement of his generalship, Chelmsford was quick to tell himself lest he got any false illusions, but rather a rallying cry and a commitment to themselves... as well as a promise to avenge their fallen comrades at the first opportunity.

With his gloom temporarily lifted he set about arranging his force in attack formation.

Their line of advance would follow the route of the dirt track. Here, at the centre, he placed his four limbered guns with the few wagons the column had taken with them immediately behind. On each side, moving by fours, were the six companies of infantry from the 2/24th, split into equal halves. Next came the NNC, the second battalion under Commandant Cooper on the right flank and Hamilton-Browne's boys of the first battalion on the left. To each side of these right and left respectively were the Mounted Police and Mounted Infantry formed in troops, and the Volunteers.

When all were in place and ready they set off into the gathering gloom.

In the near distance several fires still burned within the camp area, too large to be cooking fires but very likely burning tents and wagons. They could smell the smoke even two or three miles away. The mountain itself loomed ahead, a dark silhouette against the early evening sky.

By now the sun had set. The horizon slowly faded from red to a deep purple and then the night began to creep across the land.

They trampled on mostly in silence, their eyes straining for the first sign of the enemy. Soon they came across the first bodies.

At first there was just a sprinkling of them, all Zulus. They lay singly or in twos and threes, and the advancing line of soldiers and horsemen were able to weave their way through with little difficulty. But the further on they went, coming closer and closer to the camp, the more numerous the corpses became until the ground was carpeted with them and they had no option but to walk over the dead. Here and there men tripped and went down but they hurriedly pushed themselves back to their feet in disgust at having touched the cold flesh and the open wounds. On they went.

When they reached the line of the wide donga that cut the plain in half Chelmsford called a brief halt. The dried up watercourse was empty save for thousands of expended cartridge cases that glinted dimly in the poor light, and beyond the field of dead stretched away on the far side.

Although it was almost dark by now a few more features in the camp were distinguishable from this close. Most of the tents it seemed had either being ripped down or burnt but the centre-poles of a few were visible, and so too were the horse lines on the slope behind. Near the saddle they could make out the bulky forms of about a dozen wagons, perhaps dragged there to block the road. Chelmsford took in these details and licked his lips nervously.

Fearing that they may be walking into a trap he strode back towards the artillery commander

"Unlimber your guns would you, and fire a few rounds into the camp. It might frighten any Zulus away or at least force them to show their hand."

The men watched as the four artillery pieces were made ready, the gunners bristling around their weapons with impressive speed. Each fired a single round and the shells went trailing away through the evening sky, their fuses burning so that they seemed like short-

484

lived meteors arching across the heavens. They exploded on the saddle or against the side of the mountain with dull booms.

They provoked no reply from any Zulus still waiting in the camp. So Chelmsford ordered them on.

They crossed the donga in mesmerized awe at the visible signs of the magnitude of the battle that had raged here, the spent cases chinking under their heavy boots. A determined stand had been made here, the defenders exacting a terrible toll on the attacking Zulus, but the soldiers' fate was still a mystery. The guns and wagons were manhandled up the far side. Several men became lost in the darkness and wandered nervously about up and down the gully, calling out to their mates, and grateful when they found their way back to their units.

They moved forward for another half mile and the ground gradually started to slope upwards towards the saddle between Isandlwana and the stony hill to the left. The profusion of dead continued but now there were a number of white corpses mixed in with the Zulu warriors, stripped half-naked to reveal their terrible mutilations, vaguely visible in the black of night. Somewhere a man was weeping loudly, unable to cope with these appalling sights, whilst another vomited onto the ground because of the stench of death.

Once again Chelmsford brought the line to a stop. They were close to the camp now and as of yet the victorious Zulus had not shown themselves. He moved down towards the Imperial companies on the left and ordered Major Wilsone Black - hero of the attack on Sihayo's kraal - to take them forward and seize the stony hill. "We need to hold the high ground there if we are to keep the road to Rorke's Drift open. You must grab that position at all costs," he told the Scot.

Wilsone Black, fired up and hungry for retribution, gave a brisk salute and spun away.

"Fix your bayonets you red devils!" he called as he stomped down the line. "We have a job to do!"

They moved out cautiously, stumbling and feeling their way through the darkness, climbing up the long gradient. The ground became more and more rocky, and then steepened suddenly as they ascended up the side of the boulder-strewn hill. Behind them the four cannons fired more rounds, the shells ripping over their heads to explode on the nek. The infantry flinched and wavered at the sound.

"Keep your formation!" Wilsone Black urged, "be ready to fire a volley and charge! Let your steel do the work!"

Onwards. Upwards. Through a night of pitch.

The men sweating and panting as their anxiety reached its pinnacle.

Their eyes seeking out the enemy, who might be lurking amongst the boulders, ready to stab at them.

Then, so suddenly that it caught them by surprise, they were at the top.

They had retaken the hill without any opposition.

The Zulus, it seemed, had gone. They had slipped away in the night.

Breaking out in a loud cheer Wilsone Black's men signalled to those waiting below that it was safe to advance once more.

The remnants of Lord Chelmsford's Centre Column limped back into the destroyed campsite, towards the very heart of the bloodbath.

CHAPTER 48

The coldness of the night bit deep and Lord Chelmsford, standing slightly away from where the men rested, shivered as the chill gnawed away at his bones. Somewhere nearby he could hear some of the sentries he had posted talking quietly as they tried to stay alert. Apart from this, and the chirping of nocturnal insects, all was quiet. He had ordered the column to rest and try and get some sleep for they may have a tough day ahead of them, but he doubted whether any of them slept. How could they? Camped as they were amongst the corpses of their dead comrades.

He thought he would never enjoy another peaceful night for as long as he lived.

Not after this day.

The nightmare memory of it would haunt him forever, returning to him in the dead of night. Of that he was sure.

Chelmsford craned his neck back and stared up at the Milky Way that stretched overhead from horizon to horizon, admiring its beauty. Normally the sight would be a great comfort to him, pushing his worries to the back of his mind as he began to relax after a hard day in the saddle, and for a brief moment he thought it might help to ease the burden that weighed him down now. But then he thought about the multitude of stars he could see up there and this made him think about the countless number of lifeless, cold bodies that surrounded them, and any solace disappeared as though it was blown away on the night breeze.

Dropping his gaze he stared out into the blackness. On the horizon stretched a line of widely-spaced fires like a string of orange pearls, marking the sites of numerous burning homesteads. Some of these were over the border in Natal, an indication that the Zulus had followed up their success here by raiding over the river, hitting farms and communities far and wide and leaving a trail of more destruction in their wake.

How far would they go? he wondered. Would they launch an all-out invasion of the colony? Would they hit Greytown, Pietermaritzburg, even as far as Durban? Or across into the Transvaal to sweep away the Boer farmers? There was nothing to stop them, the border was wide open. Perhaps the disaster here was only the beginning. He just didn't have the answers.

One thing he did know with a cold certainty was that his invasion plans lay in tatters. The immediate and most paramount task now would be to try and secure the frontier and shore up Natal's defences. Once they were safely back over the river and knew precisely what the situation there was he could begin to formulate some kind of strategy, hoping against hope that he was not too late. The other two columns, Wood's to the north and Pearson's on the coast, would have to be halted and either withdrawn or ordered to hold fast in good, strong, defensive positions. There could be no more offensive movements until the situation was back under control and reinforcements arrived from home. Every border post would have to be strengthened with whatever forces he could scrape together and laagers thrown up around the towns and settlements. It would be a mammoth task needing all of his attention and the dedication of those called upon to help during this most trying of times. Only then, and not before, could he turn his thoughts to restarting the invasion and taking the war to the Zulus once more.

But before any of that they had to get through this long night and then somehow make it back to Rorke's Drift in the morning.

They were not out of the woods yet.

Just how complete the disaster was he did not know. Thankfully the night hid the worst of the horrors that surrounded them. He did not doubt for one minute that they had suffered a terrible setback with the camp having being destroyed, hundreds of tonnes of supplies and equipment lost, and large numbers of men killed: Commandant Hamilton-Browne had seen the battle unfold from a distance and he had been quite blunt in his opinions that only a few could have escaped the slaughter. Only when the new day dawned would the true scale of the defeat be revealed and Chelmsford had no intention of exposing the men to such an ordeal, for he felt certain this would shatter their already shaky morale beyond repair. No, before first light he intended that his force be on the move away from Isandlwana, thus sparing them this final torture.

He had also made it clear that no one was to go searching through the camp area. Ostensibly this was for their own safety, he told them, for it was possible that there might be Zulus still out there, but personally he thought they were probably long gone by now. The real reason for preventing the men wandering about was once again to shield them from the worst of the nightmare. They had been through enough without them stumbling and falling about amongst the stiffening bodies of lost friends and colleagues. Strangely, some of them protested against this. They wanted to absorb the details, so it seemed. They wanted to hunt about through the debris, to search for their mates, or to see what they could salvage from their tents. He refused them permission. No, they would sit tight in their little square on the crest of the nek, and then as soon as the night sky showed the first signs of brightening they would form column and set off back towards the drift.

As these and other thoughts passed through his mind, causing a painful throb to develop behind his eyes, Chelmsford became aware of soft footsteps approaching. He turned at the sound.

From out of the shadows came the ghostly figure of Colonel Crealock, holding a lantern in one hand to light his way. He strode forward with a steely look in his eye.

"Yes Colonel?"

"I've just come to inform you My Lord that I've completed my rounds. The sentries and night pickets are all in position, with orders to report any unusual sounds. Our perimeter seems secure." He spoke briskly, having overcome his earlier doubts. He was back in control again, at the General's beck and call, as attentive as always.

"Good," Chelmsford responded.

A long and drawn out silence followed, during which Crealock's eyes darted too and fro across his commander's face.

"Is there something on your mind Colonel?"

Crealock puckered his mouth and gave a gentle sigh, then said, "do you mind if I speak frankly sir?"

"By all means go ahead."

"Well... I don't like to speak ill of the dead sir... and perhaps now is not the time to raise the subject... but I can't stop thinking that... ah..." he hesitated, unsure as to whether to continue.

"Can't stop thinking what?"

He closed his eyes for several seconds as though tussling with some dangerous theory in his head. Then he snapped them open. "That Durnford must have had a hand in all this." He indicated the hidden horrors that lay out there in the night with a broad sweep of his hand.

"Go on," Chelmsford said quietly, moving closer, trying to keep the eagerness out of his own voice.

"Well, when we left camp this morning, it was made quite clear to Colonel Pulleine as commanding officer that his duty was merely to defend the camp, was it not?"

Chelmsford nodded, refraining from mentioning that it was Major Clery who had infact issued the instruction on his behalf.

"Yet later, when Durnford joined him with his column, because he is - or was, I should say - senior to Pulleine, he would automatically take over command and any such orders that had been left would devolve onto him. In simple terms the instruction to *defend* the camp was then his responsibility. Knowing Colonel Pulleine he would not have hesitated to ah hand over the reins as it were. And to rely on Durnford's experience. So from that moment henceforth he was duty-bound to obey those orders."

Chelmsford continued to listen carefully.

"Acting strictly on the defensive means just that. Retract your forces, do not push out, and under no circumstances dilute your strength. Yet on our way in sir I could not help but notice the evidence of heavy fighting in the gully out across the plain, a good mile or more from the camp. And the spread of fallen soldiers as we approached also indicate heavy fighting well away from the tents, their location indicative of a quick retreat from far advanced positions. As senior officer present any tactical decisions fell under his total authority."

Chelmsford raised a hand then to halt Crealock during mid-flow. He carefully pinched his lips together between first finger and thumb. "Do you not think your judgement is somewhat hasty, considering that we do not have all the facts available to us?"

Crealock bowed his head a fraction in acceptance of this but he continued nevertheless.

"We have to remember Durnford's past record My Lord. He has shown a degree of carelessness on numerous other occasions. Sometimes he has made choices that have been proven... unwise? Impulsive? Hare-brained? This whole tragedy smacks of the kind of personality defects Durnford is infamous for. Was for." He finished with a slight shrug of his shoulders.

Chelmsford considered what his military secretary had said, his gaze wandering off into the darkness. His points, he thought, were well put - if somewhat insensitively phrased. But then, Crealock was never one for mincing his words.

Of course, he was assuming that both Pulleine and Durnford were dead. If one of them had survived then he could give a full account of what had really happened here, without the need for all of this supposition. Yet if neither officer had survived then it would be down to him, Chelmsford, to unravel the complex chain of events, decisions and orders that had ultimately led to disaster. Including, he added to himself belatedly, his own role in things.

He did not consider himself an unforgiving man. Neither was it his style to shift the blame for things onto the shoulders of dead men. He only sought the truth.

A proper understanding of what had gone wrong.

Still - and although he did not yet know it - the seeds of doubt concerning the late Colonel Durnford RE. had already being planted into his subconciousness.

Gently he steered Crealock away. "Let us discuss this further, shall we," he said quietly.

Lying on the ground nearby, pulling a blanket up under his chin to keep out the cold - for there was an unseasonable chill about the night - Lieutenant Henry Harford surreptitiously listened in to their conversation.

At first his mind had been on other things. Like all of the other men resting there he had repeatedly been asking himself how such a frightful calamity could have happened, so quickly, with nobody aware of what was going on just a dozen miles away from where they had spent an eventful day chasing after groups of Zulus amongst the hills and valleys. It was almost too freakish to understand, let alone come to terms with. Nothing could possibly have prepared them for this, it was completely out of their experience.

As he had lain there, his mind turning things over and over, but coming to no real conclusions, Harford slowly became aware of the conversation taking place just a few feet away. To begin with he paid the two men little notice. After all, what they had to discuss was really no business of his. But when he heard the name 'Durnford' being mentioned his curiosity became suddenly aroused. Straining his ears he tried to listen to what they were saying.

What he heard (not just the actual words but also their scathing tone, delivered with poorly hidden and personally felt contempt for the man they spoke of) filled him with horror. That they could talk that way, of a person not only so recently departed but whose body in all probability lay out there perhaps just yards from them, was insensitive to say the least, and downright callous. Harford felt a horrible revulsion uncurl inside his stomach. He wanted to shout out, to implore them to stop, but despite his anger he managed to stop himself from doing so; as much as he wanted them to refrain from showing such vulgar disregard for a brave officer he knew it was not worth risking his own career over. After all, he should not be privy to their decision-making, blame-appointing, discussion.

So he said nothing.

Chose not to intervene.

Aware that he would have to live with himself but prepared for that.

Rolling over onto his side so that he could hear no more Harford pressed himself up close to the man sleeping next to him to keep warm. In the darkness he could just make out a pale face staring up at the stars overhead.

"Can't you sleep?" he asked him quietly.

The soldier didn't answer.

"Me neither. My mind is in a right state. It won't settle, won't stop spinning around and around." He turned his face to look up at the constellations that covered the dark void above them, spotting a shooting star as it raced from east to west. He gave a humourless laugh and shook his head. "What a bloody big mess!"

Somewhere in the distance came the sound of a single drunken voice singing in the night, a Zulu warrior high on brandy and victory. Harford listened for several minutes but after a while it faded away.

"I lost a lot of good friends today. Pals I've known for a long time. All gone probably. How about you, did you leave any of your mates behind in camp? Of course you did. We all did, I reckon. Well, they'll be hell to pay for this, you can count on that."

He looked over towards the prone figure lying beside him, face pale with shock. "I don't blame you for being too upset to talk."

Harford licked his lips, suddenly noticing how dry they were. Infact he was parched. He reached for his water bottle and then remembered that it was empty, and he leaned across to his new friend.

"Can you spare some of your water there?" he asked. "Mine's all gone."

Still the soldier did not say anything. Harford peered closer, and thought the man's eyes might be closed now - although he couldn't be sure because it was just too dark.

"Are you asleep?"

Nothing.

"Best that you are. They say it is the quickest way to heal one's head, sleep. To shut things out of your mind temporarily." Quietly he reached across for the soldier's water bottle, trying not to disturb him. He was sure he wouldn't mind if he took a small sip.

Suddenly his hand sank into something sticky and wet. What on earth...? Harford asked himself in surprise as his fingers were sucked in and the soft, clinging substance closed around his wrist. He froze. Bile rose into his throat as understanding dawned.

He lay there stiffly, knowing he had just reached into the soldier's jellified innards. Through a wide rent in his stomach.

The figure beside him was a dead man, cold and stiff to the touch, killed along with the hundreds of others that afternoon.

Lieutenant Harford had been unknowingly lying next to a corpse all this time! Had even been talking to it!

He pulled back with a gargled cry of revulsion and leaped to his feet, hurriedly stepping away. Sickened by what he'd done he wiped his hand on the blanket he still clutched to get rid of the blood and gore, and then he threw the blanket itself away, incase it too was stained. His stomach heaved and he bent over double, retching spasmodically, but because he had not eaten for nigh on two days nothing came up. He spat onto the ground and his eyes watered. Then he stumbled blindly away.

The shapes of dozens of prone forms covering the ground all about took on a new and frightening meaning to him for he could not tell which his resting companions were and which the butchered remains of the slain were. Numb with shock, and now terrified to lay down again, he instead went tottering through the darkness away from the bivouac area, not heeding the order to remain in one group and not to go wandering about. Surprisingly nobody stopped him.

He crossed the nek in a bewildered daze, not really aware of which direction he was going in, heading for the camp area.

Several large fires still burned where the Zulus had torched the shattered remains of tents and supply wagons and his way was lit by the fiery red glow they cast. Horror after horror was revealed to him, corpses piled high with their intestines and guts spilled out, some with limbs or heads detached, and intermixed with them the dead oxen and mules and horses, smashed crates and bottles and a thousand other pieces of camp impedimenta scattered far and wide. In his wanderings he came across the wreckage of one of the ambulance wagons, its axle snapped clean in two, the half-dozen horses dead in their traces. A strong stench of spilt chemicals wafted out of the back flap stopping him from edging any closer, but he did notice a body lying crushed into the earth just twenty or thirty feet beyond, the skull caved in where the wheels had pulverized it.

He pressed on, going from one nightmare scene to another.

Harford absorbed all the details, his mind storing them somewhere in some dark recess, from where they would be replayed dozens of times during the months and years ahead, to haunt and mock him.

He next found himself wandering within the area of ground where his own battalion of natives had been encamped, and he moved through the debris towards where his own tent had been pitched. Expecting it to have been either pulled down or burnt to the ground he was surprised to see it still standing, and he pulled back the flap to look inside, half-thinking of salvaging what he could of his own baggage.

In the dim glow from the fires he peered through the entranceway.

Everything inside had been thoroughly ransacked with his travel chest upended and emptied, his few pieces of furniture smashed or piled up into one corner, and clothes and personal effects strewn about. His various jars of preserved insects which he normally kept shut away in a small mahogany case lay about on the ground, all shattered, and his leather entomology textbooks ripped to pieces. The canvas sides of the tent were torn to shreds. At a glance he saw that many things were missing, obviously taken as plunder, and he doubted whether he would ever see them again. He took in all of this in the first two or three seconds as he stood there looking inside.

What drew his attention more than anything though were the two bodies lying amongst the mess. One lay on its back up against the side wall and the other was sprawled over the broken furniture, tossed there like a piece of rubbish. Both had been partially stripped. Both had been cut open.

Harford knew who they were for he recognized their features even in the poor light but he couldn't recall their names. They were two of his white drivers. A sense of pity about the squalid nature of their deaths struck him, for in their futile attempts to escape they had blackened their faces with boot polish in the desperate hope the Zulus would leave them alone, and he staggered against the doorway. Silently he turned and walked away from the terrible scene.

He had seen enough. His curiosity had been beaten into submission by this procession of distressing images and he had no desire to explore any further.

Harford drifted up the sloping ground behind the remnants of the camp in a stupor, moving into the shadows once more. He was still unwilling to rest after his earlier shock, preferring instead to stay on his feet until morning, and he pulled himself up over the shoulder of Isandlwana overlooking the dirt road. He knew it was dangerous to move around like this for there might still be Zulus out here somewhere... but the way he felt at that moment he didn't really care whether he was attacked or not.

He reached the edge of the shelf and stopped to rest and gather himself.

Then, in the quietness of the night, he heard something. A staccato popping sound drifting across the hills, fading in and out at first and then becoming constant and rising slightly in volume. Harford knew what it was.

The sound of prolonged gunfire, distant but clear.

He looked around and tried to pinpoint its source.

Until a few moments later he saw a sudden red flare in the western sky, illuminating one of the hills.

He knew the one, had passed it just several days earlier at the start of the invasion, its peculiar pointed tip instantly recognizable. The one the Zulus called *Shiyane* 'the eyebrow', known to the British as Oskarberg Hill, in the shadow of which lay the Swedish Mission Station of Rorke's Drift.

Their post there was on fire and under attack.

Harford watched for a few moments longer and then hurried back to inform the General.

CHAPTER 49

ISANDLWANA.
BEFORE DAWN, THURSDAY 23rd JANUARY.

As they formed up in the early morning half-light, walking amid the grim tableau of death, the men tried not to let their eyes linger on the scenes of devastation that lay all about them. They averted their gaze from the multitude of bodies, preferring instead to blankly stare straight ahead, or up at the brightening sky, or the steep side of Isandlwana that was just dimly visible - anywhere except at the corpses, except at the blood-splattered rocks, except at the gore-splashed earth.

A low-lying mist helped to shroud the carnage, but neither this nor the gloom of pre-dawn could stifle the odour. Nothing could prevent them smelling the stench of death. Of sudden death. Of sudden, violent, death. It permeated the air for already the dead were beginning to decompose a little over twelve hours since the fighting had finished. And once the men had marched away from here and the sun had risen, then the flies and vultures would descend, to devour.

Slowly, as the orders rang out, the tired and dishevelled men shuffled into position. In fifteen minutes they were in column and ready to depart. Then the word was given and off they set; they had all the appearance of an army of ghosts leaving a haunted battlefield.

At their head was their ashen-faced General, twin dark smudges beneath his eyes testimony to his long and sleepless night.

The column headed west. It crested the nek and snaked its way back to the border from whence it had begun the invasion just twelve days previously, then full of confidence and anticipation of a swift victory, but now the demoralised and beaten dregs of an army. Most of them did not glance back.

Forming a rearguard screen was the Natal Mounted Police. Their commander, Major Dartnell, rode up front with the General's staff leaving his trusty second-in-command, Inspector Mansel, in temporary charge. First making sure no stragglers were left behind they threw out squads of men to either flank and one to the rear, their eyes scanning the lightening hills, constantly on the alert for the first signs of the enemy.

Mansel himself lingered for a moment on the nek. He was the last man to leave. Twisting around in his saddle he peered back over his shoulder.

The sun was just lifting clear of the range of hills to the east, heralding a new day and casting its light across the plain towards Isandlwana, burning back the ground-hugging mist. Through the swirling vapours he caught his first sight of the carnage that lay beneath. Only a glimpse, but it was enough to chill his bones, and he quickly raised a hand to cover his eyes. Then he trotted hurriedly down the far side of the saddle, hastening after his men.

They expected to be attacked at any moment. As this was the only route back to Rorke's Drift everybody, from the General on down to the lowliest native infantryman, anticipated having to fight their way through to safety. Out here somewhere was the vast bulk of the Zulu Army, freshly emboldened after yesterday's stunning victory, and they surely would not pass up the opportunity to attack the column as it passed by. If they did the British would be hard pressed, for not only were they low on morale, they were also exhausted after yesterday's toils, plus they had little ammunition left. Their supplies had been lost when the camp fell, and so they only had what few rounds remained in their pouches and bandoliers; also, many of them had not eaten for two days. So it was debatable whether they could put up much more than a token resistance if, and when, the Zulus renewed the battle.

It was a long way back to the border. Approximately twelve miles if they stuck to the dirt track. Twelve miles of hostile terrain. Each yard, each step they took, increased the tension. Evenif they made it all the way to the river and successfully crossed over into Natal the danger would not be over, for the word had soon spread that the post at Rorke's Drift had come under attack during the night, and they had few doubts of what further appalling scenes awaited them there. The tiny garrison of less than one hundred and fifty regulars plus some native levies could not have stood a chance against the full weight of a large Zulu assault. The enemy would simply have rolled right over them.

Yet as Lord Chelmsford had noted the previous evening they had no real option but to press on. There was nowhere for them to fall back to, not with more Zulus to their rear.

So the drift it was.

They reached the Manzimyama stream with little incident and a brief ten minute halt was called to allow the men to refill their water bottles and to give their horses a drink. Mansel and his troop maintained their vigil throughout however, worried of a surprise attack whilst the column was thus preoccupied.

As he sat there in the saddle, his nervous eyes scanning the hilltops, George Mansel briefly wondered what had become of the young man he had met all those months ago at Helpmekaar, appearing as though from nowhere leading a spare horse piled high with his few possessions, and so excited at the prospect of joining the coming war. For a moment he had to think to recall his name. Brickhill, that was it. James Brickhill of Knox's store, was how he'd introduced himself. So confident. So spirited. So keen to prove his salt. What had happened to him? He'd been left behind in camp, Inspector Mansel knew that much, but had he survived the battle? Or was he dead, slain with the rest? He drew in a long breath and let it slowly out in a weary sigh, his brow creased, fearing the worst. What a waste of a wonderful person. James had been good company in the short time he'd spent with him, such a likeable young man, with his whole life ahead of him. Years of adventuring, was how he'd put it. No turning back now, he'd said. A new life. But had it been cut short so suddenly?

Yes. Mansel was sure.

But then so many fathers and sons had been lost yesterday. The tears of mourning, the heartbreaking news that awaited so many families both here and in Britain, would spread far and wide he told himself. This was more than a military disaster. More than a serious reverse for Lord Chelmsford's army. It was a catastrophe the likes of which Her Majesty's Empire had never experienced before. The repercussions would, he felt, be huge.

With a sudden blink of his eyes Mansel brought himself back to the present, kicking himself for allowing his mind to wander when he should have been alert and on the job. There would be ample time for such gloomy preoccupations later. The column was about to start out again.

Across the stream the track skirted along the edge of some low hills for a mile or so before swinging sharply to the north, then rolled over some high ground before slanting down into the wide Batshe valley. Soon, despite the General's attempts to form a compact body, the line became dangerously strung out as the men marching at the front picked up the pace in their eagerness to reach the border. Those lagging on behind, slowed by the artillery, were in danger of being isolated. Mansel knew this was the most dangerous moment, when they were at their most vulnerable. His nervousness was stretched almost to breaking point.

By the time they approached the Batshe River the sun was well above the horizon and even though the day was still young the heat was intensifying, sapping their strength still further. They trudged on.

A short while later the enemy was spotted.

One of Mansel's men saw them first. He blurted out the news, riding quickly up to his commander and jabbing over his shoulder with his thumb. Mansel immediately issued vigorous orders and the NMP hurriedly peeled away to the left and formed in skirmishing line, but remained mounted. All eyes looked towards the south.

Coming out of the wide valley around the base of a long and low hillside was a large group of warriors. Mansel estimated there were about three thousand or so, moving in one dense mass several hundred yards away to their left. They moved slowly and silently, heading in the opposite direction.

A shiver passed down his spine and he noticed several men physically flinch away and he called out in a reassuring voice, "keep yourselves together now, don't lose it boys!" and his words had an immediate effect. They took out their carbines, checking that they were loaded, and made themselves ready for the expected attack.

Mansel called over the trooper who had initially seen the Zulus. "Ride down to the head of the column. You'll find Major Dartnell there with the General. Tell him... tell him that we have some visitors."

He galloped away, steering his horse with one hand and waving his hat in the air with the other, calling out as he went. Mansel frowned in annoyance. The fool! Was he trying to cause a mass panic? This was a time for cool heads.

He looked towards the Zulus once again. He noted that they had not come any closer, had not made any provocative movements as of yet, seeming content to march quietly passed. Strange. They could have attacked immediately, using the element of total surprise to strike them in the flank. Instead they merely looked across with blank expressions on their faces. He could not understand why they did not charge or encircle them.

Then a terrible thought struck him.

These warriors were heading east, away from the border. Away from Rorke's Drift. And the reason was obvious.

Because they had just come from the fight there. A battle which had raged through the night, for the night sky had glowed red with fire and the sounds of musketry had carried all the way to Isandlwana, warning Chelmsford's force that the slaughter was not yet done. Now, after what must have been another successful assault, the Zulus were returning. Satisfied after their day's work, their spears now well and truly washed, they seemed unwilling to give battle on this morning. They passed on by, watching the British but not moving into attack position.

Mansel turned at the sound of horses approaching and saw Major Dartnell and Lord Chelmsford racing down the line towards him, and when they reined in all three of them as well as the NMP and the rest of the column - which had been ordered to a halt - looked on with grave expressions on their faces.

For several tense minutes both sides, Zulu and British, stared balefully at each other, each waiting for the other to set things off. Yet neither side seemed willing. It was a ludicrous and bizarre situation.

Finally the Zulu host slipped away, meandering over the brow of the hill until they were gone from sight.

Chelmsford, Dartnell and Mansel stared at one another. Nobody said a word.

They noticed the column of smoke rising into the still air when they were about a mile from the river. Their spirits - already battered into submission - plunged to new depths when they saw it, as any last vestiges of hope quickly faded away. Although the mission station itself was hidden from view behind the high ramparts of *Shiyane* hill they could easily visualize in their minds eye the further appalling sights that awaited them, of more scenes of butchery, the garrison defenders cut up and laying sprawled across the ground. So it was with heavy hearts that they hiked in near-silence down to the banks of the Mzinyathi.

The ponts had been anchored in mid-stream and the cables buried beneath the mud in a futile attempt to prevent the Zulus from crossing (a pointless exercise as they always waded through rivers on foot anyway) and it took several minutes to work the ferries over to their side.

The long and laborious job of shipping the infantry across to the far bank began. Lord Chelmsford and his staff, together with the various mounted units, rode over through a shallower stretch just downstream and they waited for the rest of the force to join them.

He gazed down the dirt track that led to Rorke's Drift.

He wanted to hurry and get this over with.

Then move on and ride away from this place, to begin work on his new plans.

After a few minutes he decided he could wait no longer. They needed confirmation that all of the men at the mission station had indeed perished and so he called across Lieutenant-Colonel Russell of the Mounted Infantry and ordered him to take several men and push on down the road, and to pass back the much-dreaded news.

Chelmsford watched them move tentatively away.

He waited to hear of the fate of those left behind at Rorke's Drift.

```
THOU GREAT AND MIGHTY CHIEF!
THOU WHO HAST AN ARMY...
THE RED SOLDIERS CAME:
WE DESTROYED THEM.
THE MOUNTED SOLDIERS CAME:
WE DESTROYED THEM.
THE MOUNTED POLICE CAME:
WE DESTROYED THEM...
WHEN WILL THEY DARE TO REPEAT THEIR ATTACK?
```

Zulu Victory Song - *Sung after the battle of Isandlwana*


```
"A spear has been thrust into the belly of the
nation, there are not enough tears to mourn for
the dead."
```

King Cetshwayo - *After hearing of the terrible losses sustained by his regiments in order to achieve their victory*


```
"The situation of affairs does not appear to
me to improve, and I am fairly puzzled when I
contemplate our future operations... I wish I
saw my way with honour out of this beastly
country.
```

Lord Chelmsford, 3rd February 1879

AUTHOR'S NOTE

Today, over one hundred and forty years on from that fateful day in 1879, the understanding of events surrounding the battle of Isandlwana continues to be an evolving process. Few British eyewitness accounts exist simply because of the wholesale slaughter that took place, resulting in only a handful of survivors who lived to tell the tale, and the old Zulu tradition of maintaining their history through oral means has inevitably caused a divergence of opinion amongst historians over the years. This perplexing conundrum continues to divide authors and scholars (although usually in a good-natured way) as to what the 'truth' really is. The situation is not helped by the continual discovery of new evidence, so that as soon as one theory is deemed accurate just a few years later it is quite often proven false. For instance, for the best part of a century many considered the problems that Pulleine's men had with their ammunition supply was the main contributing factor to the disaster. However, more recently, an archaeological dig at the site has unearthed a wealth of new information that may point to this as not being the case. The remains of ammunition boxes have been discovered out on the British firing line so suggesting that the men still had access to an ample supply right up to the moment that their defences cracked. Put simply, they did not run out! The truth for the terrible catastrophe may be much more straighforward, and does not always sit easily with the 'old school' of military enthusiasts -superior Zulu tactics and skill, as well as sublime timing for their final charge which coincided with Pulleine's order to fall back, is looking an increasingly plausible explanation as to why they overcame the Imperial companies and their allies. Incredible though it may seem the modem, professional and well-equiped army that Lord Chelmsford had at his disposal was outmanoeuvred and out-generaled by an inferior (or so it was thought at the time) force. By natives armed mostly with spears!

Shocking, but probably true.

So the events of the 22nd January, 1879 continue to have an impact even today.

Whatever the case, interest in the Zulu War continues to grow and grow. For most people the closest they get to re-living the drama comes through either the pages of books or the thrill of the movies. A small few have, though, gone one step further. A steady stream of enthusiasts choose to set out on what amounts to a pilgrimage to the key battlefields and sites relating to the war, wandering over hills and through valleys, and occasionally swimming rivers, in order to explore the very ground where battle was given. To some (most?) it almost amounts to a religious experience.

The following is what I hope will be a helpful guide to those who are prepared to make the journey.

THE BATTLEFIELD OF ISANDLWANA TODAY

First, a few essential tips for travel in KwaZulu-Natal.

Journeying through this part of South Africa should be, and usually is, an exciting adventure. However, because of the geographical nature of the terrain as well as its climate, and the still-lingering shadow of Apartheid, certain inherent dangers do sadly exist. Precautions have to be taken and common sense be allowed to rule. One should not be put off by this for as we all know the world can be a perilous place wherever one might wander, whether it be clinging to the side of a bush-infested crag at Isandlwana or walking down a busy city street in London. Generally KwaZulu-Natal is safe to visit and the people very friendly and helpful.

Crime in the big cities (Durban being the main worry where we are concerned) does have a reputation for running rife. Robbery is common especially against tourists so the advice is not to walk about displaying copious amounts of expensive jewellery, designer clothes or fancy cameras - keep them hidden from view. Do not visit the townships unless accompanied by a guide. Care should even be taken when in the immediate area in and around your hotel, as this is often where pick-pockets operate. Try to avoid using local transport, and only travel by taxis from firms recommended by your hotel.

Once away from the cities and large towns few problems are encountered. Still, rural Zululand is not to be taken lightly. Under no circumstances should you leave your hotel and go for a midnight stroll! Also, when you are out exploring, do not leave your vehicle unattended; the chances are that it will not be there when you return! Guards can normally be hired from most hotels for the small fee of 100 Rands (£10) per day, a price worth paying.

Apart from crime prevention there are many other 'musts' to ensure that your trip is safe and enjoyable. If you are travelling on an independent basis then good, accurate maps are essential. So too a wide brimed sunhat. A small backpack to carry plenty of water and suncream. A well-stocked first-aid kit. And maybe a walking stick - constantly tapping on the rocks and stones as you go along will scare away any snakes and scorpions. Sturdy footwear will prevent many a twisted ankle. The clothing you wear depends on the nature of the terrain; shorts are alright if visiting museums and cemeteries but longer trousers if you are going to be scrabbling about amongst the thorn bushes and aloe plants. Bright colours and camouflage patterns are not recommended.

Many of the sites associated with Isandlwana are rather remote and may require lengthy journeys down poor quality roads, so a reliable vehicle - preferably a 4x4 - should be hired for the duration of your trip. Choice of comfortable accomodation is huge with many lodges sprouting up close to - and in one case actually on - the battlefield, so use your own judgement. Traditional-style Zulu homesteads aimed at those tourists willing to 'rough it' are also available, offering such delights as open-air barbecues, Zulu beer and dancing by firelight. A marvelous experience they are well recommended.

Now onto the battlefield and other associated sites.

The main forward assembly point for the Centre Column, Helpmekaar, is well worth a visit. Situated on the windswept Biggarsberg heights, it is still a tiny hamlet consisting of three or four ramshackle buildings and a one-man policestation. It is a five minute walk to the cemetery, resting place of those men who succumbed to disease whilst stationed there following Isandlwana, and here a few traces of the old camp can still be discerned on the ground, principally the ditches and lines of the earthwork. The edge of the plateau is just beyond the fields, offering splendid views down to the Buffalo river and Zululand, with Shiyane hill and Isandlwana both easily dicernable.

From here a rough dirt road signposted 'Rorke's Drift' branches off down the steep side of the plateau. It follows the same route that Chelmsford's men took on their final march towards the border.

Rorke's Drift played a peripheral, although important, role in the battle of Isandlwana as it was the main storage site for the column's supplies. The fight that ensued during the night of the 22nd/23rd is the stuff of legend, the most well-known of all the Zulu War battles, and to go into detail here would take too long. As this is the subject of the next novel in the series a detailed description of the area will be saved for then, but a brief look here will help to set the scene for your visit. A museum now sits over the site of the burned-down hospital (Reverand Witt's old house) built pretty much to the same design - minus the thatched roof, whilst a modern day chapel has replaced the storehouse. A cemetery containing those who died during the epic defence can be found between the buildings and Shiyane hill which looms above. A road curves down to the Buffalo river a quarter of a mile away before crossing over to the far bank via a rather unsightly bridge then continues off into the distance, making for the rump of Isandlwana visible on the horizon. A shallow pool to the left of the bridge marks the spot where the ponts ferried the troops too and fro.

Head into the heart of Old Zululand along the road, over the rise into the Batshe valley, and at the junction turn left. The high crags and caves to your right are the location where the skirmish on the 12th January took place against Chief Sihayo's followers, his homestead being further along where the road swings east. Ngedla mountain, where the cavalry fought, towers above you. The exact spot of the V-shaped crevasse is debatable although a concave opening in the cliff-face is generally said to be the area where most of the fighting took place. Retrace your route and pick up the main roadway once more and continue on towards Isandlwana.

In order to visit the various sites in chronological order it would be best to save the campsite for later. Keep heading east along the road, skirting the mountain and following the line of the plateau on your left, dropping gradually southeast across the plain. The high ground on the left and right gradually closes in and you will find yourself being squeezed over the gentle saddle of Mdutshana, virtually the same route that Lord Chelmsford took during his reconnaissance on the 20th. Over the rise is the spectacular Mangeni Gorge and waterfall. Park your vehicle beyond the stream, minding the Zulu women washing their clothes, and carefully approach the southern edge. Facing you across the deep canyon is Hiazakazi, where Dartnell placed his night bivouac, whilst the open ground away to the right is the general area that Lord Chelmsford had in mind for his new camp. Below, beyond the mouth of Mangeni Gorge, is the open ground that had so worried him. Imagine, as you peer down, that you catch the faint glint of sunlight on the spearheads of the NNC as they round the bend on their way up.

Head back towards Isandlwana Mountain. On the way work your way over the Nqutu plateau to find the Ngwebeni valley. Here lay the Zulu Army, waiting patiently, on that fateful day. Looking down, you have the same view that Lieutenant Raw and Captain Shepstone had when they inadvertently stumbled across their elusive foe. From here, either drive or if you are on foot walk southwest over the rolling plateau, taking the same route that the Zulu regiments did as they deployed for attack. Along the way visit the shallow valley where Mostyn and Cavaye tried to stem the attack, just above the spur leading down to Isandlwana. Further on why not pause on the escarpment edge, at Nyoni rocks, the exact spot that the Zulu commanders watched the battle unfold from.

From here it is a short hop to St. Vincent's Mission. A Visitor's Centre has been built where the course of the battle is explained, and tickets to the actual camp area can also be obtained here. Head down the road and through the main gateway, and continue on passed the front of Isandlwana until you reach a small carpark at the foot of the Stony Hill.

The location of most of the events around the camp as depicted in this novel are still easy to spot, helped by the fact that visually the battlefield is easy to understand. Probably the best vantage point from which to initially survey the area is the summit of Isandlwana itself. There is a route to the top, manageable with care, mostly a well trod goat track that winds anticlockwise around to the rear but with the final twenty or thirty feet involving a bit of a scramble up some steep boulders. Once there you should approach the edge overlooking the carpark and plain.

Cast your eyes out towards the conical hill. Somewhere beyond this, amidst the eroded hillside below the lip of the escarpment, the Rocket Battery was over-run. Closer in you will spot a thin line of trees cutting diagonally across your front about a mile away; this marks the course of the Nyogane donga where the Colonial horsemen attempted to stop the Zulu Left Horn. Look carefully and you will see a tiny building with a red roof, now a clinic; this is roughly where Colonel Durnford

508

concentrated his defence. The British firing line lay to your left front, between the base of Isandlwana and the conical hill and roughly following the line of the escarpment. The rocky knoll marks the position of the two cannons, indicated by a memorial to the Royal Artillery that is easily distinguishable. The blocks of tents lay immediately below you running left to right as far as the stony hill just beyond the carpark. Here, on the nek and spilling over into the rough ground beyond, are the majority of the burial cairns and memorials, erected where the British fell. Climb back down and explore them.

There is the 1/24th memorial, the Natal Carbineers memorial, a small iron cross marks the spot where Lieutenant Pope died, while a large concentration of cairns near the road indicate the location of Durnford's last stand. On the shoulder of Isandlwana a giant cairn is positioned where Captain Younghusband's C. Company fought, whilst at the rear of the mountain further graves can be found where Shepstone and his men died. More and more cover the nek, then spill down towards the line of retreat, individual piles of stones or long lines of them. All a grim indication of the size and totality of the massacre.

And the Zulus, who also suffered grievous losses? They warrant just a single memorial sadly, which can be found just by the main entrance gate.

For those feeling fit and energetic it is possible to walk the Fugitives' Trail but a guide is strongly recommended as it is easy to get lost amongst the thorn valleys. At the end it is necessary to swim across the Buffalo River. The graves of Lieutenants Melvill and Coghill can be found high on the hillside opposite the crossing point, tucked just below the large rock up against which they died.

PERIPHERAL SITES ASSOCIATED WITH ISANDLWANA

North of Durban lies the mouth of the Thukela River. Just a few miles inland is the Lower Drift, and here can be found the remains of the Ultimatum tree where the British announced their intention to invade Zululand unless its strict conditions were met. Smith's Hotel is long since gone but would have occupied the low rise just thirty to forty feet back from the river. Walk back from the bank and follow a path beside a new road bridge, which takes you up to the top of the high bluff above. Here are the earthwork remains of Fort Pearson, together with a tiny cemetery known as Euphorbia Redoubt. Scattered about are numerous information boards and centres to help explain.

South of here is a small town called Stanger. On the main street can be found a large statue of King Shaka, founder of the Zulu nation, placed over his grave.

At modern day Ulundi (Ondini) Cetshwayo's *Ikhanda* has been partially rebuilt and is wonderful to explore in order to gain some idea of what his enormous kraal would have looked like at the time of the war. There is also the KwaZulu Cultural Museum on the site.

At Pietermaritzburg many of the old Colonial buildings still remain. The Town Hall has hardly changed, so too Government House on Longmarket Street. Statues and memorials can be found throughout the city centre. On the outskirts nothing much remains of Fort Napier except the cemetery, containing a number of men who died during the war, most notably Colonel Durnford whose body was recovered from Isandlwana and buried here. A high and rather ugly fence surrounds the graves as though to discourage people from corning to pay their respects but it is possible to climb through a hole if you try. It is a peaceful spot. Well kept, so at least somebody must come to tend to the graves. Just across the way, funnily enough, is the local lunatic asylum!

Forgiveness came hard for Durnford it seems.

It goes without saying that to do justice to these places would require a timeframe of several days - or even weeks in order to fully explore them in depth. Hopefully this summary has given you a helpful guide to enable you to plan a much more detailed trip.

Happy trekking!

Mark Hobson
June 2019 – August 2020

Bibliography

Ashe, W and Wyatt-Edgell, *The Story of the Zulu Campaign* (London 1880)

Binns, C.T., *The Last Zulu King: The Life and Death of Cetshwayo* (Longman, London 1963)

Boyden, Peter, and Guy, Alan, and Harding, Marion (ed.), *Ashes and Blood: The British Army in South Africa 1795-1914* (National Army Museum 1999)

Castle, Ian, *Zulu War – Volunteers, Irregulars and Auxiliaries* (Osprey Publishing, Oxford 2003)

Castle, Ian, *British Infantryman in South Africa 1877-81* (Osprey Publishing, Oxford 2003

Clarke, Sonia (ed.), *Invasion of Zululand 1879* (Brenthurst Press, Houghton 1979)

Colenso, Francis E, *My Chief and I* (London 1994 Edition)

Drooglever, R.W.F., *The Road to Isandhlwana* (Collins, London 1948)

Featherstone, Donald, *Weapons & Equipment of the Victorian Soldier* (London 1996)

French, Maj. The Hon. G., *Lord Chelmsford and the Zulu War* (London 1939)

Gon, Philip, *The Road to Isandlwana: The Years of an Imperial Battalion* (Donker, Johannesburg, 1970

Greaves, Adrian, and Best, Brian (eds), *The Curling Letters of the Zulu War* (Pen and Sword, Barnsley 2001

Hamilton-Browne, G, *A Lost Legionary in South Africa* (T. Werner Laurie, London 1913)

Jackson, F.W.D., *Hill of the Sphinx* (Westerners Publication, London 2003)

Jones, Huw. M, *The Boiling Cauldron: Utrecht District and the Anglo-Zulu War, 1879* (The Shermershill Press, Gloucestershire 2006)

Knight, Ian, *Brave Men's Blood* (Greenhill Books, London 1990)

Knight, Ian, *Zulu: The Battles of Isandlwana and Rorke's Drift* (Windrow and Greene, London 1992)

Knight, Ian, *The Anatomy of the Zulu Army* (Greenhill Books, London 1995)

Knight, Ian, *Great Zulu Commanders* (Arms and Armour Press, London 1999)

Knight, Ian, *By The Orders of the Great White Queen* (Greenhill Books, London 1992)

Knight, Ian, *Zulu Rising* (Macmillan 2010)

Laband, John, *The Rise and Fall of the Zulu Nation* (Arms and Armour Press, London 1997)

Laband, John, and Thompson, Paul, *Kingdom and Colony at War* (N&S Press, Pietermaritzburg 1990)

Laband, John, and Thompson, Paul, and Henderson, S, *The Buffalo Border 1879* (Pietermaritzburg 1983)

Lock, Ron, and Quantrill, Peter, *Zulu Victory: The Epic of Isandlwana and the Cover-Up* (Greenhill Books, London 2002)

Machin, I, *Antbears and Targets for Zulu Assegais* (Durban 2002)

McKenzie, John. R, *Uncivilized Races in all Countries of the World Vol 1 & 2* (Rood, Hawley & Company, New York 1880)

Morris, Donald. R, *The Washing of the Spears* (Jonathan Cape, London 1966

Nathan, M, *The Voortrekkers of South Africa* (London 1937)

Roberts, B, *The Zulu Kings* (London 1974)

Snook, Lt. Col. Mike, *How Can Man Die Better: The Secrets of Isandlwana Revealed* (Greenhill Books, London 2005)

Strawson, John, *Beggars in Red: The British Army 1789-1889* (Pen and Sword, Barnsley 2003)

Thompson, P.S, *The Natal Native Contingent in the Anglo-Zulu War* (Brevitas, Pietermaritzburg 1997)

Wilkinson-Latham, C, *Uniforms and Weapons of the Zulu War* (London 1978)

Whitehouse, H, *Battle in Africa, 1879-1914* (Mansfield 1987)

ABOUT THE AUTHOR

Mark Hobson first gained an interest in the Anglo-Zulu War in 1977 aged just 7 years old. A number of years later he began to study the subject much more carefully. He has travelled extensively throughout KwaZulu-Natal, visiting the battlefield of Isandlwana on a number of occasions. In 2000 he was elected a Fellow of the Anglo-Zulu War Historical Society.
He lives at home in Yorkshire with his 3 cats.

Now May Men Weep is his first novel.